DAY HIKES AROUND
Los
Angeles

160 GREAT HIKES

Robert Stone

6th EDITION

Day Hike Books, Inc.
RED LODGE, MONTANA

Published by Day Hike Books, Inc.
P.O. Box 865 · Red Lodge, Montana 59068
www.dayhikebooks.com

Distributed by National Book Network
800-243-0495 (direct order) · 800-820-2329 (fax order)

Front cover photograph by Roy Mata
Back cover photograph by Robert Stone
Design and maps by Paula Doherty

The author has made every attempt to provide accurate information in this book. However, trail routes and features may change— please use common sense and forethought, and be mindful of your own capabilities. Let this book guide you, but be aware that each hiker assumes responsibility for their own safety. The author and publisher do not assume any responsibility for loss, damage, or injury caused through the use of this book.

Copyright © 2015 by Day Hike Books, Inc.
6th Edition
ISBN: 978-1-57342-071-6

Cover photo:
Point Dume, Hike 113

Back cover photo:
Mesa Peak from Malibu Canyon, Hike 103

Awards for Day Hikes Around Los Angeles

Best In Show Award
Rocky Mountain Outdoor Writers and Photographers

Best Guidebook Award
Outdoor Writers Association of California

Best Guidebook Award
Northwest Outdoor Writers Association

Best Guidebook Award
Rocky Mountain Outdoor Writers and Photographers

and...
Los Angeles Times Bestseller

Table of Contents

The Hikes

CENTRAL LOS ANGELES

Griffith Park and Hollywood Hills

Los Angeles Basin Coastline
Santa Monica to Marina Del Rey Harbor Channel

Palos Verdes Peninsula
Manhattan Beach to Long Beach

EASTERN SANTA MONICA MOUNTAINS
Beverly Hills to Malibu Canyon Road

Beverly Hills to 405 Freeway

**405 Freeway to Pacific Palisades
Will Rogers State Park**

Topanga State Park

Topanga Canyon to Malibu Canyon
Cold Creek Area

WESTERN SANTA MONICA MOUNTAINS
Malibu Canyon to Point Mugu

Malibu Canyon to Kanan Dume Road

Point Dume • Kanan Dume Road

Decker Road to Point Mugu State Park

Point Mugu State Park
Rancho Sierra Vista/Satwiwa

SIMI HILLS · SANTA SUSANA MOUNTAINS

Cheeseboro/Palo Comado Canyons
Upper Las Virgenes Canyon

Simi Valley · Santa Susana Mountains

Eastern Santa Susana Mountains

Hiking the Los Angeles area

Despite the widespread presence of the Los Angeles metropolis, there exist thousands of acres of natural, undeveloped land and countless out-of-the-way hiking trails. Now in its 6th edition, *Day Hikes Around Los Angeles* includes 160 day hikes within a 50-mile radius of the city, providing access to the area's cherished green space and disclosing many entry points to the coast. Most hikes are located in public open space (local, state, and national), wilderness areas, in the expansive Santa Monica Mountains National Recreation Area, and within the San Gabriel Mountain Range. A few metropolitan strolls are included as well.

These hikes provide an excellent cross-section of scenery and difficulty levels, ranging from coastal beach walks to steep canyon climbs with far-reaching views. Hiking times range from 30 minutes to seven hours, although the majority of hikes are 2—6 miles in length. Relevant maps are listed under the statistics to lengthen the hike. A quick glance at the hikes' statistics and summaries will allow you to choose a hike that is appropriate to your ability and intentions. An overall map on page 16 identifies the general locations of the hikes and major access roads. Several other regional maps (underlined in the table of contents), as well as maps for each hike, provide the essential details. The Thomas Guide, or other comparable street guide, is useful for navigating through the metropolitan areas.

A few basic necessities are recommended. Wear supportive, comfortable hiking shoes and layered clothing. Take along hats, sunscreen, sunglasses, drinking water, snacks, and appropriate outerwear for variable weather. Insects, including ticks, may be prolific and poison oak flourishes in some of the canyons and shady areas. Exercise caution by using insect repellent and staying on the trails. A basic first aid kit is always a good idea.

Please note that wildfires are common in southern California. For the latest updates on trail conditions, closures, and routes, check with the Forest Service.

Use good judgement about your capabilities—reference the hiking statistics for an approximation of difficulty—and allow extra time for exploration.

The National Forest Adventure Pass is a parking permit required by the U.S. Forest Service and issued for a fee. Adventure Passes are required in the Angeles National Forest, Los Padres National Forest, Cleveland National Forest, and San Bernardino National Forest. Nearly all of the hikes in the San Gabriel Mountains section of this book will require the pass, which needs to be displayed in the vehicles. The daily or annual Adventure Passes can be purchased online, at any Forest Service facility, or at various local outdoor shops and sporting goods stores. (Other parking lots may charge fees as well.)

San Gabriel Mountains and Verdugo Mountains

The San Gabriel Mountains are at the northern end of Los Angeles County. The range lies between the Los Angeles basin (to the south) and the Mojave Desert (to the north). The highest peak is over 10,000 feet in elevation. The Verdugo Mountains are a small off-shoot range along the western end of the San Gabriels. Hikes 1—27 are located in these surprisingly remote and rugged mountains. Many of the hikes lead up stream-fed, wooded canyons to waterfalls. Fire roads and old wagon routes are often utilized to access overlooks with magnificent vistas of the greater Los Angeles area and coastline.

Hollywood Hills and Griffith Park

Hollywood Hills and Griffith Park sit at the eastern terminus of the Santa Monica Mountain Range. Thirteen hikes (28—40) are located in this area, just minutes from downtown Los Angeles. Griffith Park, the largest municipal park in the United States, has both tourist attractions and solitary retreats within its 4,100 acres. The urban wilderness contains a 53-mile network of hiking and equestrian trails through semi-arid foothills, oak groves, and wooded glens. The mountains and steep interior canyons of the Hollywood Hills, directly to the west of Griffith Park, are largely undeveloped and offer a haven for humans and animals in the midst of Los Angeles.

Highlights include overlooks of the city, secluded canyons, gardens, the Hollywood Reservoir, Griffith Park Observatory and Planetarium, a 1926 merry-go-round, and a hike up to the famous "HOLLYWOOD" sign.

Los Angeles Basin Coastline:
Santa Monica to Marina Del Rey

Hikes 41—46 explore the metropolitan oceanfront and its interesting culture along Santa Monica Bay. A continuous series of oceanside paths and boardwalks connect the beaches, from Santa Monica to Marina Del Rey. Well-known Venice Beach and the Venice Canals are located here.

Palos Verdes Peninsula: Torrance to Long Beach

Hikes 47—59 are found along the coast of the Palos Verdes Peninsula and San Pedro Bay at the southernmost point of Los Angeles County. This geographically interesting area includes ocean-side cliffs, beaches, coves, grassy bluffs, actively slipping landslides, and some of the best tidepools in the area. A beautiful lighthouse sits at the tip of Point Fermin.

Eastern Santa Monica Mountains
Hollywood Hills to Malibu Canyon

The Santa Monica Mountains extend roughly 50 miles directly east and west, from Griffith Park in central Los Angeles to Point Mugu. The mountains, which lie along the San Andreas Fault, run parallel to the coast and are 8—12 miles wide. Elevations extend from sea level to just over 3,000 feet at Sandstone Peak. Beaches and coastal communities lie interspersed along the Pacific Coast Highway (Highway 1), the access road to the hikes.

Because of the mountainous landscape, the canyons and slopes were slower to develop as Los Angeles expanded. Hundreds of acres of land were preserved from further encroachment and converted to public parklands. Past the 405, the undeveloped acreage increases. Stream-fed wooded canyons drain from the ridgeline to the ocean. Rocky outcroppings offer spectacular mountain-to-coast views. The sprawling 11,525-acre Topanga State Park is actually entirely within the Los Angeles city limits. Hikes 60—93 are all located in the eastern half of the Santa Monica range.

Western Santa Monica Mountains
Malibu Canyon to Point Mugu

From Malibu Canyon, the Santa Monica Mountains continue westward, past Point Dume, Sandstone Peak, and Point Mugu, where the range ends abruptly in flat farmland. Hikes 94—135 are located in the western half of the Santa Monica Range. A large number of trails are found along coastal bluffs and beaches. Many other trails meander across foothills, traverse peaks and ridges, and drop down across the northern side of the range into the rolling landscape of interior California. Highlights include sweeping views of the coast, unusual geological formations, waterfalls, cliff overlooks, ridge walks, canyons, old ranch roads (including Ronald Reagan's ranch), filming locations, and shady retreats. Many state parks link with designated wilderness across the greater part of the western Santa Monicas. The undeveloped acreage includes the expansive Point Mugu State Park and Malibu Creek State Park.

Simi Hills to Santa Susana Mountains

Hikes 136—149 are located in and around the Simi Hills, a low, rocky range that divides Simi Valley from San Fernando Valley. Connected to the hills on the northeast, across Santa Susana Pass and the 118 Freeway, are the Santa Susana Mountains. The range stretches westward from the San Gabriels (west of I-5) and includes Hikes 150—160.

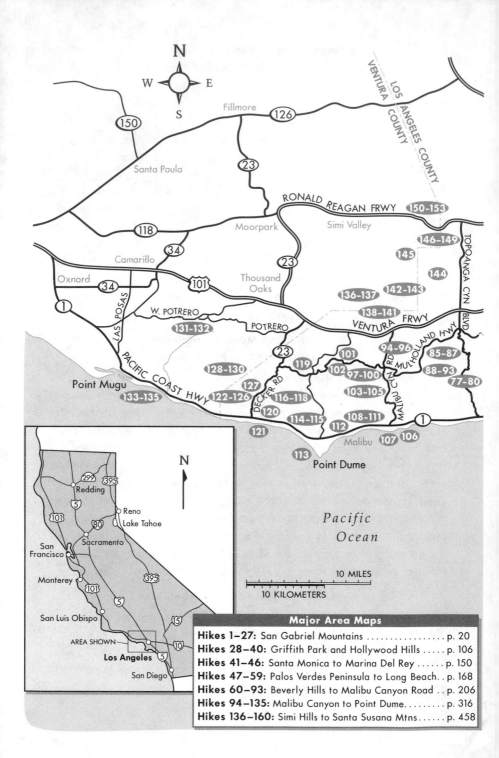

Point Mugu

Point Dume

Pacific Ocean

10 MILES
10 KILOMETERS

Redding
Reno
Lake Tahoe
San Francisco
Sacramento
Monterey
San Luis Obispo
AREA SHOWN
Los Angeles
San Diego

| Major Area Maps |

MAP of the HIKES
LOS ANGELES and VICINITY

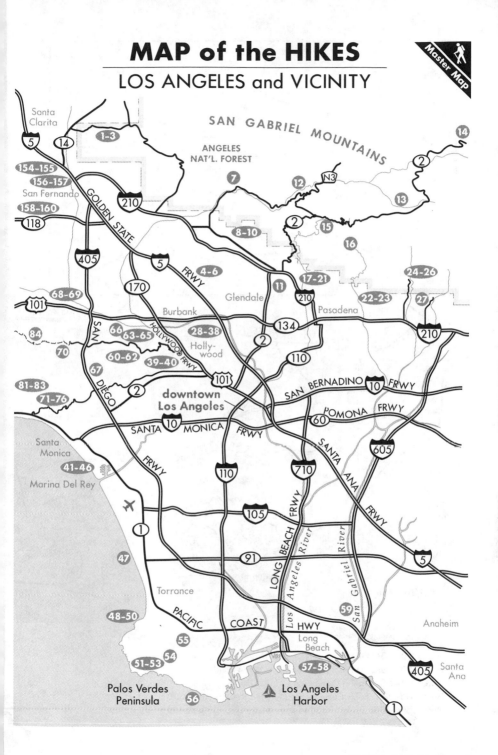

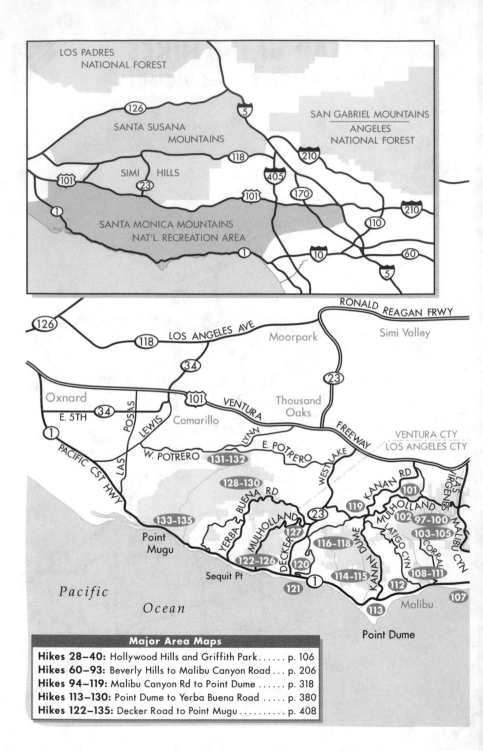

LOS PADRES
NATIONAL FOREST

126

5

SANTA SUSANA
MOUNTAINS

118

210

SAN GABRIEL MOUNTAINS
ANGELES
NATIONAL FOREST

101

SIMI   HILLS
23

405

101

170

210

1

110

SANTA MONICA MOUNTAINS
NAT'L. RECREATION AREA

1

10

60

5

RONALD REAGAN FRWY

126

118

LOS ANGELES AVE

Moorpark

Simi Valley

34

23

Oxnard

101

VENTURA

Thousand
Oaks

E. 5TH

34

Camarillo

FREEWAY

VENTURA CTY
LOS ANGELES CTY

1

W. POTRERO

E. POTRERO

WESTLAKE

KANAN RD

101

131-132

119

102

97-100

128-130

23

103-105

133-135

127

116-118

108-111

Point
Mugu

122-126

120

114-115

112

107

Sequit Pt

1

121

113

Malibu

Pacific

Ocean

Point Dume

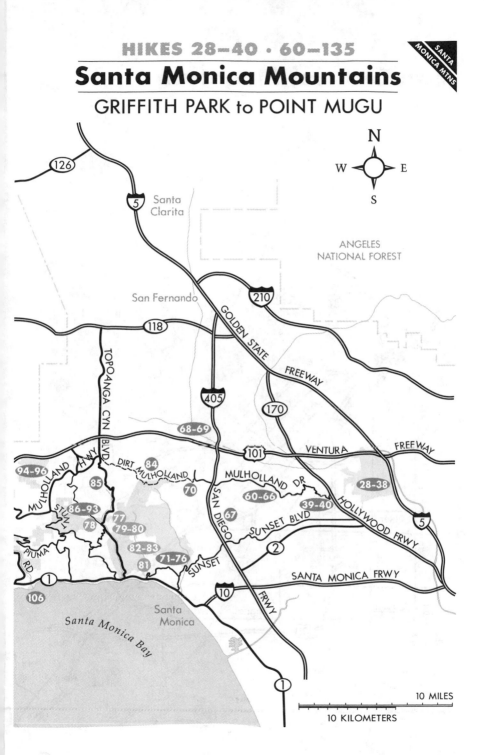

Santa Monica Mountains
GRIFFITH PARK to POINT MUGU

SANTA MONICA MTNS

N
W E
S

126

5 Santa
Clarita

ANGELES
NATIONAL FOREST

San Fernando

118

210

GOLDEN STATE

FREEWAY

TOPANGA CYN BLVD

405

170

68–69

101 VENTURA FREEWAY

94–96

MULHOLLAND HWY

DIRT MULHOLLAND

84

85

MULHOLLAND DR

70

60–66

28–38

STUNT RD

86–93

SAN DIEGO

67

39–40

HOLLYWOOD FRWY

5

78

77

79–80

SUNSET BLVD

82–83

71–76

2

PIUMA RD

81

SUNSET

SANTA MONICA FRWY

1

10

FRWY

106

Santa
Monica

Santa Monica Bay

1

10 MILES

10 KILOMETERS

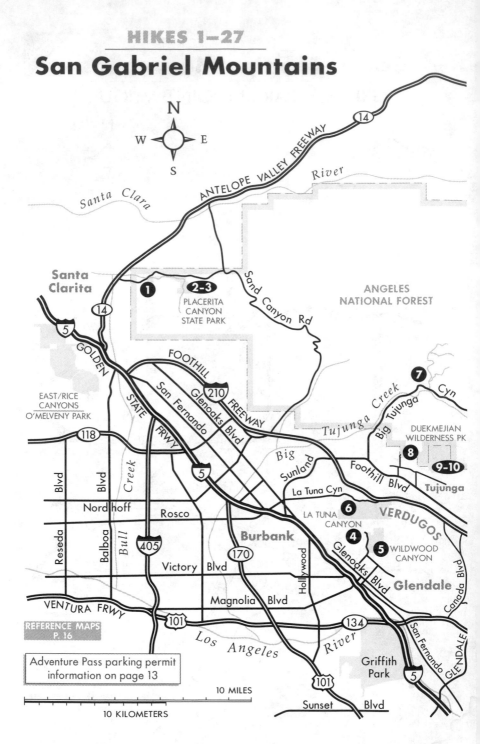

San Gabriel Mountains

N
W E
S

14

ANTELOPE VALLEY FREEWAY

Santa Clara

River

Sand Canyon Rd

Santa Clarita

14

5

❶

❷-❸

PLACERITA CANYON STATE PARK

ANGELES NATIONAL FOREST

GOLDEN

STATE

FRWY

FOOTHILL

210

FREEWAY

San Fernando

Glenoaks Blvd

EAST/RICE CANYONS O'MELVENY PARK

118

Creek

5

Tujunga Creek

❼

Cyn

Big Tujunga

DUEKMEJIAN WILDERNESS PK

❽

❾-❿

Tujunga

Big

Sunland

Foothill Blvd

Blvd

Blvd

Nordhoff

Rosco

Bull

405

La Tuna Cyn

LA TUNA CANYON

❻

VERDUGOS

Reseda

Balboa

Burbank

170

Victory Blvd

Hollywood

Magnolia Blvd

❹

❺ WILDWOOD CANYON

Glenoaks Blvd

Glendale

Canada Blvd

VENTURA FRWY

101

Los Angeles

River

134

San Fernando

GLENDALE

REFERENCE MAPS P. 16

Adventure Pass parking permit information on page 13

10 MILES

10 KILOMETERS

Griffith Park

101

Sunset Blvd

5

In the summer of 2009, the Station Fire swept through the San Gabriel Mountains. The fire burned more than 160,000 acres of the pristine forestland, including the Vetter Mountain Fire Lookout, the last remaining lookout in the mountain range. The western third of the San Gabriel Mountains was reduced to charred timber, ash, and crumbling rock. Since that time, many of the trails have been restored and the vegetation has been slowly returning.

Wildfires are common in southern California. For the latest updates on trail conditions, closures, and routes, check with the Forest Service before venturing out on any of these hikes.

SAN GABRIEL MOUNTAINS

Angeles Forest Hwy

N3

WINSTON ▲

(14)

2

WATERMAN ▲

Big
Tujunga
Res.

(12)

VETTER ▲

(13)

ANGELES
NATIONAL FOREST

Rd

N3

Crest Hwy

LAWLOR ▲

Angeles

(15)

Cogswell Res.

San Gabriel River

2

HAHAMONGNA
WATERSHED PK

(16)

Mt Wilson Rd

▲WILSON

La
Crescenta

(19-21)

LOWE ▲

(17)

(18)

▲ECHO

(24-26)

Lincoln

EATON
CANYON PK

Santa Anita

11

Altadena Dr

(22-23)

(27)

MONROVIA
CANYON PK

Flintridge

210

Lake

Altadena

Monrovia

2

134

Seco

California

Eaton Wash

Rosewood

Arcadia

Wash

210

110

Pasadena

Arroyo

Sawpit

605

1. Placerita Canyon Trail

PLACERITA CANYON STATE PARK and NATURAL AREA

19152 Placerita Canyon Road · Newhall

Hiking distance: 4 miles round trip
Hiking time: 2 hours
Configuration: out-and-back
Elevation gain: 250 feet
Exposure: mostly shaded canyon
Difficulty: easy
Dogs: allowed
Maps: U.S.G.S. Mint Canyon · Harrison: Angeles Front Country Trail Map
　　　　Placerita Canyon Natural Area Map

Placerita Canyon State Park is a designated state historic land-mark. The canyon is the site of the original gold discovery in California, dating back to 1842, six years prior to the famous discovery of gold by John Marshall at Sutter's Mill in the north-ern town of Coloma. This 350-acre natural area is located on the north slope of the San Gabriel Mountains, overlooking the

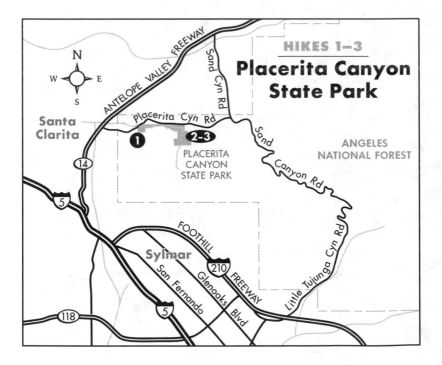

Santa Clarita Valley. The park sits in a transition zone between the San Gabriel Mountains and the Mohave Desert. The east–west running canyon links the Angeles National Forest with the Santa Susana Mountains, the Simi Hills, and the Santa Monica Mountains. Placerita Canyon is home to sandstone formations, seasonal streams, and riparian woodlands with stands of oaks, sycamores, cottonwoods, and willows.

This hike begins at the nature center and follows the picturesque canyon and meandering creek east into the Walker Ranch Campground. The camp is named for Frank Walker, who built his home on the historic ranch in the 1920s.

To the trailhead

From the Golden State Freeway (I-5) in Newhall, take the Antelope Valley Freeway (H-14) east. Continue 3 miles and exit on Placerita Canyon Road. Turn right and drive 1.4 miles to the signed Placerita Canyon State Park on the right. Turn right and continue 0.1 mile to the nature center. Park in the spaces on the left. An Adventure Pass is required for parking.

The hike

From the nature center, cross the drainage to a junction. The Hillside Trail climbs the hill to the south. Stay in Placerita Canyon and continue up canyon to the east. Follow the rock-lined path on the south edge of the seasonal creek under oaks, willows, cottonwoods, alders, and sycamores. The rock-walled drainage narrows to a gorge, and the footpath crosses the transient drainage four times. Pass through a beautiful oak grove and a seasonal drainage on the right by a 10-foot ephemeral waterfall at one mile. The canyon widens out and the grade remains relatively level. Climb a short slope and curve left by signpost 19 at a bubbling spring with a mixture of oil and water (known as *white oil*) on the right. At two miles enter the Walker Ranch Campground on a grassy flat covered in majestic oaks, reaching a signed junction with Los Pinetos Trail and the Placerita Waterfall Trail (Hikes 1 and 2).

To extend the hike, continue with Hike 2 to Placerita Falls or Hike 3 to the crest of the San Gabriel Mountains, overlooking the San Fernando Valley. ▥

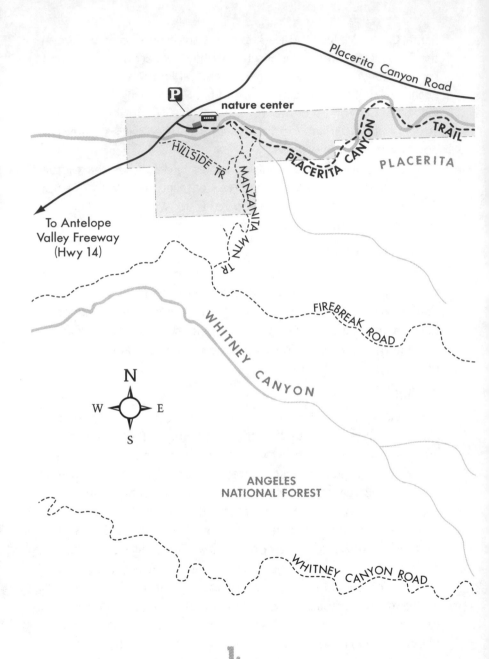

1.

Placerita Canyon Trail
PLACERITA CANYON STATE PARK

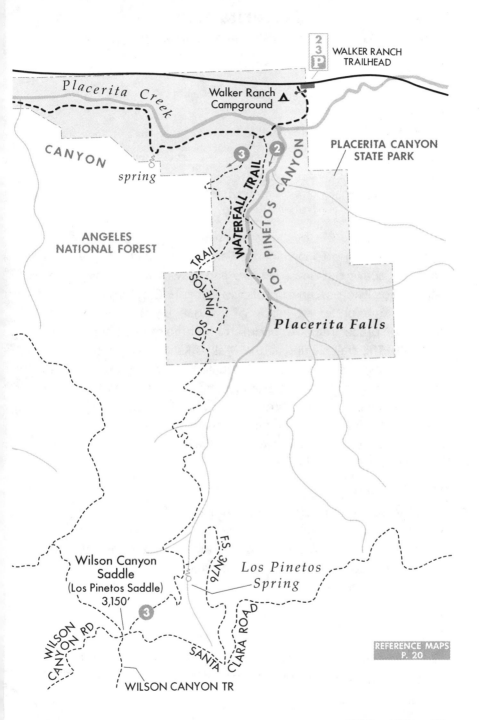

WALKER RANCH
TRAILHEAD

Placerita Creek

Walker Ranch
Campground

PLACERITA CANYON
STATE PARK

CANYON

spring

ANGELES
NATIONAL FOREST

WATERFALL TRAIL

LOS PINETOS TRAIL

LOS PINETOS CANYON

Placerita Falls

Wilson Canyon
Saddle
(Los Pinetos Saddle)
3,150'

F.S. 3N76

Los Pinetos
Spring

SANTA CLARA ROAD

WILSON CANYON RD

WILSON CANYON TR

REFERENCE MAPS
P. 20

2. Placerita Falls

PLACERITA CANYON STATE PARK and NATURAL AREA

Hiking distance: 1.5 miles round trip
Hiking time: 1 hour
Configuration: out-and-back
Elevation gain: 250 feet
Exposure: mostly shaded canyon
Difficulty: easy
Dogs: allowed
Maps: U.S.G.S. Mint Canyon and San Fernando
Harrison: Angeles Front Country Trail Map
Placerita Canyon Natural Area Map

Placerita Falls is a 25-foot seasonal waterfall tucked into a cool, rock-enclosed grotto in Placerita Canyon State Park. (The falls is generally active between January and May.) The easy hike into narrow Los Pinetos Canyon follows Placerita Creek through the shaded gorge under a canopy of live oak, big leaf maple, and big cone spruce trees. An understory of moist ferns surrounds the path. The trail begins at the Walker Ranch Campground by historic remnants of a settler's cottage built in the early 1900s. The cement foundation and chimney are still intact. En route, the trail meanders along the waterway, crossing the ephemeral creek seven times. The path scrambles over water-polished metamorphic rock to the trail's end in a steep-walled box canyon, where the creek slides over the rock wall.

To the trailhead

From the Golden State Freeway (I-5) in Newhall, take the Antelope Valley Freeway (H-14) east. Continue 3 miles and exit on Placerita Canyon Road. Turn right and drive 3.1 miles to the signed Walker Ranch Trailhead parking area on the right. An Adventure Pass is required for parking.

The hike

Pass through the vehicle gate and walk down the dirt road. Descend and cross the seasonal stream into the Walker Ranch Campground to the Placerita Canyon Trail (Hike 1). Veer right a

few yards to the Placerita Waterfall Trail on the left. Pass a sm.
rock wall and head up the oak-dotted canyon on the west side
of the transient creek. The Los Pinetos Trail (Hike 3) can be seen
perched on the west canyon wall. Climb steps and traverse the
oak-covered hillside just above the canyon floor. The canyon
narrows and follows the edge of the seasonal stream to a rock
grotto and pool. Curve left and cross the stream for the first of
seven crossings. At the fifth crossing, the canyon bends left. The
trail ends in a box canyon with vertical rock walls. The vernal falls
drops down the face of the cliff. ■

2.
Placerita Falls
PLACERITA CANYON STATE PARK

3. Los Pinetos Trail
to Wilson Canyon Saddle
PLACERITA CANYON STATE PARK and NATURAL AREA

Hiking distance: 4.7 miles round trip
Hiking time: 3 hours
Configuration: out-and-back with small loop atop saddle
Elevation gain: 1,300 feet
Exposure: a mix of shaded woodland and open chaparral slopes
Difficulty: moderate to somewhat strenuous
Dogs: allowed
Maps: U.S.G.S. Mint Canyon and San Fernando
　　　　Harrison: Angeles Front Country Trail Map
　　　　Placerita Canyon Natural Area Map

Los Pinetos Trail is a moderately steep trail that climbs from the Walker Ranch Campground in Placerita Canyon to the crest of the San Gabriel Mountains at Wilson Canyon Saddle. The hike begins in Placerita Canyon State Park, on the northwest corner of the San Gabriel Mountains, and enters the Angeles National Forest along the way. The route weaves up the west slope of Los Pinetos Canyon through riparian, chaparral, and oak woodland habitats. From the summit are northern views of Placerita Canyon and Santa Clarita Valley and southern vistas across the urban sprawl of the San Fernando Valley and downtown Los Angeles.

To the trailhead

From the Golden State Freeway (I-5) in Newhall, take the Antelope Valley Freeway (H-14) east. Continue 3 miles and exit on Placerita Canyon Road. Turn right and drive 3.1 miles to the signed Walker Ranch. The trailhead parking area is on the right. An Adventure Pass is required for parking.

The hike

Pass through the vehicle gate and walk down the dirt road. Descend and cross the seasonal stream into the Walker Ranch Campground to the Placerita Canyon Trail (Hike 1). Veer right, passing the Placerita Waterfall Trail on the left (Hike 2) to the posted Los Pinetos Trail, also on the left.

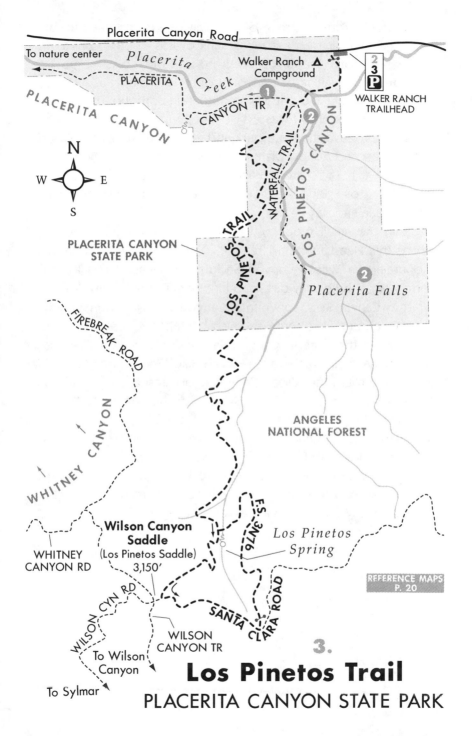

Placerita Canyon Road

To nature center
Placerita
PLACERITA
Creek
Walker Ranch
Campground
2 3 P
WALKER RANCH
TRAILHEAD

PLACERITA CANYON

CANYON TR ①

N
W ⊕ E
S

WATERFALL TRAIL

LOS PINETOS CANYON

②

PLACERITA CANYON
STATE PARK

LOS PINETOS

Placerita Falls
②

TRAIL

FIREBREAK ROAD

ANGELES
NATIONAL FOREST

WHITNEY CANYON

F.S. 3N76

**Wilson Canyon
Saddle**
*Los Pinetos
Spring*

WHITNEY
CANYON RD
(Los Pinetos Saddle)
3,150'

REFERENCE MAPS
P. 20

WILSON CYN RD

SANTA CLARA ROAD

To Wilson
Canyon
WILSON
CANYON TR

To Sylmar

3.
Los Pinetos Trail
PLACERITA CANYON STATE PARK

Bear left through a grove of coast live oaks and head up the foothill. Begin climbing the west flank of Los Pinetos Canyon to an overlook of Placerita Canyon, the oak-dotted campground, and forested Los Pinetos Canyon. Continue climbing at a steady incline, curving in and out of the mountain contours from sunny, exposed chaparral to forested pockets with manzanita and oak. At 1.5 miles, leave the state park and enter the Angeles National Forest. Descend a short distance through the forest, then begin climbing again. Loop around and cross a drainage to a trail split by Los Pinetos Spring and a cement water tank in a shaded glen with spruce and oak.

Begin the small loop by veering right, staying on the Los Pintos Trail. Head up the hill, reaching the crest of the San Gabriel Mountains on Wilson Canyon Saddle (also called Los Pinetos Saddle) at a three-way dirt road junction. The right fork follows Whitney Canyon Road to Whitney Canyon and a junction with the Firebreak Road. (This route can also be taken as an 8-mile loop, returning to the Placerita Canyon Nature Center via the Firebreak Trail and Manzanita Mountain Trail. See Hike 1 map.) Straight ahead, across the road, the Wilson Canyon Road descends into Wilson Canyon and leads to the city of Sylmar. For this hike, go to the left on the Santa Clara Road and head east, parallel to the ridge on its north side. Continue 0.3 miles on the dirt road to a left bend at an overlook with far-reaching views across the San Fernando Valley. On the bend is gated Forest Service Road 3N76. Bear left on the side road and weave downhill, completing the loop at Los Pinetos Spring. Retrace your steps to the right. ▓

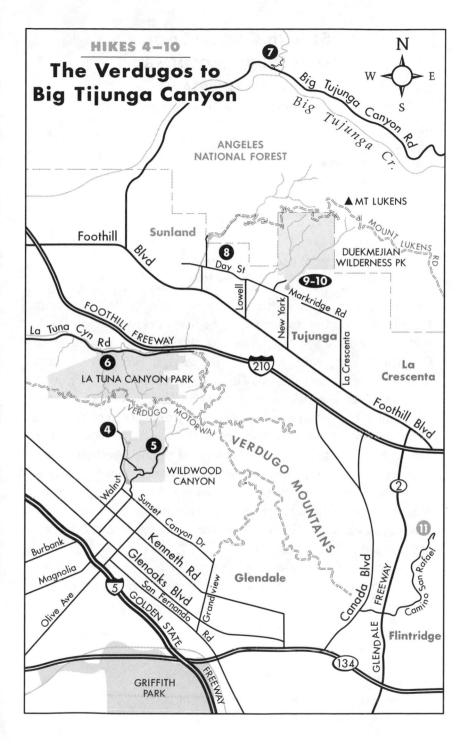

HIKES 4–10

The Verdugos to Big Tijunga Canyon

N
W E
S

7

Big Tujunga Canyon Rd

Big Tujunga Cr.

ANGELES
NATIONAL FOREST

▲ MT LUKENS

MOUNT LUKENS RD

Foothill   Sunland

Blvd

DUEKMEJIAN
WILDERNESS PK

8

Day St

Lowell

9–10

Markridge Rd

New York

Tujunga

FOOTHILL FREEWAY

La Tuna Cyn Rd

La Crescenta

6

LA TUNA CANYON PARK

210

Foothill Blvd

VERDUGO MOTORWAY

4

5

WILDWOOD
CANYON

VERDUGO MOUNTAINS

2

Walnut

Sunset Canyon Dr

11

Kenneth Rd

Burbank

Glenoaks Blvd

Glendale

Magnolia

San Fernando

Grandview Rd

Camino San Rafael

Canada Blvd

GLENDALE FREEWAY

Olive Ave

5

GOLDEN STATE

Flintridge

FREEWAY

GRIFFITH
PARK

134

4. Stough Canyon Loop to Verdugo Motorway

VERDUGO MOUNTAINS

2300 Walnut Avenue · Burbank

Hiking distance: 2.3-mile loop
Hiking time: 1.5 hours
Configuration: loop
Elevation gain: 650 feet
Exposure: exposed slope
Difficulty: easy to moderate
Dogs: allowed
Maps: U.S.G.S. Burbank
        Harrison: Angeles Front Country Trail Map
        Harrison: Verdugo Mountains Trail Map

Stough Canyon sits on the southern slope of the Verdugo Mountains, an urban mountain range rising above the northern edge of Burbank and Glendale. Stough Canyon is named after Oliver J. Stough, who purchased the land in 1883 and deeded it to the city of Burbank in 1916 as a gift to be used as public parkland. This hike begins at the Stough Canyon Nature Center, a beautiful facility opened in 1991 with exhibits and interpretive displays that highlight the natural history, native plants, and Native Americans. This loop hike follows a sun-baked dirt road up the brushy slopes of the canyon to the Verdugo Motorway, a well-maintained fire road that follows the crest of the Verdugo Mountains. From the ridge are dramatic vistas of the San Fernando Valley, Los Angeles, Griffith Park, the Santa Monica Mountains, and the San Gabriel Mountains.

The next three hikes lead up to the Verdugo Motorway from three different trailheads. This is the shortest and easiest access to the ridge.

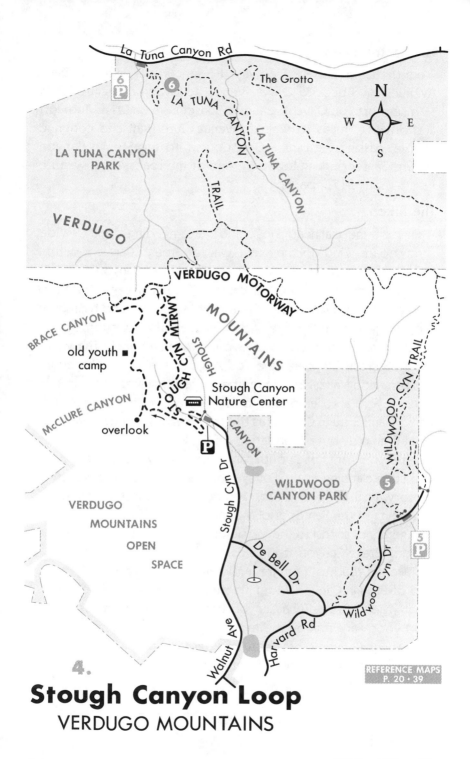

Stough Canyon Loop
VERDUGO MOUNTAINS

La Tuna Canyon Rd

The Grotto

N
W E
S

6 P

6

LA TUNA CANYON

LA TUNA CANYON

LA TUNA CANYON

TRAIL

LA TUNA CANYON PARK

VERDUGO

VERDUGO MOTORWAY

MOUNTAINS

BRACE CANYON

VRDUGO CYN MTRWY

STOUGH

old youth camp

STOUGH CANYON

Stough Canyon Nature Center

WILDWOOD CYN TRAIL

McCLURE CANYON

overlook

P

WILDWOOD CANYON PARK

5

5 P

VERDUGO

MOUNTAINS

OPEN

SPACE

Stough Cyn Dr

De Bell Dr

Wildwood Cyn Dr

Walnut Ave

Harvard Rd

REFERENCE MAPS
P. 20 • 39

To the trailhead

From the Golden State Freeway (I-5) in Burbank, exit on Olive Avenue. Wind back to Olive Avenue, following the signs. Head 1.2 miles north on Olive Avenue to Sunset Canyon Drive. Turn left and drive 0.7 miles to Walnut Avenue. Turn right and continue 1.1 mile, passing the DeBell Golf Course, to the Stough Canyon Nature Center parking lot at the end of the road. An Adventure Pass is required for parking.

The hike

Walk past the trailhead kiosk and gate, heading up the wide, sandy road. Wind up the west wall of Stough Canyon, with a view of the ridge towering over Wildwood Canyon (Hike 5). Steadily climb to a posted junction at 0.4 miles. Begin the loop to the left, leaving the Stough Canyon Motorway and hiking the loop clockwise. Follow the wide trail to another junction. Detour ninety yards to the left to an overlook with a bench. The vistas extend across Glendale, the Los Angeles Basin, and the entire San Fernando Valley. Continue on the main trail among scrub oak, sage, toyon, and lemonade berry while overlooking McClure Canyon and Stough Canyon as the trail narrows to a footpath. On a flat is an old house foundation on the left with a 30-foot brick chimney, remnants of a youth camp from the 1920s. Cross the flat and start climbing again. Follow the trail signs toward Verdugo Motorway, the fire road atop the ridge. Top the slope to northern views of the San Gabriel Mountains above Tujunga. Veer left and gently descend to the Verdugo Motorway in a saddle at the head of Brace Canyon at 1.1 miles.

Take the road to the right, and head 0.3 miles downhill to the top of Stough Canyon and a junction. The ridge road continues a half mile to the La Tuna Canyon Trail (Hike 6) and 2 miles to the Wildwood Park Trail by the radio towers (Hike 5). Bear right on the Stough Canyon Motorway, and descend along the west canyon wall, completing the loop at 1.9 miles. Retrace your steps to the nature center. ■

5. Wildwood Canyon Trail to Verdugo Motorway and Wardens Grove

VERDUGO MOUNTAINS: WILDWOOD CANYON PARK

1701 Wildwood Canyon Drive · Burbank

Hiking distance: 4 miles round trip
Hiking time: 2.5 hours
Configuration: out-and-back
Elevation gain: 1,300 feet
Exposure: exposed
Difficulty: moderate
Dogs: allowed
Maps: U.S.G.S. Burbank · Harrison: Angeles Front Country Trail Map
Harrison: Verdugo Mountains Trail Map

The Verdugo Mountains are a small, three-mile-wide mountain range running parallel to the western end of the San Gabriel Mountains, forming part of the eastern boundary of the San Fernando Valley. The Verdugo Range stretches for eight miles above the cities of Burbank and Glendale (on the southwest) and Sunland, Tujunga, and La Crescenta (on the northeast). The Verdugos sit amidst greenspace that is entirely surrounded by urban development.

Wildwood Canyon, located in Burbank on the south-facing slope, is a 500-acre park with an open grassland, picnic areas, and this two-mile trail up to the Verdugo Motorway. Wildwood Canyon Trail is a steep, spine-climbing trail. The hike gains 1,300 feet from the lower foothills to the 2,900-foot ridge, located less than a mile west of 3,126-foot Verdugo Peak, the highest point in the range. Atop the ridgeline, the Verdugo Motorway, an unpaved, vehicle-restricted fire road, leads to fenced radio towers and Wardens Grove, a pine forest on the mountain's crest. Throughout the shadeless, aerobic climb are spectacular vistas of Los Angeles, the San Fernando Valley, Griffith Park, the Santa Monica Mountains, and the San Gabriel Mountains.

To the trailhead

From the Golden State Freeway (I-5) in Burbank, exit on Olive Avenue. Wind back to Olive Avenue, following the signs. Head 1.2 miles north on Olive Avenue to Sunset Canyon Drive. Turn left and drive 0.4 miles to Harvard Road. Turn right and continue 0.6 miles to the signed park entrance. Turn right into the park, and go 0.6 miles to the posted trailhead on the left. Park in the spaces on the right. An Adventure Pass is required for parking.

The hike

Pass the trailhead gate (located by the restrooms) and bend left. Follow the unpaved fire road and curve around the water tanks to the footpath. Loop around the contour of the mountain on a steep uphill grade to the ridge and a T-junction at 0.2 miles. The left fork descends south to the lower trailheads. Bear right and follow the narrow ridge above Wildwood Canyon. Climb to another junction at 0.4 miles. Savor the great views of the urban basin below and the Santa Monica Mountains, including Griffith Park. To the right is a picnic area and overlook, which continues down to the terminus of the park road.

Veer left on the footpath and zigzag up at a very steep grade. Cross a narrow spine on a level stretch, then climb again to a trail split. Both routes rejoin a short distance ahead; the right fork is the longer but easier route. Follow the ridge and climb a series of short but steep switchbacks on the sun-drenched chaparral slope. The trail reaches a dirt road on a U-bend at 1.4 miles. To the right is a radio tower. Veer to the left and go downhill to a road split at the Verdugo Motorway, with north and west vistas. The left fork leads 1.5 miles to La Tuna Canyon (Hike 6) and 2 miles to Stough Canyon (Hike 4). The right fork meanders through Wardens Grove, a partially burned pine grove atop the ridge that was planted by the Los Angeles County Department of Forestry in the 1930s. Return along the same route. ▪

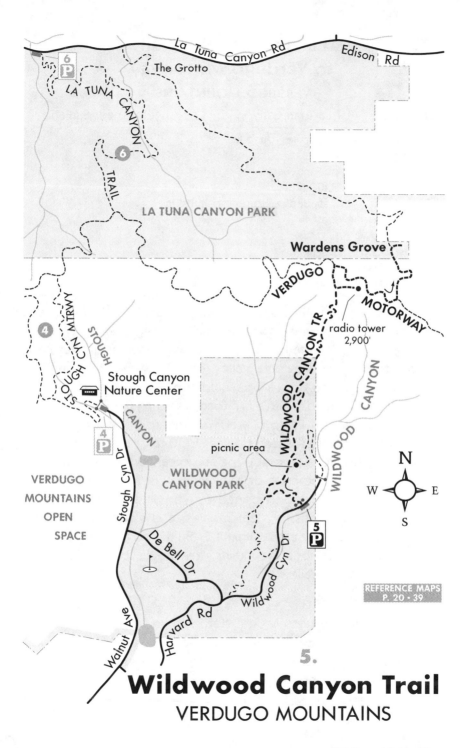

La Tuna Canyon Rd

Edison Rd

The Grotto

6 P

LA TUNA CANYON

6

TRAIL

LA TUNA CANYON PARK

Wardens Grove

VERDUGO

MOTORWAY

STOUGH CYN MTRWY

4

STOUGH CANYON

radio tower
2,900'

WILDWOOD CANYON TR

WILDWOOD CANYON

Stough Canyon
Nature Center

4 P

picnic area

WILDWOOD
CANYON PARK

VERDUGO
MOUNTAINS
OPEN
SPACE

Stough Cyn Dr

De Bell Dr

WILDWOOD

5 P

Wildwood Cyn Dr

N
W · E
S

REFERENCE MAPS
P. 20 - 39

Walnut Ave

Harvard Rd

Wildwood Cyn Dr

5.

Wildwood Canyon Trail
VERDUGO MOUNTAINS

6. La Tuna Canyon Trail to Verdugo Motorway

VERDUGO MOUNTAINS

8000 block of La Tuna Canyon Rd · Los Angeles (near Sunland)

Hiking distance: 4.4 miles round trip
Hiking time: 2.5 hours
Configuration: out-and-back
Elevation gain: 1,100 feet
Exposure: mix of shaded canyon and open slopes
Difficulty: moderate
Dogs: allowed
Maps: U.S.G.S. Burbank
Harrison: Angeles Front Country Trail Map
Harrison: Verdugo Mountains Trail Map

The Verdugo Mountains, an offshoot range of the San Gabriel Mountains, were named for the Jose Verdugo family, owners of the land during the late 1700s. The two mountain ranges are separated by the Crescenta Valley, containing the communities of Sunland, Tujunga, and La Crescenta. A network of trails weave though the Verdugos, with a fire road bisecting the ridge.

La Tuna Canyon Park, located on the north slope of the Verdugo Mountains, encompasses 1,100 acres. The undeveloped park provides access up the steep canyon to the Verdugo Motorway atop the crest of the range. This 2.2-mile-long trail climbs through a quiet, tree-lined canyon among mature coast live oaks, bay laurels, big leaf maples, and sycamores to the scrub-covered slope at the summit. From the ridge are sweeping views of the San Gabriel Mountains, downtown Los Angeles, and the San Fernando Valley.

To the trailhead

From the Foothill Freeway (Interstate 210) in Tujunga, exit on La Tuna Canyon Road. Drive 1.1 mile west to the signed trailhead on the left. Park in the signed pullout by the trailhead. An Adventure Pass is required for parking.

The hike

From the east end of the parking pullout, take the signed trail into an unnamed canyon. Drop down along the east side of the drainage among oaks and sycamores. Zigzag up the canyon wall on five switchbacks, then traverse the mountain. Follow the contours on a steady uphill grade. At 0.8 miles, the trail levels out on the north-facing slope and crosses into La Tuna Canyon.

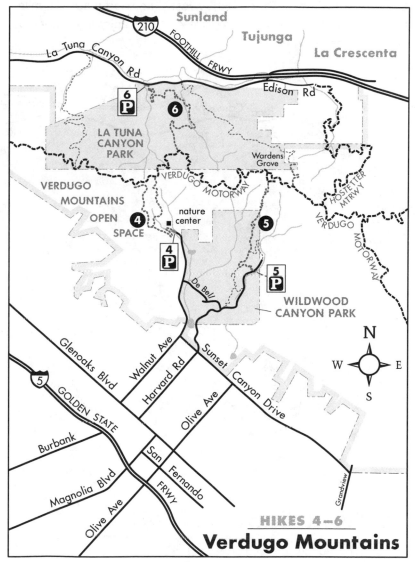

Descend into the forested canyon and cross the seasonal drainage. Ascend the east canyon slope and return to the streambed. Follow the drainage under the shaded canopy and cross the stream. Climb the west canyon slope, winding to a ridge. Make a horseshoe left bend and follow the ridge south, reaching the Verdugo Motorway at 2.2 miles. To the left (east), the dirt fire road leads 1.5 miles to Wardens Grove and the Wildwood Canyon Trail (Hike 5). To the right (west), the road leads 0.5 miles to the head of Stough Canyon (Hike 4). After enjoying the views, return by retracing your route. ■

6.
La Tuna Canyon Trail
VERDUGO MOUNTAINS

7. Trail Canyon Falls
BIG TUJUNGA CANYON

Hiking distance: 3 miles round trip
Hiking time: 1.5 hours
Configuration: out-and-back
Elevation gain: 700 feet
Exposure: mix of shaded woodland and open slopes
Difficulty: easy to moderate
Dogs: allowed
Maps: U.S.G.S. Sunland
Harrison: Angeles Front Country Trail Map

Trail Canyon Creek forms on the southern slope of Iron Mountain in the San Gabriel Mountains. The creek drops five miles down the steep, rocky canyon before joining Big Tujunga Creek. On its downward journey, Trail Canyon Falls freefalls 40 feet off a granite precipice into a pool etched into the metamorphic rock. This hike begins in Big Tujunga Canyon and follows the creek up Trail Canyon to the crest of the falls. The trail starts on a closed fire road that passes through a cluster of private cabins that date back to the 1920s. The diverse hike leads through streamside vegetation with sycamores, alders, and cottonwoods, then traverses an exposed chaparral-covered canyon wall to the falls.

To the trailhead

From the Foothill Freeway (Interstate 210) in Sunland, exit on Sunland Boulevard. Drive 0.7 miles east on Foothill Boulevard to Oro Vista Avenue and turn left. Continue 0.8 miles to Big Tujunga Canyon Road and curve right. Drive 4.4 miles to a dirt road on the left, directly across the road from a "Delta Flats" sign. (If you reach Ottie Road, you have gone 0.1 mile too far.) Turn left on Trail Canyon Road (Forest Service Road 3N34), and wind 0.4 miles on the narrow dirt road to the trailhead parking area at the end of the road. An Adventure Pass is required for parking.

The hike

From the trailhead kiosk, take the gated fire road. Pass a group of privately owned cabins, and follow the winding road on the east wall of Trail Canyon. Pass a small waterfall on the left, and drop into the canopy of oaks, alders, and cottonwoods. Cross a tributary and climb over an exposed scrub-covered slope. Leave the road at a sharp left bend, and veer right on a footpath. Cross Trail Canyon Creek and stroll up the shaded canyon floor along the west side of the creek. Cross the boulder-filled creek four more times, then leave the canyon bottom. Climb up the open chaparral-clad hillside to great views up and down Trail Canyon. Traverse the canyon wall on an upward slope. As the path levels out, bend left to an overlook of Trail Canyon Falls, dropping off a rounded granite rock lip. Continue on a sweeping curve, and pass a couple of steep paths with loose gravel on the right that descend to the base of the falls and pool. A short distance ahead, another side path on the right leads to an overlook from the brink of the falls. Return by retracing your steps.

To extend the hike, the trail follows the creek two miles to Tom Lucas Camp on a grassy flat with lush vegetation along the banks of Trail Canyon Creek. Beyond the camp, the trail continues up the east flank of Iron Mountain. ■

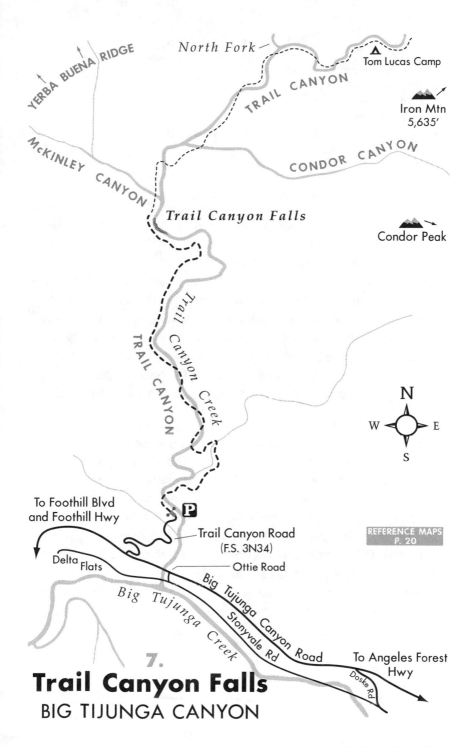

YERBA BUENA RIDGE

McKINLEY CANYON

North Fork

TRAIL CANYON

CONDOR CANYON

Tom Lucas Camp

Iron Mtn
5,635'

Condor Peak

Trail Canyon Falls

TRAIL CANYON

Trail Canyon Creek

N
W ◆ E
S

To Foothill Blvd
and Foothill Hwy

P

Trail Canyon Road
(F.S. 3N34)

REFERENCE MAPS
P. 20

Delta Flats

Ottie Road

Big Tujunga Creek

Big Tujunga Canyon Road

Stonyvale Rd

Doske Rd

To Angeles Forest
Hwy

7.
Trail Canyon Falls
BIG TIJUNGA CANYON

8. Haines Canyon

Hiking distance: 3 miles round trip
Hiking time: 1.5 hours
Configuration: out-and-back
Elevation gain: 1,000 feet
Exposure: mix of open slopes and forested pockets
Difficulty: moderate
Dogs: allowed
Maps: U.S.G.S. Sunland
Harrison: Angeles Front Country Trail Map

Haines Creek forms on the west slope of Mount Lukens on the western end of the San Gabriel Mountains. The creek flows through the canyon, emptying into the Haines Canyon Reservoir on the northeast corner of Tujunga. The basin is a catch-all for rocks and brush washed down the drainage. The Haines Canyon Trail begins at the dam and catch basin, following the waterway up canyon. The trail is an often-used route to the summit of Mount Lukens, the highest peak in Los Angeles. Instead of climbing up the 5,074-foot mountain, this hike follows the canyon bottom through a jungle of riparian habitat to a lush spring with ferns.

To the trailhead

Heading westbound on the Foothill Freeway (Interstate 210) in La Crescenta, exit on Lowell Avenue. Drive 0.3 miles straight ahead on Honolulu Avenue to Tujunga Canyon Boulevard. Veer right on Tujunga Canyon Boulevard, and go 1.3 miles to Haines Canyon Avenue. Turn right and continue 0.2 miles to Day Street. Turn right and go one block, returning to Haines Canyon Avenue. Turn left and drive 0.6 miles to the end of the road at the trailhead gate. An Adventure Pass is required for parking.

Heading eastbound on the Foothill Freeway (Interstate 210) in La Crescenta, exit on La Tuna Canyon Road. Turn left under the freeway and drive 1.3 miles to Tujunga Canyon Boulevard. Turn left and continue with the directions above.

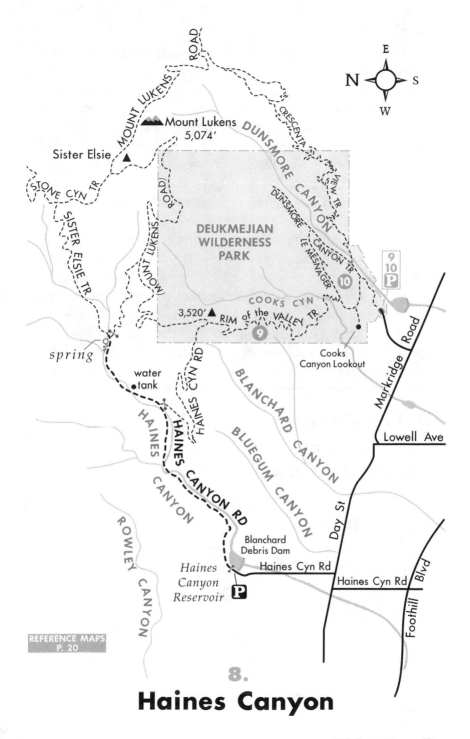

N
E
S
W

MOUNT LUKENS ROAD

Mount Lukens
5,074'

Sister Elsie

CRESCENTA

DUNSMORE CANYON

STONE CYN TR

SISTER ELSIE TR

MOUNT LUKENS ROAD

DEUKMEJIAN
WILDERNESS
PARK

DUNSMORE

VIEW TR

CANYON TR

LE MESNAGER

10

spring

water
tank

3,520'

RIM of the VALLEY TR

COOKS CYN

9

Cooks
Canyon Lookout

9
10
P

Markridge Road

HAINES CYN RD

HAINES CANYON

BLANCHARD CANYON

BLUEGUM CANYON

Day St

Lowell Ave

HAINES CANYON RD

ROWLEY CANYON

Blanchard
Debris Dam

Haines Cyn Rd

Haines
Canyon
Reservoir

P

Haines Cyn Rd

Foothill Blvd

REFERENCE MAPS
P. 20

8.

Haines Canyon

The hike

Head up the dirt fire road and pass the vehicle gate, following the left side of the Blanchard debris dam and the Haines Canyon Reservoir. Stay on the main road, passing a dirt road coming in from the left and another from the right. Steadily climb along the west edge of Haines Canyon under oaks and sycamores. The road levels out at one mile, and the canyon bends left at a trail split. Haines Canyon Road (also known as Mount Lukens Road) veers to the right, passing another vehicle gate. The fire road climbs the south-facing slope to the summit of 5,074-foot Mount Lukens.

For this hike, take the left fork, staying in Haines Canyon. The forested canyon quickly narrows, and the dirt road becomes a footpath. Pass a cement water tank on the right, and cross Haines Creek under a lush canopy. Continue up canyon, curving right along the drainage to a signed fork at a fern-filled spring. The left fork follows the Sister Elsie Trail to the Stone Canyon Trail. The right fork continues one mile to the Haines Canyon Road. Choose your own turn around spot. ■

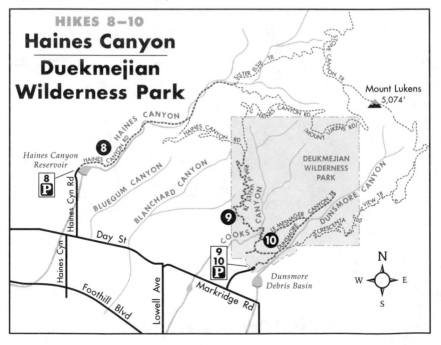

9. Rim of the Valley Trail

DEUKMEJIAN WILDERNESS PARK

3429 Markridge Road · La Crescenta

Hiking distance: 3.5 miles round trip
Hiking time: 2 hours
Configuration: out-and-back
Elevation gain: 1,200 feet
Exposure: mix of forested canyon and open slopes
Difficulty: moderate to somewhat strenuous
Dogs: allowed
Maps: U.S.G.S. Sunland and Condor Peak
　　　　Harrison: Angeles Front Country Trail Map
　　　　Deukmejian Wilderness Park Trail Map

Deukmejian Wilderness Park is a rugged 702-acre park on the north edge of Glendale in the foothills of the San Gabriel Mountains. The park is named for George Deukmejian, the former governor of California. The wilderness park is home to Cooks Canyon and Dunsmore Canyon, two stream-fed drainages with riparian woodland habitats and steep chaparral-covered slopes. The Rim of the Valley Trail passes through lush Cooks Canyon, teaming with native plants. The path crosses bridges over gorges to the arid upper slopes and Haines Canyon Road, a narrow dirt fire road that weaves up to 5,074-foot Mount Lukens, the highest peak in Los Angeles. From the upper foothills at the end of this hike are great vistas across the San Fernando Valley.

To the trailhead

From the Foothill Freeway (Interstate 210) in La Crescenta, exit on Pennsylvania Avenue. Drive 0.4 miles north to Foothill Boulevard. Turn left and go 0.3 miles to New York Avenue. Turn right and continue 0.9 miles to Markridge Road. Turn left and drive 0.1 mile to the park entrance on the right. Turn right, enter the park, and go 0.2 miles uphill to the trailhead parking lots on both sides of the road. An Adventure Pass is required for parking.

The hike

From the far north end of the parking lot, take the gravel path through the landscaped grounds to the map kiosk. Head up the canyon on the Dunsmore Canyon Trail, staying on the west side of the drainage to a posted junction. Leave the Dunsmore Canyon Trail, and bear left on the Rim of the Valley Trail. Ascend the west canyon wall to a signed Y-fork with the Cooks Canyon Lookout Trail. Detour to the left, and follow a narrow ridge 265 yards on the southeast rim of Cooks Canyon. The side path ends at an overlook of the Verdugo Mountains, the San Gabriel Mountains, the San Gabriel Valley, and the San Fernando Valley.

Return to the main trail, and continue 130 yards to a junction with the Le Mesnager Loop Trail. Bear left, staying on the Rim of the Valley Trail. Descend into Cooks Canyon to the forested canyon floor. Follow the narrow, stream-fed canyon bottom and cross the stream. Climb wooden steps to a bridge, and cross over the steep-walled ravine. Traverse the west wall of Cooks Canyon, zigzagging up the hillside. Steadily gain elevation to magnificent views. The pines of Wardens Grove can be spotted atop Verdugo Ridge (Hike 5). Near the top, cross a ridge to views across the entire San Fernando Valley, from the Santa Susana Mountains to the Santa Monica Mountains. Follow the ridge between Blanchard Canyon and Cooks Canyon. Zipper up two more switchbacks, arriving at Haines Canyon Road, a narrow dirt road at the upper end of the trail at 3,520 feet. ▪

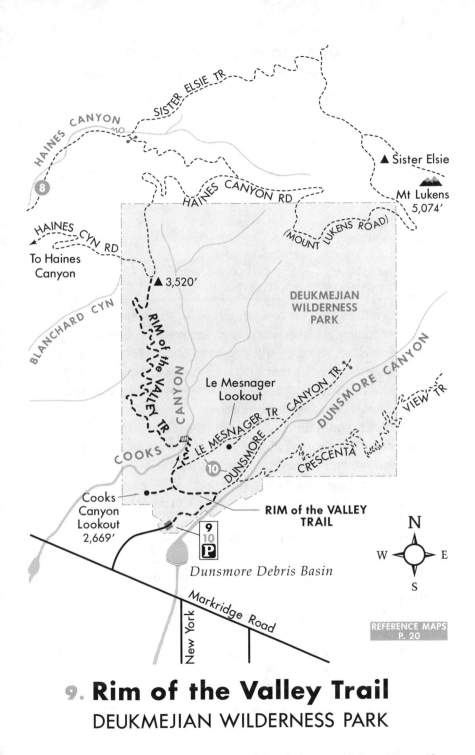

SISTER ELSIE TR

HAINES CANYON

▲ Sister Elsie

Mt Lukens
5,074'

8

HAINES CANYON RD

(MOUNT LUKENS ROAD)

HAINES CYN RD

To Haines
Canyon

▲ 3,520'

DEUKMEJIAN
WILDERNESS
PARK

BLANCHARD CYN

RIM of the VALLEY TR

COOKS CANYON

Le Mesnager
Lookout

LE MESNAGER TR

DUNSMORE CANYON TR

DUNSMORE CANYON

VIEW TR

DUNSMORE

CRESCENTA

10

Cooks
Canyon
Lookout
2,669'

RIM of the VALLEY
TRAIL

9
10
P

Dunsmore Debris Basin

N

W ✦ E

S

New York

Markridge Road

REFERENCE MAPS
P. 20

9. **Rim of the Valley Trail**
DEUKMEJIAN WILDERNESS PARK

10. Dunsmore Canyon Loop
Le Mesnager Trail • Cooks Canyon Lookout
DEUKMEJIAN WILDERNESS PARK
3429 Markridge Road · La Crescenta

Hiking distance: 2 miles round trip
Hiking time: 1 hour
Configuration: loop with three short spur trails
Elevation gain: 700 feet
Exposure: mix of forested canyon and open slopes
Difficulty: easy to slightly moderate
Dogs: allowed
Maps: U.S.G.S. Sunland and Condor Peak
        Harrison: Angeles Front Country Trail Map
        Deukmejian Wilderness Park Trail Map

Dunsmore Canyon is the main drainage in Deukmejian Wilderness Park. The canyon is tucked into the mountains above the Crescenta Valley and is bordered by the Angeles National Forest. The elevations range from 2,159 feet at the park's southern end to 4,775 feet in the northeast corner. Aside from the lower 12 acres, the rustic terrain is relatively undisturbed.

This hike makes a loop up Dunsmore Canyon and returns on Le Mesnager Trail, stopping at a couple of overlooks. It is a popular hiking, biking, and equestrian route. The Dunsmore Canyon Trail parallels the creek for nearly one mile on an easy uphill grade. The trail passes a series of low dams used to control the flow of water and contain sediments. The Le Mesnager Trail winds along the east-facing hillside through native chaparral, connecting with short spur trails to Le Mesnager Lookout and Cooks Canyon Lookout. The lookouts sit atop knolls that overlook the Verdugo Mountains, Glendale, the San Fernando Valley, the Los Angeles basin, and the San Gabriel Valley.

The Le Mesnager Trail is named for George Le Mesnager, an immigrant and World War 1 veteran who originally purchased the land in 1898 and began a wine growing operation. The old two-story granite stone building at the trailhead were built in

1914 and used for the storage of Le Mesnager's equipment and grapes. Later it was converted into the ranch house. The ranch was purchased by the city of Glendale in 1988.

To the trailhead

From the Foothill Freeway (Interstate 210) in La Crescenta, exit on Pennsylvania Avenue. Drive 0.4 miles north to Foothill Boulevard. Turn left and go 0.3 miles to New York Avenue. Turn right and continue 0.9 miles to Markridge Road. Turn left and drive 0.1 mile to the park entrance on the right. Turn right, enter the park, and go 0.2 miles uphill to the trailhead parking lots on both sides of the road. An Adventure Pass is required for parking.

The hike

From the far north end of the parking lot, take the gravel path through the landscaped grounds to the map kiosk. Head up the canyon 300 yards on the Dunsmore Canyon Trail (a fire road), staying on the west side of the drainage to a posted junction. The Rim of the Valley Trail goes to the left. Stay to the right on the Dunsmore Canyon Trail for another 70 yards to a second signed junction. The Crescenta View Trail veers off to the right. Stay left, following the west side of the drainage to Le Mesnager Loop Trail on the left—our return route. Continue climbing straight ahead as the canyon narrows. The trail ends by the seasonal stream under the shade of oaks and alders by a concrete weir.

Descend back to Le Mesnager Loop Trail, losing 325 feet in elevation. Bear right and head up the slope on the west wall of the canyon. Climb the chaparral-cloaked hillside, topping a rise to great views of the Verdugo Mountains and the pocket communities of La Crescenta and Tujunga. Detour left on Le Mesnager Lookout Trail for 40 yards to a knoll with a bench and expansive vistas of Dunsmore Canyon, the urban basins, and the surrounding mountain ranges. Return to the main trail and head downhill. Pass the Rim of the Valley Trail heading off to the right (Hike 9), and continue to Cooks Canyon Lookout Trail, also on the right. Detour to the right and follow a narrow ridge 265 yards on the southeast rim of Cooks Canyon to an overlook. From this spot are additional vast views of the cities and mountains. The main trail drops back down into Dunsmore Canyon, completing the loop. Return to the trailhead on the right. ■

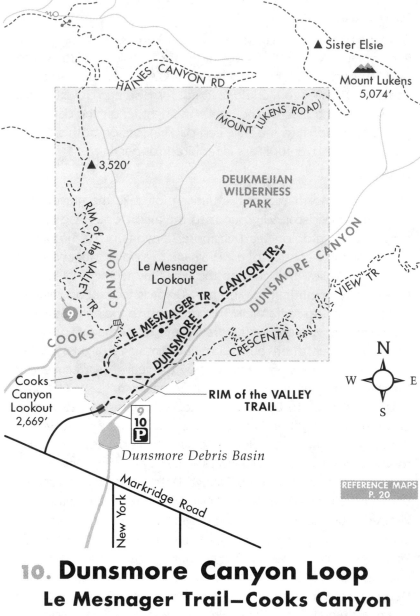

10. Dunsmore Canyon Loop
Le Mesnager Trail–Cooks Canyon
DEUKMEJIAN WILDERNESS PARK

11. Cerro Negro (Black Hill)
SAN RAFAEL HILLS

Hiking distance: 1.5 miles round trip
Hiking time: 45 minutes
Configuration: out-and-back
Elevation gain: 200 feet
Exposure: exposed hilltop
Difficulty: easy
Dogs: allowed
Maps: U.S.G.S. Pasadena

The San Rafael Hills are a small mountain rise on the eastern flank of the Verdugo Mountains at the east end of Glendale. The hills are bordered by the Verdugo Canyon, the Arroyo Seco Drainage, and La Crescenta Valley. A network of fire road trails weave through the San Rafael Hills.

This hike begins off Camino San Rafael and climbs through native chaparral habitat to an out-of-service fire lookout tower atop Cerro Negro. Cerro Negro, Spanish for *black hills*, is the second highest peak in the hills at 1,887 feet, two feet shorter than Flint Peak to its south. From the summit are sweeping 360-degree vistas of the San Gabriel Mountains, the Verdugo Mountains, La Crescenta Valley, and the Los Angeles Basin.

To the trailhead

From the Glendale Freeway (Highway 2) in Glendale, exit on Mountain Street. Drive east on Mountain Street, which becomes Camino San Rafael en route. At 1.9 miles, the road tops a ridge by two gated fire roads on the left. The northern (right) road is the trail. Park along the side of the road. An Adventure Pass is required for parking.

The hike

Walk past the vehicle gate, and head up the paved road 100 yards to the end of the pavement. Continue up the dirt road to westward views of Glendale, La Crescenta, Tujunga, the San Gabriel Mountains, and the east face of the Verdugo Mountains. Top the slope to a Y-fork. Stay left and gently descend to a view of the fire lookout tower. Drop down to the edge of the subdivision, passing another trail access at the north end of Camino San Rafael. Skirt the west flank of the homes along the back side of Flintridge Drive. Ascend the hill to a junction and veer right, staying on the Ridge Motorway. Pass the lookout tower above to an overlook and bench, with vistas east along the San Gabriel Range and across Pasadena. The road continues to the right up to the fenced lookout tower, with views of Hollywood and the Los Angeles Basin. ■

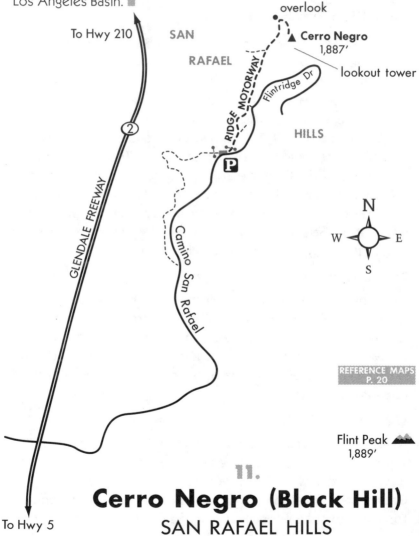

11.
Cerro Negro (Black Hill)
SAN RAFAEL HILLS

12. Fall Creek Falls
BIG TUJUNGA CANYON

Hiking distance: 4 miles round trip
Hiking time: 2 hours
Configuration: out-and-back
Elevation gain: 600 feet
Exposure: mostly exposed
Difficulty: easy to moderate
Dogs: allowed
Maps: U.S.G.S. Condor Peak · Harrison: Angeles Front Country Trail Map
 Harrison: Mt. Wilson Trail Map

Fall Creek Falls is a four-tiered waterfall that tumbles down the cliff walls for more than 250 feet. The waterfall is located on Fall Creek in Big Tujunga Canyon, just above its confluence with Big Tujunga Creek. All four drops have a pool at their base. The Fall Creek Trail descends on a dirt fire road into Big Tujunga Canyon, a mile upstream from Big Tujunga Reservoir. The road/trail drops 700 feet down the south canyon wall to the creek. En route is a spectacular view of Big Tujunga Canyon and an overlook of the waterfall, seen across the scenic canyon. To see Fall Creek Falls in its glory, it is best to go after a rain.

To the trailhead

From the Foothill Freeway (Interstate 210) in La Canada, exit on the Angeles Crest Highway (Highway 2). Drive 9.4 miles north to the signed Angeles Forest Highway. Turn left and continue 3.8 miles to Big Tujunga Canyon Road. Turn left and go 0.6 miles to a wide parking pullout on the right. An Adventure Pass is not required.

The hike

Pass the vehicle gate and head down the old dirt road (Forest Service Road 3N27). Curve right to the spectacular view of Big Tujunga Canyon from a perch 600 feet above. Steadily descend on the serpentine road at an easy grade. Follow the contours of the mountain beneath the eroding rock wall. At 1.7 miles, the road lies directly across the canyon from Fall Creek and Fall Creek Falls.

This is the best vantage point to view portions of the four-tiered cataract. Parts of the waterfall are obscured by a dense pocket of alder trees.

Continue down the road to the canyon floor and Big Tujunga Creek. At the creek is very primitive Fall Creek Camp, precariously tucked within the boulders and brush. To reach the base of the lower 80-foot falls, rock-hop and bushwack a quarter mile downstream, carving out your own route. To see the upper falls, climb less than a half mile up Fall Creek Road (on the north wall of the canyon) to views of all four tiers. Return by retracing your steps. ■

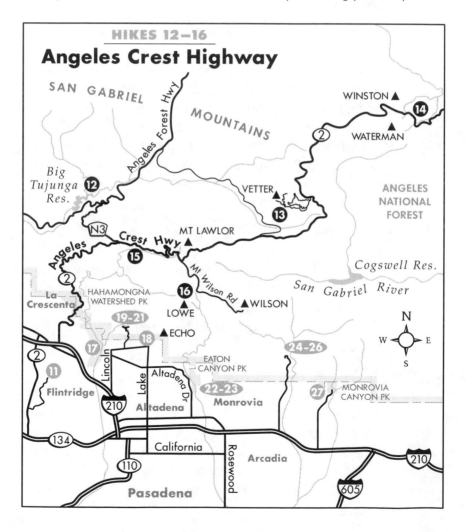

HIKES 12–16
Angeles Crest Highway

SAN GABRIEL

Angeles Forest Hwy

MOUNTAINS

WINSTON ▲

14

② WATERMAN ▲

Big Tujunga Res. 12

VETTER ▲

13

ANGELES NATIONAL FOREST

N3 Crest Hwy MT LAWLOR ▲

Angeles

15

②

La Crescenta

HAHAMONGNA WATERSHED PK

16

LOWE ▲

Mt Wilson Rd

▲ WILSON

Cogswell Res.

San Gabriel River

N
W ✦ E
S

19-21

17

18

▲ ECHO

EATON CANYON PK

24-26

Lincoln

Altadena Dr

11

Flintridge

Lake

22-23

Monrovia

27

MONROVIA CANYON PK

210 Altadena

134

California

110

Rosewood

Arcadia

210

605

Pasadena

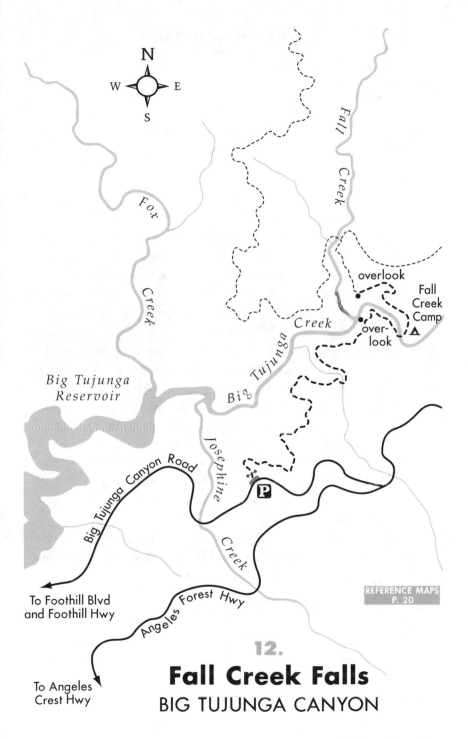

N
W E
S

Fall Creek

Fox Creek

overlook

Fall Creek Camp

Creek

over-look

Big Tujunga

Big Tujunga Reservoir

Big Tujunga Canyon Road

Josephine Creek

P

REFERENCE MAPS
P. 20

To Foothill Blvd and Foothill Hwy

Angeles Forest Hwy

To Angeles Crest Hwy

12.
Fall Creek Falls
BIG TUJUNGA CANYON

13. Vetter Mountain

Hiking distance: 1.8-mile loop
Hiking time: 1 hour
Configuration: loop
Elevation gain: 400 feet
Exposure: mix of open hilltop and forested groves
Difficulty: easy
Dogs: allowed
Maps: U.S.G.S. Chilao Flat · Harrison: Angeles Front Country Trail Map
Harrison: Mt. Wilson Trail Map

Vetter Mountain (formerly called Pine Mountain) rises 5,908 feet in the front range of the San Gabriel Mountains. The mountain sits between the hot and dry Chaparral Zone to the south and the Montane Forest Zone to the north, home to big cone spruce, Jeffrey pine, sugar pine, white fir, incense cedar, and canyon oak. Previously perched atop the summit was a fire lookout built by the U.S. Forest Service in 1937. The historic Vetter Lookout was, unfortunately, destroyed in the 2009 Station Fire. The summit, however, still offers spectacular 360-degree panoramas that include San Gabriel Peak, Mount Wilson, Fox Mountain, Condor Peak, Mount Gleason, Mount Waterman, and Mount Baldy. On the east flank of the summit is Charlton Flat, a picnic area. The Vetter Mountain Trail, a 1.5-mile-long trail, leads from the picnic area to the summit. This hike includes just the upper section of the trail through a shallow draw, utilizing a gated dirt road to form a loop. The trail winds through chaparral and a conifer forest across both ecological zones.

A segment of the 53-mile Silver Moccasin Trail runs through Charlton Flat, connecting the Angeles Crest Highway to Chilao Flat.

To the trailhead

From the Foothill Freeway (Interstate 210) in La Canada, exit on the Angeles Crest Highway (Highway 2). Drive 23.2 miles north to the Charlton Flat Picnic Area turnoff (Forest Service Road 3N16) on the left. Turn left and continue 1.3 miles, staying left at the junctions, to a Y-fork and gated dirt road. Park on the side of the road. An Adventure Pass is required for parking.

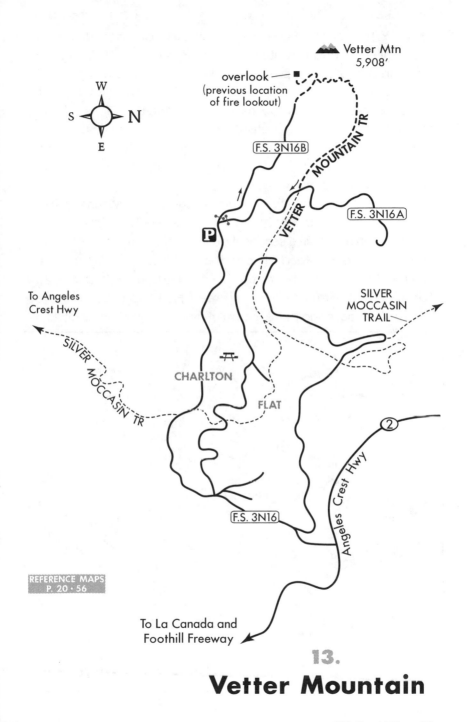

Vetter Mtn
5,908'

overlook
(previous location
of fire lookout)

F.S. 3N16B

VETTER MOUNTAIN TR

F.S. 3N16A

W
S — N
E

P

To Angeles
Crest Hwy

SILVER MOCCASIN TR

SILVER
MOCCASIN
TRAIL

CHARLTON

FLAT

2

Angeles Crest Hwy

F.S. 3N16

REFERENCE MAPS
P. 20 · 56

To La Canada and
Foothill Freeway

13.
Vetter Mountain

The hike

At the Y-fork, Forest Service Road 3N16 divides into 3N16A on the right—our return route—and 3N16B on the left. Begin the loop on the left fork, passing the vehicle gate. Follow the dirt road parallel to the north side of the ridge. The gentle uphill slope gains 300 feet in 0.7 miles to the remains of the Vetter Mountain Lookout. Just before reaching the summit, pass the posted Vetter Mountain Trail on the right, the return route. Veer left, then right, forming an S-pattern to the open overlook with sweeping 360-degree vistas.

After savoring the views, return to the Vetter Mountain Trail. Leave the road and zigzag down eleven switchbacks on the footpath. Stroll down a seasonal drainage through chaparral and under oaks to F.S. Road 3N16A. The trail continues across the road and leads 0.7 miles to the lower Charlton Flat Picnic Area. For this hike, bear right on the dirt road. Head up the serpentine road among oaks and pines, completing the loop at the Y-fork. ■

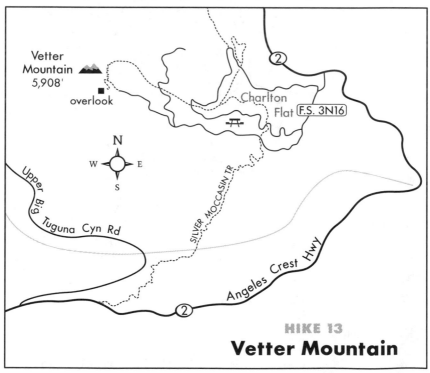

14. Cooper Canyon Falls
via Burkhart Trail

Hiking distance: 3.6 miles round trip
Hiking time: 2 hours
Configuration: out-and-back
Elevation gain: 750 feet
Exposure: mostly forested canyon
Difficulty: moderate
Dogs: allowed
Maps: U.S.G.S. Waterman Mountain
        Harrison: Angeles High Country Trail Map

Cooper Canyon Falls drops 30 feet off a moss-covered rock wall into a lush grotto with a pool. The cataract is set within the San Gabriel Wilderness in a deep canyon northeast of Waterman Mountain. The pristine, 6,000-foot-high landscape is rich with a fragrant forest of towering incense cedar, Jeffrey and sugar pine, fir, oak, alder, and perennial cascading waters. The Burkhart Trail descends through Buckhorn Canyon to Cooper Canyon and follows Cooper Creek to the waterfall, where the trail joins with the Pacific Crest Trail.

The Pacific Crest Trail runs for 2,650 miles, from Mexico to Canada, passing through California, Oregon, and Washington.

To the trailhead

From the Foothill Freeway (Interstate 210) in La Canada, exit on the Angeles Crest Highway (Highway 2). Drive 34 miles north to the signed Buckhorn Campground on the left. Turn left and wind one mile down the narrow paved road to the day use trailhead parking area. An Adventure Pass is required for parking.

The hike

From the far end of the parking area, head northeast on the signed trail. Follow the sandy footpath on the west side of the forested canyon high above Buckhorn Creek. Steadily descend among the towering cedars, pines, firs, and pockets of ferns. Pass overlooks of the stream-fed Buckhorn Canyon, which offers views of beautiful outcrops. When the outcrops on the east canyon wall come into view, three spur trails on the right descend to the stream by small falls and pools. The Burkhart Trail veers left into Cooper Canyon, then switchbacks to the right. Traverse the south canyon wall, and parallel Cooper Creek to the base of Buckhorn Canyon by majestic cedar trees with multiple trunks grown together. Rock hop over Buckhorn Creek above its confluence with Cooper Canyon Creek. Continue downstream to the east, passing more cedars. At 1.7 miles is a T-junction with the Pacific Crest Trail. The left fork leads 1.1 mile to Cooper Canyon Camp. Go to the right and walk 100 yards to the top of Cooper Canyon Falls on the left. Continue 30 yards to an unsigned fork. (If you reach the crossing of Little Rock Creek, you have gone 0.2 miles past the fork.) The short, steep spur trail on the left descends to the base of the falls in a vertical rock bowl. If descending to the base, use caution, as this path has loose rock and is steep. ■

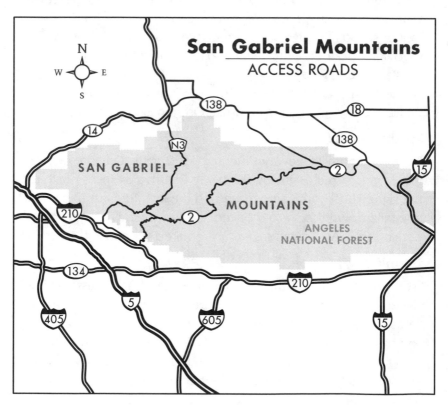

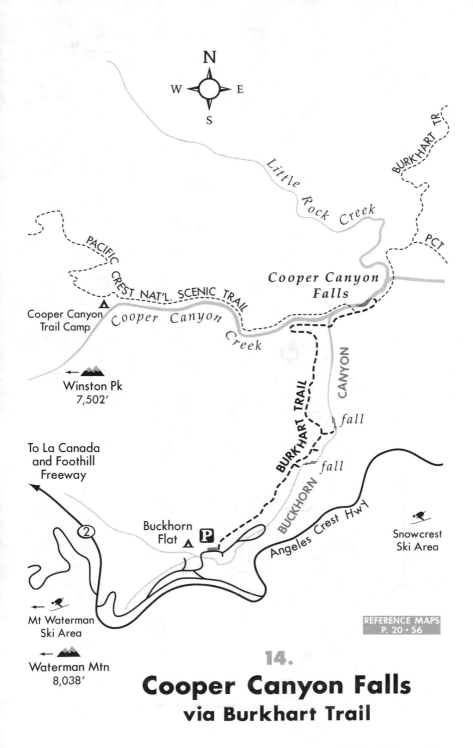

N
W E
S

BURKHART TR

Little Rock Creek

PACIFIC

PCT

CREST NAT'L. SCENIC TRAIL

Cooper Canyon Falls

Cooper Canyon
Trail Camp

Cooper Canyon Creek

CANYON

Winston Pk
7,502'

BURKHART TRAIL

fall

To La Canada
and Foothill
Freeway

fall

BUCKHORN

Buckhorn
Flat

P

Angeles Crest Hwy

Snowcrest
Ski Area

2

Mt Waterman
Ski Area

REFERENCE MAPS
P. 20 • 56

Waterman Mtn
8,038'

14.

Cooper Canyon Falls
via Burkhart Trail

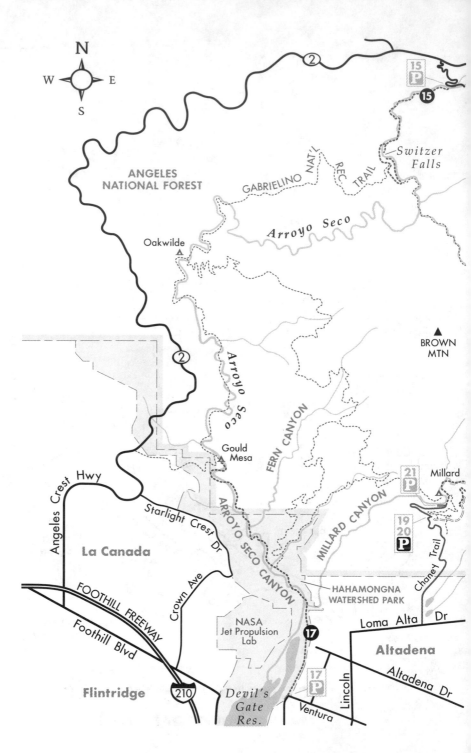

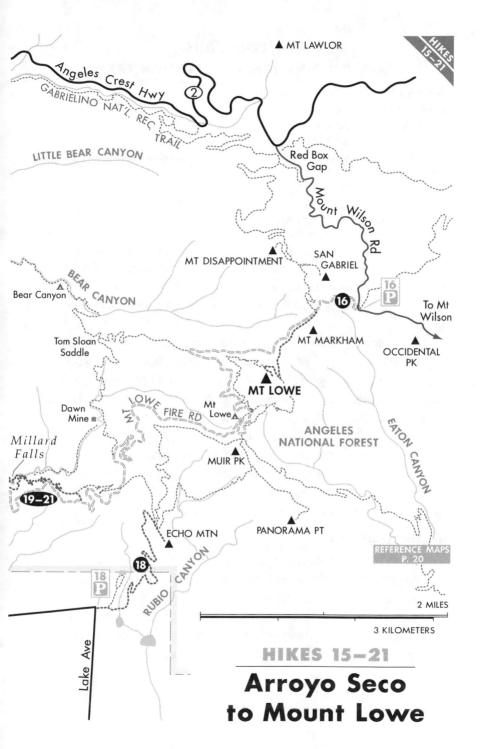

▲ MT LAWLOR

Angeles Crest Hwy

②

GABRIELINO NAT'L. REC. TRAIL

LITTLE BEAR CANYON

Red Box
Gap

Mount Wilson Rd

BEAR CANYON

Bear Canyon ▲

MT DISAPPOINTMENT ▲

SAN
GABRIEL ▲

16 P

16

To Mt
Wilson

Tom Sloan
Saddle

MT MARKHAM ▲

OCCIDENTAL
PK ▲

Dawn
Mine ■

MT LOWE FIRE RD

Mt
Lowe ▲

MT LOWE ▲

ANGELES
NATIONAL FOREST

EATON CANYON

Millard
Falls

19-21

MUIR PK ▲

ECHO MTN ▲

PANORAMA PT ▲

REFERENCE MAPS
P. 20

18

18 P

RUBIO CANYON

2 MILES

3 KILOMETERS

Lake Ave

HIKES 15-21

Arroyo Seco
to Mount Lowe

15. Switzer Falls
GABRIELINO NATIONAL RECREATION TRAIL

Hiking distance: 4.6 miles round trip
Hiking time: 2.5 hours
Configuration: out-and-back
Elevation gain: 600 feet
Exposure: mostly forested canyon with some exposed sections
Difficulty: moderate
Dogs: allowed
Maps: U.S.G.S. Condor Peak · Harrison: Angeles Front Country Trail Map
Harrison: Mt. Wilson Trail Map

Switzer Falls is a gorgeous 50-foot, two-tiered waterfall deep in Arroyo Seco Canyon. The upper falls drops through a narrow gorge into a pool naturally carved into the rock. The 15-foot lower falls is tucked into a steep-walled rock grotto with a small pool.

The trailhead to Switzer Falls is located off the Angeles Crest Highway (Highway 2) at the mouth of the canyon by the Switzer Picnic Area. The hike follows Arroyo Seco Creek through intimate creekside habitat with granite boulders, numerous pools, and the shade of alder, oak, maple, spruce, and willow trees. The trail leads to primitive Commodore Switzer Camp, traverses sheer rock walls, passes overlooks of the upper falls, and doubles back along the creek to the base of the lower falls. The trail follows a section of the Gabrielino National Recreation Trail, a 28-mile trail that runs through the Angeles National Forest.

To the trailhead

From the Foothill Freeway (Interstate 210) in La Canada, exit on the Angeles Crest Highway (Highway 2). Drive 9.9 miles north to the signed Switzer Picnic Area turnoff on the right. (The turnoff is located 0.5 miles past the Angeles Forest Highway.) Turn right and wind a half mile down the paved road to the parking lot at the end of the road. An Adventure Pass is required for parking.

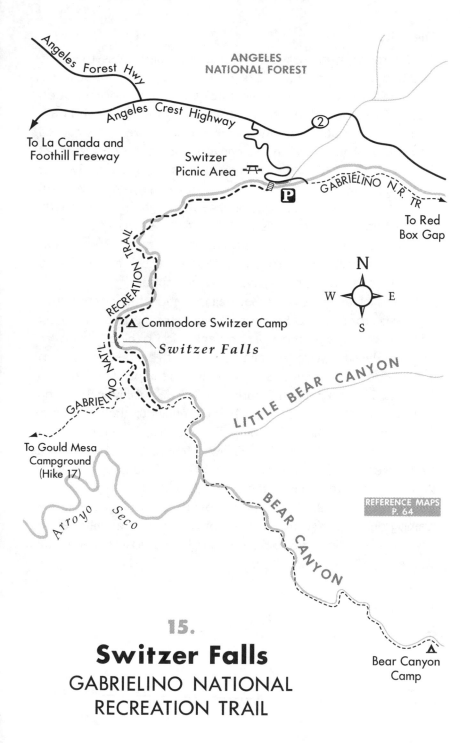

ANGELES
NATIONAL FOREST

Angeles Forest Hwy

Angeles Crest Highway

ANGELES NATIONAL FOREST

2

To La Canada and
Foothill Freeway

Switzer
Picnic Area

P

GABRIELINO N.R. TR

To Red
Box Gap

RECREATION TRAIL

N
W E
S

▲ Commodore Switzer Camp

Switzer Falls

GABRIELINO NAT'L

LITTLE BEAR CANYON

To Gould Mesa
Campground
(Hike 17)

Arroyo Seco

BEAR CANYON

REFERENCE MAPS
P. 64

15.
Switzer Falls
GABRIELINO NATIONAL
RECREATION TRAIL

Bear Canyon
Camp
▲

The hike

Walk across the oak-covered picnic area, and cross the foot-bridge over Arroyo Seco Creek. Follow the paved path downhill, parallel to the south side of the creek through the cool wooded glades. Pass pools along the rock-filled creek as the paved path turns to a dirt path. Cross the creek, passing more pools carved into the bedrock. Stay on the canyon floor, crossing the creek five more times. After the sixth crossing is Commodore Switzer Camp, a primitive camp on the banks of Arroyo Seco Creek. An undesignated path leads straight ahead through the camp to the brink of upper Switzer Falls on the edge of steep, rocky walls. This overlook is dangerous with unstable, slippery rock. It has been the scene of numerous falling deaths and is an ill-advised route. If you take this route, use extreme caution!

Bear right at the signed Gabrielino National Recreation Trail sign, and cross Arroyo Seco Creek. Head up the exposed west canyon wall, leaving the riparian vegetation behind. Pass overlooks of the narrow, rock-walled chasm, with bird's-eye views of the 50-foot upper tier of Switzer Falls and the pool etched into the rock. At 1.4 miles is a Y-fork with the Bear Canyon Trail. The Gabrielino National Recreation Trail continues to the right, leading 3.7 miles to Oakwilde Camp and 6.5 miles to Gould Mesa Camp (Hike 17). Take the Bear Canyon Trail to the left, perched on the vertical canyon wall. Descend 0.7 miles and reunite with Arroyo Seco Creek under the shade of oaks to a posted fork. To the right, the Bear Canyon Trail continues to the Bear Canyon Campground. To hike to the base of lower Switzer Falls, go to the left and follow the rocky creek 0.2 miles upstream into the gorge. ■

16. Mount Lowe Summit from Eaton Saddle

Hiking distance: 3 miles round trip
Hiking time: 1.5 hours
Configuration: out-and-back
Elevation gain: 500 feet
Exposure: mix of exposed hills and forested groves
Difficulty: easy to moderate
Dogs: allowed
Maps: U.S.G.S. Mount Wilson
Harrison: Angeles Front Country Trail Map
Harrison: Mt. Wilson Trail Map

Mount Lowe is located 1.5 miles west of Mount Wilson and its observatories. The 5,603-foot peak was named for Thaddeus Lowe by his friends on their first horseback ride to the summit on September 24, 1892. Known as Oak Mountain until that time, Lowe built the Mount Lowe Railway from Echo Mountain to the foot of Mount Lowe, a thousand feet shy of the summit. A trolley then offered access to the Mount Lowe Alpine Tavern, a Swiss-style hotel. The historic site, located south of the peak at the current location of the Mount Lowe Trail Camp, operated from 1893 through 1935. The railway enabled guests to ride from Altadena to Mount Lowe via a tram up Rubio Canyon to the Echo Mountain Resort (Hike 18). The trolley took guests a few miles farther, from Echo Mountain to the Mount Lowe Tavern. The tavern burned down in 1936. Several foundations and rock wall ruins remain, along with interpretive panels describing the tavern and its history.

The scenic 5,603-foot summit of Mount Lowe also has interpretive panels and viewing scopes of Mount Disappointment, Mount Markham, Mount Baldy, San Gabriel Peak, Mount Wilson, and Mount Harvard. This hike begins off of Mount Wilson Road on Eaton Saddle (also known as Mount Lowe East). The trailhead is tucked between San Gabriel Peak and Occidental Peak. The trail route passes through a tunnel built in 1942 to Markham Saddle between Mount Markham and Mount Disappointment. Atop Mount Lowe are comprehensive views of the urban basins below and sighting tubes which identify the surrounding peaks.

To the trailhead

From the Foothill Freeway (Interstate 210) in La Canada, exit on the Angeles Crest Highway (Highway 2). Drive 14 miles north to the signed Mount Wilson Road turnoff on the right. Turn right and continue 2.3 miles to Eaton Saddle by a metal vehicle gate on the right. Park in the dirt pullouts on either side of the road. An Adventure Pass is required for parking.

The hike

Walk around the trailhead gate to a close-up view of Mount Markham and San Gabriel Peak. Follow the Mount Lowe Fire Road, an old gravel road perched on a vertical south cliff of San Gabriel Peak. Along the road are great vistas that span from the head of Eaton Canyon to the San Gabriel Valley. At 0.3 miles, walk through Mueller Tunnel, carved through the southern base of San Gabriel Peak in 1942. At a half mile, the historic road reaches Markham Saddle and a posted junction. To the right, the trail leads 0.8 miles to Mount Disappointment and 1.1 mile to San Gabriel Peak. Straight ahead, the fire road descends and circles Mount Lowe counterclockwise to Mount Lowe Trail Camp, nestled in a grove of oaks and big cone spruce.

Instead, take the footpath to the left. Enter a shaded oak canopy and a chaparral landscape. Traverse the west slope of Mount Markham at a level grade, directly toward Mount Lowe to a saddle between the two mountains. Continue 220 yards through a pocket of oaks to an unsigned fork. The Mount Lowe East Trail goes straight ahead to Mount Lowe Trail Camp. Go sharply right on the Mount Lowe West Trail, and climb 0.3 miles to a signed fork. The right fork—Mount Lowe West Trail—descends to Mount Lowe Trail Camp as well. Veer left on the undesignated Mount Lowe Summit Trail, and continue less than 0.1 mile to the exposed summit. From the 5,603-foot peak are metal sighting tubes directed at the surrounding mountains and views across the San Gabriel Valley, the Verdugo Mountains, Griffith Park, downtown Los Angeles, and the San Fernando Valley. Return by retracing your steps. ∎

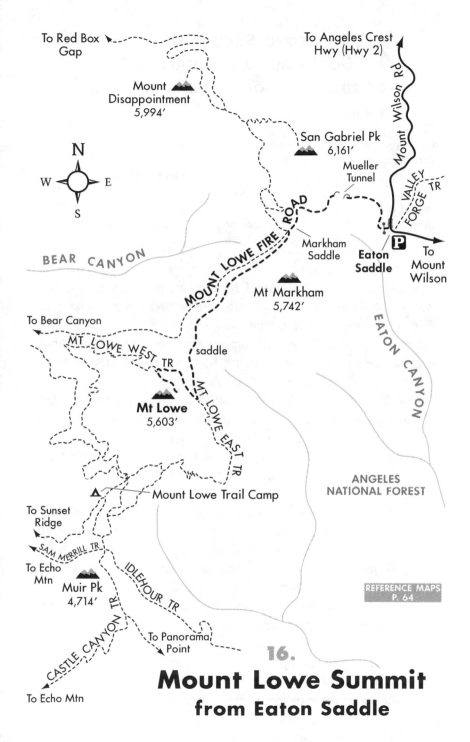

To Red Box Gap

To Angeles Crest Hwy (Hwy 2)

Mount Wilson Rd

Mount Disappointment
5,994'

San Gabriel Pk
6,161'

Mueller Tunnel

N
W   E
S

ROAD

VALLEY FORGE TR

BEAR CANYON

MOUNT LOWE FIRE

Markham Saddle

P

Eaton Saddle

To Mount Wilson

Mt Markham
5,742'

EATON CANYON

To Bear Canyon

MT LOWE WEST TR

saddle

MT LOWE EAST TR

Mt Lowe
5,603'

Mount Lowe Trail Camp

ANGELES NATIONAL FOREST

To Sunset Ridge

SAM MERRILL TR

To Echo Mtn

Muir Pk
4,714'

IDLEHOUR TR

REFERENCE MAPS
P. 64

CASTLE CANYON TR

To Panorama Point

To Echo Mtn

16.

Mount Lowe Summit
from Eaton Saddle

17. Arroyo Seco Trail to Gould Mesa Campground

GABRIELINO NATIONAL RECREATION TRAIL

Hiking distance: 4.8 miles round trip
Hiking time: 2.5 hours
Configuration: out-and-back
Elevation gain: 230 feet
Exposure: mostly forested canyon with some exposed areas
Difficulty: easy to slightly moderate
Dogs: allowed
Maps: U.S.G.S. Pasadena · Harrison: Angeles Front Country Trail Map
   Harrison: Mt. Wilson Trail Map

Arroyo Seco Creek forms from three stream forks near Red Box Gap on the south flank of Mount Lawlor. The scenic creek weaves through the deeply cut canyon from the upper San Gabriel Mountains. The perennial waterway flows through the communities of La Canada, Altadena, Pasadena, South Pasadena, and northeast Los Angeles to its terminus at the Los Angeles River, just north of downtown Los Angeles.

The Gabrielino National Recreation Trail follows the Arroyo Seco through the canyon, from the foothills on the northwest corner of Pasadena to the headwaters at Red Box Gap. The 28-mile-long Gabrielino Trail continues east from Red Box Gap through Santa Anita Canyon to Chandry Flat north of Arcadia (Hike 24).

This hike follows the lower portion of the Gabrielino Trail from Hahamongna Watershed Park, a 1,300-acre park with oak groves, picnic areas, and walking paths (formerly called Oak Grove Park). The trail passes the NASA Jet Propulsion Laboratory, then enters the gorgeous stream-fed canyon. The trail was originally a road in the 1920s that provided access into the canyon to resorts and rustic cabins. Now the multi-use trail follows this historic route along the creek through dense groves of big leaf maples, white alders, sycamores, Douglas firs, and live oaks. The trail leads to Gould Mesa Camp—the turn-around point for this hike—then continues up canyon to the Angeles Crest Highway.

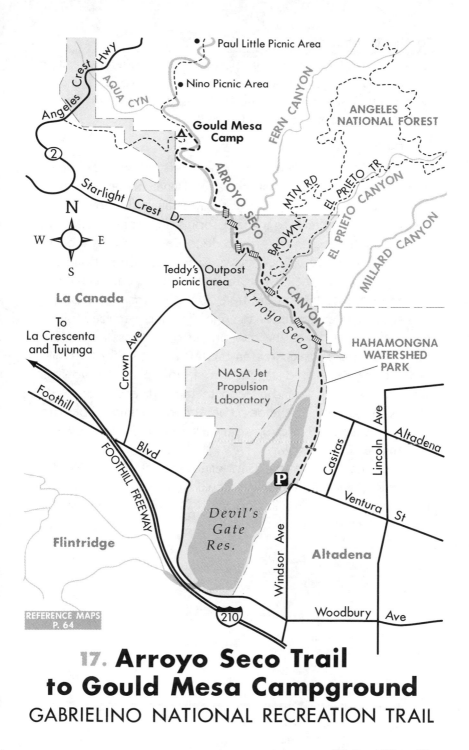

17. Arroyo Seco Trail to Gould Mesa Campground

GABRIELINO NATIONAL RECREATION TRAIL

To the trailhead

From the Foothill Freeway (Interstate 210) in Altadena, exit on Windsor Ave. Drive 0.9 miles north on Windsor Ave to its junction with Ventura Street. Park in the trailhead parking lot on the left. An Adventure Pass is required for parking.

The hike

Walk to the posted trailhead at the north end of Windsor Avenue. Head north along the east edge of Hahamongna Watershed Natural Park. Take the signed Gabrielino Trail, and follow the gated, paved road parallel to the jet propulsion laboratory. At a half mile, enter the mouth of Arroyo Seco Canyon. Cross a bridge over the creek into an oak grove. Cross a second bridge to a signed Y-fork with the Lower Brown Mountain Road on the right at one mile. Stay left on the trail closest to the creek, passing Forest Service residences on the right. The unpaved road follows the canyon bottom as the canyon narrows. Cross a bridge to Teddy's Outpost Picnic Area on the left at just under two miles. Cross three more bridges, then rock-hop over Arroyo Seco Creek three times. Round a bend to the left, and enter Gould Mesa Campground, a developed backcountry camp. A road/trail on the left leads 1.3 miles up to a trailhead on the lower end of the Angeles Crest Highway.

To extend the hike, the Gabrielino National Recreation Trail continues 0.6 miles to the Nino Picnic Area, 1.6 miles to the Paul Little Picnic Area, 2.6 miles north to Oakwilde Camp, and 4.3 miles to Switzer Falls (Hike 15). ■

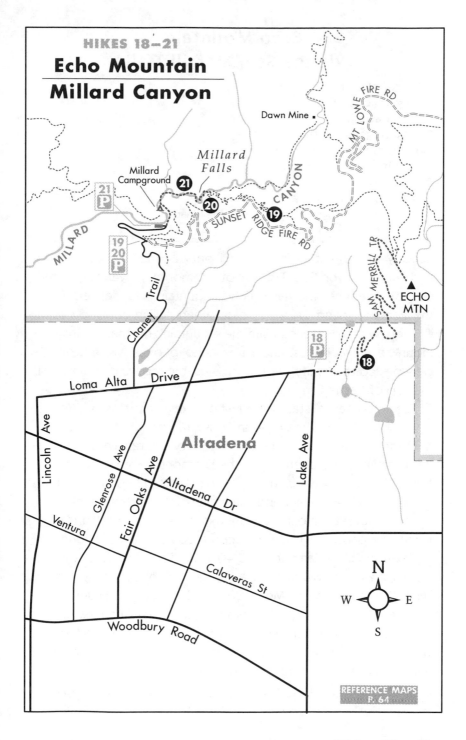

HIKES 18-21

Echo Mountain
Millard Canyon

Dawn Mine ∎

MT LOWE FIRE RD

Millard Falls

Millard Campground

MILLARD CANYON

21

20

19

SUNSET RIDGE FIRE RD

Millard

Chaney Trail

SAM MERRILL TR

▲ ECHO MTN

21 P

19 20 P

18 P

18

Loma Alta Drive

Lincoln Ave

Glenrose Ave

Fair Oaks Ave

Ventura

Altadena

Altadena Dr

Lake Ave

Calaveras St

Woodbury Road

N
W ◆ E
S

REFERENCE MAPS
P. 64

18. Echo Mountain
via the Sam Merrill Trail

Hiking distance: 5.8 miles round trip
Hiking time: 2.5 hours
Configuration: out-and-back
Elevation gain: 1,400 feet
Exposure: mostly exposed slope
Difficulty: moderate to strenuous
Dogs: allowed
Maps: U.S.G.S. Pasadena and Mount Wilson
Harrison: Angeles Front Country Trail Map
Harrison: Mt. Wilson Trail Map

Echo Mountain, jutting southward between Las Flores Canyon and Rubio Canyon, is a 3,250-foot promontory overlooking the city of Altadena. The name Echo Mountain was derived from the echoing sound of one's voice when calling out into Castle Canyon, which descends from the mountain's northeast. Ground-mounted megaphones, known as echo-phones, were strategically placed to amplify the sound. A usable replica is mounted at the top of Castle Canyon.

Echo Mountain is listed on the National Register of Historic Places. It was the site of White City, an active mountaintop resort from 1893 through 1936. The ruins of White City still remain, creating a museum-like atmosphere. Atop the promontory are rock foundations, old retaining walls, rusting Pacific Electric railroad parts, iron tracks, abandoned gears, and ball wheels. Interpretive panels with historic photos are mounted in the exact spot they were originally taken. The photos highlight the Echo Mountain House, a four-story, 70-room Victorian hotel; the 40-room Echo Chalet; as well as dormitories, the powerhouse, a car barn, an observatory, casino, dance hall, and zoo. The Mount Lowe Railway shuttled guests seven miles and 1,300 feet up Rubio Canyon, from Altadena to the top of the Echo Mountain promontory. The trip continued to the base of Mount Lowe via 18 trestles and 127 hairpin curves. The multi-stage trip included electric trolleys, cable cars, and open-air railway cars. For four decades, the tourist attraction thrived. In 1900, a fire destroyed the Echo Mountain House. Another fire and

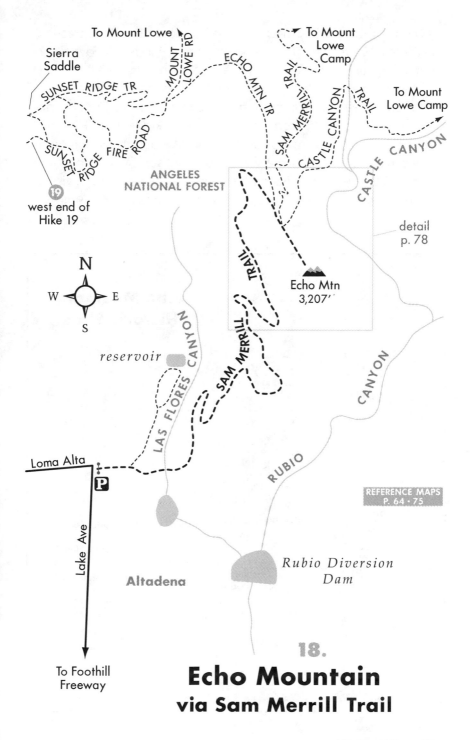

To Mount Lowe

Sierra
Saddle

SUNSET RIDGE TR

MOUNT LOWE RD

ECHO MTN TR

To Mount
Lowe
Camp

SAM MERRILL TRAIL

CASTLE CANYON TRAIL

To Mount
Lowe Camp

CASTLE CANYON

SUNSET RIDGE FIRE ROAD

ANGELES
NATIONAL FOREST

19

west end of
Hike 19

detail
p. 78

N
W E
S

TRAIL

Echo Mtn
3,207'

SAM MERRILL

reservoir

LAS FLORES CANYON

RUBIO CANYON

Loma Alta

P

REFERENCE MAPS
P. 64 · 75

Lake Ave

Altadena

Rubio Diversion
Dam

To Foothill
Freeway

18.

Echo Mountain
via Sam Merrill Trail

a windstorm in 1905 burned additional structures and the trestles. In the late 1930s, flash floods and gale force winds wiped out the remaining buildings. The railway was abandoned in 1938.

The Sam Merrill Trail, located at the top of Lake Avenue in Altadena, is a major hiking route to Echo Mountain. The historic site can also be accessed from the Sunset Ridge Trail (Hike 19), which is a longer (3.7-mile) route. This hike along the Sam Merrill Trail zigzags 2.5 miles up the scrub-covered, southwest mountain slope to the ruins atop Echo Mountain. En route are grand vistas of the rugged canyons, the surrounding mountains, Los Angeles, and the San Gabriel Valley.

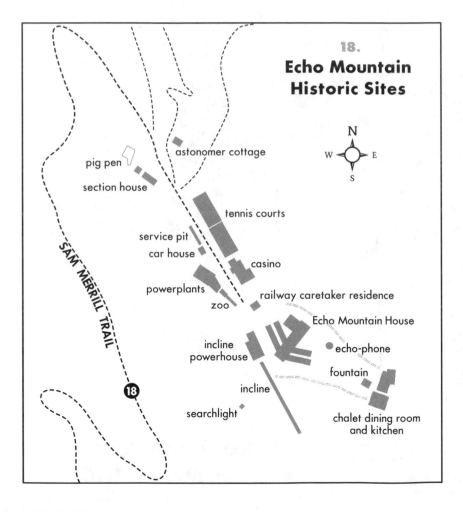

18.

Echo Mountain Historic Sites

N
W → ◇ ← E
S

astonomer cottage

pig pen

section house

tennis courts

service pit
car house

casino

powerplants

zoo

railway caretaker residence

Echo Mountain House

incline
powerhouse

echo-phone

fountain

incline

searchlight

chalet dining room
and kitchen

SAM MERRILL TRAIL

18

To the trailhead

From the Foothill Freeway (Interstate 210) in Altadena, exit on Lake Avenue. Drive 3.6 miles north on Lake Avenue to its end at Loma Alta Drive. Park along the side of the road. An Adventure Pass is required for parking.

The hike

From the corner of Loma Alta Drive and Lake Avenue, pass through the stone-pillared gate of the former Cobb Estate, now part of the Angeles National Forest. Follow the rutted road 100 yards east to a left bend, and veer right at the "trail" sign to the posted Sam Merrill Trailhead at the base of Las Flores Canyon. Cross the dry riverbed and zigzag up the southwest slope of Echo Mountain. Steadily climb the east canyon wall, overlooking the seasonal watershed and a network of walking paths that lead to an enclosed reservoir. Continue up the serpentine, cliff-hugging path cut into the steep cliffs to the upper reaches of the canyon. The amazing views extend across the San Gabriel Valley and Los Angeles Basin to the Pacific Ocean. Curve through a small pocket of oaks, reaching a junction at 2.7 miles. The Echo Mountain Trail cuts sharply left and leads to Mount Lowe Road and Sunset Ridge Trail.

Stay to the right on the south-heading Echo Mountain Trail. Pass the Sam Merrill Trail on the left in about 65 yards, which leads 3 miles to the Mount Lowe Trail Camp (see Hike 16). Ten yards farther is the Castle Canyon Trail, also on the left, which leads 2 miles to Inspiration Point and 2.5 miles to Mount Lowe Trail Camp. Continue descending south to the historic promontory of Echo Mountain, passing a picnic area on the left. Explore the ruins and overlooks, choosing your own route. ▪

19. Millard Canyon— Sunset Ridge Loop

Hiking distance: 3.3-mile loop
Hiking time: 1:45 hours
Configuration: loop
Elevation gain: 1,000 feet
Exposure: mostly exposed with forest pockets
Difficulty: moderate
Dogs: allowed
Maps: U.S.G.S. Pasadena
   Harrison: Angeles Front Country Trail Map
   Harrison: Mt. Wilson Trail Map

This hike makes a long loop that contours the upper, south-facing slope of Millard Canyon, then returns on a fire road along Sunset Ridge. The Sunset Ridge Fire Road is a historic route that leads to the ruins at the Mount Lowe Trail Camp. Informational signs along the road tell the story of the Mount Lowe Railway, the resorts atop Echo Mountain and Mount Lowe, and about the fire and floods that destroyed the resorts over the past century. The route travels through a mix of pine forests and brushy slopes blanketed with sage, scrub oak, toyon, and lemonade berry. After zigzagging up to the ridge, the trail reveals deep canyon views and sweeping vistas across the San Gabriel and Los Angeles basins.

To the trailhead

From the Foothill Freeway (Interstate 210) in Altadena, exit on Lake Avenue. Drive 3.6 miles north on Lake Avenue to its end. Turn left on Loma Alta Drive, and go one mile to Chaney Trail. Turn right and continue 1.1 mile, staying left at a fork, to a sharp left bend in the road and a vehicle gate on the right. Park along the side of the road. An Adventure Pass is required for parking.

The hike

Walk past the vehicle gate and follow the Sunset Ridge Fire Road, a narrow, paved road. Pass an access trail on the left, leading to the Millard Campground. Stay on the road, which overlooks

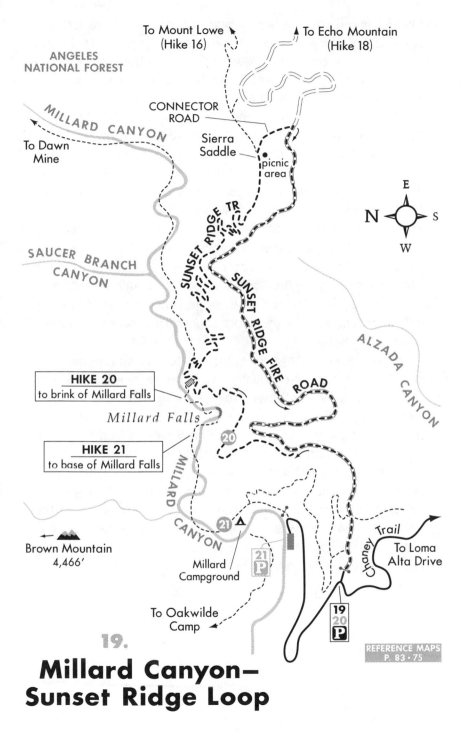

To Mount Lowe ↖
(Hike 16)

▲ To Echo Mountain
(Hike 18)

ANGELES
NATIONAL FOREST

CONNECTOR
ROAD

MILLARD CANYON

Sierra
Saddle

● picnic
area

To Dawn
Mine

SUNSET RIDGE TR

SUNSET RIDGE FIRE

ROAD

E
N ✦ S
W

SAUCER BRANCH
CANYON

ALZADA CANYON

HIKE 20
to brink of Millard Falls

Millard Falls

20

HIKE 21
to base of Millard Falls

MILLARD CANYON

Brown Mountain
4,466'

21 ▲

Chaney Trail

To Loma
Alta Drive

Millard
Campground

21
P

To Oakwilde
Camp ◄

19
20
P

REFERENCE MAPS
P. 83 · 75

19.

Millard Canyon—
Sunset Ridge Loop

Millard Canyon and the San Gabriel Mountains on the left and Altadena, Pasadena, and Los Angeles on the right. At 0.4 miles is a fork. Leave the Sunset Ridge Fire Road—the return route—and veer left on the Sunset Ridge Trail. Skirt the upper slope of Millard Canyon, weaving along the contours of the hills to a signed junction at 0.9 miles. The left fork crosses an old bridge and leads to the brink of Millard Falls (Hike 20).

Stay on the Sunset Ridge Trail to the right, and ascend the mountain with the aid of fourteen switchbacks. At the ninth switchback is a view up Saucer Branch Canyon. Zigzag under tall oaks and Coulter pines past beautiful fern-covered rock walls, steadily climbing to views of Glendale and the Verdugo Mountains. At 1.6 miles, the trail emerges at the Sierra Saddle by a junction with a short connector to Sunset Ridge Road. On the right is a picnic area. The Sunset Ridge Trail continues one mile, connecting again with the Sunset Ridge Fire Road just a mile shy of Echo Mountain. Take the short connector road to the paved Sunset Ridge Road.

(To make a much longer hike, the left fork continues one mile uphill to a junction. The Mount Lowe Road veers left and winds 3.5 miles up to Mount Lowe Trail Camp, nestled in a grove of oaks and big cone spruce—see Hike 16. The right fork, the Echo Mountain Trail, leads 0.8 miles on the old railway bed to the historic ruins atop Echo Mountain—see Hike 18.)

For this much shorter loop hike, head downhill (west) on the Sunset Ridge Fire Road along the exposed, south-facing slope. The spectacular vistas span across the urban basin as far as the haze will allow. Follow the upper south wall of Millard Canyon, completing the loop back at the junction with the Sunset Ridge Trail. Return a quarter mile to the trailhead. ▪

20. Brink of Millard Falls

Hiking distance: 2.2 miles round trip
Hiking time: 1 hour
Configuration: out-and-back
Elevation gain: 300 feet
Exposure: mix of exposed hillside and forested canyon
Difficulty: easy
Dogs: allowed
Maps: U.S.G.S. Pasadena · Harrison: Angeles Front Country Trail Map
Harrison: Mt. Wilson Trail Map

Millard Canyon, tucked between Sunset Ridge and Brown Mountain, is filled with a lush forest of oaks, alders, maples, and Douglas firs. Millard Creek flows through the mossy, boulder-strewn canyon. On a bend in the creek, Millard Falls tumbles 50 feet through chockstones wedged into the vertical cleft to a pool surrounded by boulders. The water filters through the gaps in the boulders to the box canyon below. By carefully peering over the sheer rock wall, people can be spotted in the boulder-strewn grotto below (accessed from Hike 21).

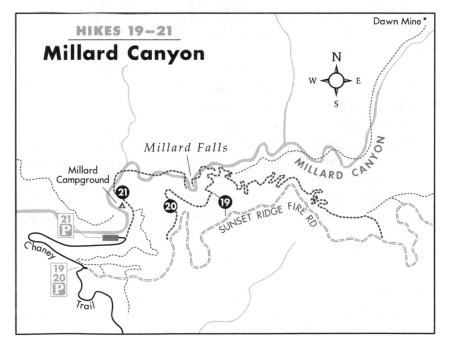

This trail begins on Sunset Ridge along the upper south slope of Millard Canyon. A footpath descends to the serene, shaded canyon floor and downstream to the brink of the falls.

To extend the hike, an old trail weaves up canyon along the creek to Dawn Mine. The abandoned gold mine, perched on the west canyon slope, was active from 1895 until the 1950s. This 1.5-mile path entails a considerable amount of hopping over boulders, crossing the creek, and climbing over down logs. The path is partially washed away and fades in and out. The rough but atmospheric route passes cascades, pools, old mining machinery, and assorted rusty paraphernalia.

To the trailhead

From the Foothill Freeway (Interstate 210) in Altadena, exit on Lake Avenue. Drive 3.6 miles north on Lake Avenue to its end. Turn left on Loma Alta Drive, and go one mile to Chaney Trail. Turn right and continue 1.1 mile, staying left at a fork, to a sharp left bend in the road and a vehicle gate on the right. Park along the side of the road. An Adventure Pass is required for parking.

The hike

Walk past the vehicle gate and follow the Sunset Ridge Fire Road, a narrow, paved road. Pass an access trail on the left, leading to the Millard Campground. Stay on the road, which overlooks Millard Canyon and the San Gabriel Mountains on the left and Altadena, Pasadena, and Los Angeles on the right. At 0.4 miles is a fork. Leave the Sunset Ridge Fire Road, and veer left on the Sunset Ridge Trail. Skirt the upper slope of Millard Canyon, weaving along the contours of the hills to a signed junction at 0.9 miles. The right fork stays on the Sunset Ridge Trail and climbs the hillside to Sierra Saddle, forming a loop with the Sunset Ridge Fire Road (Hike 19). For this hike, stay left and cross an old metal bridge. Pass a cabin on the right, and descend through the lush forest thick with ferns, mosses, and live oak trees to Millard Creek on the canyon floor. Bear left and head downstream along the south side of the creek. Pass rock-formed pools, crossing the creek three times in the shady, rock-walled canyon. The trail ends at a jumble of huge boulders at the brink of the falls. ▪

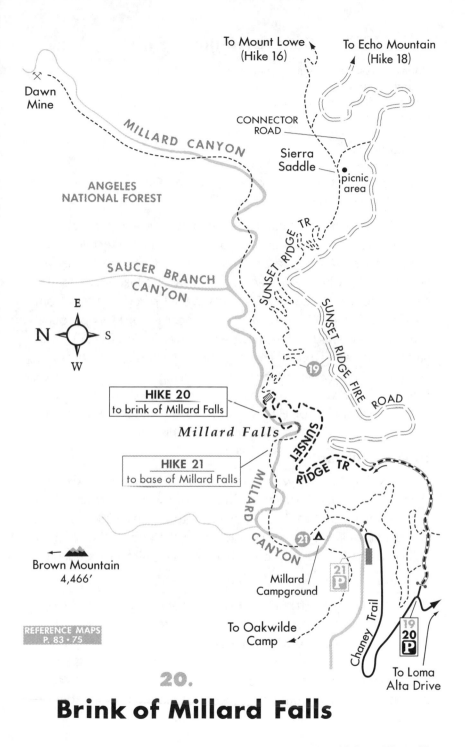

To Mount Lowe
(Hike 16)

To Echo Mountain
(Hike 18)

Dawn
Mine

MILLARD CANYON

CONNECTOR
ROAD

Sierra
Saddle

picnic
area

ANGELES
NATIONAL FOREST

SUNSET RIDGE TR

SAUCER BRANCH
CANYON

SUNSET RIDGE FIRE ROAD

E

N   S

W

19

HIKE 20
to brink of Millard Falls

SUNSET

Millard Falls

HIKE 21
to base of Millard Falls

RIDGE TR

MILLARD CANYON

19

21

Brown Mountain
4,466'

Millard
Campground

21
P

REFERENCE MAPS
P. 83 · 75

To Oakwilde
Camp

Chaney Trail

19
20
P

To Loma
Alta Drive

20.
Brink of Millard Falls

21. Base of Millard Falls

Hiking distance: 1.5 miles round trip
Hiking time: 1 hour
Configuration: out-and-back
Elevation gain: 150 feet
Exposure: forested canyon
Difficulty: easy
Dogs: allowed
Maps: U.S.G.S. Pasadena · Harrison: Angeles Front Country Trail Map
Harrison: Mt. Wilson Trail Map

Millard Falls is a 50-foot cataract that drops over a moss-covered vertical rock face deep in Millard Canyon. The waterfall braids through a jumble of huge boulders, wedged into the V-shaped notch, to a pool in a narrow box canyon. This hike leads to the base of the falls, while Hike 20 leads to the brink of the falls from the Sunset Ridge Trail. The hike begins near Millard Campground in a small tree-shaded flat. The trail follows Millard Creek up the narrow boulder-strewn canyon under towering alders, oaks, sycamores, and willow trees to the falls in a cool, lush grotto. Millard Canyon was originally known as Church Canyon. The canyon was renamed for Henry Millard, a beekeeper who homesteaded in the mouth of the canyon with his family in 1862.

To the trailhead

From the Foothill Freeway (Interstate 210) in Altadena, exit on Lake Avenue. Drive 3.6 miles north on Lake Avenue to its end. Turn left on Loma Alta Drive and go one mile to Chaney Trail. Turn right and continue 1.7 miles to a parking lot at the end of the road by Millard Campground. An Adventure Pass is required for parking.

The hike

Walk to the upper (front) end of the parking lot by the kiosk. Take the gated dirt road under the shaded forest canopy. Follow the serpentine course of Millard Creek into Millard Campground. Veer right on the footpath, staying close to the creek. Pass pools and small waterfalls as the steep-walled canyon narrows. Weave among the boulders under a canopy of alders. Pass a cabin on the right, and follow the course of the stream up canyon. Cross the creek six times, reaching the falls from the south (right) side of the creek. The trail ends at the base of the falls in a box canyon with moss and ferns growing from the vertical rock walls. ■

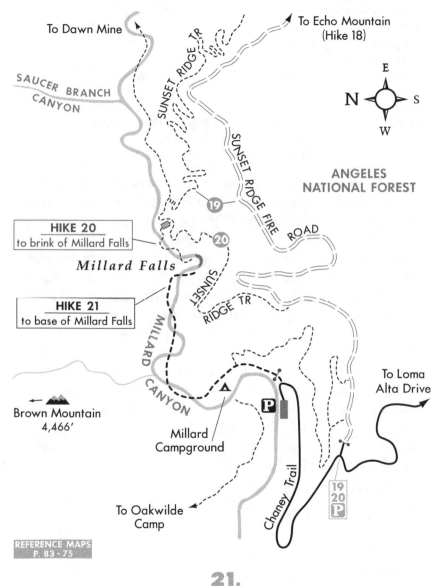

21.
Base of Millard Falls

22. Eaton Canyon Falls

EATON CANYON COUNTY PARK and NATURAL AREA

1750 N. Altadena Drive · Pasadena

Hiking distance: 3 miles round trip
Hiking time: 1.5 hours
Configuration: out-and-back
Elevation gain: 400 feet
Exposure: mix of exposed wash and forested canyon
Difficulty: easy
Dogs: allowed
Maps: U.S.G.S. Mount Wilson · Harrison: Mt. Wilson Trail Map
Harrison: Angeles Front Country Trail Map
Eaton Canyon Natural Area County Park map

Eaton Canyon is a major drainage that stretches from the upper San Gabriel Mountain slopes at Eaton Saddle, between Mount Markham and Occidental Peak, to the mouth of the canyon at Eaton Canyon County Park in Altadena, where this hike begins. Eaton Creek flows through the canyon, emerges from the foothills, and continues south through Eaton Wash and Pasadena to the Los Angeles River. The county park encompasses 190 acres in the foothills of the mountain range. The popular park includes a nature center and picnic areas. It is a staging area for hikes into Eaton Canyon and the gateway to Henninger Flats, Idlehour Campground, and Mount Wilson via the Mount Wilson Toll Road.

This hike winds through the natural area along Eaton Wash, then enters the canyon to Eaton Canyon Falls. The falls drops 40 feet off the rock cliffs through a jagged, V-shaped notch in the bedrock into the pool below. En route to the falls, the trail crosses the Mount Wilson Toll Road.

To the trailhead

From the Foothill Freeway (Interstate 210) in Pasadena, exit on Altadena Drive. Drive 1.6 miles north on Altadena Drive to the signed Eaton Canyon County Park on the right. Turn right into the park and park 0.2 miles ahead by the nature center. Parking is free.

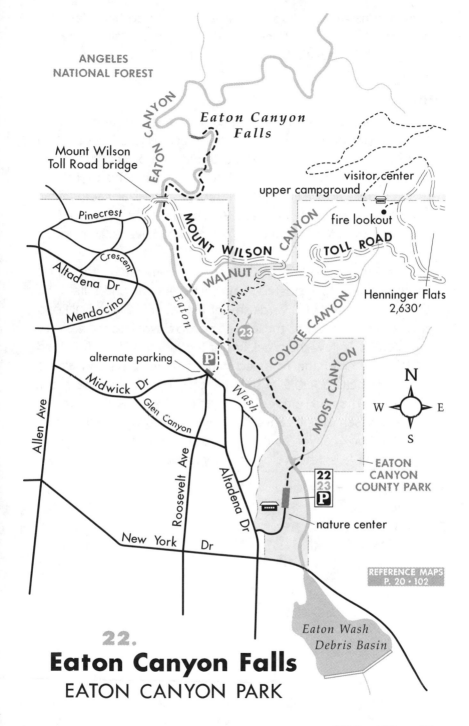

ANGELES
NATIONAL FOREST

EATON CANYON

Eaton Canyon
Falls

Mount Wilson
Toll Road bridge

visitor center
upper campground

Pinecrest

fire lookout

MOUNT WILSON CANYON

TOLL ROAD

Crescent

WALNUT

Altadena Dr

Henninger Flats
2,630'

Mendocino

Eaton

COYOTE CANYON

23

MOIST CANYON

alternate parking

P

Midwick Dr

Wash

Glen Canyon

N

W ◆ E

S

Allen Ave

Roosevelt Ave

EATON
CANYON
COUNTY PARK

Altadena Dr

22
23
P

New York   Dr

nature center

REFERENCE MAPS
P. 20 • 102

Eaton Wash
Debris Basin

22.
Eaton Canyon Falls
EATON CANYON PARK

An alternative trailhead pullout is also located 0.5 miles past the turnoff into Eaton Canyon Park. It is on the right, directly across from Roosevelt Avenue and Midwick Drive. This trailhead will shorten the hike by one mile round trip.

The hike

From the far (north) end of the parking lot, pass the gate and take the wide dirt path north. Follow the west edge of Eaton Wash towards the mountains, passing a picnic area on the left. Cross the rocky wash and enter an oak grove. Continue north, following the terrace above Eaton Wash through chaparral, cactus, scattered maples, willows, and oaks. At a half mile is a posted Y-fork at the mouth of Walnut Canyon. The right fork leads 2.9 miles to Henninger Flats (Hike 23).

Veer left, passing Walnut Canyon, and continue up the Eaton Creek drainage to a posted fork on the left at one mile. (The junction is located 200 yards shy of the Mount Wilson Toll Road bridge.) Take the fork to the left, and drop down into the wash to Eaton Creek. Follow the creek under the Mount Wilson Toll Road bridge, and enter the forested canyon under oaks and alders. Pass pools, cascades, and small waterfalls, crossing the creek two times. The rock-embedded path curves along the floor of the narrow, serpentine canyon amongst vertical rock cliffs. Curve left into a box canyon at the base of Eaton Canyon Falls. After enjoying the falls, return along the same route. ▪

23. Mount Wilson Toll Road

Eaton Canyon Park to Henninger Flats

EATON CANYON COUNTY PARK AND NATURAL AREA

1750 N. Altadena Drive · Pasadena

Hiking distance: 7 miles round trip
Hiking time: 3.5 hours
Configuration: out-and-back
Elevation gain: 1,600 feet
Exposure: mostly exposed with forested pockets
Difficulty: strenuous
Dogs: allowed
Maps: U.S.G.S. Mount Wilson · Harrison: Angeles Front Country Trail Map
Harrison: Mt. Wilson Trail Map

The Mount Wilson Toll Road is a historic wagon road that begins in the foothills of Altadena and ascends nine miles to the summit of Mount Wilson. The road, active from 1891 through 1936, was closed to vehicles when the Angeles Crest Highway was completed. The old road was then turned over to the U.S. Forest Service and became a hiking, biking, and equestrian route. The road climbs the exposed, chaparral-covered slopes to Henninger Flats, a forested flat above Altadena with incense cedar, sequoia, cypress, and a variety of pines. William Henninger settled on the mesa above Altadena in the early 1880s. He built a home and planted fruits, vegetables, grasses, and nut trees. He also started an experimental reforestation project at Henninger Flats. After his death, the flat was used as a high-elevation forest nursery.

The hike to Henninger Flats follows the exposed dirt fire road, with exceptional vistas of Los Angeles and the San Gabriel Valley. Set amid the trees on the 2,600-foot bench is a nature center, picnic area, campground, and a historic fire lookout, relocated here from Castro Peak in the Santa Monica Mountains.

In the past, the toll road has been closed intermittently for repairs. Call ahead to the nature center to verify conditions: (626) 398-5420.

To the trailhead

From the Foothill Freeway (Interstate 210) in Pasadena, exit on Altadena Drive. Drive 1.6 miles north on Altadena Drive to the signed Eaton Canyon County Park on the right. Turn right into the park and park 0.2 miles ahead by the nature center. Parking is free.

An alternative trailhead pullout is also located 0.5 miles past the turnoff into Eaton Canyon Park. It is on the right, directly across from Roosevelt Avenue and Midwick Drive. This trailhead will shorten the hike by one mile round trip.

The hike

From the far (north) end of the parking lot, take the wide dirt path north. Follow the west edge of Eaton Wash towards the mountains. Cross the rocky wash and enter an oak grove. Continue north, following the rim of Eaton Wash through chaparral, cactus, scattered maples, willows, and oaks. At a half mile is a posted Y-fork at the mouth of Walnut Canyon. The left fork continues up Eaton Canyon to Eaton Canyon Falls (Hike 22). Stay to the right and head up the north wall of Walnut Canyon. Zigzag a half mile up the mountain to Mount Wilson Toll Road, a narrow dirt road on a U-bend. En route, pass two overlooks of Eaton Canyon, Altadena, Pasadena, and the San Gabriel Valley. The left fork descends 0.8 miles to the toll road bridge that crosses Eaton Wash at the mouth of Eaton Canyon.

Bear right on the one-lane dirt road, which frequently narrows to a footpath due to erosion. Head uphill at a moderate grade. The views span from the Verdugo Mountains and the San Rafael Hills to the Los Angeles basin. At 3.3 miles, enter the shade of the forested Lower Henninger Flats Campground and a trail split. On the left is the visitor center and the old Castro Peak Fire Lookout from the Santa Monica Mountains, in service from 1925 through 1971. Continue up the slope on the Mount Wilson Toll Road to a signed fork. The main road curves right and continues 6 miles to Mount Wilson at 5,710 feet.

For this hike, go to the left and loop back above the visitor center. Walk a half mile to the upper campground, perched on the end of a 2,600-foot forested ridge with spectacular vistas. ∎

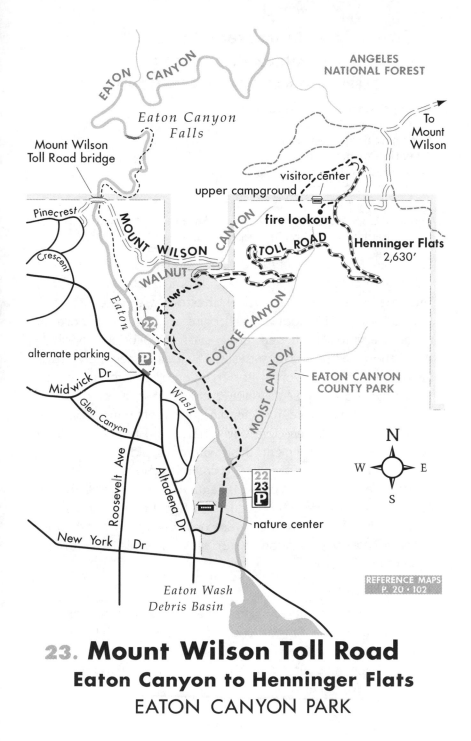

ANGELES
NATIONAL FOREST

EATON CANYON

Eaton Canyon
Falls

Mount Wilson
Toll Road bridge

To
Mount
Wilson

visitor center
upper campground

Pinecrest

MOUNT WILSON CANYON

fire lookout

TOLL ROAD

Henninger Flats
2,630'

Crescent

WALNUT

Eaton

22

alternate parking

COYOTE CANYON

P

Midwick Dr

Wash

EATON CANYON
COUNTY PARK

Glen Canyon

MOIST CANYON

Roosevelt Ave

N

Altadena Dr

22
23
P

W   E

nature center

New York Dr

S

Eaton Wash
Debris Basin

REFERENCE MAPS
P. 20 • 102

23. **Mount Wilson Toll Road**
Eaton Canyon to Henninger Flats
EATON CANYON PARK

24. Sturtevant Falls

SANTA ANITA CANYON

GABRIELINO NATIONAL RECREATION TRAIL

Hiking distance: 4.3 miles round trip
Hiking time: 2.5 hours
Configuration: out-and-back
Elevation gain: 650 feet
Exposure: shaded canyon
Difficulty: easy to moderate
Dogs: allowed
Maps: U.S.G.S. Mount Wilson · Harrison: Angeles Front Country Trail Map
Harrison: Mt. Wilson Trail Map

Sturtevant Falls is a beautiful 50-foot waterfall tucked into a lush gulch with colorful moss-covered cliffs in Santa Anita Canyon. The creek freefalls over a vertical limestone precipice into a natural rock bowl. This popular hike begins at Chantry Flat, north of Arcadia, and follows the eastern end of the Gabrielino National Recreation Trail to Sturtevant Falls. The trail immediately drops into Santa Anita Canyon at Roberts Camp, a historic vacation lodge nestled along Santa Anita Creek. Built in 1912, the stone lodge, dining hall, store, rustic cabins, and tents remained active until 1931. The trail meanders along the stream-fed canyon floor in a jungle-like environment, thick with oaks, alders, spruce, cedars, willows, ferns, and vines. Old charming cabins are scattered beside the trail. The path parallels Santa Anita Creek, dotted with large granite boulders and occasional flood control dams. The dams, built in the early 1960s, are now overgrown with moss, ferns, and leafy vegetation. Waterfalls and pools have formed around the structures.

To the trailhead

From the Foothill Freeway (Interstate 210) in Arcadia, exit on Santa Anita Avenue. Turn left and head 4.8 miles north to the end of the road and the Chantry Flat parking lots on the right. En route, the road becomes Santa Anita Canyon Road. An Adventure Pass is required for parking.

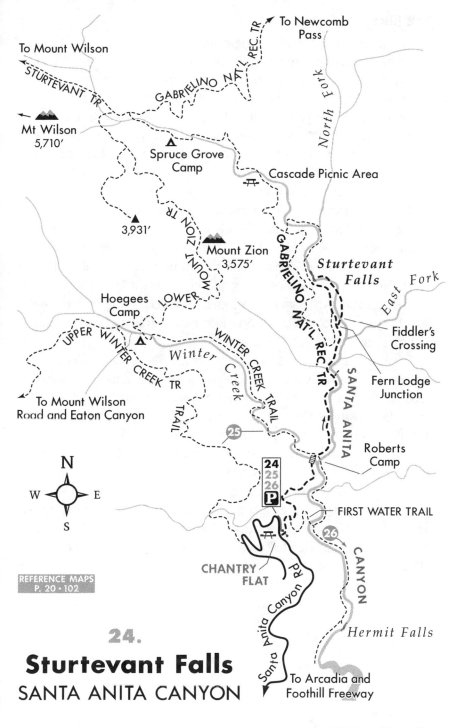

To Newcomb Pass

To Mount Wilson

STURTEVANT TR

GABRIELINO NAT'L REC. TR

North Fork

Mt Wilson
5,710'

Spruce Grove Camp

Cascade Picnic Area

3,931'

MOUNT ZION TR

Mount Zion
3,575'

GABRIELINO NAT'L REC. TR

Sturtevant Falls

East Fork

Hoegees Camp

LOWER

WINTER CREEK TRAIL

Winter Creek

Fiddler's Crossing

UPPER WINTER CREEK TR

Fern Lodge Junction

To Mount Wilson Road and Eaton Canyon

TRAIL

SANTA ANITA

25

Roberts Camp

N

W ● E

S

24
25
26
P

FIRST WATER TRAIL

26

CANYON

CHANTRY FLAT

Santa Anita Canyon Rd

Hermit Falls

REFERENCE MAPS
P. 20 · 102

To Arcadia and Foothill Freeway

24.
Sturtevant Falls
SANTA ANITA CANYON

The hike

From the top (front end) of the parking lot, take the signed trail downhill. Follow the winding, paved fire road on the west wall of Santa Anita Canyon to Roberts Camp on the canyon floor at 0.6 miles. Cross a metal bridge over Winter Creek above its confluence with Santa Anita Creek. Just after the bridge is a 4-way junction. The right fork follows the creek down canyon past a group of turn-of-the-century cabins to Hermit Falls, located just above Santa Anita Dam (Hike 26). The Winter Creek Trail bears left, following the creek (Hike 25).

Continue straight ahead in the lush riparian scenery, staying in Santa Anita Canyon on the Gabrielino National Recreation Trail. Stroll through the shade of the forest along the boulder-filled creek, passing rustic cabins with beautiful rock walls and chimneys. Flood control dams along the creek form 20-foot waterfalls and pools. At 1.5 miles is a signed junction at the Fern Lodge Junction. The Gabrielino National Recreation Trail goes to the left 0.3 miles to the top of Sturtevant Falls.

For now, stay to the right and cross Santa Anita Creek at Fiddler's Crossing. Cross the creek two more times. Scramble over river rock to the base of Sturtevant Falls and a rock-lined pool in a vertical-walled box canyon. After enjoying the falls, return to Fern Lodge Junction. Bear right and wind up the hillside on the west canyon wall. Traverse the slope, perched on a precipitous cliff, to various views of Sturtevant Falls. Return to the trailhead by retracing your steps.

From the Fern Lodge Junction, the Gabrielino National Recreation Trail continues another 2.25 miles to Spruce Grove Campground, 4.5 miles to Newcomb Pass, and 5.5 miles to Mount Wilson. ▪

25. Winter Creek Canyon to Hoegees Camp

SANTA ANITA CANYON · WINTER CREEK CANYON

Hiking distance: 6-mile loop
Hiking time: 3 hours
Configuration: loop
Elevation gain: 950 feet
Exposure: mostly shaded canyon with some exposed chaparral slopes
Difficulty: moderate
Dogs: allowed
Maps: U.S.G.S. Mount Wilson · Harrison: Angeles Front Country Trail Map
Harrison: Mt. Wilson Trail Map

Winter Creek, a major tributary of Santa Anita Creek, forms on the upper south slope of Mount Wilson. Winter Creek Canyon, a shady, deeply cut canyon, is an arboreal haven with stately alders, three varieties of oaks, California bays, big leaf maples, sycamores, willows, and a lush understory of giant ferns and ivy. This hike begins on the lower (south) end of the 28-mile Gabrielino National Recreation Trail at Chantry Flat. The trail descends into bucolic Santa Anita Canyon, then veers up perennial Winter Creek. The route passes historic stone and wood cottages built in the early 1900s, huge granite boulders, stacked concrete dams that form 20-foot cascades, and rock-scoured pools. At the upper end of this loop hike, the Winter Creek Trail passes through rustic Hoegee's Camp, a deep, wooded trail camp on the south bank of the creek. It is named for Arie Hoegee, who built and operated a resort camp at the site from 1908 to 1938. The resort buildings were ruined in the floods of 1938 and burned during the Monrovia Peak Fire of 1953.

To the trailhead

From the Foothill Freeway (Interstate 210) in Arcadia, exit on Santa Anita Avenue. Turn left and head 4.8 miles north to the end of the road and the Chantry Flat parking lots on the right. En route, the road becomes Santa Anita Canyon Road. An Adventure Pass is required for parking.

The hike

From the top (front end) of the parking lot, take the signed trail downhill. Follow the winding, paved fire road on the west wall of Santa Anita Canyon to the historic Roberts Camp on the canyon floor at 0.6 miles. Cross a metal bridge over Winter Creek above its confluence with Santa Anita Creek. Just after the bridge is a 4-way junction. The right fork follows the creek down canyon past a group of turn-of-the-century cabins to Hermit Falls, located just above Santa Anita Dam (Hike 26). Sturtevant Falls is straight ahead another 1.25 miles (Hike 24).

For this hike, bear left on the Winter Creek Trail. Enter the narrow, scenic canyon. Cross the creek and head upstream, passing pools under a mix of alder, willow, bay, and oak trees. Cross the creek at the base of a flood control dam and head up the hillside past a small group of cabins. Climb the hillside, passing a small waterfall and a deep pool on the left beneath a vertical rock wall. Walk through a camp, following the trail signs. Cross the creek and ascend the hillside into Hoegees Camp beneath big cone spruce at 2.1 miles. Meander through the shaded camp, and cross Winter Creek to a posted junction on the right with the Lower Mount Zion Trail. The Lower Mount Zion Trail leads 1.25 miles north to the 3,575-foot summit of Mount Zion, then another 1.25 miles to the Gabrielino National Recreation Trail.

Instead, continue straight and cross the creek to a junction with the Upper Winter Creek Trail—the return route. The Winter Creek Trail continues to the right 4.5 miles to Eaton Canyon and the summit of Mount Wilson. Stay to the left on the Upper Winter Creek Trail, and loop around a side canyon. Traverse the upper south canyon wall under a canopy of bay trees and an understory of ferns and vines. Follow the contours of the steep mountainside, weaving in and out of shady side canyons and exposed chaparral. Slowly descend, overlooking Chantry Flat. The footpath ends at the paved access road. Bear left on the road and wind downhill into Chantry Flat, completing the loop at the parking lot. ■

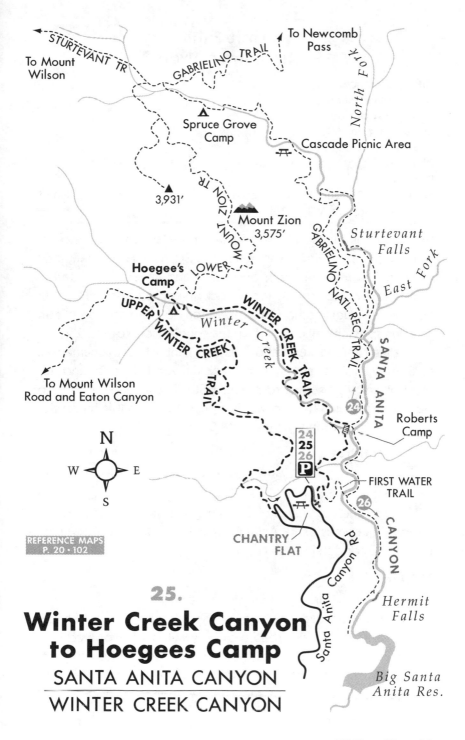

To Newcomb Pass

STURTEVANT TR

To Mount Wilson

GABRIELINO TRAIL

North Fork

△ Spruce Grove Camp

Cascade Picnic Area

MOUNT ZION TR

3,931'

▲▲ Mount Zion 3,575'

GABRIELINO NATL. REC. TRAIL

Sturtevant Falls

East Fork

Hoegee's Camp

LOWER

UPPER WINTER CREEK

Winter Creek

WINTER CREEK TRAIL

SANTA ANITA

To Mount Wilson Road and Eaton Canyon

TRAIL

24

Roberts Camp

N
W — E
S

24
25
26
P

FIRST WATER TRAIL

26

CANYON

REFERENCE MAPS
P. 20 • 102

CHANTRY FLAT

Santa Anita Canyon Rd

Hermit Falls

25.

Winter Creek Canyon to Hoegees Camp
SANTA ANITA CANYON
WINTER CREEK CANYON

Big Santa Anita Res.

26. Hermit Falls
SANTA ANITA CANYON

Hiking distance: 3 miles round trip
Hiking time: 2 hours
Configuration: out-and-back
Elevation gain: 600 feet
Exposure: shaded canyon
Difficulty: easy to slightly moderate
Dogs: allowed
Maps: U.S.G.S. Mount Wilson · Harrison: Angeles Front Country Trail Map
Harrison: Mt. Wilson Trail Map

Hermit Falls is tucked away in Santa Anita Canyon, downstream from well-known Sturtevant Falls. The 30-foot falls sits among huge rock formations with overhangs and caves. The cataract spills out of water chutes in the rock, joined by a series of four descending pools etched into the water-polished granite. It is an amazing spot. The hike begins on the southern end of the 28-mile Gabrielino National Recreation Trail at Chantry Flat, the same trail to Sturtevant Falls and Winter Creek Canyon (Hikes 24 and 25). Most hikers are headed to popular Sturtevant Falls; the trip to Hermit Falls avoids the crowds in a quiet forest that is thick with foliage along perennial Santa Anita Creek.

To the trailhead

From the Foothill Freeway (Interstate 210) in Arcadia, exit on Santa Anita Avenue. Turn left and head 4.8 miles north to the end of the road and the Chantry Flat parking lots on the right. En route, the road becomes Santa Anita Canyon Road. An Adventure Pass is required for parking.

The hike

From the top (front end) of the parking lot, take the signed trail downhill on the west wall of Santa Anita Canyon. Follow the winding, paved fire road a quarter mile to the posted First Water Trail on the right. Take the footpath, perched on the cliff covered with chaparral and yucca, and weave downhill along the mountain contours. At the canyon floor is a flood control

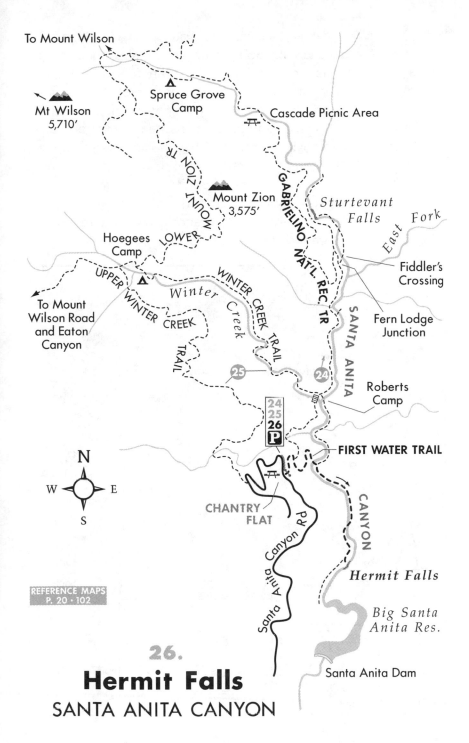

To Mount Wilson

Mt Wilson
5,710'

Spruce Grove
Camp

Cascade Picnic Area

MOUNT ZION TR

Mount Zion
3,575'

*Sturtevant
Falls*

East Fork

Hoegees
Camp

LOWER

GABRIELINO NATL. REC. TR

Fiddler's
Crossing

To Mount
Wilson Road
and Eaton
Canyon

UPPER WINTER CREEK TRAIL

WINTER CREEK TRAIL

Winter Creek

SANTA ANITA

Fern Lodge
Junction

25

24

Roberts
Camp

24
25
26
P

FIRST WATER TRAIL

CHANTRY
FLAT

Santa Anita Canyon Rd

CANYON

Hermit Falls

*Big Santa
Anita Res.*

REFERENCE MAPS
P. 20 · 102

Santa Anita Dam

26.
Hermit Falls
SANTA ANITA CANYON

dam, forming a pool and a manmade waterfall in a lush riparian canopy of alders and oaks. Boulder-hop over Santa Anita Creek to a posted T-junction at 0.75 miles. The left fork follows the creek 0.75 miles up canyon past a group of turn-of-the-century cabins to the historic Roberts Camp and a 4-way junction.

Instead, go to the right and descend past another flood control dam. Stroll through the quiet of the shaded forest among giant sword, chain, and maidenhair ferns to a stream crossing. Cross the creek and head up the west canyon hillside. Traverse the slope, slowly descending to a Y-fork among gorgeous rock formations and pools. Take the left branch down to Hermit Falls. Explore the area, choosing your own route. ■

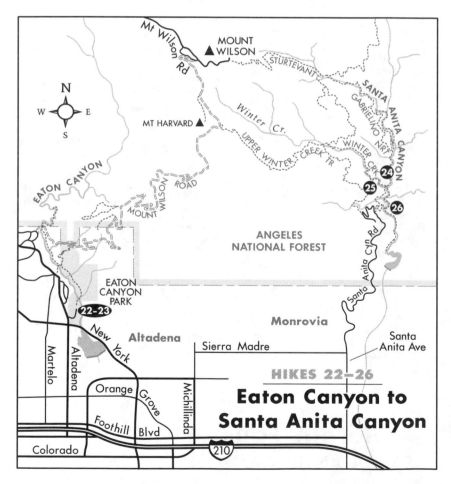

27. Monrovia Canyon Falls

MONROVIA CANYON PARK

1200 North Canyon Boulevard · Monrovia

Hiking distance: 2 miles round trip
Hiking time: 1 hour
Configuration: out-and-back
Elevation gain: 350 feet
Exposure: mostly shaded canyon
Difficulty: easy
Dogs: allowed
Maps: U.S.G.S. Azusa · Monrovia Canyon Park Trail Guide
Harrison: Angeles High Country Trail Map

Monrovia Canyon Falls is a 40-foot, two-tiered cataract fed by year-round springs from the upper slopes of Clamshell Peak and Rankin Peak. The perennial waterfall cascades off a granite ledge in a verdant box canyon, fronted by a pool and large, smooth boulders. The picturesque cataract is located in 80-acre Monrovia Canyon Park in the foothills above the city of Monrovia. The popular park contains shady picnic areas, a nature center, a lush canyon with check dams to control the power of the stream, hiking trails, and the boulder-flanked waterfall.

Three different trailheads offer access to the waterfall. From the lower (south) end of the park by the entrance station, the Bill Cull Trail forms a 3.4-mile round-trip hike. The shortest route, a 1.5-mile round-trip hike, begins by the nature center at the upper end of the park road. This hike begins between the two, midway up the park road by a picnic area, where the Bill Cull Trail connects with the Falls Trail. This route extends the walk through the beautiful canyon. The Falls Trail stays close to Monrovia Creek through rich oak woodland and riparian habitat under a lush canopy of coast live oak, big leaf maple, white alder, sycamores, and ferns. The path leads up narrow Monrovia Canyon and dead-ends by the pool at the base of the falls.

To the trailhead

From the Foothill Freeway (Interstate 210) in Monrovia, exit on Myrtle Avenue. Turn left and drive 0.8 miles to Foothill Boulevard. Turn right (west) and go 0.25 miles to Canyon Boulevard. Turn left and continue 1.2 miles north. Veer to the right, staying on Canyon Boulevard for one mile and following signs to the park entrance. Drive 0.3 miles to the middle parking area, just after crossing over a bridge. Parking spaces are on the right to the east of the restroom building. A parking fee is required.

The hike

Walk fifty yards up the road. As the road veers right, take the signed footpath straight ahead, veering left. Enter the dense forest under the shade of alders, bays, sycamores, and oaks. Follow the east side of the canyon, and pass a junction on the right, which leads up the hill among pines and oak to the nature center and picnic area. Gently wind up canyon and cross the creek just above a manmade waterfall. Traverse the west canyon wall above the stream, weaving past rock formations and through a tunnel of vegetation. Return to the stream and follow the canyon floor. Pass a couple more flood control dams with waterfalls. At just under one mile, cross the stream and boulder hop a short distance to Monrovia Falls and a pool in the rock-walled grotto at the end of the trail. ■

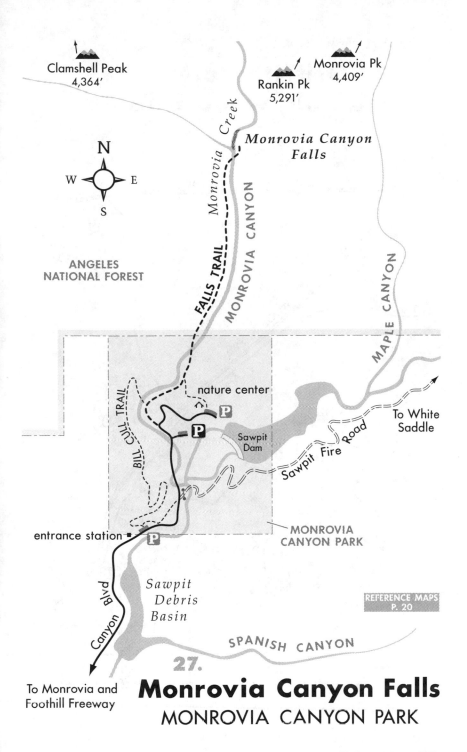

Clamshell Peak
4,364'

Rankin Pk
5,291'

Monrovia Pk
4,409'

Monrovia Creek

Monrovia Canyon
Falls

FALLS TRAIL

MONROVIA CANYON

MAPLE CANYON

N
W   E
S

ANGELES
NATIONAL FOREST

BILL CULL TRAIL

nature center

Sawpit
Dam

Sawpit Fire Road

To White
Saddle

entrance station

MONROVIA
CANYON PARK

REFERENCE MAPS
P. 20

Canyon Blvd

Sawpit
Debris
Basin

SPANISH CANYON

To Monrovia and
Foothill Freeway

27.
Monrovia Canyon Falls
MONROVIA CANYON PARK

Griffith Park
and Hollywood Hills

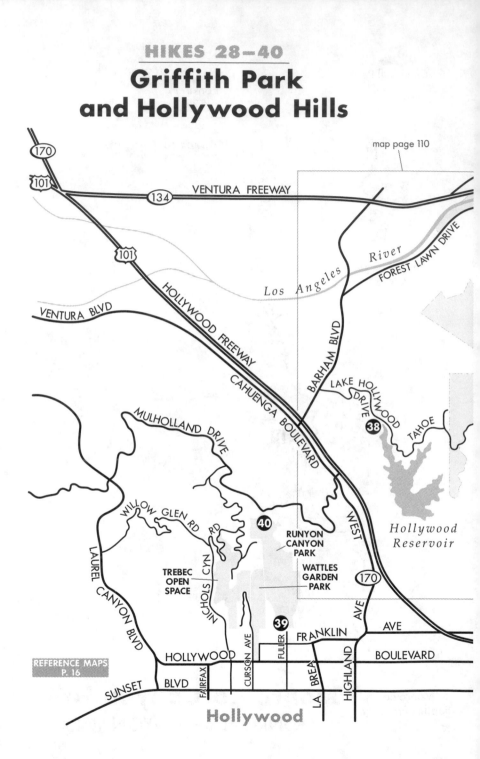

map page 110

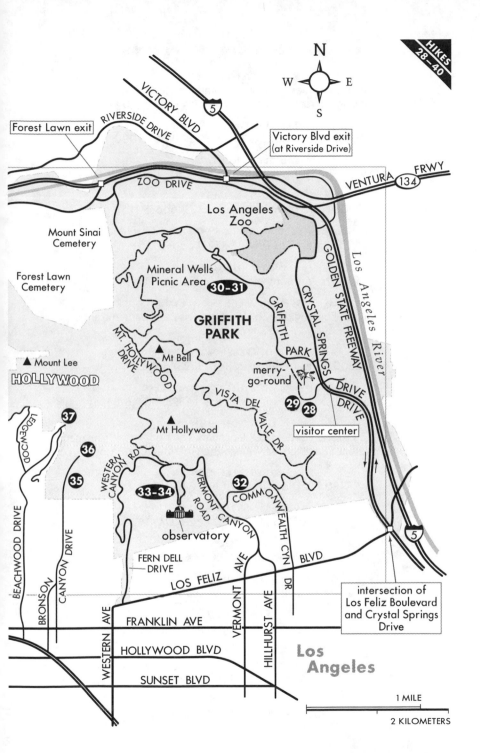

N
W E
S

VICTORY BLVD

RIVERSIDE DRIVE

5

Forest Lawn exit

Victory Blvd exit
(at Riverside Drive)

ZOO DRIVE

VENTURA FRWY 134

Los Angeles Zoo

Los Angeles River

Mount Sinai
Cemetery

Mineral Wells
Picnic Area

30-31

Forest Lawn
Cemetery

GRIFFITH
PARK

GRIFFITH PARK DRIVE

GOLDEN STATE FREEWAY

CRYSTAL SPRINGS

Mt Bell

MT. HOLLYWOOD DRIVE

▲ Mount Lee

HOLLYWOOD

merry-
go-round

PARK

DRIVE

29 28

Mt Hollywood

VISTA DEL VALLE DR

visitor center

37

36

35

BRONSON CANYON

WESTERN CANYON RD

33-34

VERMONT CANYON ROAD

observatory

32

COMMONWEALTH CYN

DRIVE

5

BEACHWOOD DRIVE

BRONSON

CANYON DRIVE

FERN DELL
DRIVE

LOS FELIZ

VERMONT AVE

HILLHURST AVE

COMMONWEALTH CYN BLVD

intersection of
Los Feliz Boulevard
and Crystal Springs
Drive

WESTERN AVE

FRANKLIN AVE

HOLLYWOOD BLVD

SUNSET BLVD

Los
Angeles

1 MILE

2 KILOMETERS

ATTRACTIONS and ACTIVITIES

FACILITIES
athletic facilities · soccer · swimming · tennis · golf
picnicking · horseback riding · camping · hiking · jogging

AUTRY NATIONAL CENTER
4700 Western Heritage Drive · (323) 667-2000

BICYCLE RENTAL
4730 Crystal Springs Drive at ranger station · (323) 653-4099

BIRD SANTUARY
2900 N. Vermont Avenue · (323) 666-5046

FERNDELL NATURE MUSEUM • WESTERN CANYON
5375 Red Oak Drive · (323) 666-5046

GREEK THEATER
2700 N. Vermont Avenue · (323) 665-1927

GRIFFITH PARK MERRY-GO-ROUND
between the Los Angeles Zoo and the Los Feliz park entrance
(323) 665-3051

GRIFFITH OBSERVATORY
2800 E. Observatory Road · (323) 664-1191

GRIFFITH PARK SOUTHERN RAILROAD
Corner Los Feliz/Riverside Drive · (323) 664-6788

HOLLYWOOD SIGN
Views of the historic Los Angeles landmark can be gained from many
hiking trails in the Park as well as the Griffith Observatory

L.A. EQUESTRIAN CENTER
480 Riverside Drive · (323) 840-9063

L.A. LIVE STEAMERS
5200 Zoo Dr · (323) 662-5874

L.A. ZOO
5333 Zoo Drive · (323) 666-4650

PONY RIDES
Corner Los Feliz/Riverside Drive · (323) 664-3266

STATUARY
Statues are found throughout Griffith Park

SYMPHONY IN THE GLEN
Free concert program has been based in Griffith Park at the
Old Zoo Picnic Area · www.symphonyintheglen.org

TRAVEL TOWN
5200 Zoo Drive · (323) 662-5874

Griffith Park

Griffith Park is an emerald gem in the midst of the Los Angeles metropolis. The 4,217-acre park (equal to five square miles) is the largest municipal park in the United States. It is nearly three times the size of New York City's Central Park. This rugged urban wilderness contains ridges and peaks with overlooks, secluded canyons, creeks, springs, and gardens. Large portions of the park remain virtually unchanged from its original natural state. The mountains and steep interior canyons of Griffith Park, as well as the adjacent Hollywood Hills, are largely undeveloped and offer a natural haven for humans and animals.

Griffith Park lies on the easternmost tip of the Santa Monica Mountains. It is surrounded by the cities of Burbank, Hollywood, Glendale, and Los Angeles. To the east, the park faces the Verdugo Mountains and San Gabriel Mountains. The preserved parkland is bound along its borders by major thoroughfares as well as the Los Angeles River.

Colonel Griffith J. Griffith donated over 3,000 acres to create this parkland in 1896. Griffith was a Welsh immigrant who made his fortune in gold and silver mining speculation. He deeded the land as a Christmas gift to the people of Los Angeles as "a place of rest and relaxation for the masses." Additional land acquisitions since this time have expanded the park to 4,217 acres.

A 56-mile network of hiking and equestrian trails weaves across the semi-arid foothills, chaparral-cloaked hills, oak groves, and wooded glens. The trail system combines single-track footpaths, unpaved fire roads, and paved (but gated) roads. The park's elevation ranges from 384 feet to 1,625 feet at the summit of Mount Hollywood. From the trails are some of the best views of the Los Angeles basin.

Numerous attractions are located with the park, in addition to the well-known Griffith Observatory and Greek Theater (see left). The next 10 hikes include some of these points of interest, including the historic merry-go-round, the Old Zoo, Mount Hollywood, Amir's Garden, Ferndell Park, the Bronson Caves, and the HOLLYWOOD sign (arguably the best-known site within the park). For a complete list of events and attractions, go to the observatory (2800 East Observatory Road) or the visitor center (4730 Crystal Springs Drive).

Note: Leashed dogs are allowed on all the trails within the park.

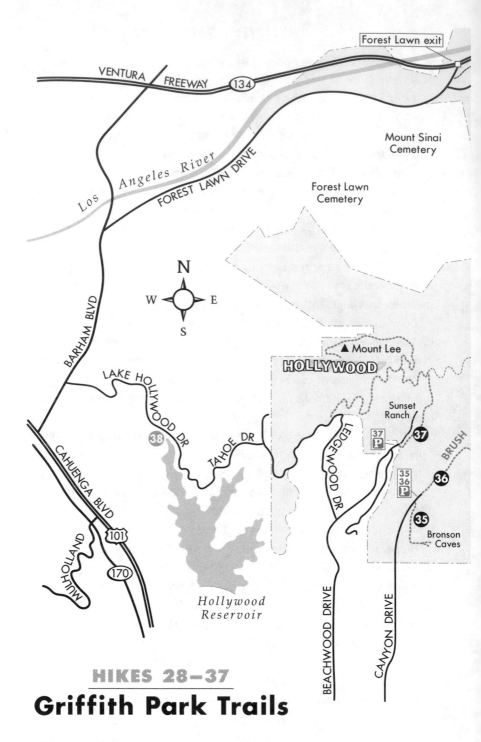

HIKES 28–37

Griffith Park Trails

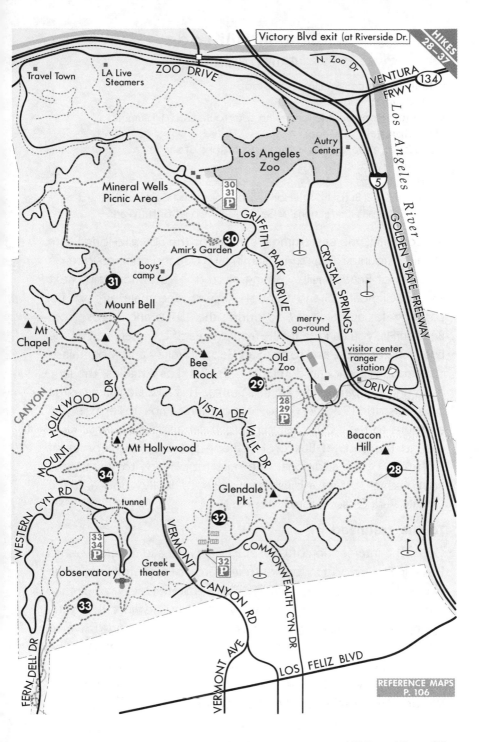

Victory Blvd exit (at Riverside Dr.)

HIKES 28–37

N. Zoo Dr

ZOO DRIVE

VENTURA FRWY

134

Travel Town

LA Live Steamers

Los Angeles River

5

GOLDEN STATE FREEWAY

Autry Center

Los Angeles Zoo

Mineral Wells Picnic Area

30 31 P

GRIFFITH PARK DRIVE

CRYSTAL SPRINGS

Amir's Garden

30

boys' camp

31

Mount Bell

Mt Chapel

Bee Rock

merry-go-round

Old Zoo

29

visitor center ranger station

DRIVE

MOUNT HOLLYWOOD DR

CANYON

VISTA DEL VALLE DR

28 29 P

Beacon Hill

28

Mt Hollywood

34

Glendale Pk

32

tunnel

WESTERN CYN RD

33 34 P

observatory

33

Greek theater

VERMONT CANYON RD

32 P

COMMONWEALTH CYN DR

FERN DELL DR

VERMONT AVE

LOS FELIZ BLVD

REFERENCE MAPS P. 106

28. Beacon Hill Loop
GRIFFITH PARK

Hiking distance: 5-mile double loop
Hiking time: 3 hours
Configuration: double loop with spur to Beacon Hill summit
Elevation gain: 650 feet
Exposure: exposed hills with short sections of shade
Difficulty: moderate
Dogs: allowed
Maps: U.S.G.S. Burbank and Hollywood · Map and Guide of Griffith Park
Hileman's Recreational & Geological Map of Griffith Park

Beacon Hill is the easternmost summit of the 50-mile-long Santa Monica Mountain Range. An illuminated beacon once resided on the top of Beacon Hill, warning aircraft of the mountains next to the Glendale Grand Central Airport, the main airport for Los Angeles and Hollywood during the 1910s and 1920s. From Beacon Hill you can see it all—from the Pacific Ocean, across the Los Angeles Basin, and to the San Gabriel Valley and Mountains.

Beacon Hill is located in Griffith Park in Los Angeles, the largest municipal park in the United States. This hike begins near the park's historic 1926 merry-go-round, then climbs up Fern Canyon en route to the 1,001-foot summit. The trail forms a large loop around the base of Beacon Hill along the southeast corner of Griffith Park. An additional one-mile loop leads to Vista View Point, which offers a bird's-eye view of Hollywood and the Griffith Park Observatory.

To the trailhead

Go to the intersection of Los Feliz Boulevard and Crystal Springs Drive in Hollywood in the southeast area of Griffith Park. (To arrive at this intersection from the Golden State Freeway/I-5, take the Los Feliz Boulevard Exit. Drive west a short distance to Crystal Springs Drive.) Drive 1.3 miles north on Crystal Springs Drive to the merry-go-round turnoff on the left. Turn left and park in the first parking lot.

From Highway 134/Ventura Freeway in Burbank, take the Victory Boulevard exit. Drive south to a T-junction with Zoo Drive.

Turn left on Zoo Drive and continue 2.1 miles to the merry-go-round turnoff on the right. (En route, Zoo Drive becomes Griffith Park Drive.) Turn right and park in the first parking lot.

The hike

From the parking lot, walk back to the entrance road and the vehicle gate. The Lower Beacon Trail, our return route, is directly across the road. Walk 75 yards to the right on the paved road to the Fern Canyon Nature Trail on the left. Continue on the paved road for 55 yards (straight ahead) to a second junction. Leave the paved road and veer left on the Fern Canyon Trail, a dirt road. Pass two junctions on the right that form a loop through the Old Zoo (Hike 29). Pass a side path on the left that descends into Fern Canyon and the amphitheater. Steadily climb the west canyon wall, following the curvature of the mountains. Cross over to the east slope of Fern Canyon, reaching the 5-Points junction on a ridge overlooking the San Gabriel Valley and Los Angeles at one mile. Straight ahead is the Coolidge Trail, the return route. The two trails to the right form the smaller one-mile loop.

For now, bear left on a spur trail to the summit of Beacon Hill. Walk east along the eucalyptus-lined ridge at a near-level grade. Make a short but steep ascent to the rounded, 1,001-foot summit at 1.25 miles. Below is the Golden State (I-5) Freeway and the Los Angeles River. To the east and north are Glendale, Eagle Rock, Burbank, the Verdugo Mountains, and the San Gabriel Mountains. To the south and west are downtown Los Angeles and the entire Los Angeles basin to Palos Verdes.

Return to the 5-Points junction. To add a one-mile loop to the hike, take the second trail to the right. Traverse the mountain westward, perched on the steep slope. Climb to Vista Del Valle Drive, stretching along the head of Fern Canyon and directly across from Vista View Point. The overlook offers more sweeping views of Hollywood, Los Angeles, and the Griffith Park Observatory. Across the road is the Hogback Trail and Riverside Trail (Hike 32). Follow the path to the left, above and parallel to Vista Del Valle Drive. The path joins the road along a U-bend in Vista Del Valle Drive. Pick up the posted trail on the outside bend.

Descend east, completing the loop at the 5-Points junction.

To continue on the large loop, take the Coolidge Trail to the right, descending on the south-facing slope. As the path nears the Marty Tregnan Golf Academy, look north to a great view of Beacon Hill. Descend to a trail split at the southeast corner of Griffith Park. The right fork drops down to Crystal Springs Drive. Veer left on the Lower Beacon Trail, skirting the east flank of Beacon Hill above the freeway on the undulating path. Curve left (west) and climb to northern park views. Descend to the park road, directly across from the trailhead parking area. ■

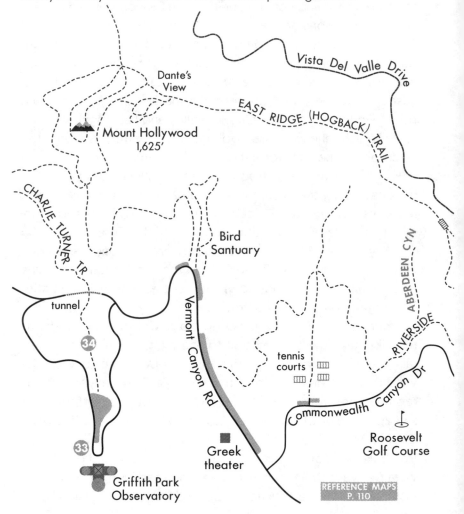

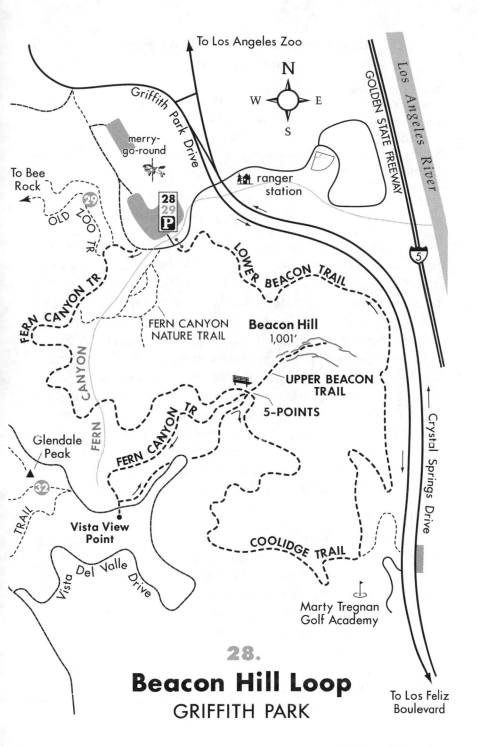

To Los Angeles Zoo

N
W E
S

Griffith Park Drive

merry-go-round

ranger station

GOLDEN STATE FREEWAY

Los Angeles River

To Bee Rock

29

OLD ZOO TR

28 29 P

To Los Angeles River

FERN CANYON TR

LOWER BEACON TRAIL

FERN CANYON NATURE TRAIL

FERN CANYON

Beacon Hill
1,001'

UPPER BEACON TRAIL

5-POINTS

FERN CANYON TR

Glendale Peak

32

TRAIL

Vista View Point

Vista Del Valle Drive

COOLIDGE TRAIL

5

Crystal Springs Drive

Marty Tregnan Golf Academy

28.
Beacon Hill Loop
GRIFFITH PARK

To Los Feliz Boulevard

29. Bee Rock and Old Zoo Park
GRIFFITH PARK

Hiking distance: 2.2-mile loop
Hiking time: 1.5 hours
Configuration: loop with spur to Bee Rock
Elevation gain: 600 feet
Exposure: mostly exposed with sections of shade
Difficulty: easy with moderate ascent to Bee Rock
Dogs: allowed
Maps: U.S.G.S. Burbank · Map and Guide of Griffith Park
Hileman's Recreational & Geological Map of Griffith Park

Bee Rock is a large, cavernous sandstone outcropping that is naturally sculpted into the shape of a beehive near the center of Griffith Park. From atop the 1,056-foot rock formation are impressive views across the massive park. The hike returns through the Old Los Angeles Zoo, which was converted into a park after the new zoo was built. The Old Los Angeles Zoo operated from 1912 through 1965 at this location before moving to the current location two miles north. The historic enclosures, walls, and grottoes, built in the 1930s to house the animals, are still intact. The trail winds past the abandoned animal cages with an eerie animal ghost town atmosphere. The trails are on the old walking paths and expansive lawns. This hike begins at the at the merry-go-round and follows a dirt road that circles the back side of the Old Zoo to Bee Rock, then returns through the Old Zoo.

To the trailhead

Go to the intersection of Los Feliz Boulevard and Crystal Springs Drive in Hollywood in the southeast area of Griffith Park. (To arrive at this intersection from the Golden State Freeway/I-5, take the Los Feliz Boulevard exit. Drive west a short distance to Crystal Springs Drive.) Drive 1.3 miles north on Crystal Springs Drive to the merry-go-round turnoff on the left. Turn left and park in the first parking lot.

From Highway 134/Ventura Freeway in Burbank, take the Victory Boulevard exit. Drive south to a T-junction with Zoo Drive.

Turn left on Zoo Drive and continue 2.1 miles to the merry-go-round turnoff on the right. (En route, Zoo Drive becomes Crystal Springs Drive.) Turn right and park in the first parking lot.

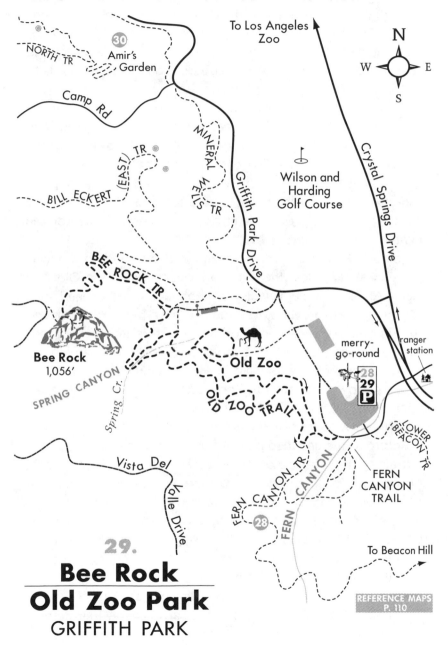

29.
Bee Rock
Old Zoo Park
GRIFFITH PARK

The hike

From the parking lot, walk back to the entrance road and the vehicle gate. The Lower Beacon Trail is directly across the road. Walk 75 yards to the right on the paved road to the Fern Canyon Nature Trail on the left. Continue on the paved road for 55 yards (straight ahead) to a second junction. Leave the paved road and veer left on the Fern Canyon Trail, a dirt road. Walk 80 yards to a Y-fork. Begin the loop to the left, staying on the Fern Canyon Trail for 60 yards to a junction with the Old Zoo Trail. The left fork (straight ahead) leads to Beacon Hill (Hike 28). Instead, veer right on the Old Zoo Trail and head uphill into the trees. Skirt the back (west) side of the Old Zoo as prominent Bee Rock comes into view at a half mile. Gently descend into the shade of pines and oaks. On a horseshoe right bend is seasonal Spring Creek and a rock grotto. Cross over the stream to an unsigned trail on the right, our return route.

For now, continue straight ahead and descend to a 4-way junction at 0.7 miles. The right fork descends to the Old Zoo Picnic Area. The Mineral Wells Trail continues straight ahead, then curves right. For this hike, take the Bee Rock Trail to the left, and traverse the south canyon slope with scattered oaks. The road/trail curves left and ends by a footpath. Bear left on the path and weave uphill at a steeper grade. Head generally south on the steep, narrow trail. Concrete steps lead up to the perch atop Bee Rock. From the fenced 1,056-foot summit are great vistas of the San Gabriel Mountains and the San Fernando Valley.

Return to the unsigned path at Spring Canyon. Descend to the left along the left side of the waterway to a paved path, part of the Old Zoo pathway. Go to the right, passing old cell-like cages built in the 1930s that once housed the animals. On the left are expansive lawns. At 100 yards is a junction. The main trail (straight head) weaves downhill, passing abandoned rock animal habitats and returning to the parking lots by the merry-go-round. Take the narrower paved path to the right. Wind along the contours of the hillside, passing more animal cages. Parallel the Old Zoo Trail, completing the loop at the Fern Canyon Trail. Retrace your steps back to the trailhead parking lot. ▪

30. Amir's Garden
GRIFFITH PARK

Hiking distance: 1.5 miles round trip
Hiking time: 1 hour
Configuration: out-and-back with interconnected pathways in garden
Elevation gain: 300 feet
Exposure: exposed hills with shaded pockets
Difficulty: easy
Dogs: allowed
Maps: U.S.G.S. Burbank · Map and Guide of Griffith Park
Hileman's Recreational & Geological Map of Griffith Park

Amir's Garden is a beautifully landscaped garden with rock-lined paths, benches, and picnic tables on layered terraces in Griffith Park. The nearly five-acre oasis contains several species of trees (including pines, palm, eucalyptus, jacaranda, and pepper), ferns, ice plants, geraniums, rose bushes, yucca, and a wide variety of succulents. A network of trails and stairways lead through the lush, shaded grove. The garden was once a barren hillside. Amir Dialameh, a Persian immigrant, created, designed, planted, nurtured, and maintained this idyllic landscape as a labor of love from 1971 until his death in 2003. The garden is currently cared for by volunteers. This hike begins at the Mineral Wells Picnic Area and climbs the hillside to the tranquil garden.

To the trailhead

Go to the intersection of Los Feliz Boulevard and Crystal Springs Drive in Hollywood in the southeast area of Griffith Park. (To arrive at this intersection from the Golden State Freeway/I-5, take the Los Feliz Boulevard exit. Drive west a short distance to Crystal Springs Drive.) Drive 1.5 miles north on Crystal Springs Drive to Griffith Park Drive—just past the merry-go-round—and turn left. Drive 1.3 miles to the Mineral Wells Picnic Area and park alongside the road.

From Highway 134/Ventura Freeway in Burbank, take the Victory Boulevard exit. Drive south to a T-junction with Zoo Drive. Turn right and drive 2.3 miles to the Mineral Wells Picnic Area. (En route, Zoo Drive becomes Griffith Park Drive.) Park along the road.

The hike

At the trailhead is a 3-way junction. The Mineral Wells Trail heads left and right, connecting the Bill Eckert Trail by the Old Zoo with Mount Hollywood Drive. For this hike, bear right and immediately go left onto the unsigned North Trail. Switchback to the left and curve around a water tank to views of Burbank, Glendale, the Verdugo Mountains, and the majestic San Gabriel Mountains. At a half mile is a trail split. The North Trail continues to the right. Bear left into Amir's Garden, the lush oasis on the southeast mountain slope. Explore along your own route as the garden paths zigzag across the hillside. Stroll to overlooks and benches among the landscaped grounds. Return along the same route.

To extend the hike, continue up the hill on the North Trail, leading to Mount Bell and Mount Hollywood (Hike 31). ■

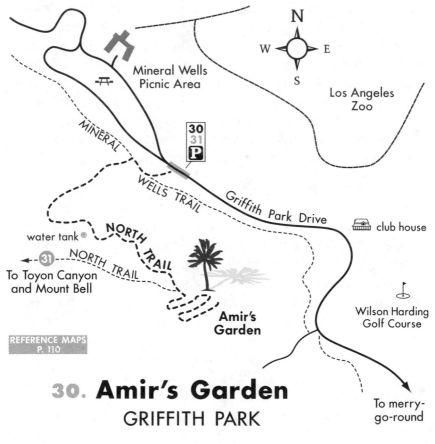

Mineral Wells Picnic Area

Los Angeles Zoo

N
W   E
S

30
31
P

MINERAL WELLS TRAIL

Griffith Park Drive

club house

water tank ◉

NORTH TRAIL

31
NORTH TRAIL
To Toyon Canyon and Mount Bell

Amir's Garden

Wilson Harding Golf Course

REFERENCE MAPS
P. 110

To merry-go-round

30. **Amir's Garden**
GRIFFITH PARK

31. Mount Bell from Mineral Wells Picnic Area

GRIFFITH PARK

Hiking distance: 4.2-miles round trip
Hiking time: 2.5 hours
Configuration: out-and-back with loop; side-trip to Amir's Garden
Elevation gain: 900 feet
Exposure: exposed hills
Difficulty: moderate
Dogs: allowed
Maps: U.S.G.S. Burbank · Map and Guide of Griffith Park
Hileman's Recreational & Geological Map of Griffith Park

Mount Bell sits in the geographic center of Griffith Park at an elevation of 1,582 feet. It is less than a half mile north of Mount Hollywood, the highest peak in the park. This hike begins at the Mineral Wells Picnic Area and climbs high into the park's backcountry to Mount Bell. The trail circles the summit, offering spectacular vistas in every direction. En route, the trail visits Amir's Garden, a 5-acre hillside oasis.

To the trailhead

Go to the intersection of Los Feliz Boulevard and Crystal Springs Drive in Hollywood in the southeast area of Griffith Park. (To arrive at this intersection from the Golden State Freeway/I-5, take the Los Feliz Boulevard exit. Drive west a short distance to Crystal Springs Drive.) Drive 1.5 miles north on Crystal Springs Drive to Griffith Park Drive—just past the merry-go-round—and turn left. Drive 1.3 miles to the Mineral Wells Picnic Area and park alongside the road.

From Highway 134/Ventura Freeway in Burbank, take the Forest Lawn Drive exit. Turn right and drive one block to Zoo Drive. Turn left and go 0.2 miles to Griffith Park Drive. Turn right and continue 1.4 miles to the signed Mineral Wells Picnic Area. Park alongside the road.

The hike

At the trailhead is a 3-way junction. The Mineral Wells Trail heads left and right, connecting the Bill Eckert Trail by the Old Zoo with Mount Hollywood Drive. For this hike, bear right and immediately go left onto the unsigned North Trail. Switchback to the left and curve around a water tank to views of Burbank, Glendale, the Verdugo Mountains, and the majestic San Gabriel Mountains. At a half mile is a trail split. The North Trail continues to the right. First, detour left into Amir's Garden, a lush oasis on the southeast mountain slope.

After exploring the garden, return to the North Trail and continue uphill. Follow the ridge overlooking the Griffith Park Boys Camp (in the canyon to the left) to a T-junction by a water tank. The right fork leads to an irrigated, terraced hillside, part of the Toyon Canyon Restoration Project. Go to the left, curving around the right side of the water tank. Walk 100 yards to an unmarked junction at one mile. The Toyon Trail, a footpath, goes to the right and heads downhill. Stay on the fire road to the left, now the Mount Hollywood Trail. Head south and climb to Vista Del Valle Drive as views open up across the San Fernando Valley. Walk 30 yards to the left on the paved road, and pick up the trail on the right. Traverse the slope above Vista Del Valle Drive, passing rock formations and admiring the far-reaching vistas, to a trail fork by power poles at 1.5 miles.

Begin the loop sharply to the right on the north flank of Mount Bell. Climb across the north face of Mount Bell to a T-junction. A view spans across Los Angeles, extending from the towering buildings of Hollywood, Century City, and Westwood to the Pacific Ocean. The right fork leads to Mount Hollywood Drive. Bear left and cross the south side of Mount Bell above Brush Canyon. Walk beyond Mount Bell to an overlook by a spring on the right, and drop down to another junction. The right fork leads to Mount Hollywood, which can be seen ahead, and Dante's View. Go to the left and descend to a trail on the right that leads to Bee Rock and the Old Zoo (Hike 29). Walk straight ahead and continue downhill, completing the loop. Return by retracing your steps. ■

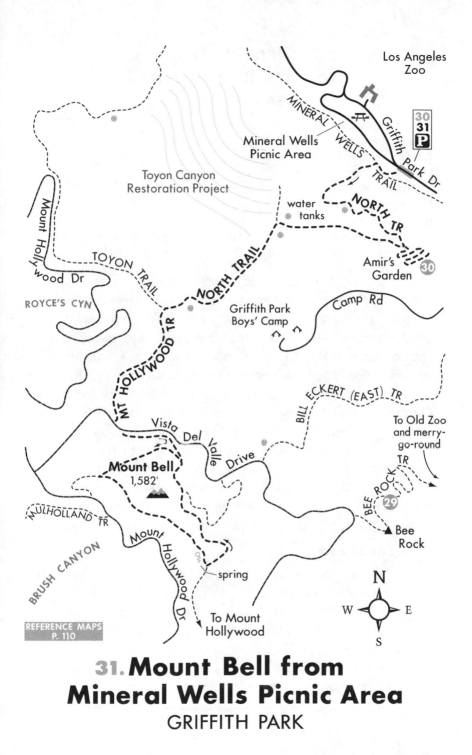

Los Angeles Zoo

MINERAL WELLS TRAIL

Griffith Park Dr

30
31
P

Mineral Wells
Picnic Area

Toyon Canyon
Restoration Project

water
tanks

NORTH TR

TOYON TRAIL

NORTH TRAIL

Mount Hollywood Dr

ROYCE'S CYN

MT HOLLYWOOD TR

Amir's
Garden

30

Griffith Park
Boys' Camp

Camp Rd

BILL ECKERT (EAST) TR

To Old Zoo
and merry-
go-round

TR

BEE ROCK

29

Vista Del Valle Drive

Mount Bell
1,582'

MULHOLLAND TR

Mount Hollywood Dr

BRUSH CANYON

spring

To Mount
Hollywood

Bee
Rock

N
W   E
S

REFERENCE MAPS
P. 110

31. Mount Bell from
Mineral Wells Picnic Area
GRIFFITH PARK

32. Glendale Peak
from the Riverside Trail
GRIFFITH PARK

Hiking distance: 2.8 miles round trip
Hiking time: 1.5 hours
Configuration: out-and-back
Elevation gain: 400 feet
Exposure: exposed hills
Difficulty: easy to moderate
Dogs: allowed
Maps: U.S.G.S. Hollywood and Burbank · Map and Guide of Griffith Park
Hileman's Recreational & Geological Map of Griffith Park

Glendale Peak is a 1,184-foot mountain on the southeast corner of Griffith Park between Mount Hollywood and Beacon Hill. From the peak are sweeping vistas that span from downtown Los Angeles to Glendale and from the San Gabriel Valley to the Pacific Ocean. A short, quarter-mile memorial trail climbs to the summit of Glendale Peak. The narrow footpath—Henry's Trail—is named for the late Henry Shamma, former chairman of the Sierra Club. (He was also a long-time friend of Amir Dialameh, who created Amir's Garden from Hike 30.) Henry worked on many of Griffith Park's trails and gardens. This hike begins on the Riverside Trail, traversing the mountain slopes with views of the nearby Griffith Park Observatory. For an extended hike, the East Ridge (Hogback) Trail connects Glendale Peak to Dante's View and Mount Hollywood, following the ridge of the steep hillside.

To the trailhead

From the intersection of Los Feliz Boulevard and Vermont Avenue in Hollywood, drive 0.7 miles north on Vermont Avenue to Commonwealth Canyon Drive on the right. It is located just before the Greek Theatre. (En route, Vermont Avenue curves into Vermont Canyon Road.) Turn right on Commonwealth Canyon Drive, and go 0.15 miles to the parking lot for the Vermont Canyon tennis courts on the left. Turn left and park.

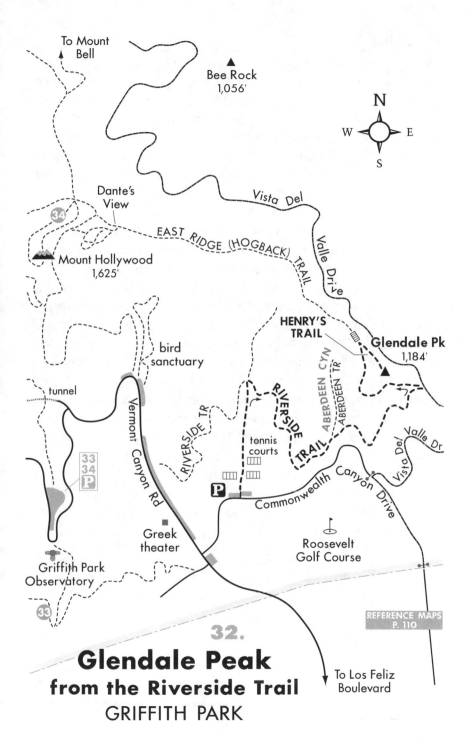

To Mount Bell

Bee Rock
1,056'

N
W E
S

Dante's View

34

EAST RIDGE (HOGBACK) TRAIL

Mount Hollywood
1,625'

Vista Del

Valle Drive

HENRY'S TRAIL

Glendale Pk
1,184'

bird sanctuary

RIVERSIDE

ABERDEEN CYN

ABERDEEN TR

tunnel

RIVERSIDE TR

Vermont Canyon Rd

TRAIL

tennis courts

33
34
P

P

Commonwealth Canyon Drive

Vista Del

Valle Dr

Greek theater

Roosevelt
Golf Course

Griffith Park
Observatory

33

REFERENCE MAPS
P. 110

32.

Glendale Peak
from the Riverside Trail
GRIFFITH PARK

To Los Feliz
Boulevard

The hike

Walk up the paved lane between the tennis courts to a 3-way junction with the Riverside Trail (formerly called the Aberdeen Trail). The footpath straight ahead is a dead-end path that leads to the north end of the canyon. To the left, the Riverside Trail leads to Vermont Canyon Road south of the bird sanctuary.

Take the right fork of the Riverside Trail. Traverse the hillside slope on a gentle uphill grade to an overlook of downtown Los Angeles, Hollywood, the Hollywood Hills, and the Griffith Park Observatory. Follow the contours of the hillside, and slowly descend into Aberdeen Canyon. At the mouth of the canyon, the Aberdeen Trail, a narrow footpath spur, veers left up the canyon. Stay on the Riverside Trail straight ahead, and ascend the hillside to a junction with Vista Del Valle Drive at one mile. Take the switchback to the left on the East Ridge (Hogback) Trail, savoring the views overlooking the entire Los Angeles basin. Loop clockwise around Glendale Peak to a metal bridge over a narrow ridge at the head of Aberdeen Canyon. From the bridge is a view below of Fern Canyon, Beacon Hill, and the merry-go-round. Just before crossing the bridge, bear sharply right on Henry's Trail, the access trail to Glendale Peak. Take the footpath and follow the ridge south 0.1 mile to the 1,184-foot summit, where there are great 360-degree views. Return by retracing your route.

To extend the hike from the bridge, the East Ridge (Hogback) Trail steeply climbs the serpentine spine of the mountain 0.8 miles to Dante's View, then a short distance farther to the overlook atop Mount Hollywood. Throughout the hike are spectacular vistas. ■

33. Griffith Park Observatory to Ferndell Park

GRIFFITH PARK

Hiking distance: 2.5 miles round trip
Hiking time: 1.5 hours
Configuration: out-and-back with central loop
Elevation gain: 500 feet
Exposure: exposed hills and sun-filtered shade in Ferndell Park
Difficulty: easy to slightly moderate
Dogs: allowed
Maps: U.S.G.S. Hollywood · Map and Guide of Griffith Park
Hileman's Recreational & Geological Map of Griffith Park

The copper-domed Griffith Park Observatory is a Los Angeles landmark and one of Griffith Park's most popular attractions. The historic observatory is perched on the south-facing slope of Mount Hollywood, overlooking the city. The facilities include a planetarium, laser programs, gift shop, and a variety of science displays. An observation deck with telescopes winds around the south side of this architectural landmark, with views across Hollywood and the expansive metropolitan area.

This hike begins at the observatory and descends the mountain slope to the waterway in Ferndell Park. The park is a lush, stream-fed oasis in Western Canyon down the hillside from the observatory. The upper portion of the park is a shaded glen with mature oaks, sycamores, spruce, alders, and coast redwoods. At the southern end of the park is an exotic tropical garden with a stone-lined path, a tree-shaded brook, charming footbridges, small waterfalls, stone retaining walls, a variety of ferns, succulents, and moss-covered rocks.

To the trailhead

OPTION 1: From Los Feliz Boulevard in Hollywood, take Fern Dell Drive north 2.3 miles to the Griffith Park Observatory parking lot. (Fern Dell Drive becomes Western Canyon Road after the hairpin turn.)

OPTION 2: From Los Feliz Boulevard in Hollywood, take Vermont Avenue north 1.8 miles to the observatory parking lot. (En route, Vermont Avenue curves into Vermont Canyon Road.) Both directions offer a beautiful, curving drive through Griffith Park.

The hike

From the parking lot, walk towards the observatory. Take the unpaved trail to the left (east) of the magnificent structure to an overlook and trail split at a quarter mile. The left fork descends to the Greek Theater at Vermont Canyon Road. For this hike, bear right another quarter mile to a second junction. Begin the loop to the right on the West Observatory Trail, a dirt road. Continue down the hillside, leaving the chaparral-clad hillside into forested Western Canyon at Ferndell Park (also known as Fern Dell). At the canyon floor is an old adobe restroom and a junction with the East Observatory Trail, the return route.

For now, detour down canyon to the south through Ferndell Park under towering sycamore and oak trees. Pass through the picnic grounds to the brook. Stroll along the quarter-mile path, meandering along the park's stream, crossing over bridges, passing waterfalls and pools, and meandering through the lush gardens and glen.

Return to the trail junction by the adobe restroom, and now take the East Observatory Trail. Climb up the side canyon under the three domes of the observatory, completing the loop. Bear right and return a half mile to the trailhead at the observatory. ▪

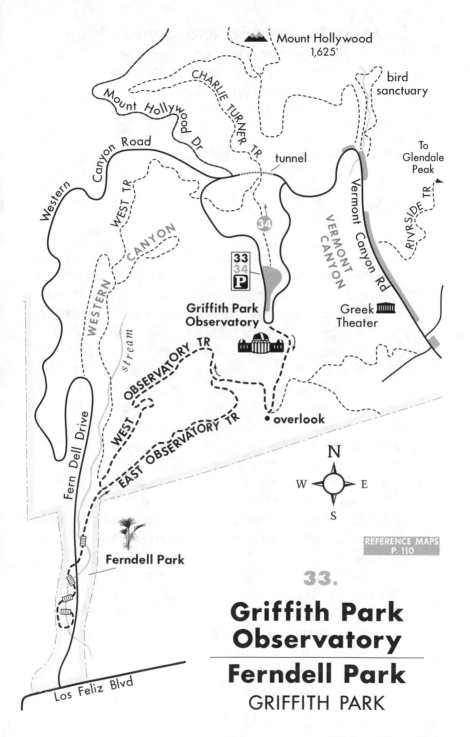

Mount Hollywood
1,625'

bird sanctuary

CHARLIE TURNER TR

Mount Hollywood Dr

Western Canyon Road

WEST TR

tunnel

To Glendale Peak

Vermont Canyon Rd

RIVRSIDE TR

WESTERN CANYON

34

33
34
P

Griffith Park Observatory

VERMONT CANYON

Greek Theater

stream

WEST OBSERVATORY TR

EAST OBSERVATORY TR

overlook

Fern Dell Drive

N
W   E
S

REFERENCE MAPS
P. 110

Ferndell Park

33.

Griffith Park Observatory
Ferndell Park
GRIFFITH PARK

Los Feliz Blvd

34. Mount Hollywood and Dante's View
CHARLIE TURNER TRAIL from the
GRIFFITH PARK OBSERVATORY
GRIFFITH PARK

Hiking distance: 3 miles round trip
Hiking time: 1.5 hours
Configuration: out-and-back with loop
Elevation gain: 500 feet
Exposure: exposed hills
Difficulty: easy to moderate
Dogs: allowed
Maps: U.S.G.S. Hollywood and Burbank · Map and Guide of Griffith Park
Hileman's Recreational & Geological Map of Griffith Park

Mount Hollywood, the highest peak in Griffith Park, is perched at 1,625 feet in elevation. From the bald, flat summit is an overlook with commanding vistas of the Los Angeles basin, the San Fernando Valley, the San Gabriel Mountains, the majestic Griffith Park Observatory, and a view of the landmark "HOLLYWOOD" sign.

East of Mount Hollywood is Dante's View, a terraced, two-acre garden oasis planted in 1964 by Dante Orgolini, a Brazilian-born Italian immigrant. Dante maintained and cared for the garden until he died in 1978. Charlie Turner became caretaker of the famed arboretum for 15 years until he passed away in 1997. The picturesque garden has been maintained since by volunteers. The south-facing Dante's View overlooks the observatory with picnic benches and shade trees along its intertwining trail.

The Charlie Turner Trail, likely the most popular trail in the park, connects the Griffith Park Observatory with the lookout atop Mount Hollywood and Dante's View. This hike begins just north of the historic observatory, built in 1935. The triple-domed landmark has excellent science exhibits, a planetarium, gift shop, and an observation deck with telescopes. Throughout the hike are panoramic vistas. Mount Hollywood can also be accessed from the north via several other routes.

To the trailhead

OPTION 1: From Los Feliz Boulevard in Hollywood, take Fern Dell Drive north 2.3 miles to the Griffith Park Observatory parking lot. (Fern Dell Drive becomes Western Canyon Road after the hairpin turn.)

OPTION 2: From Los Feliz Boulevard in Hollywood, take Vermont Avenue north 1.8 miles to the observatory parking lot. (En route, Vermont Avenue curves into Vermont Canyon Road.) Both directions offer a beautiful, curving drive through Griffith Park.

Griffith Park Observatory

2800 East Observatory Road • Los Angeles
213-473-0800 • general information

Hours:

Wednesday—Friday • Noon—10 p.m.
Saturday—Sunday • 10 a.m.—10 p.m.
Monday—Tuesday • closed
closed on major holidays (call ahead to confirm)

Admission:

free to observatory • small admission to planetarium

History of Griffith Park:

Griffith J. Griffith donated over 3,000 acres to create this parkland in 1896. Griffith was a Welsh immigrant who made his fortune in mine speculation. Additional land acquisitions since this time have expanded the park to 4,217 acres, making it the largest municipal park in the United States.

Attractions within the Park:

Griffith Park Observatory • Greek Theater
Los Angeles Zoo and Botanical Gardens
Travel Town Transportation Museum • Los Angeles Live Steamers
Griffith Park and Southern Railroad (miniature railroad)
Autry National Center • Los Angeles Equestrian Center
Historic 1926 Merry-Go-Round • golf courses
Griffith Park Boys' Camp • Camp Hollywoodland (girls' camp)
Bird Sanctuary • Amir's Garden • Ferndell Park
The Hollywood Sign • Bronson Caves

The hike

From the parking lot, hike north (opposite from the observatory) to the well-marked and landscaped Charlie Turner trailhead. Climb the tree-lined ridge between Vermont Canyon and Western Canyon to the Berlin Forest, a friendship park between the people of Berlin and Los Angeles. From the pine-dotted knoll with picnic benches are great views across Los Angeles. Cross over the Vermont Canyon Road tunnel. Meander up the sage- and chaparral-covered hillside at an easy grade. At the hairpin right bend is a close-up view of the "HOLLYWOOD" sign.

At 0.8 miles is a 4-way junction on the ridge below Mount Hollywood. Begin a clockwise loop on the left fork. Pass Captain's Roost on the left by a row of towering palm trees. The landscaped plateau offers additional vistas across Los Angeles. Continue uphill to the north (back) side of Mount Hollywood to another 4-way junction. The two trails on the right form a short 0.2-mile loop to the 1,625-foot summit. From the flat, rounded peak are 360-degree vistas, including a picture-perfect view of the observatory.

After marveling at the views, return to the 4-way junction. Curve right (east), skirting the elevated picnic area on the knoll. Descend 100 yards to a junction at Dante's View. The Hogback (East Ridge) Trail continues straight ahead to Glendale Peak (Hike 32). The landscaped two-acre garden takes in the southeast corner, with access from both trails. After exploring the terraced slope, continue southwest on the loop around Mount Hollywood, completing the loop on the ridge below the summit. Return down the hill, retracing your route. ■

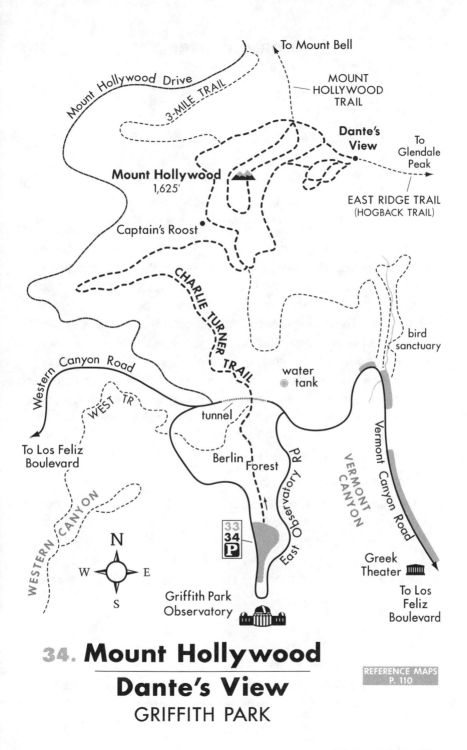

To Mount Bell

Mount Hollywood Drive

3-MILE TRAIL

MOUNT
HOLLYWOOD
TRAIL

**Dante's
View**

To
Glendale
Peak

Mount Hollywood
1,625'

EAST RIDGE TRAIL
(HOGBACK TRAIL)

Captain's Roost

CHARLIE TURNER TRAIL

bird
sanctuary

Western Canyon Road

WEST TR

water
tank

To Los Feliz
Boulevard

tunnel

Berlin Forest

East Observatory Rd

VERMONT
CANYON

Vermont Canyon Road

WESTERN CANYON

N
W   E
S

33
34 P

Greek
Theater 🏛

To Los
Feliz
Boulevard

Griffith Park
Observatory

**34. Mount Hollywood
Dante's View**
GRIFFITH PARK

REFERENCE MAPS
P. 110

35. Bronson Caves
GRIFFITH PARK

Hiking distance: 0.6 miles round trip
Hiking time: 0.5 hours
Configuration: out-and-back
Elevation gain: 40 feet
Exposure: exposed
Difficulty: very easy
Dogs: allowed
Maps: U.S.G.S. Hollywood · Map and Guide of Griffith Park
Hileman's Recreational & Geological Map of Griffith Park

At the southwest corner of Griffith Park is a short, historical hike to one of Hollywood's most frequently filmed caves—the Bronson Caves. First used as a quarry in 1907, the crushed rock from the area was used to pave the streets of a growing Hollywood. The quarry ceased operation in the late 1920s, leaving the manmade caves. The two caves were originally created as access tunnels through the huge rock, which sat within the abandoned quarry. The tunnels were used to reach the granite cliffs as a source for crushed rock. Many western and science fiction movies have shot on location at these caves, including *Star Trek*, *Mission Impossible*, *Gunsmoke*, *Bonanza*, *Little House on the Prairie*, and the *Batman* series.

To the trailhead

At the intersection of Hollywood Boulevard and Western Avenue in Hollywood, drive 0.5 miles west on Hollywood Boulevard to Bronson Avenue. Turn right (north) and continue 1.5 miles on Bronson Avenue (which merges with Canyon Drive) past Bronson Park to the end of the road. Park in the lot on the left.

The hike

From the parking lot, hike back along the park road 100 feet to the trailhead on the left (east) side of the road. The trail gently climbs a quarter mile to the caves backed by granite cliffs. From here you may walk through the caves and around the hill. Return along the same path. ■

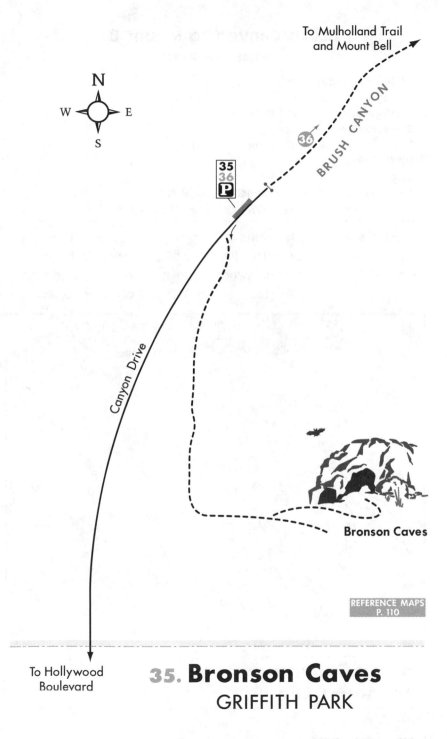

N
W E
S

To Mulholland Trail
and Mount Bell

BRUSH CANYON

36

35
36
P

Canyon Drive

Bronson Caves

REFERENCE MAPS
P. 110

To Hollywood
Boulevard

35. **Bronson Caves**
GRIFFITH PARK

36. Brush Canyon to Mount Bell
GRIFFITH PARK

Hiking distance: 3.3 miles round trip
Hiking time: 2.5 hours
Configuration: out-and-back
Elevation gain: 850 feet
Exposure: shaded canyon and exposed hills
Difficulty: moderate
Dogs: allowed
Maps: U.S.G.S. Hollywood and Burbank · Map and Guide of Griffith Park
    Hileman's Recreational & Geological Map of Griffith Park

Brush Canyon is a beautiful yet lightly traveled trail from the southwest corner of Griffith Park. This hike begins from the north end of Canyon Drive and winds through a forest of large sycamore and oak trees in the canyon. The trail climbs into a drier

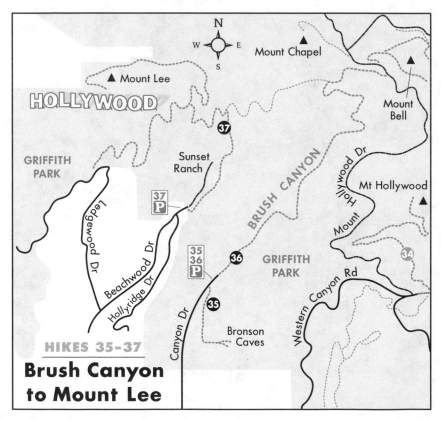

chaparral and shrub terrain in the undeveloped mountainous interior of Griffith Park, leading up the southwest slope of Mount Bell. The 1,582-foot peak is located in the geographic center of Griffith Park. From the summit are fantastic views of secluded canyons, Hollywood, and the Los Angeles Basin. Mount Bell can also be accessed from the Mineral Wells Picnic Area (Hike 31) or from the park's merry-go-round (Hike 29).

To the trailhead

At the intersection of Hollywood Boulevard and Western Avenue in Hollywood, drive 0.5 miles west on Hollywood Boulevard to Bronson Avenue. Turn right and continue 1.5 miles on Bronson Avenue (which merges with Canyon Drive) past Bronson Park to the end of the road. Park in the lot on the left.

The hike

From the parking lot, walk uphill on the road to the north. Pass the vehicle gate and continue on the unpaved fire road parallel to Brush Creek. The fire road follows along the perennial stream in a thicket of oak, manzanita, and sage. Pass the Pacific Electric Quarry and bend right (east), crossing over the creek to an expansive park and picnic area on the right at a quarter mile. After passing the park, climb out of the canyon, leaving the shade of the forest for the drought-resistant shrubs and a view of Mount Lee and the "HOLLYWOOD" sign. Continue up the canyon wall, with views of Mount Hollywood and Mount Bell, reaching the Mulholland Trail junction at one mile. To the left, the Mulholland Trail heads 1.5 miles west to the "HOLLYWOOD" sign on Mount Lee (Hike 37). Take the Mulholland Trail to the right 0.3 miles to Mount Hollywood Drive, a paved and gated road.

To continue up the final ascent to Mount Bell, take Mount Hollywood Drive 0.1 mile to the left. Pick up the dirt path on the right, and head up the slope. Stay to the right at a junction on a saddle and skirt the south flank of Mount Bell. To ascend the 1,582-foot summit, watch for a narrow path that scrambles through brush to the peak. Return by retracing your steps. ▪

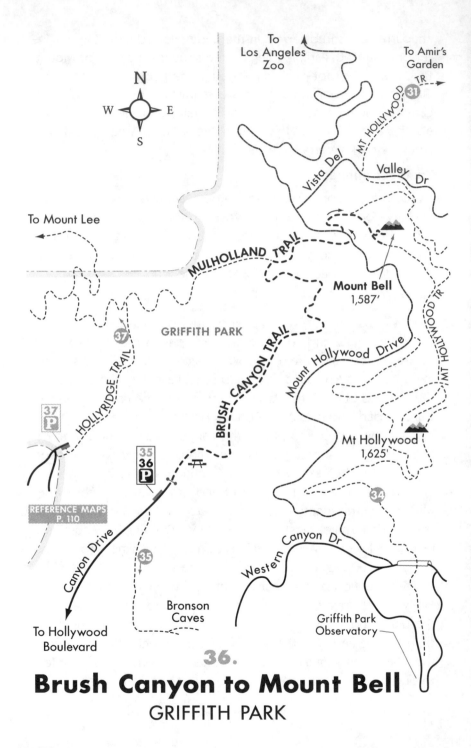

To
Los Angeles
Zoo

To Amir's
Garden

N

W   E

S

To Mount Lee

Vista Del

Valley Dr

MT HOLLYWOOD TR

31

MULHOLLAND TRAIL

Mount Bell
1,587'

GRIFFITH PARK

37

BRUSH CANYON TRAIL

Mount Hollywood Drive

MT HOLLYWOOD TR

HOLLYRIDGE TRAIL

37
P

35
36
P

Mt Hollywood
1,625'

REFERENCE MAPS
P. 110

34

Canyon Drive

35

Western Canyon Dr

To Hollywood
Boulevard

Bronson
Caves

Griffith Park
Observatory

36.

Brush Canyon to Mount Bell
GRIFFITH PARK

37. Mount Lee and the "Hollywood" sign
GRIFFITH PARK

Hiking distance: 3 miles round trip
Hiking time: 1.5 hours
Configuration: out-and-back
Elevation gain: 550 feet
Exposure: exposed hillside and ridges
Difficulty: easy to moderate
Dogs: allowed
Maps: U.S.G.S. Hollywood and Burbank · Map and Guide of Griffith Park

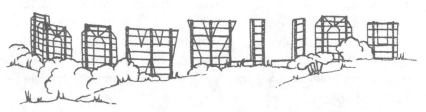

This hike offers an interesting view of the
"Hollywood" sign from the back.

This hike up the Hollyridge Trail leads to the famous "HOLLYWOOD" sign on the south slope of Mount Lee in the far west end of Griffith Park. The historic Los Angeles landmark was originally built in the 1920s to read "HOLLYWOODLAND" to promote real estate development in Beachwood Canyon. In 1978, entertainment celebrities donated money to replace the original sign, which was worn from time, weather, and vandalism. The sign now measures 50 feet high by 450 feet long. It sits just below the Mount Lee summit.

The trail leads to close-up views of both the front and back of the sign, although the sign itself is fenced off from direct visitation to prevent vandalism. From the trail, the letters are immense. In addition, the panoramic views from atop Mount Lee are superb. The vistas extend far beyond the "HOLLYWOOD" letters to the Los Angeles basin and the San Fernando Valley.

To the trailhead

At the intersection of Franklin Avenue and Western Avenue in Hollywood, drive 0.7 miles west on Franklin Avenue to Beachwood Drive. Turn right (north) and continue 1.8 miles up Beachwood Drive to the signed trailhead parking area on the right at the end of the public road.

The hike

Head up the signed slope to a T-junction on a ridge overlooking Hollywood and Los Angeles. From the ridge is a picture-perfect view of the "HOLLYWOOD" sign. The right fork descends to the old trailhead access, which is now fenced off. Bear left and follow the ridge northeast, overlooking the Sunset Horse Ranch on the left and a view of the Griffith Park Observatory to the right. Continue 0.5 miles to an intersection with the unmarked Mulholland Trail. The right fork leads to Brush Canyon and Mount Bell (Hike 36).

Take a sharp left up the Mulholland Trail as it heads west. The winding fire road leads 0.3 miles to the paved and gated Mount Lee Drive. The left fork leads a short distance to an excellent frontal view of the sign. Go uphill to the right and steadily climb to the ridge. Head west along the north slope of Mount Lee, overlooking the San Fernando Valley. Pass below the telecommunication towers atop Mount Lee to a horseshoe left bend. Loop around the bend to the end of the road, perched above and 30 yards behind the "HOLLYWOOD" sign. A fence prohibits access to the sign (along with several warnings), but there is a view of the back of the towering letters and the skeletal support structure. The vistas extend across the Los Angeles basin to the south—to the downtown skyline and beyond on clear days—and to the San Fernando Valley to the north. Return along the same route. ■

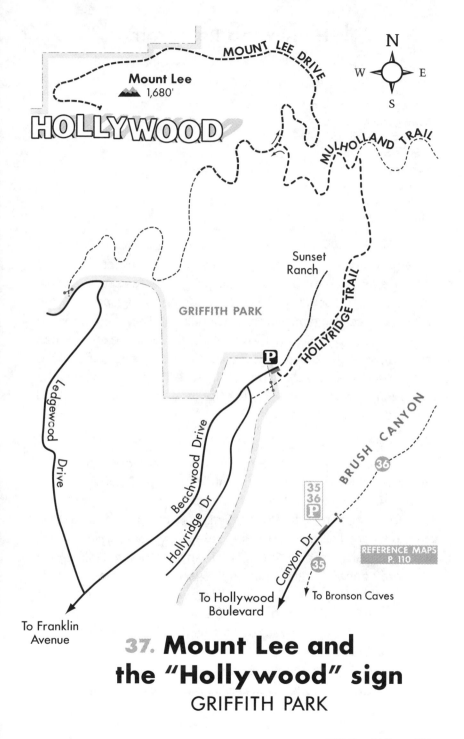

N
W E
S

MOUNT LEE DRIVE

Mount Lee
▲▲▲ 1,680'

HOLLYWOOD

MULHOLLAND TRAIL

Sunset
Ranch

GRIFFITH PARK

HOLLYRIDGE TRAIL

P

Ledgewood Drive

Beachwood Drive

Hollyridge Dr

BRUSH CANYON

36

35
36
P

Canyon Dr

35

REFERENCE MAPS
P. 110

To Hollywood
Boulevard

To Bronson Caves

To Franklin
Avenue

37. Mount Lee and the "Hollywood" sign
GRIFFITH PARK

38. Hollywood Reservoir

Open weekdays 6:30—10 a.m. and 2—5 p.m.

Open weekends 6:30 a.m. to 5 p.m.

Hiking distance: 4-mile loop
Hiking time: 1.5 hours
Configuration: loop
Elevation gain: level
Exposure: mostly shaded
Difficulty: easy
Dogs: not allowed
Maps: U.S.G.S. Hollywood and Burbank

This hike follows the perimeter of the Hollywood Reservoir on an asphalt service road that is closed to vehicles. The road, which is landscaped on both sides, is a rural retreat inside the city that is frequently used as a walking and jogging trail. The lake is fenced, preventing access to the shoreline. The tall foliage along the trail obscures full views of the reservoir except when crossing Mulholland Dam, but the dam crossing is magnificent. To the north is Mount Lee and the "Hollywood" sign overlooking the beautiful reservoir below. To the south is a view of Hollywood and the Los Angeles Basin.

To the trailhead

From Hollywood, take Highland Avenue north past the Hollywood Bowl, curving left onto Cahuenga Boulevard West. Continue one mile to Barham Boulevard. Turn right and cross over the Hollywood Freeway. Drive 0.2 miles to Lake Hollywood Drive and turn right. Follow the winding Lake Hollywood Drive through a residential neighborhood for 0.8 miles to the Hollywood Reservoir entrance gate on the right. Park alongside the road.

From the Hollywood Freeway/Highway 101, take the Barham Boulevard Exit, and head north 0.2 miles to Lake Hollywood Drive. Turn right and drive 0.8 miles to the Hollywood Reservoir entrance gate on the right.

The hike

The reservoir entrance is on the right (south). The paved path follows the perimeter of the reservoir through the shaded evergreen forest. At the south end of the reservoir, cross Mulholland Dam. The path then loops north to Tahoe Drive. Bear left along the road, returning to the parking area. ■

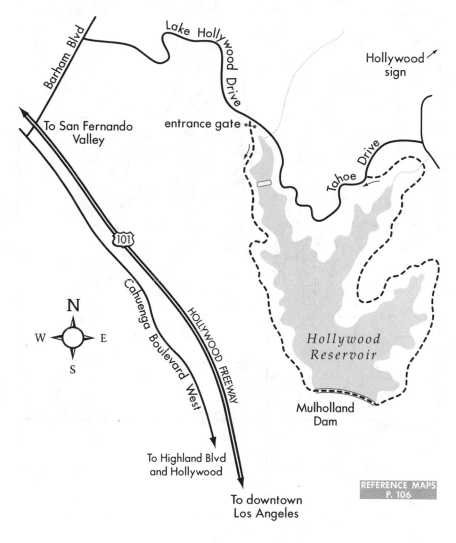

38. Hollywood Reservoir

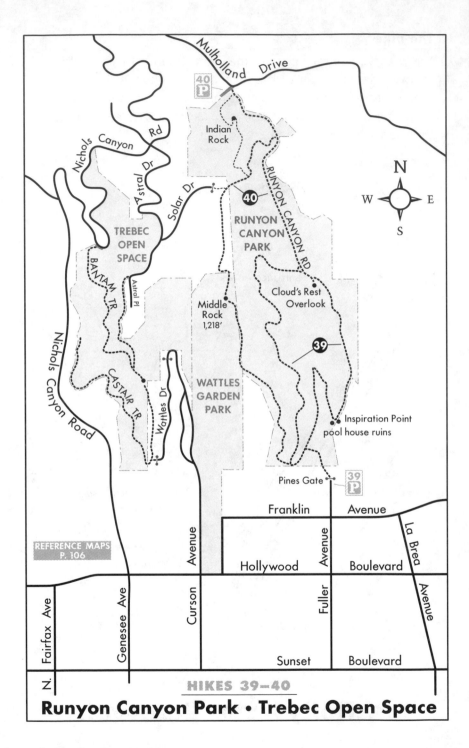

Mulholland Drive

40 P

Indian Rock

Nichols Canyon Rd

Astral Dr

Solar Dr

TREBEC
OPEN
SPACE

Astral Pl

BANTAM TR

Nichols Canyon Road

CASTAIR TR

Wattles Dr

RUNYON CANYON RD

40

RUNYON
CANYON
PARK

Cloud's Rest
Overlook

Middle
Rock
1,218'

39

WATTLES
GARDEN
PARK

Inspiration Point
pool house ruins

Pines Gate

39 P

N
W   E
S

REFERENCE MAPS
P. 106

Franklin   Avenue

La Brea

Avenue

Hollywood   Boulevard

Genesee Ave

Curson

Fuller

Avenue

Avenue

Fairfax Ave

N.

Sunset   Boulevard

HIKES 39-40

Runyon Canyon Park • Trebec Open Space

39. Runyon Canyon Loop
from Fuller Avenue

RUNYON CANYON PARK: Lower Trailhead

Hiking distance: 2-mile loop
Hiking time: 1 hour
Configuration: loop
Elevation gain: 500 feet
Exposure: exposed hills
Difficulty: easy
Dogs: allowed
Maps: U.S.G.S. Hollywood · Runyon Canyon Park map
Trails Illustrated Santa Monica Mountains Nat'l. Rec. Area

Runyon Canyon Park is a sprawling 130-acre preserve minutes from the heart of Hollywood. The popular preserve was purchased by the Santa Monica Mountains Conservancy and the city of Los Angeles in the mid 1980s. The off-leash dog park is among the most popular and heavily used open spaces in the Santa Monica Mountains. This hike begins from the lower trailhead at the north end of Fuller Ave, just two blocks north of Hollywood Boulevard. The trail loops around the chaparral-clad hillsides of Runyon Canyon and crosses a broad gorge overlooking the urban canyon wilderness and Hollywood. The loop passes the ruins of a pool house designed by Frank Lloyd Wright and occupied by Errol Flynn in the late 1950s. Remnants of the old foundation, tennis courts, and exotic landscaping are all that remain of the ruined oasis.

To the trailhead

At the intersection of Franklin Avenue and Highland Avenue in Hollywood, drive 0.3 miles west on Franklin to Fuller Avenue. Turn right (north) and continue 0.5 miles to The Pines gate at the end of the road. Park along the street where a space is available.

The hike

Walk through The Pines entrance gate at the north end of Fuller Avenue into Runyon Canyon Park. A short distance past the entrance is a trail junction. Begin the loop to the left, hiking clockwise.

Curve along the south end of the park to a second trail split. The left fork, straight ahead, climbs the west ridge of Runyon Canyon (Hike 40). Instead, veer right and traverse the west canyon slope, parallel to the canyon floor on the paved path. Follow the chaparral-covered hillside with drought-resistant evergreens on a gentle uphill grade. Make a horseshoe right bend to the east side of the canyon and a posted junction. The left fork climbs to the upper trailhead at Mulholland Drive. For this hike, veer right to Cloud's Rest, an overlook on the right with benches and 360-degree panoramas. The main trail continues along the east canyon ridge, descending to Inspiration Point, a level area with a bench that overlooks Hollywood. Pass the Wright/Flynn pool house ruins, and descend to the canyon floor, completing the loop. Return to the trailhead on the left. ■

40. Runyon Canyon Loop from Mulholland Drive
RUNYON CANYON PARK: Upper Trailhead

Hiking distance: 2.5-mile loop
Hiking time: 1.5 hours
Configuration: loop
Elevation gain: 500 feet
Exposure: exposed hills
Difficulty: easy to slightly moderate
Dogs: allowed
Maps: U.S.G.S. Hollywood · Runyon Canyon Park map
       Trails Illustrated Santa Monica Mountains Nat'l Rec. Area

Runyon Canyon Park is a gorgeous mountain park in the Hollywood Hills. The 130-acre park stretches from the base of the mountains at the congested edge of Hollywood to Mulholland Drive atop the scenic mountain ridge. A vehicle-restricted fire road runs through the center of the park. The park is an extremely popular hiking, jogging, and off-leash dog-walking park. (It is especially crowded on weekends.) This hike begins from the upper reaches of the park, with spectacular views of the surrounding

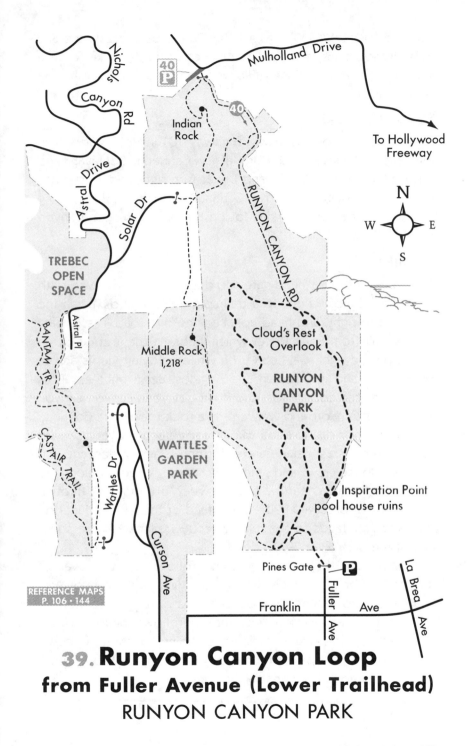

39. Runyon Canyon Loop
from Fuller Avenue (Lower Trailhead)
RUNYON CANYON PARK

hills, the "HOLLYWOOD" sign, Griffith Park Observatory, the San Gabriel Mountains, and the Los Angeles basin. The hike forms a loop along the west ridge of Runyon Canyon and returns up the canyon floor.

To the trailhead

From the Hollywood Freeway/Highway 101 in Hollywood, take the Barham Boulevard exit. Turn left on Cahuenga Boulevard and drive a half mile to Mulholland Drive. Turn right and an immediate left onto Mulholland Drive. Continue 1.5 miles on the winding road to the trailhead parking lot on the left at Runyon Canyon Road.

The hike

Pass through the trailhead gate and descend on the paved path. Skirt around Indian Rock to a trail split at 300 yards. Begin the loop to the right, and head uphill on the dirt road. Pass a park access trail from Solar Drive, which leads to the Trebec Open Space on the right. Gain elevation while enjoying views across Hollywood and downtown Los Angeles. Bend right as vistas open up to the coast. Cross the ridge between Runyon Canyon and Nichols Canyon, and weave over a rock formation. Continue south atop the ridge to Middle Rock, a spectacular overlook with 360-degree vistas. Using careful footing, sharply descend the knoll on a loose gravel and sand path. Steadily descend along the spine to a flat area near the bottom. Veer left and walk through a eucalyptus forest along the south face of the hill to a junction. The right fork leads to the Fuller Avenue Trailhead at the south end of the park (Hike 39).

Bear left on the paved path, and follow the west wall of Runyon Canyon on a gentle uphill grade. Wind up the canyon wall, and make a horseshoe right bend to the east side of the canyon and a posted junction. The right fork follows the lower loop, leading to Cloud's Rest and Inspiration Point. For this hike, curve left, staying on the paved path and completing the loop. Return to the trailhead 300 yards straight ahead. ▪

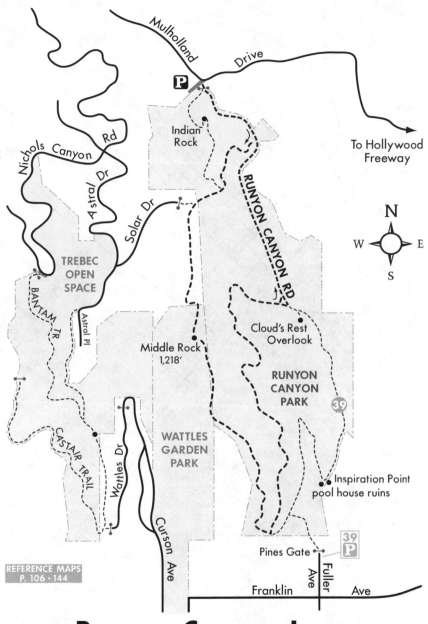

Mulholland Drive

P

To Hollywood
Freeway

Indian
Rock

Nichols Canyon Rd

Astral Dr

Solar Dr

RUNYON CANYON RD

N
W   E
S

TREBEC
OPEN
SPACE

BANTAM TR

Astral Pl

Cloud's Rest
Overlook

Middle Rock
1,218'

RUNYON
CANYON
PARK

39

CASTAIR TRAIL

Wattles Dr

WATTLES
GARDEN
PARK

Inspiration Point
pool house ruins

Curson Ave

Pines Gate

39
P

REFERENCE MAPS
P. 106 · 144

Franklin

Fuller Ave

Ave

40. Runyon Canyon Loop
from Mulholland Drive (Upper Trailhead)
RUNYON CANYON PARK

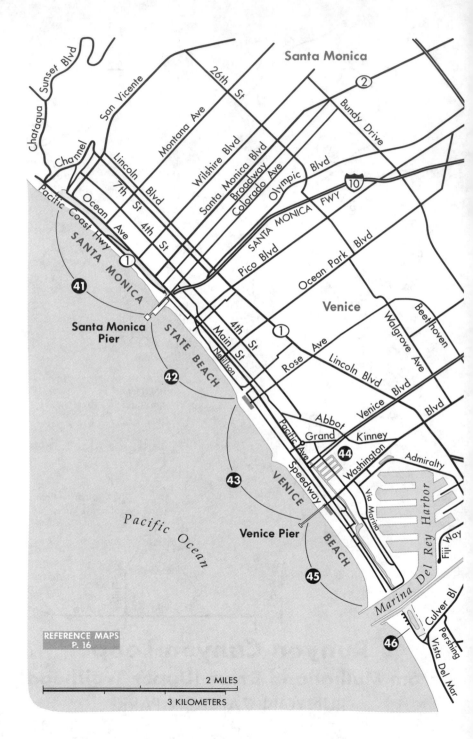

Santa Monica

Chataqua

Sunset Blvd

San Vicente

26th St

Bundy Drive

Montana Ave

Wilshire Blvd

Channel

Lincoln Blvd

7th St

4th St

Ocean Ave

Santa Monica Blvd

Broadway

Colorado Ave

Olympic Blvd

SANTA MONICA FWY

10

Pacific Coast Hwy

SANTA MONICA

1

41

SANTA MONICA

STATE BEACH

Santa Monica
Pier

42

Neilson

Main St

4th St

Pico Blvd

Ocean Park Blvd

Venice

Walgrove Ave

Beethoven

1

Rose Ave

Lincoln Blvd

Venice Blvd

Blvd

Abbot

Grand

Kinney

44

Washington

Admiralty

Via Marina

43

Pacific Ave

VENICE BEACH

Speedway

Venice Pier

Marina Del Rey Harbor

Fiji Way

45

Pacific Ocean

REFERENCE MAPS
P. 16

Culver Bl

46

Pershing

Vista Del Mar

2 MILES

3 KILOMETERS

HIKES 41–46

Santa Monica to
Marina Del Rey Harbor Channel

41. Palisades Park and Santa Monica Pier

Hiking distance: 3.5 miles round trip
Hiking time: 2 hours
Configuration: loop along bluffs and ocean side boardwalk;
side trip to Santa Monica Pier
Elevation gain: 100 feet
Exposure: exposed coastline
Difficulty: easy
Dogs: allowed
Maps: U.S.G.S. Topanga and Beverly Hills

Palisades Park is perched on the eroding 100-foot bluffs above the Pacific Coast Highway, overlooking Santa Monica State Beach, the Santa Monica Pier, and the entire bay. The 26-acre park stretches 1.6 miles between Ocean Avenue and the sandstone cliffs. The gorgeous landscaped grounds are filled with palm, oak, and eucalyptus trees lining the paved and natural paths. Throughout the park are gardens with exotic and native plants, benches, and a few gazebos. A pedestrian bridge and stairway connect the park to the wide, sandy beach. The south end of the park has direct access onto the Santa Monica Pier.

To the trailhead

Palisades Park is on the oceanfront bluffs in Santa Monica. The 1.6-mile-long park is located at the west end of Colorado Avenue, Santa Monica Boulevard, Wilshire Boulevard, Montana Avenue, and San Vicente Boulevard. Park along the oceanfront park in an available metered parking space. Parking may also be available on the Santa Monica Pier at the end of Colorado Avenue.

The hike

Begin the hike by strolling along the bluffs on the parallel paths, enjoying the vistas, people, and landscaping. From the south end of the park—at Colorado Avenue—bear right and head out onto the Santa Monica Pier.

To return, descend steps on the north side of the pier, and follow the paved boardwalk 400 yards to the bridge crossing over the PCH. Cross the bridge and climb the eroding cliffs on brick steps, re-entering Palisades Park by the historic cannon.

To continue along the coast from the Santa Monica Pier, hike south on the Santa Monica Beach Promenade (Hike 42). ■

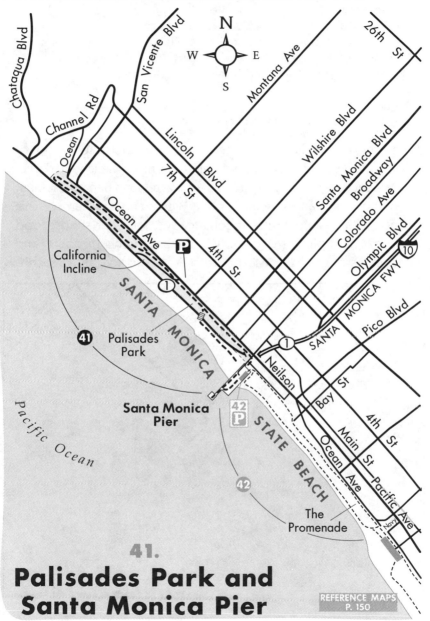

41.

Palisades Park and Santa Monica Pier

REFERENCE MAPS
P. 150

42. Santa Monica Pier to Venice Beach

Hiking distance: 2.5 miles round trip
Hiking time: 1.5 hours
Configuration: out-and-back or loop along oceanfront;
side trip to Santa Monica Pier
Elevation gain: level
Exposure: exposed beach coastline
Difficulty: easy
Dogs: allowed
Maps: U.S.G.S. Beverly Hills and Venice

The Santa Monica Pier sits beneath sandstone bluffs at the foot of Colorado Avenue in downtown Santa Monica. The landmark pier dates back to the early 1900s as a privately owned amusement center. It is still an amusement park, with an historic turn-of-the-century carousel, a ferris wheel, arcades, souvenir shops, food vendors, and pier fishing. Stairways from the north, south, and east sides of the pier descend onto Santa Monica State Beach.

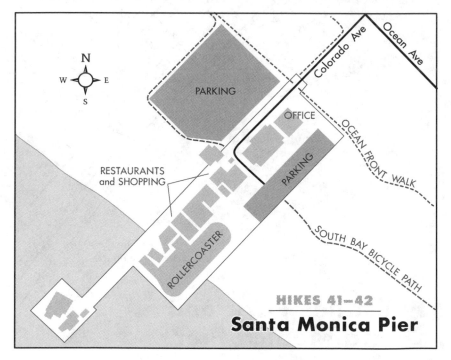

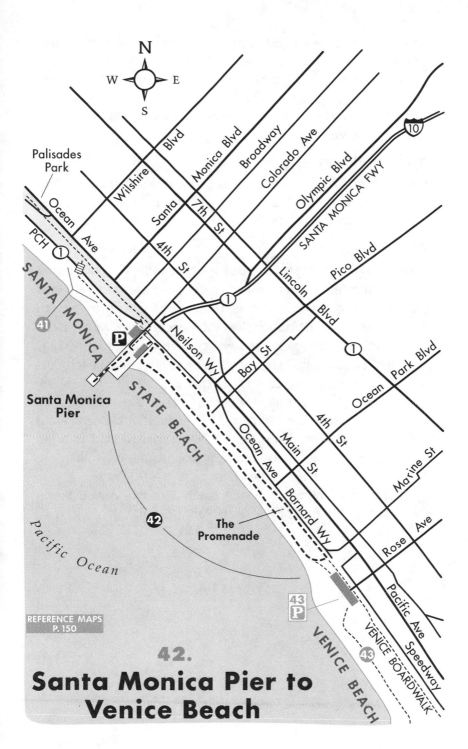

N
W E
S

Palisades
Park

Blvd

Santa Monica Blvd

Broadway

Colorado Ave

Olympic Blvd

SANTA MONICA FWY

10

Wilshire

Santa

7th St

Ocean

Ave

PCH

1

4th

St

Pico Blvd

Lincoln

1

Blvd

SANTA MONICA

41

P

Neilson Wy

Bay St

1

Ocean Park Blvd

Santa Monica
Pier

STATE

BEACH

Ocean Ave

Main

St

4th

St

Marine St

Pacific Ocean

42

The
Promenade

Barnard Wy

Rose

Ave

Pacific

Ave

REFERENCE MAPS
P. 150

43
P

VENICE BOARDWALK

Venice Speedway

VENICE BEACH

43

42.
Santa Monica Pier to
Venice Beach

Santa Monica State Beach is a broad stretch of white sand that stretches 3 miles from Chautauqua Boulevard to Venice Beach. Along the backside of the beach are the South Bay Bicycle Trail and a walking path. The bicycle trail extends over 20 miles, from Will Rogers State Beach south to Redondo Beach (Hike 47) at the base of Palos Verdes.

To the trailhead

From downtown Santa Monica, take Colorado Avenue west to Ocean Avenue. Cross Ocean Avenue onto the Santa Monica Pier. Park on the pier in the lots to the left.

The hike

Before hiking the Santa Monica Beach Promenade, walk out on the pier past the ferris wheel, roller coaster, bumper cars, arcades, and curio shops to view the ocean and coastline from the end of the pier. Return to the parking lot, and descend the wood steps to the promenade. Follow the wide, paved path south (right), passing old historic buildings and the original Muscle Beach. Just past the west end of Pico Boulevard at Bay Street, the walking path curves right and continues parallel to the biking path. At 1.2 miles from the pier, the promenade connects with Ocean Front Walk at the north end of the Venice Beach Boardwalk. This is the turn-around spot. Return by retracing your route, or walk to the shoreline and return along the water.

For extended hiking, continue south through Venice Beach (Hike 43) or north through Palisades Park (Hike 41). ▓

43. Venice Beach

Hiking distance: 3 miles round trip
Hiking time: 2 hours
Configuration: out-and-back on boardwalk or loop along shoreline
Elevation gain: level
Exposure: exposed beach coastline
Difficulty: easy
Dogs: allowed
Maps: U.S.G.S. Venice

Venice Beach is a unique wedge of Los Angeles between Ocean Park (in Santa Monica) and the Marina Del Rey Harbor Channel. The famous Venice Beach Boardwalk is on Ocean Front Walk, an asphalt walkway that runs parallel to the back end of the wide, sandy beach. It extends south from Navy Street to the Venice Pier at the foot of Washington Boulevard. The 1.5-mile promenade, built in 1905, is lined with beachfront businesses, cafes, hawkers, vendors, bodybuilders, musicians, comedians, artists, jugglers, fortune-tellers, dancers, drunks, hiking book authors, panhandlers, spectators, and a vast array of other unique characters. The calm of the ocean is only steps away from the endless parade of people. Winding through the sand between the boardwalk and the water is the 20-mile South Bay Bicycle Trail.

To the trailhead

Venice Beach can be accessed from numerous east-west streets, including Washington Boulevard, Venice Boulevard, Windward Avenue, and Rose Avenue. This hike begins from the north end of Venice Beach off of Rose Avenue.

From the Santa Monica (10) Freeway in Santa Monica, exit on Lincoln Boulevard. Head 1.4 miles south to Rose Avenue. Turn right and follow Rose Avenue 0.9 miles into the Venice Beach oceanfront parking lot. A parking fee is required.

The hike

From the north end of Venice Beach, walk south along the board-walk, passing cafes and beautiful old brick buildings. Stroll through the parade of humanity, marveling at the diverse circus. At one mile is the Venice Pavilion and an outdoor roller skating area on the right. To the left is Windward Avenue, showcasing massive murals and charming Italian-style buildings with colonnades that date back to 1905. Just past Windward Avenue are paddle tennis courts, basketball courts, and an outdoor weight-lifting arena known as Muscle Beach (named after the historical Muscle Beach south of the Santa Monica Pier). The active, theatrical portion of the boardwalk ends at 1.5 miles by Venice Pier, a 1,100-foot pier at the west end of Washington Boulevard. Return along the boardwalk or go to the shoreline and return along the ocean.

To extend the hike, continue south to the mouth of the Marina Del Rey Harbor Channel 1.1 miles ahead (Hike 45), north along Ocean Front Walk (Hike 42), or 2 blocks inland to the Venice Canals (Hike 44). ■

PARKING AROUND VENICE BEACH
(rates vary by season and location)

City parking lots that are located near the beach

North Venice Boulevard and Ocean Front Walk

Washington Boulevard and Ocean Front Walk

Rose Avenue and Ocean Front Walk

Other parking options

Westminster Elementary School on Main Street—Weekends only

1697 Pacific Avenue

Windward Avenue and Speedway

301 Ocean Front Walk

110 Navy Street

42 North Venice Boulevard

100 North Venice Boulevard

Electric Avenue (east of Abbot Kinney)—several lots available

Marina Del Rey—shuttles are available from some parking lots

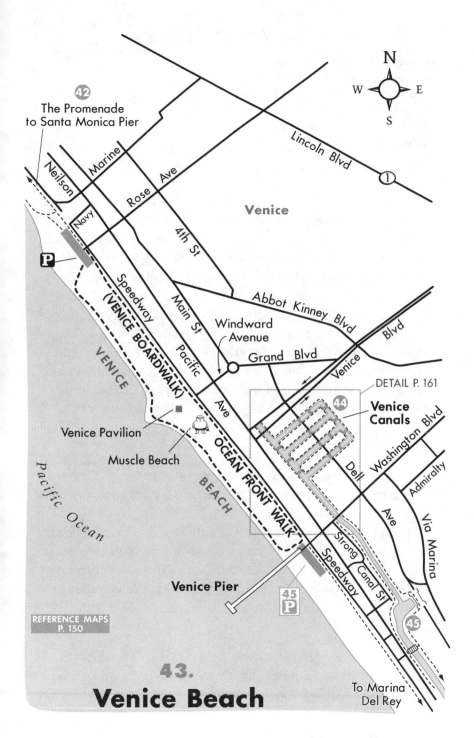

N
W · E
S

42
The Promenade
to Santa Monica Pier

Lincoln Blvd
①

Neilson

Marine

Rose Ave

Venice

Navy

4th St

P

Speedway (VENICE BOARDWALK)

Main St

Pacific Ave

Abbot Kinney Blvd

Windward
Avenue

Grand Blvd

Venice Blvd

DETAIL P. 161

44

VENICE

Venice Pavilion

Muscle Beach

OCEAN FRONT WALK

Venice
Canals

Washington Blvd

Admiralty

Dell

Pacific Ocean

BEACH

Strong Canal St

Ave

Via Marina

Venice Pier

45
P

Speedway

45

REFERENCE MAPS
P. 150

43.
Venice Beach

To Marina
Del Rey

44. The Venice Canals

Hiking distance: 1 mile or more
Hiking time: 20 minutes to 1 hour
Configuration: several inter-connecting loops
Elevation gain: level
Exposure: exposed walkways
Difficulty: very easy
Dogs: allowed
Maps: U.S.G.S. Venice · City of Venice map

The Venice Canals are located between Venice Boulevard and Washington Boulevard, two blocks inland from Venice Beach. In 1904, Abbott Kinney purchased 160 acres of coastal marshland, part of the Ballona Creek wetlands, to develop a new cultural center. He dreamed of, then developed, "Venice in America," a seaside resort recreating the canals of Venice, Italy. The area was embellished with lagoons, arched Venetian-style bridges, gondolas imported from Italy, and a network of 16 interconnected canals. What remains are six interwoven water canals flowing through a charming seaside community with landscaped walkways, diverse architecture, and 14 bridges. Canoes, paddle boats, and ducks grace the waterways, adding to an enchanting and unique experience.

To the trailhead

From the San Diego Freeway/Interstate 405 in Culver City, take the Washington Boulevard exit, and drive 3.5 miles west towards the ocean to Dell Avenue.

The Venice Canals are located near the Pacific Coast between Washington Boulevard and Venice Boulevard, two blocks east of Pacific Avenue, which parallels the ocean. Dell Avenue crosses over the canals via four arched bridges. Park on Dell Avenue anywhere along the residential street.

The hike

Walking paths border the canals on each side. Fourteen bridges span the canals, connecting all the walkways. Choose your own path. The Grand Canal continues south across Washington

Boulevard a little over one mile to the Marina Del Rey harbor channel (Hike 45)

One block west of the Grand Canal is Venice Beach and the Venice Boardwalk. The boardwalk parallels the oceanfront, from Washington Boulevard for 2.5 miles north to the Santa Monica Pier (Hike 43). ■

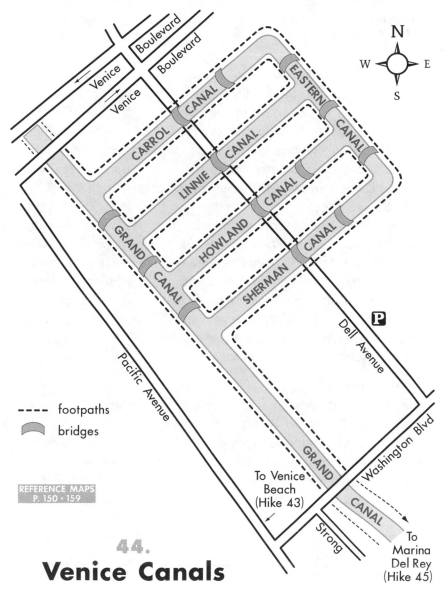

- - - - footpaths

bridges

REFERENCE MAPS
P. 150 · 159

N
W ◆ E
S

To Venice Beach (Hike 43)

To Marina Del Rey (Hike 45)

44.
Venice Canals

45. Ballona Lagoon Marine Preserve

GRAND CANAL to MARINA DEL REY HARBOR CHANNEL

Hiking distance: 2.4-mile loop
Hiking time: 1.5 hours
Configuration: loop
Elevation gain: level
Exposure: mostly exposed
Difficulty: easy
Dogs: allowed
Maps: U.S.G.S. Venice

The Ballona Lagoon Marine Preserve is a 16.3-acre natural salt-water estuary between Hurricane Street (south of Washington Boulevard) and the Marina Del Rey Harbor Channel, one block inland from Venice Beach. The ocean-fed lagoon connects to Grand Canal, the main channel of the Venice Canals (Hike 44). Ballona Lagoon was originally part of the once-extensive 1,700-acre Ballona Creek wetlands, extending from Playa Del Rey to Santa Monica. The lagoon was cut off from the wetlands with the development of Marina Del Rey. The lagoon is on the 2,000-mile migratory route for birds between Alaska and Latin America, known as the Pacific Flyway. The preserve is a protected habitat for hundreds of birds, native plants, animals, and marine life. It is one of the last tidal wetlands in southern California, with high and low tides twice daily. This route utilizes natural and paved paths, making a loop around the channel.

To the trailhead

The Ballona Lagoon Marine Preserve is located between Washington Boulevard and the north side of the Marina Del Rey Harbor Channel, one block east of Pacific Avenue in Venice. From the 405 (San Diego) Freeway, take the Washington Boulevard exit, and drive 3.5 miles west towards the ocean. The trail can be accessed from several locations. This hike begins on the 300 block of Washington Boulevard. Park alongside the street or on the side streets where a parking space is available. At the west end of Washington Boulevard, 2 blocks past the lagoon, is an oceanfront parking lot for a fee.

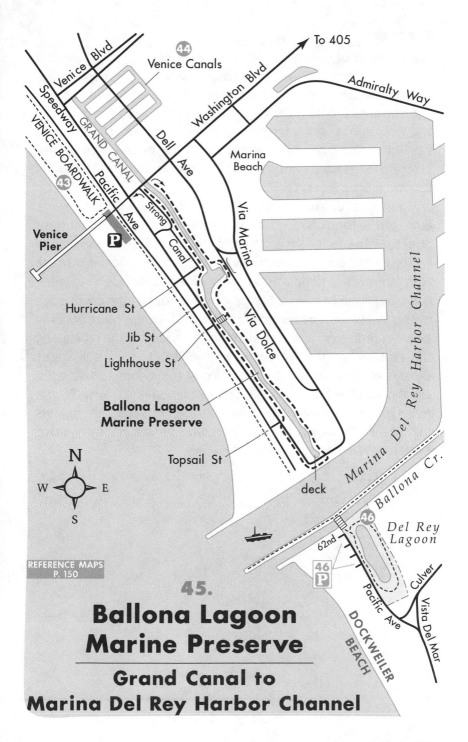

To 405

Venice Blvd

44 Venice Canals

Washington Blvd

Admiralty Way

Speedway

VENICE BOARDWALK

GRAND CANAL

Pacific Ave

Dell Ave

Marina Beach

Via Marina

43

Venice Pier

P

Strong Canal

Via Dolce

Marina Del Rey Harbor Channel

Hurricane St

Jib St

Lighthouse St

Ballona Lagoon Marine Preserve

N

W — E

S

Topsail St

deck

Ballona Cr.

Marina Del Rey Harbor Channel

46 Del Rey Lagoon

62nd

46 P

Pacific Ave

Culver

Vista Del Mar

DOCKWEILER BEACH

REFERENCE MAPS
P. 150

45.

Ballona Lagoon Marine Preserve

Grand Canal to Marina Del Rey Harbor Channel

The hike

The trailhead begins on the 300 block of Washington Boulevard, just east of Strong Drive. Head south along the east bank of the Grand Canal on the narrow footpath. Under a canopy of lush foliage, the natural path changes to a paved path between the canal and homes. At 0.4 miles, near the end of the path, curve left to Via Dolce. Cross over the wetlands on the bridge to the right. Take the rail-fenced walkway to the right, and enter the Ballona Lagoon Marine Preserve.

Continue southeast through the preserve. Pass a cement bridge over the lagoon that leads to Pacific Avenue by Lighthouse Street. At the far south end of the path, just before Via Marina by the harbor channel, a boardwalk leads to an observation deck with interpretive panels about the preserve. Across Via Marina is Austin Park, a narrow, landscaped park fronting the north edge of the Marina Del Rey Harbor Channel. It is a great place to view boats entering and leaving the marina. Continue to the right along the sidewalk on the west side of the street to Topsail Street. Cross the street to the dirt path along the lagoon, passing the Lighthouse Street Bridge to Jib Street. Curve right, leaving Pacific Avenue while staying close to the lagoon. A paved path follows the west bank of Grand Canal and returns parallel to Strong Drive back to Washington Boulevard. ▪

46. Del Rey Lagoon and Ballona Creek
MARINA DEL REY HARBOR CHANNEL

Hiking distance: 2.8 miles round trip
Hiking time: 1.5 hours
Configuration: out-and-back with two spur trails
Elevation gain: level
Exposure: exposed
Difficulty: easy
Dogs: allowed
Maps: U.S.G.S. Venice

The Del Rey Lagoon in Playa Del Rey, near the Marina Del Rey Harbor Channel, is tucked between the north end of Dockweiler Beach and Ballona Creek. The 13-acre lagoon is surrounded by a grassy park with geese and ducks. It is a remnant of the original 1,700-acre Ballona Creek wetlands, stretching from Playa Del Rey to Santa Monica. Ballona Creek borders the south edge of the harbor channel and heads 9 miles inland through Culver City to the north side of the Santa Monica Freeway. This hike begins at Del Rey Lagoon and follows Ballona Creek seaward to the mouth of the harbor and inland along the creek. A section of the path follows the boulder levee that forms the south side of the harbor channel, utilizing a paved walking and biking path over the boulders.

To the trailhead

From the south side of Marina Del Rey at the intersection of Lincoln Boulevard and Culver Boulevard in Marina Del Rey, head 1.5 miles southwest on Culver Boulevard (towards the ocean) to Vista Del Mar at a traffic light. Stay to the right on Culver Boulevard 2 blocks to Pacific Avenue. Turn right and drive 0.4 miles to the vehicle-restricted bridge at 62nd Avenue. Park along the road where a space is available.

From the 405 (San Diego) Freeway in Culver City, take the Culver Boulevard exit and head 2.25 miles southwest (towards the ocean) to Lincoln Boulevard. Proceed with the directions above.

The hike

Walk into Del Rey Lagoon Park, and stroll through the grassy park along the lagoon. Return to Pacific Avenue and head north. Cross the vehicle-restricted bridge over Ballona Creek to the walking and biking path on the levee separating Ballona Creek from the Marina Del Rey Harbor Channel. The left fork follows the paved, built-on-boulders path between the two waterways. The path leads beyond the shoreline to the end of the harbor channel, a great spot for observing boats coming in and out of the harbor. Use caution and good judgment if venturing west across the cemented boulders along the last 100 yards.

Return and follow the levee inland. At a half mile past the bridge, the harbor channel curves north, away from Ballona Creek and the hiking/biking path. Continue along the paved path, or take the dirt trail to the north of the paved trail. A short distance ahead, a path curves left to Fisherman's Village, a tourist area resembling a New England seaport town with shops, galleries, and boat docks. This is the turn-around spot.

To hike farther, continue on the main trail along Ballona Creek, reaching the Lincoln Boulevard underpass 0.8 miles ahead. ▪

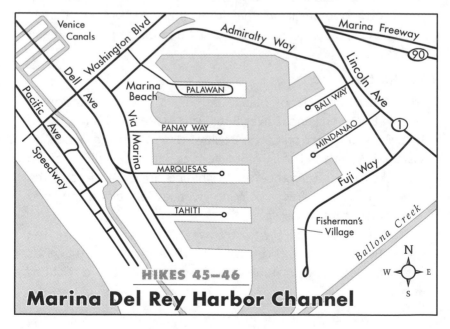

HIKES 45-46

Marina Del Rey Harbor Channel

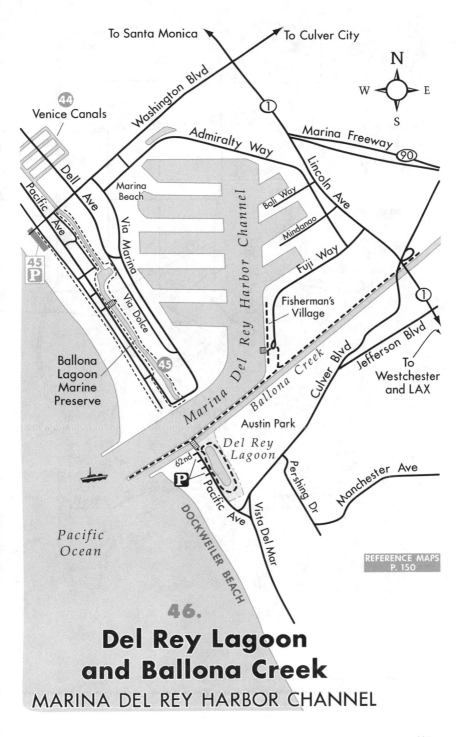

To Santa Monica

To Culver City

N
W   E
S

Venice Canals
44

Washington Blvd

Admiralty Way

Marina Freeway

90

Dell Ave

Pacific Ave

Marina Beach

Via Marina

Via Dolce

45 P

Bali Way

Lincoln Ave

Mindanao

Fuji Way

Marina Del Rey Harbor Channel

Fisherman's Village

45

Ballona Lagoon Marine Preserve

Ballona Creek

Culver Blvd

Jefferson Blvd

To Westchester and LAX

Austin Park

Del Rey Lagoon

Pershing Dr

Manchester Ave

62nd
P

Pacific Ave

Vista Del Mar

Pacific Ocean

DOCKWEILER BEACH

REFERENCE MAPS
P. 150

46.
Del Rey Lagoon
and Ballona Creek
MARINA DEL REY HARBOR CHANNEL

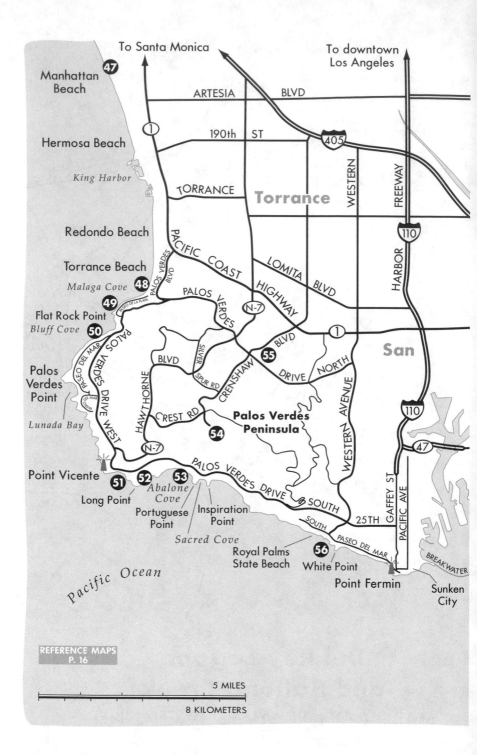

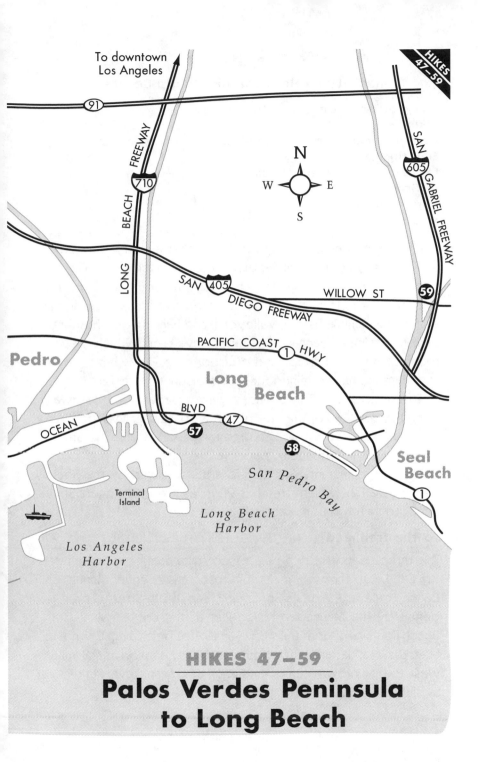

To downtown
Los Angeles

91

N

W   E

S

710

SAN GABRIEL FREEWAY

605

BEACH FREEWAY

LONG

SAN 405

DIEGO FREEWAY

WILLOW ST

59

PACIFIC COAST 1 HWY

Pedro

Long
Beach

BLVD 47

57

OCEAN

58

Seal
Beach

1

San Pedro Bay

Terminal
Island

Long Beach
Harbor

Los Angeles
Harbor

HIKES 47–59
Palos Verdes Peninsula
to Long Beach

47. The Strand
Manhattan • Hermosa • Redondo Beaches

Hiking distance: 6 miles round trip
Hiking time: 3 hours
Configuration: out-and-back with side trips to three beach piers
Elevation gain: level
Exposure: exposed beach coastline
Difficulty: easy to slightly moderate
Dogs: allowed
Maps: U.S.G.S. Redondo Beach and Venice

Manhattan, Hermosa, and Redondo Beaches are strung together along the southern end of Santa Monica Bay in the area known as South Bay. They are laid-back, quintessential southern California beaches with clean, broad, white sand beaches, popular for surfing, swimming, fishing, volleyball, and hanging out. The three well-maintained beach communities have piers, which are surrounded by quaint shops and outdoor cafes. They have grown together, yet have retained their own distinct characters.

This hike follows The Strand, a paved pedestrian boardwalk lining the back end of the beaches. The boardwalk links the three towns and is used by walkers, joggers, and skaters. The Strand connects to an aquarium, parks, and three beach piers with shops and restaurants. The towns are also linked by the South Bay Bicycle Trail, which stretches 20 miles from Will Rogers State Beach to its terminus at Redondo Beach.

To the trailhead

The three beaches can be accessed from numerous routes off the San Diego Freeway, including Rosecrans Avenue, Manhattan Beach Boulevard, Artesia Boulevard, and 190th Street. This hike begins by the Manhattan Beach Pier at the end of Manhattan Beach Boulevard. From the 405 (San Diego) Freeway in Lawndale, take the Manhattan Beach Boulevard exit, and drive 2.8 miles west to downtown Manhattan Beach at Ocean Drive. Park in an available metered parking space.

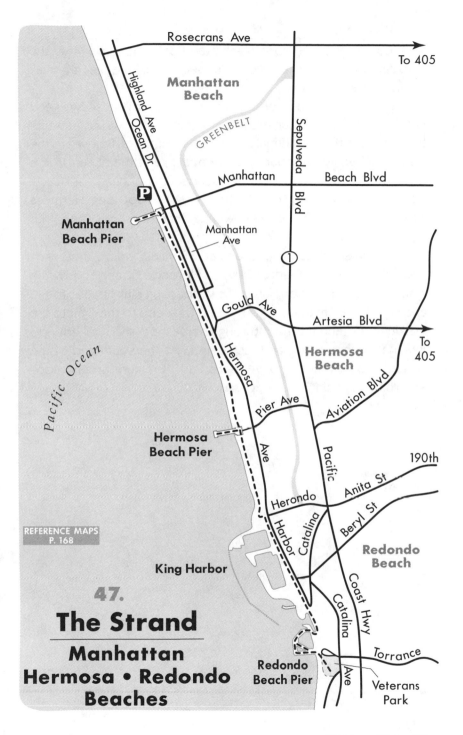

Rosecrans Ave

To 405

Manhattan
Beach

GREENBELT

Highland Ave

Ocean Dr

Sepulveda Blvd

Manhattan   Beach Blvd

P

Manhattan
Beach Pier

Manhattan
Ave

①

Gould Ave

Artesia Blvd

To
405

Hermosa
Beach

Hermosa

Aviation Blvd

Pier Ave

Ave

Pacific

190th

Hermosa
Beach Pier

Pacific Ocean

Herondo

Anita St

Beryl St

Catalina

Harbor

Redondo
Beach

REFERENCE MAPS
P. 168

King Harbor

Coast Hwy

Catalina

Torrance

47.

The Strand

Manhattan
Hermosa • Redondo
Beaches

Redondo
Beach Pier

Ave

Veterans
Park

The hike

Walk out on the 900-foot Manhattan Beach Pier, and view the coastline from offshore. At the rounded end of the pier is a small marine lab and aquarium.

Return to The Strand on the low bluffs atop the seawall and head south, passing numerous pedestrian-only walking streets that connect the residential streets to The Strand. Below are the biking trail, volleyball courts, sandy beach, and the ocean. In less than a half mile, cross into Hermosa Beach. Continue past beach-front homes and apartments to the 900-foot-long Hermosa Beach Pier at the foot of Pier Avenue. Pier Avenue is lined with outdoor restaurants and interesting shops.

Continue south to King Harbor at 2.3 miles, where the beach ends. Walk inland to Harbor Drive at Herondo Street. Follow the sidewalk to the right on Harbor Drive, passing King Harbor to the end of the road at a parking structure. Descend to the right to the walking path, and meander through horseshoe-shaped Redondo Beach Pier amid shops and restaurants. At the south end of the pier, the path leads into Veterans Park, the turn-around spot. Return by retracing your steps. ■

48. Malaga Cove and Flat Rock Point

Hiking distance: 4 miles round trip
Hiking time: 2 hours
Configuration: out-and-back with loop
Elevation gain: 300 feet
Exposure: exposed beach coastline
Difficulty: easy
Dogs: allowed
Maps: U.S.G.S. Redondo Beach

Malaga Cove and Flat Rock Point are at the north end of the Palos Verdes Peninsula. Malaga Canyon, formed by a major water drainage, slices through the northern slopes of the peninsula and empties into the ocean at Malaga Cove. Flat Rock Point borders the north end of Bluff Cove under soaring 300-foot cliffs. The point has some of the best tidepools in the area. This hike begins on sandy Torrance County Beach and quickly reaches the rocky tidepools and near-vertical cliffs at Malaga Cove. The trail continues along the rugged, rocky shoreline along the base of the eroded cliffs to Flat Rock Point. For extended hiking, Hikes 48—50 are adjacent to each other with connecting trails.

To the trailhead

From the Pacific Coast Highway/Highway 1 at the south end of Redondo Beach, turn south on Palos Verdes Boulevard. Drive 1.1 mile to Paseo De La Playa and turn right. Continue 0.7 miles to Torrance County Beach. Park in the lot on the left. A parking fee is required seasonally.

The hike

Take the ramp down from the bluffs to the sandy beach. Head south (left), strolling on the sand towards the Palos Verdes cliffs. The views extend out to Palos Verdes Point (Hike 49). At 0.7 miles, the sand gives way to rock at the foot of the cliffs. Curve west and follow the wide walking path into Malaga Cove. Just before reaching the Palos Verdes Beach Club, a paved access path—our return route—follows stream-fed Malaga Canyon up an easy grade to the bluffs at Via Corta and Paseo Del Mar. Continue along the shoreline beneath the steep cliffs on the rounded shoreline rocks, passing Malaga Cove and the beach club. The shoreline reaches Flat Rock Point and the tidepools at 1.7 miles. From the point, cross over the rocky ridge into Bluff Cove. Curve into the crescent-shaped cove to an access trail. Hike 49 continues along the shoreline.

To return, ascend the cliffs on the wide, easy path for a quarter mile to the bluffs on Paseo Del Mar. Follow Paseo Del Mar to the left a half mile to Via Arroyo. Walk through the intersection into the parking lot on Via Arroyo, on the ocean side of Malaga Cove School. Pick up the paved Malaga Canyon Trail on the left, and descend through the canyon to the ocean, completing the loop. Return to Torrance Beach on the right. ■

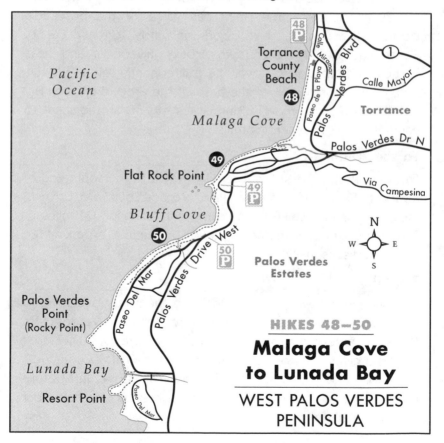

HIKES 48–50

Malaga Cove to Lunada Bay

WEST PALOS VERDES PENINSULA

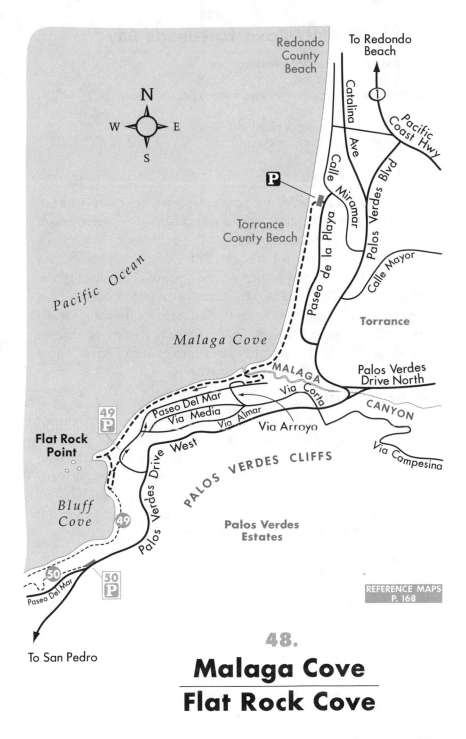

Redondo County Beach

To Redondo Beach

Pacific Coast Hwy

Catalina Ave

Calle Miramar

Palos Verdes Blvd

P

Torrance County Beach

Calle Mayor

Paseo de la Playa

Torrance

Pacific Ocean

Malaga Cove

Palos Verdes Drive North

MALAGA

Via Corta

CANYON

Paseo Del Mar

Via Media

Via Almar

Via Arroyo

Via Campesina

49 P

Flat Rock Point

Palos Verdes Drive West

PALOS VERDES CLIFFS

Bluff Cove

49

Palos Verdes Estates

50

Paseo Del Mar

50 P

REFERENCE MAPS
P. 168

To San Pedro

48.

Malaga Cove
Flat Rock Cove

49. Bluff Cove to Lunada Bay

Hiking distance: 6 miles round trip
Hiking time: 3 hours
Configuration: loop with return on Paseo Del Mar
Elevation gain: 300 feet
Exposure: exposed beach coastline
Difficulty: easy to slightly moderate
Dogs: allowed
Maps: U.S.G.S. Redondo Beach

Bluff Cove and Lunada Bay are both crescent-shaped rocky beach pockets resting beneath sheer, terraced cliffs. They are popular with surfers and tidepool explorers. The path begins at Flat Rock Point and leads down to the rocky Bluff Cove. The jagged shore is lined with cliffs and numerous small coves. The horseshoe-shaped Lunada Bay is framed by Palos Verdes Point (also known as Rocky Point) and Resort Point. In 1961, a Greek freighter named *Dominator*, en route from Vancouver, Canada, to the Los Angeles Harbor, ran aground in thick fog just north of Rocky Point. Watch for the rusted remnants of the abandoned ship.

To the trailhead

From the Pacific Coast Highway/Highway 1 at the south end of Redondo Beach, turn south on Palos Verdes Boulevard. Drive 1.5 miles and curve to the right onto Palos Verdes Drive West to the first stop sign. Turn right on Via Corta. Drive 0.4 miles and turn right on Via Arroyo. Drive one block to Paseo Del Mar. Turn left and continue 0.5 miles to a distinct path on a left bend in the road. Surfers' vehicles are often parked along this bend.

The hike

Take the wide path down the cliffs on an easy, tapered grade overlooking the rock formations at Flat Rock Point. At the north end of Bluff Cove, a steep side path descends to the tidepools at Flat Rock Point. The main trail curves left into the rocky beach at crescent-shaped Bluff Cove. Slowly follow the shoreline southwest, walking over the eroded boulders under the 300-foot

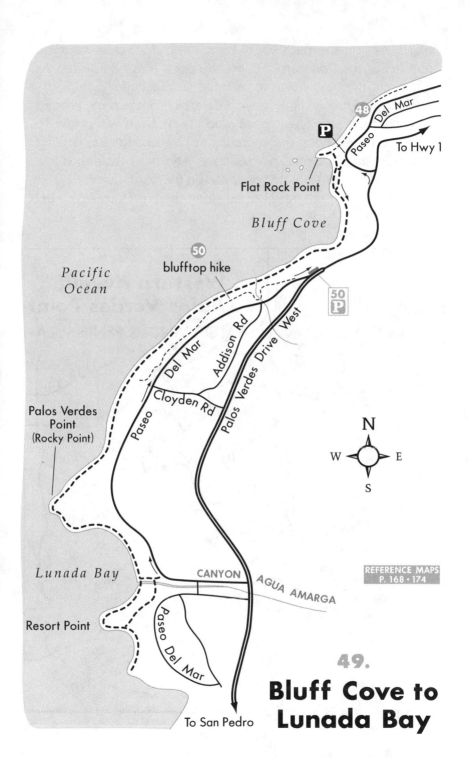

P

48

Paseo Del Mar

To Hwy 1

Flat Rock Point

Bluff Cove

Pacific Ocean

50

blufftop hike

50
P

Paseo Del Mar

Addison Rd

Cloyden Rd

Palos Verdes Drive West

Palos Verdes Point (Rocky Point)

N

W ◇ E

S

Lunada Bay

CANYON

AGUA AMARGA

REFERENCE MAPS
P. 168 • 174

Resort Point

Paseo Del Mar

To San Pedro

49.
Bluff Cove to Lunada Bay

bluffs. As you approach Rocky Point, watch for some scattered remains of the *Dominator*. Follow the point into Lunada Bay. As you circle the bay, watch for a steep path ascending the cliffs, just before Agua Amarga Canyon. Carefully climb up the eroded cliffs to the grassy open space atop the bluffs. If you prefer to continue hiking along the shoreline, follow Lunada Bay around Resort Point into a small pocket cove. Another precipitous trail ascends the cliffs to the open space on the bluffs.

For a loop, return northbound along the bluffs on Paseo Del Mar and Palos Verdes Drive. ▦

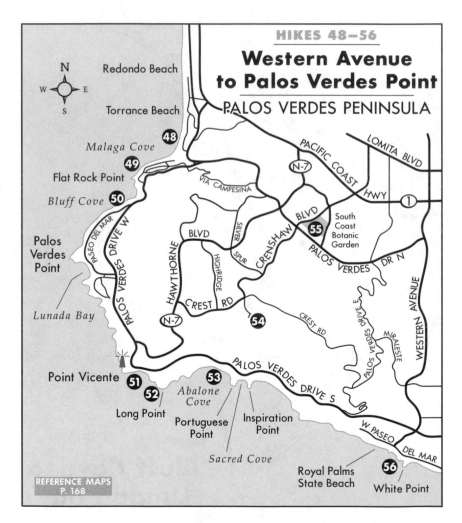

HIKES 48–56

**Western Avenue
to Palos Verdes Point**

PALOS VERDES PENINSULA

N

Redondo Beach

Torrance Beach

Malaga Cove

Flat Rock Point

Bluff Cove

Palos Verdes Point

Lunada Bay

Point Vicente

Long Point

Abalone Cove

Portuguese Point

Inspiration Point

Sacred Cove

Royal Palms State Beach

White Point

PACIFIC COAST HWY

LOMITA BLVD

N-7

VIA CAMPESINA

BLVD

South Coast Botanic Garden

PALOS VERDES DR N

PASEO DEL MAR

PALOS VERDES DRIVE W

HAWTHORNE

BLVD

SILVER SPUR

CRENSHAW

HIGHRIDGE

CREST RD

N-7

CREST RD

PALOS VERDES DRIVE E

PALOS VERDES DRIVE S

MIRALESTE

WESTERN AVENUE

W PASEO DEL MAR

REFERENCE MAPS
P. 168

50. Paseo Del Mar Bluffs
PALOS VERDES ESTATES SHORELINE PRESERVE

Hiking distance: 1.3 miles round trip
Hiking time: 45 minutes
Configuration: out-and-back
Elevation gain: level
Exposure: easy
Difficulty: exposed coastline
Dogs: allowed
Maps: U.S.G.S. Redondo Beach

The Palos Verdes Estates Shoreline Preserve is a 130-acre undeveloped stretch of land running 4.5 miles along the southwest coast of the peninsula. The city-owned preserve includes scalloped blufftop parklands, footpaths that lead from the overlooks to the rocky shore, plus the adjacent submerged offshore land. This hike follows the grassy oceanfront bluffs high above Bluff Cove (Hike 49), parallel to Paseo Del Mar. From the cliff's edge are incredible views of Bluff Cove, Catalina Island, the Channel Islands, and the beach cities along Santa Monica Bay to Point Dume. It is also a great area to view migrating gray whales.

To the trailhead

From the Pacific Coast Highway/Highway 1 at the south end of Redondo Beach, turn south on Palos Verdes Boulevard. Drive 1.5 miles and curve to the right onto Palos Verdes Drive West to the first stop sign at Via Corta. Continue straight ahead for 1.7 miles to a parking lot on the right, just before the Paseo Del Mar turnoff.

The hike

Take the grassy blufftop path from the south end of Bluff Cove. The parkland parallels the crenelated cliffs bordered by Paseo Del Mar. The level, cliff-top trail leaves the edge of the cliffs and curves inland, looping around a stream-carved gorge before returning to the cliffs. The meandering path ends at a row of palm trees adjacent to an oceanfront residence across from Cloyden Road. Return along the same route. ∎

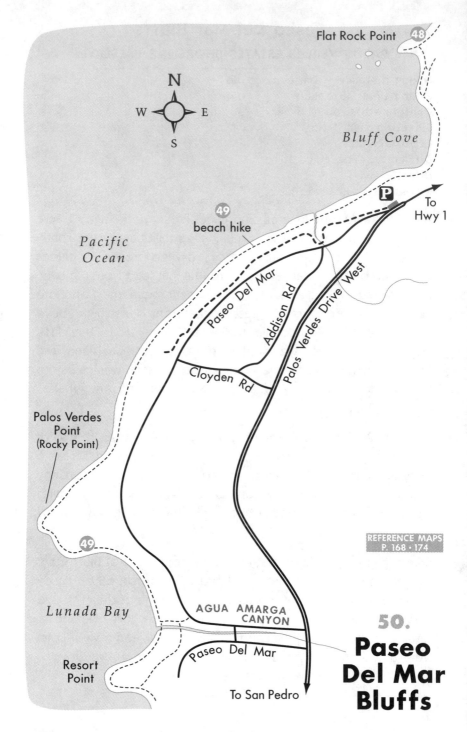

N
W · E
S

Flat Rock Point

48

Bluff Cove

P

To Hwy 1

49
beach hike

Pacific Ocean

Paseo Del Mar

Addison Rd

Palos Verdes Drive West

Cloyden Rd

Palos Verdes Point
(Rocky Point)

REFERENCE MAPS
P. 168 · 174

49

Lunada Bay

AGUA AMARGA CANYON

Resort Point

Paseo Del Mar

To San Pedro

50.
Paseo Del Mar Bluffs

51. Point Vicente

POINT VICENTE FISHING ACCESS TRAIL

Hiking distance: 1.5 miles round trip
Hiking time: 1 hour
Configuration: out-and-back
Elevation gain: 140 feet
Exposure: exposed coastline
Difficulty: easy
Dogs: allowed
Maps: U.S.G.S. Redondo Beach

Point Vicente is situated on the southwest point of the Palos Verdes Peninsula. Perched on the cliffs high above the shore is the historic 67-foot Point Vicente Lighthouse, built in 1926. The lighthouse warned ships of the rocky shoals in the Catalina Channel. From the 140-foot scalloped bluffs are vistas of the lighthouse, Santa Catalina Island, and Long Point, the former site of Marineland on the southeast end of the bay. This is a premier spot to observe migrating gray whales from mid-December through March.

The Point Vicente Fishing Access Trail descends the eroding cliffs to the rounded cobblestone beach beneath Point Vicente and Long Point, where the tidepools are teeming with marine life. The crescent-shaped bay with large offshore rocks is a popular site for scuba divers, surfers, and anglers.

To the trailhead

From the Pacific Coast Highway (Highway 1) at the south end of Torrance, take Hawthorne Boulevard south 7.3 miles to its terminus at the coast. Turn left on Palos Verdes Drive South, and drive 0.8 miles to the posted fishing access. Park in the lot on the right.

The hike

Walk to the west (upper) end of the parking lot. Take the well-defined dirt path, just beyond the restrooms. Descend the cliffs on an easy grade towards the prominent Point Vicente Lighthouse. Halfway down the slope, switchback left, dropping down to the rocky cobblestone shoreline. The beach pocket is bordered on the west by steep cliffs and a natural rock jetty. On the south end, the beach ends near Long Point, where the cliffs drop 100 feet into the sea near the offshore rock outcroppings. ▪

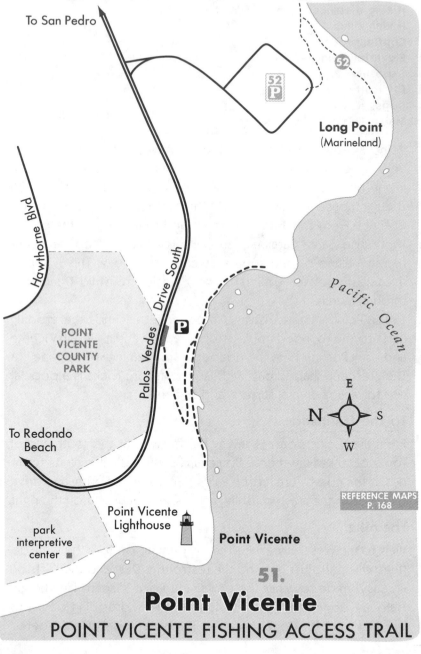

To San Pedro

52
P

52

Long Point
(Marineland)

Hawthorne Blvd

Palos Verdes Drive South

POINT VICENTE COUNTY PARK

P

Pacific Ocean

To Redondo Beach

E

N — S

W

REFERENCE MAPS
P. 168

park interpretive center ▪

Point Vicente Lighthouse

Point Vicente

51.
Point Vicente
POINT VICENTE FISHING ACCESS TRAIL

52. Long Point
(MARINELAND)

Hiking distance: 1 mile round trip
Hiking time: 45 minutes
Configuration: out-and-back
Elevation gain: 100 feet
Exposure: exposed coastline
Difficulty: easy
Dogs: allowed
Maps: U.S.G.S. Redondo Beach

Long Point extends seaward at the southwest point of the Palos Verdes Peninsula. Marineland, a defunct 108-acre marine amusement park, was situated on the bluffs atop Long Point from 1954 to 1987. It closed due to its remoteness and competition from modern aquatic parks and aquariums. Beach access is still permitted from the enormous Marineland parking lot atop the 100-foot bluffs. The trail descends the eroded cliffs to an isolated beach pocket at the base of the vertical cliffs. It is a popular snorkeling and scuba diving area.

To the trailhead

From the Pacific Coast Highway (Highway 1) at the south end of Torrance, take Hawthorne Boulevard south 7.3 miles to its terminus at the coast. Turn left on Palos Verdes Drive South, and drive 1.3 miles to the Long Point turnoff, the old entrance to Marineland. Turn right and drive 0.4 miles to the far southwest corner of the parking lot.

The hike

Take the partially paved road/trail past the vehicle barrier. Descend to the east, overlooking Abalone Cove and Portuguese Point (Hike 53). Halfway down the descent is a large flat area and trail split. The road continues straight ahead to the sheer, eroding cliffs and rocky beach pocket. Watch for a narrow, intermittent waterfall dropping 60 feet off the cliffs. After exploring the tidepools and rock formations at the beach, return to the trail split. Bear left, leaving the road, and take the dirt path along the edge of the 100-foot bluffs. Slowly descend to the tip of rocky Long Point, where pelicans often line the ridge. Return along the same route. ▦

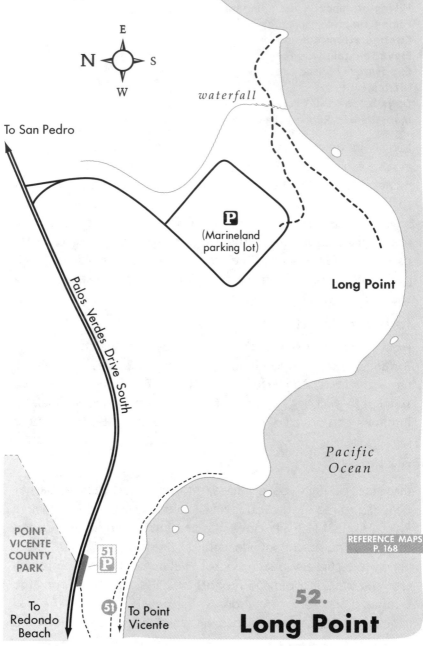

53. Abalone Cove and Portuguese Point

5970 Palos Verdes Drive South

Hiking distance: 2 miles round trip
Hiking time: 1 hour
Configuration: two loops
Elevation gain: 150 feet
Exposure: exposed coastline
Difficulty: easy
Dogs: allowed
Maps: U.S.G.S. Redondo Beach and San Pedro

Abalone Cove Shoreline Park and Ecological Preserve is a federal reserve where grassy 180-foot bluffs offer easy access to the rocky shoreline. The 80-acre preserve extends from Abalone Cove to Portuguese Point and Sacred Cove (also known as Smugglers Cove). Sacred Cove is bordered by tidepools at both points. From Portuguese Point are magnificent views of Abalone Cove, Long Point (Hike 52), Sacred Cove, Inspiration Point, White Point, Point Fermin (Hike 56), and Catalina Island. The oceanfront park sits at the foot of the unstable and actively slipping Portuguese Bend landslide area.

To the trailhead

From the Pacific Coast Highway/Highway 1 at the south end of Torrance, take Hawthorne Boulevard south 7.3 miles to its terminus at the coast. Turn left on Palos Verdes Drive South, and drive 2.2 miles to the posted Abalone Cove Shoreline Park entrance. Turn right and park in the lot. A parking fee is required.

The hike

From the east end of the parking lot, cross the grassy picnic area onto a wide gravel path. Continue to a vehicle-restricted road. Bear left and wind up the hillside on the vehicle-restricted road to Palos Verdes Drive. Bear to the left on the narrow path, parallel to the highway, for 0.2 miles to the Portuguese Point access. Walk up the curving, gated road to the north edge of the peninsula and a trail split. First, take the left fork out to Portuguese Point, which stays atop the peninsula and loops around the perimeter.

After enjoying the awesome coastal views from the point, return to the trail split Take the left fork down to the beach and tidepools near an old rock enclosure. The trail to the left leads to the base of the cliffs at Portuguese Point. To return, follow the shoreline trail back along Abalone Cove for 0.4 miles to Upper Beach, a raised, man-made sandy beach and lifeguard station just above the rocky shore. Curve right and take the old paved road to a trail junction. The footpath to the left ascends the cliffs through the dense brush, back to the parking lot. ■

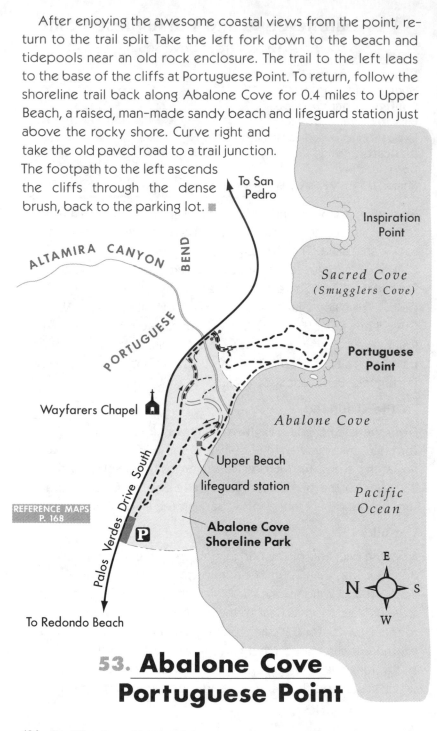

Inspiration Point

ALTAMIRA CANYON

BEND

To San Pedro

Sacred Cove
(Smugglers Cove)

PORTUGUESE

Portuguese Point

Wayfarers Chapel

Abalone Cove

Upper Beach

lifeguard station

Pacific Ocean

Palos Verdes Drive South

REFERENCE MAPS
P. 168

P

Abalone Cove
Shoreline Park

E

N ←✦→ S

W

To Redondo Beach

53. Abalone Cove
Portuguese Point

54. Portuguese Bend Overlook

CRENSHAW EXTENSION TRAIL from DEL CERRO PARK

Hiking distance: 2.8 miles round trip
Hiking time: 1.5 hours
Configuration: out-and-back with loop
Elevation gain: 500 feet
Exposure: exposed with shaded pockets
Difficulty: easy to moderate
Dogs: allowed
Maps: U.S.G.S. Torrance

This hike begins in Del Cerro Park in Rancho Palos Verdes, which sits atop the Palos Verdes Peninsula at more than 1,100 feet. From the park overlook are spectacular southern views of the 13 distinct marine terraces that make up the peninsula and the massive 270-acre landslide area of Portuguese Bend. The Crenshaw Extension Trail descends from Del Cerro Park into the precarious bowl-shaped canyon, still active with faults and shifting ground. A trail system winds through the rolling green hills and ancient wave-cut terraces to the shady Portuguese Bend Overlook, perched high above Portuguese Bend, Portuguese Point, and Inspiration Point (Hike 53).

To the trailhead

From the Pacific Coast Highway/Highway 1 at the south end of Torrance, take Crenshaw Boulevard south 3.9 miles to the trailhead at the end of the road.

The hike

Before starting down the trail, walk 30 yards up the road, and bear left into Del Cerro Park for a bird's-eye view of the surrounding hills, coastline, and the trails you are about to hike. Return to the metal trailhead gate, and take the unpaved road, passing a few hilltop homes. Descend into the unspoiled open space overlooking layers of rolling hills, the magnificent Palos Verdes coastline, and the island of Catalina. At just under a half mile is a 3-way trail split by a water tank on the left. Follow the main road, curving to the right a quarter mile to an unsigned footpath on the left. Detour left to the distinctive 950-foot knoll dotted with pine trees. From the overlook are sweeping coastal views, including Point Vicente, Portuguese Point, Inspiration Point, and Catalina Island.

Return from the overlook to the main trail. Continue downhill, curving left on a wide horseshoe bend. Just beyond the bend, a road veers off to the right, leading to Narcissa Drive. Twelve yards past this road split is a distinct footpath on the left. Leave the road and take this path through a forest of feathery sweet fennel plants. The path curves left, overlooking Portuguese Canyon. A switchback cuts back to the west and climbs the hillside to a ridge at a T-junction. The right fork follows the ridge uphill to the summit again, completing a loop on the pine-covered knoll. Descend from the knoll to the main trail (the same route hiked earlier). Bear right, returning to the trailhead. ■

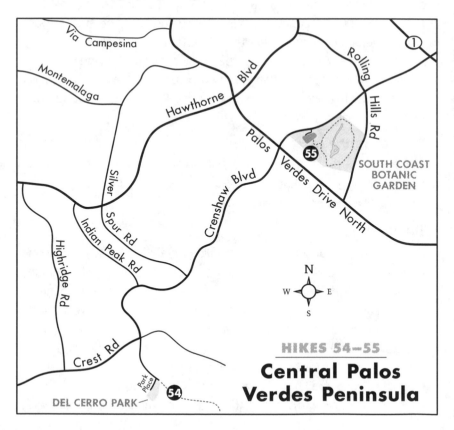

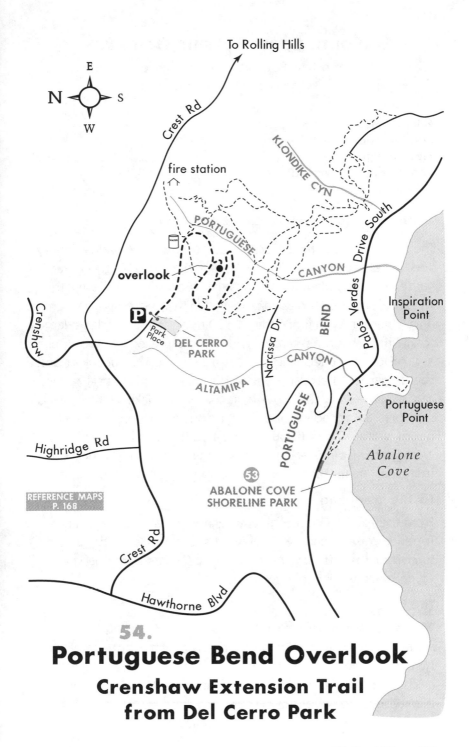

54.
Portuguese Bend Overlook
Crenshaw Extension Trail
from Del Cerro Park

55. South Coast Botanic Garden

26300 Crenshaw Boulevard · Palos Verdes Peninsula
Open daily 9 a.m.—5 p.m.

Hiking distance: 1—2 miles round trip
Hiking time: 1—2 hours
Configuration: many inter-connecting paths
Elevation gain: 100 feet
Exposure: mixed sun and shade
Difficulty: very easy
Dogs: not allowed
Maps: U.S.G.S. Torrance · South Coast Botanic Garden map

The South Coast Botanic Garden, owned by Los Angeles County, was developed on a sanitary landfill site in 1959. The 87-acre garden includes plant collections that represent southern Africa, Australia, and the Mediterranean. Within this impressive garden is a rose garden with more than 1,600 hybrids that circles a large fountain, a children's garden with a miniature enchanted house, a gazebo, an arched bridge over a fish pond, a succulent and cactus garden, herb and vegetable gardens, a fuchsia garden, and a water-wise garden. A large man-made lake with an island supports an abundant bird population. A canyon with a channel of water winds through riparian and marshland habitats, a woodland of pines and junipers, coastal redwoods, flowering fruit trees, palm trees, and over 50 species of eucalyptus trees.

To the trailhead

From the Pacific Coast Highway/Highway 1 at the south end of Torrance, take Crenshaw Boulevard south 1 mile to the posted turnoff on the left. Turn left and drive 0.2 miles to the parking lot. An entrance fee is required.

The hike

Walk past the gift shop to a hub of trails at the top of the garden. A paved road/trail circles the perimeter of the botanic garden. Numerous unpaved roads and trails weave through the tiered landscape leading to the lake. Let your interests lead you through the gardens along your own route. ■

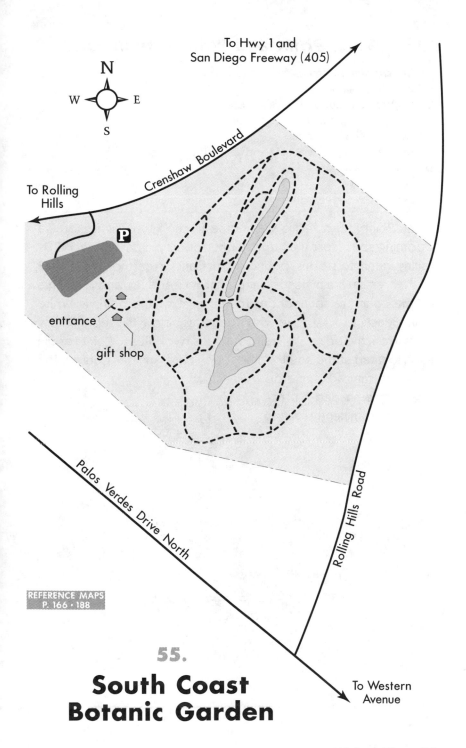

To Hwy 1 and
San Diego Freeway (405)

N
W E
S

Crenshaw Boulevard

To Rolling
Hills

P

entrance

gift shop

Palos Verdes Drive North

Rolling Hills Road

REFERENCE MAPS
P. 166 · 188

55.

South Coast
Botanic Garden

To Western
Avenue

56. White Point and Point Fermin Park

Hiking distance: 4 miles round trip
Hiking time: 2 hours
Configuration: out-and-back or return along
South Paseo Del Mar for a loop
Elevation gain: 100 feet
Exposure: exposed coastline and shady blufftop park
Difficulty: easy
Dogs: allowed
Maps: U.S.G.S. San Pedro

White Point in San Pedro was home to the Royal Palms Hotel, a booming spa resort with hot sulphur pools predating the 1920s. Falling victim to storms, pounding surf, and an earthquake in 1933, all that remain are majestic palms, garden terraces, and remnants of the concrete foundation. To the east of the point is White Point Beach, a rocky cove with tidepools below the sedimentary cliffs. From the point, the trail continues two miles to Point Fermin Park, located at the southernmost tip in Los Angeles County. The long coastal park sits atop grassy tree-shaded bluffs that jut prominently out

The Point Fermin Lighthouse was built in 1874.

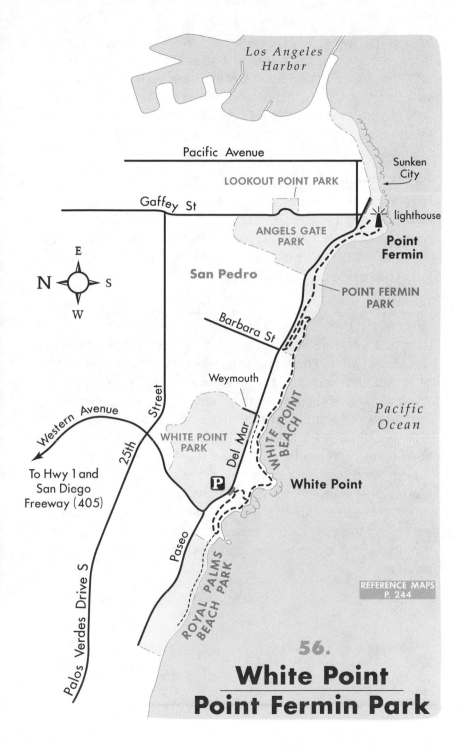

Los Angeles Harbor

Pacific Avenue

LOOKOUT POINT PARK

Gaffey St

Sunken City

lighthouse

ANGELS GATE PARK

Point Fermin

San Pedro

POINT FERMIN PARK

E

N ⬦ S

W

Barbara St

Weymouth

Pacific Ocean

Western Avenue

Street

WHITE POINT PARK

Del Mar

WHITE POINT BEACH

25th

To Hwy 1 and San Diego Freeway (405)

P

White Point

Paseo

Palos Verdes Drive S

ROYAL PALMS BEACH PARK

REFERENCE MAPS
P. 244

56.
White Point
Point Fermin Park

to sea. The scenic 37-acre park has flower gardens, mature fig trees, and curving pathways that lead from the bluffs to the rocky shoreline. Point Fermin Lighthouse is an historic Victorian structure that sits on the edge of the vertical cliffs. It was built in 1874 with lumber and bricks shipped around Cape Horn. The lighthouse was in use for nearly a century. It is now a museum and open for tours (Tuesday through Sunday).

To the trailhead

From the intersection of Western Avenue and 25th Street in San Pedro, drive 0.5 miles south to the end of Western Avenue at the coastline. Curve left onto Paseo Del Mar, and drive 0.1 mile to the White Point Bluff Park parking lot on the right. Park in the lot for a fee or alongside the road for free.

The hike

Descend the cliffs on the dirt path or walk west down the paved road to Royal Palms Beach Park. Head east and follow the coastline around White Point, crossing over small boulders and slabs of rock. Stroll along the rocky shore of White Point Beach below the ruins of the Royal Palms Hotel. Continue following the shoreline past a group of old homes at the base of the sheer 120-foot cliffs. At 1.2 miles, take the distinct path on the left, and head up the cliffs to the west. Half way up, the path becomes paved. Wind through a palm tree grove and to the top of the bluffs across from Barbara Street, at the west end of Point Fermin Park. Continue east for one mile through the narrow tree-shaded park along the edge of the grassy bluffs to Point Fermin and the lighthouse. This is the turn-around point. Return along the same path. ▩

57. Long Beach Oceanfront Trail to Belmont Pier

Long Beach City Beach

Hiking distance: 7 miles round trip
Hiking time: 3.5 hours
Configuration: out-and-back; optional side trip out onto Belmont Pier
Elevation gain: level
Exposure: exposed beach coastline
Difficulty: easy to moderate
Dogs: not allowed
Maps: U.S.G.S. Long Beach

The Long Beach Oceanfront Trail is a paved walking and biking path along the San Pedro Bay coastline in Long Beach. Long Beach is the southernmost coastal city in Los Angeles County. Long Beach City Beach, which fronts the path, extends four miles from the Long Beach Harbor to the Alamitos Peninsula and San Gabriel River on the Orange County line.

This hike begins at the mouth of the Los Angeles River in Queensway Bay by Shoreline Village, a tourist attraction with shops and restaurants. The path follows the coastline along Long Beach City Beach to Belmont Pier. En route is Bluff Park, an elevated grassy park above the wide, sandy beach overlooking San Pedro Bay. Bluff Park backs the beach and runs parallel to Ocean Boulevard. Offshore from the beach and path are four artificial tropical islands with postcard-perfect fronts. They are actually landscaped oil drilling platforms.

Belmont Pier—the destination for the hike—is a 1,600-foot T-shaped pier that bisects Long Beach City Beach. The pier was built in 1968 at the foot of 39th Place in Belmont Shore, a charming seaside community filled with shops and eateries. After Belmont Pier, the coastal path continues to Alamitos Bay—Hike 58.

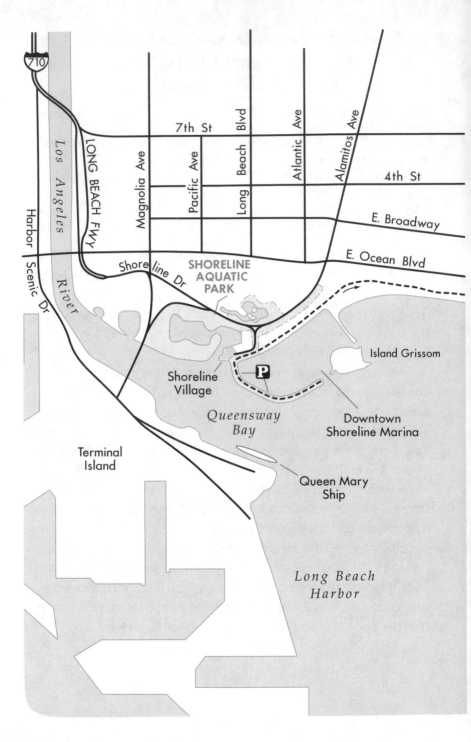

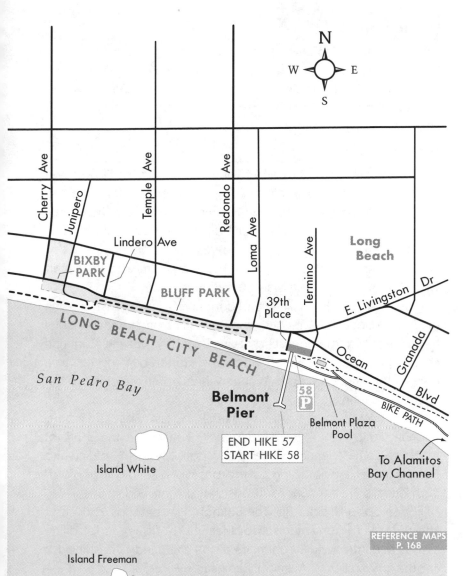

N
W • E
S

Cherry Ave
Junipero
Temple Ave
Redondo Ave
Lindero Ave
Loma Ave
Termino Ave

BIXBY PARK
BLUFF PARK

Long Beach
E. Livingston Dr
Granada
Blvd

39th Place

LONG BEACH CITY BEACH

San Pedro Bay

Ocean

BIKE PATH

Belmont Pier

58 P

Belmont Plaza Pool

Island White

END HIKE 57
START HIKE 58

To Alamitos Bay Channel

REFERENCE MAPS P. 168

Island Freeman

Island Chaffe

57.
Long Beach Oceanfront Trail to Belmont Pier
LONG BEACH CITY BEACH

To the trailhead

From the 405 (San Diego) Freeway in Long Beach, take 710 (Long Beach Freeway) south to its end. Follow the Downtown Long Beach/Aquarium signs onto Shoreline Drive. Turn right and curve into the huge Long Beach Marina parking lot and park near Shoreline Village. A parking fee is required.

The hike

Follow the paved walking and biking path along the Downtown Shoreline Marina to Shoreline Village. Curve left along the narrow, palm-lined breakwater in Queensway Bay. Pass the Queen Mary, an 81,000-ton luxury liner built in 1934 and retired after more than a thousand transatlantic voyages. Continue past several short fishing and overlook piers for a half mile to the breakwater's end, across from Island Grissom.

Return to Shoreline Village and continue 0.5 miles east, passing the marina boat slips. The path curves away from the small marina to the back end of wide, sandy Long Beach City Beach. Continue east, curving past the historic lifeguard station built in 1938, to a parking lot where Junipero Avenue winds down the bluffs to the shoreline parking lot.

Climb up the stairs to grassy Bluff Park, just west of Lindero Avenue. Follow the tree-filled park 0.8 miles on the 40-foot bluffs to Loma Avenue. Descend the stairway to the beach and follow the coastline, rising to the base of Belmont Pier off of 39th Place in Belmont Shore. This is the turn-around spot.

For an optional side trip, The Belmont Pier extends 1,600 feet into the bay. The long pier is a popular site for fishing and strolling.

The oceanfront trail continues along the sandy coastline for another two miles to Alamitos Peninsula—Hike 58. ■

58. Belmont Pier
to Alamitos Peninsula and Bay
Long Beach City Beach

Hiking distance: 4 miles round trip
Hiking time: 2 hours
Configuration: out-and-back with loop around peninsula
Elevation gain: level
Exposure: exposed beach coastline
Difficulty: easy
Dogs: allowed
Maps: U.S.G.S. Long Beach and Seal Beach

Long Beach City Beach stretches over 4 miles, from the port of Long Beach to the Alamitos Bay entrance channel at the Orange County border. This hike begins at Belmont Pier near the middle of the coastal beach. The 1,620-foot-long, T-shaped pier extends from the foot of 39th Place. The hike explores both shores of the narrow Alamitos Peninsula to the mouth of Alamitos Bay. The route follows the Seaside Walk (a wooden boardwalk) and Bay Shore Walk (a paved walkway) along the San Pedro Bay coastline. From Belmont Pier, the hike can be extended west on the Long Beach Oceanfront Trail—Hike 57.

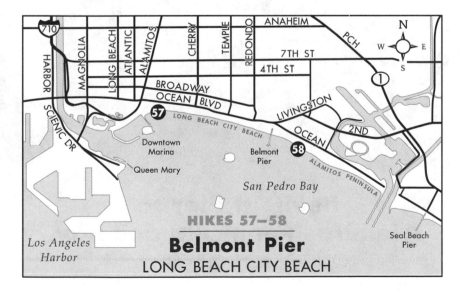

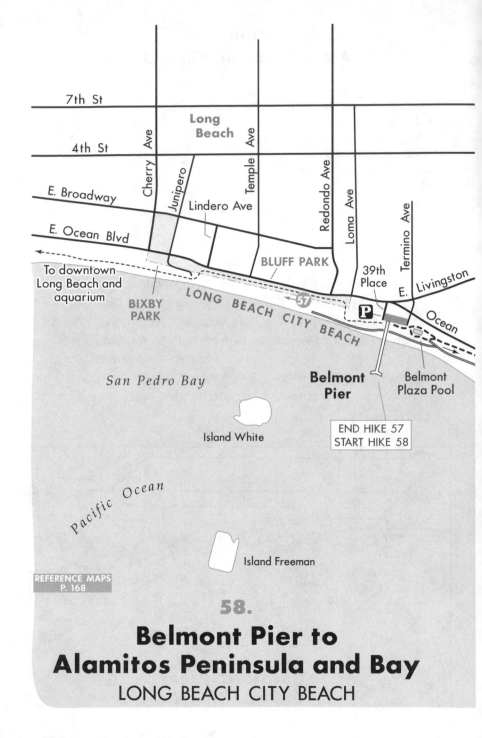

7th St

Long Beach

4th St

Cherry Ave

Junipero

Temple Ave

Long Beach Ave

Redondo Ave

Loma Ave

E. Termino Ave

E. Broadway

Lindero Ave

E. Ocean Blvd

To downtown Long Beach and aquarium

BIXBY PARK

BLUFF PARK

39th Place

E. Livingston

P

Ocean

LONG BEACH CITY BEACH

San Pedro Bay

Belmont Pier

Belmont Plaza Pool

Island White

END HIKE 57
START HIKE 58

Pacific Ocean

Island Freeman

REFERENCE MAPS
P. 168

58.

Belmont Pier to Alamitos Peninsula and Bay

LONG BEACH CITY BEACH

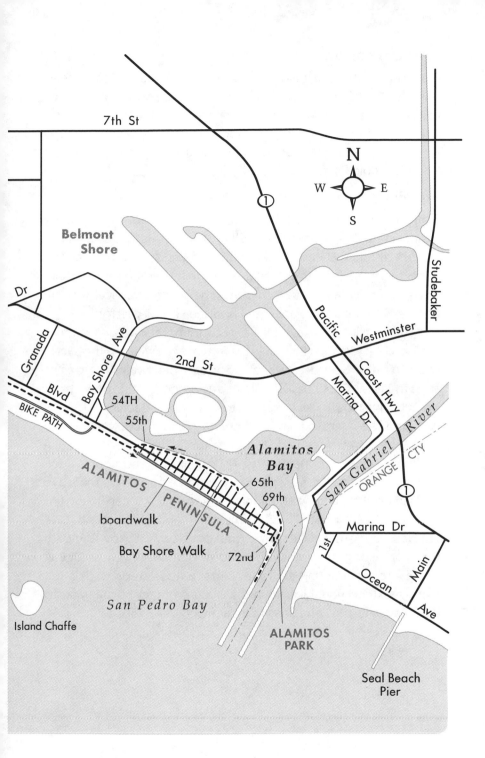

To the trailhead

From the Pacific Coast Highway (Highway 1) in Seal Beach, head north to 2nd Street in Long Beach. Turn left and drive 1.7 miles to Livingston Drive. Veer left and continue 0.4 miles to Termino Avenue. Turn left and drive 2 blocks into the beachfront parking lot on the east side of Belmont Pier, adjacent to the Belmont Plaza Olympic Pool.

The hike

From Belmont Pier, head east on the paved boardwalk along either side of the Belmont Plaza Olympic Pool. Both routes merge a short distance ahead. A bike path also winds east through the wide sandy beach. At just over a half mile, pass a row of palm trees by Granada Avenue. Offshore, the scenic, tropical-looking islands with palm trees are actually disguised oil platforms.

At one mile, the paved bike path joins the walking path at the head of Alamitos Peninsula by 54th Place. Walk on the sandy strand to the Seaside Walk, a wooden boardwalk that begins at 55th Place. Continue 0.7 miles to the end of the oceanfront boardwalk at 69th Place. Return to the sand, reaching Alamitos Park and the Alamitos Bay Channel by 72nd Place. Walk to the right, passing the lifeguard station to the jetty. Atop the jetty, a rock-lined path, frequented by fisherman, extends out to sea. Return to the small grassy park. A paved path follows the edge of Alamitos Bay, ending at the marina. Return to Ocean Boulevard and walk west to 65th Place. At the north end of the street, pick up the Bay Shore Walk, a paved public walkway. Follow the path 0.4 miles along the bay to the end at 55th Place. Cross Ocean Boulevard, completing the loop. Retrace your steps to Belmont Pier. To extend your hike along the oceanfront, continue west to Bluff Park and the Long Beach Oceanfront Trail—Hike 57. ▩

59. El Dorado Nature Center

EL DORADO PARK

7550 E. Spring Street · Long Beach · Open Tues.—Sun.

Hiking distance: 2-mile loop
Hiking time: 1 hour
Configuration: loop with optional cut-across
Elevation gain: level
Exposure: shade with some exposed pathways
Difficulty: easy
Dogs: not allowed
Maps: U.S.G.S. Los Alamitos · El Dorado Nature Center Trail Map

El Dorado Park is a 450-acre parkland in Long Beach just west of the Los Angeles-Orange County line. The park includes fishing lakes, tree groves, picnic shelters, a petting zoo, 4.5 miles of paved biking trails, and a nature center. The park is divided into an east section and a west section. The developed west section has a golf course and athletic fields. The west section has interconnecting roads and paved walkways.

This hike makes a loop through the least developed section of the park in the southwest corner. The pastoral 105-acre area is known as the El Dorado Nature Center. An interpretive trail loops around two lakes and meanders through the sanctuary along rolling hills, tree-lined meadows, chaparral communities, oak woodlands, and a stream connecting the two lakes. An interpretive trail pamphlet is available at the museum.

To the trailhead

From the 405 (San Diego) Freeway in Long Beach, take the Studebaker Road exit. Drive 1.4 miles north to Spring Street and turn right. Continue 0.8 miles to the park entrance on the right. Park just beyond the entrance station, near the posted trailhead on the right. A parking fee is required.

The hike

Enter the lush, forested parkland on the paved path to the bridge. Cross the bridge to the nature center building, perched on an island in North Lake. After visiting the center, loop clockwise to the backside of the buildings. Cross another bridge, leaving the island to a 3-way junction. The two trails on the right comprise a paved quarter-mile, handicapped-accessible loop. Take the unpaved left fork along the west edge of North Lake to a junction.

Begin the One-Mile Trail and Two-Mile Trail loops to the right. Parallel North Lake's outlet stream, and zigzag up the chaparral-covered hillside, passing the observation tower on the right, the highest point in the preserve. Descend and cross the bridges over the stream two times. Wind through eucalyptus and oak groves, and cross another bridge over the stream to a junction. The One-Mile Trail continues to the left for a shorter loop. Stay to the right on the Two-Mile Trail, and descend to the north shore of South Lake. Follow the west edge of the lake to the inlet stream. Cross a bridge and return to the south end of the lake. The meandering path returns to the north, completing the loop at North Lake. Return to the right. ▪

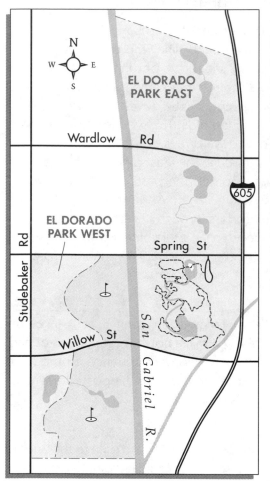

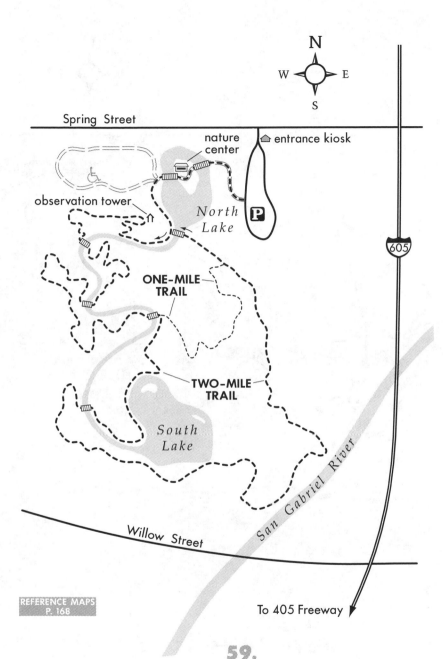

59.
El Dorado Nature Center
EL DORADO PARK

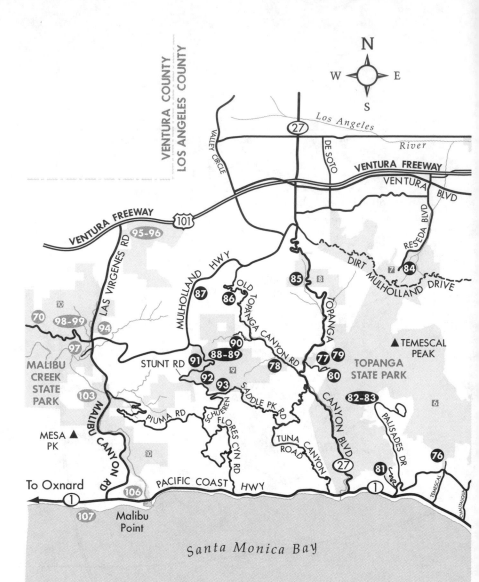

HIKES 60–93
Beverly Hills to
Malibu Canyon Road
EASTERN SANTA MONICA MOUNTAINS

Public Lands

1. Franklin Canyon Park
2. Coldwater Canyon–Wilacre Parks
3. Fryman Canyon Park
4. Sepulveda Basin Recreation Area
5. Will Rogers State Park
6. Topanga State Park
7. Marvin Braude Mulholland Gateway Park
8. Summit Valley–Edelman Park
9. Cold Creek Preserve
10. Malibu Creek State Park

HIKES 60–93

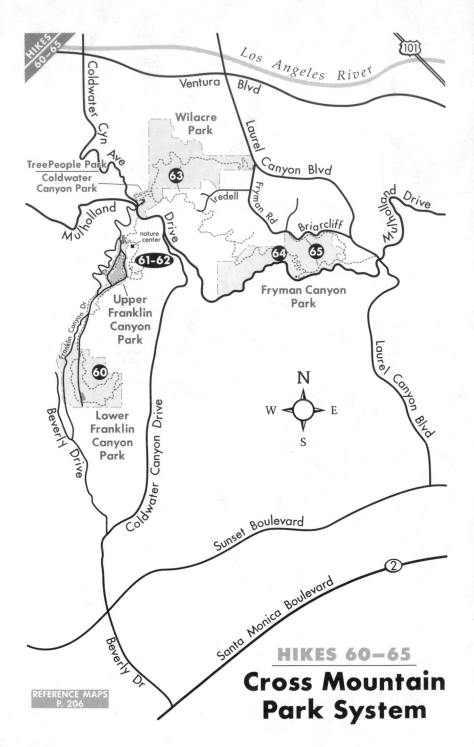

101

Los Angeles River

Ventura Blvd

Coldwater Cyn Ave

Wilacre
Park

Laurel Canyon Blvd

Fryman Rd

Mulholland Drive

TreePeople Park
Coldwater
Canyon Park

63

Iredell

Briarcliff

Mulholland Drive

nature
center

61-62

64   65

Upper
Franklin
Canyon
Park

Fryman Canyon
Park

Franklin Canyon Dr.

60

N

W   E

S

Beverly Drive

Lower
Franklin
Canyon
Park

Coldwater Canyon Drive

Laurel Canyon Blvd

Sunset Boulevard

2

Santa Monica Boulevard

Beverly Dr

HIKES 60—65
Cross Mountain
Park System

60. Hastian—Discovery Loop
LOWER FRANKLIN CANYON PARK
CROSS MOUNTAIN PARK SYSTEM

Hiking distance: 3-mile loop
Hiking time: 1.5 hours
Configuration: loop
Elevation gain: 400 feet
Difficulty: easy
Exposure: exposed slopes and shaded canyon
Dogs: allowed
Maps: U.S.G.S. Beverly Hills · Franklin Canyon Park Nature Trails map

The Hastian—Discovery Loop in Lower Franklin Canyon Park winds through the 105-acre Franklin Canyon Ranch site. The ranch is nestled in a deep valley in the mountains above Beverly Hills. These two trails form a loop through the canyon bottom woodlands to the chaparral-covered slopes. The Hastian Trail climbs the east wall of Franklin Canyon on a fire road to spectacular vistas of the lower canyon, Franklin Canyon Reservoir, West Los Angeles, and the Pacific Ocean. The Discovery Trail follows the canyon floor through groves of sycamore, oak, and black walnut trees.

To the trailhead

From Sunset Boulevard in Beverly Hills, head north on Beverly Drive for 0.6 miles. At the fork, go left on Beverly Drive, where the main road continues as Coldwater Canyon Drive. Continue 0.8 miles and curve right onto Franklin Canyon Drive. Drive 1.1 mile to Lake Drive. Turn right and drive 0.3 miles to the posted trailhead parking area on the left.

From the Ventura Freeway/Highway 101 in Studio City, exit on Coldwater Canyon Drive. Head 2.5 miles south to the intersection with Mulholland Drive by the Coldwater Canyon Park/ TreePeople Park. Make a 90-degree right turn onto Franklin Canyon Drive. Continue 1.4 miles to Lake Drive. Curve left onto Lake Drive, and go 0.3 miles to the posted trailhead parking area on the left.

The hike

Take the posted Hastian Trail (a fire road) past the trail gate. Traverse the hillside high above Lake Drive. The easy uphill grade climbs the east canyon wall. The trail curves left and makes a wide sweeping loop around a side canyon, steadily gaining elevation to an overlook of Lower Franklin Canyon, Santa Monica, Westwood, and the ocean. The main trail curves left and continues up to the ridge, leaving Franklin Canyon and the park. Take the narrow footpath on the right by the wood pole and wind down the hill. The serpentine path exits the hillside at 2.3 miles on a broad grassy lawn by the old Doheny ranch house, a Spanish-style stucco house built in 1935. Cross Lake Road to the Discovery Trail. Curve right and head north, parallel to the park road along the lower west canyon slope. The forested trail joins Lake Drive 50 yards south of the trailhead. Return to the left. ■

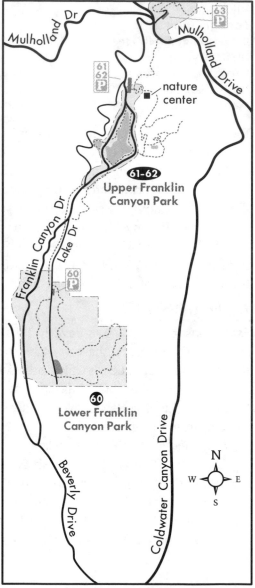

Upper and Lower Franklin Canyon Parks

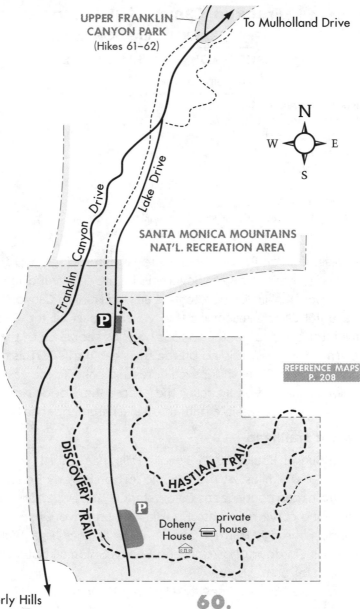

UPPER FRANKLIN
CANYON PARK
(Hikes 61–62)

To Mulholland Drive

N
W E
S

Franklin Canyon Drive

Lake Drive

SANTA MONICA MOUNTAINS
NAT'L. RECREATION AREA

P

REFERENCE MAPS
P. 208

DISCOVERY TRAIL

HASTIAN TRAIL

P

Doheny
House

private
house

To Beverly Hills

60.
Hastian Discovery Loop
LOWER FRANKLIN CANYON PARK
CROSS MOUNTAIN PARK SYSTEM

61. Franklin Canyon Lake Loop

UPPER FRANKLIN CANYON PARK

CROSS MOUNTAIN PARK SYSTEM

1500 Franklin Canyon Drive · Beverly Hills

Hiking distance: 1-mile loop
Hiking time: 30 minutes
Configuration: loop
Elevation gain: 30 feet
Difficulty: very easy
Exposure: exposed hills and shaded canyon
Dogs: allowed
Maps: U.S.G.S. Beverly Hills · N.P.S. Franklin Canyon Site
Franklin Canyon Park Nature Trails map

Franklin Canyon Park is a 605-acre wildlife refuge and tranquil retreat just minutes from Beverly Hills. The pastoral open space of Upper Franklin Canyon centers around Franklin Canyon Lake, a beautiful, 9-acre manmade lake which is part of the California migratory bird route. The famous opening sequence of the *Andy Griffith Show* was filmed on the trail near the lake. This hike circles the serene lake under sycamores and oaks. To the east of the lake is Heavenly Pond. Circling the pond is the Wodoc Nature Trail, a wheelchair-accessible path through a natural riparian habitat.

To the trailhead

From Sunset Boulevard in Beverly Hills, head north on Beverly Drive for 0.6 miles. At the fork, go left on Beverly Drive, where the main road continues as Coldwater Canyon Drive. Continue 0.8 miles and curve right onto Franklin Canyon Drive. Drive 1.8 miles, winding through Franklin Canyon Park, to the large William O. Douglas Outdoor Classroom and Sooky Goldman Nature Center parking lot on the right.

From the Ventura Freeway/Highway 101 in Studio City, exit on Coldwater Canyon Drive. Head 2.5 miles south to the intersection with Mulholland Drive by the Coldwater Canyon Park/TreePeople Park. Make a 90-degree right turn onto Franklin Canyon Drive. Continue 0.7 miles to the William O. Douglas Outdoor Classroom and Sooky Goldman Nature Center parking lot on the left.

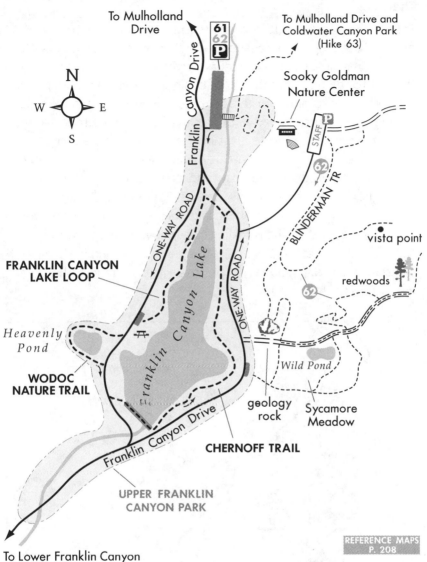

To Mulholland Drive

To Mulholland Drive and Coldwater Canyon Park (Hike 63)

61 62 P

Franklin Canyon Drive

Sooky Goldman Nature Center

P STAFF

N
W E
S

BLINDERMAN TR

62

vista point

redwoods

ONE-WAY ROAD

FRANKLIN CANYON LAKE LOOP

Franklin Canyon Lake

ONE-WAY ROAD

62

Heavenly Pond

WODOC NATURE TRAIL

Wild Pond

geology rock

Sycamore Meadow

Franklin Canyon Drive

CHERNOFF TRAIL

UPPER FRANKLIN CANYON PARK

To Lower Franklin Canyon and Beverly Hills

REFERENCE MAPS P. 208

61.
Franklin Canyon Lake Loop
UPPER FRANKLIN CANYON PARK
CROSS MOUNTAIN PARK SYSTEM

The hike

Follow the park road to the left (south) for 30 yards to a road on the right by the maintenance shop. To hike counter-clockwise around Franklin Canyon Lake, curve right and descend steps on the left to the trail. Pass the surge basin to a trail split. Both paths parallel the lake and merge at a picnic area by the park road. (The left fork skirts the edge of the lake.) Follow the road to the left 50 yards to the Wodoc Nature Trail at Heavenly Pond. Loop around the serene pond on the paved path. Back at the road, continue south above the lake, and cross the dam at the end of the lake. After crossing, descend steps on the Chernoff Trail, and follow the east banks of the lake through a shady woodland and a picnic area. At the Franklin Lake spillway, curve right to the road, and bear left 100 yards, returning to the parking area. (If the spillway is dry, you may cross over it to complete the loop and return to the right.) ▪

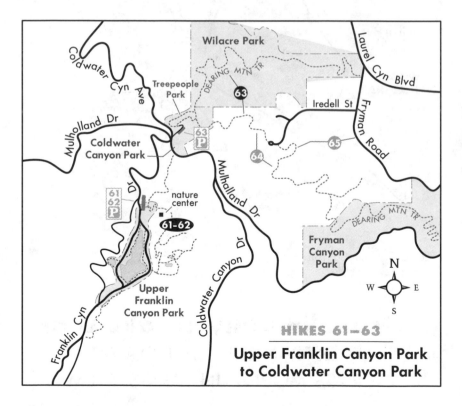

HIKES 61–63

**Upper Franklin Canyon Park
to Coldwater Canyon Park**

62. Blinderman Trail

UPPER FRANKLIN CANYON PARK

CROSS MOUNTAIN PARK SYSTEM

1500 Franklin Canyon Drive · Beverly Hills

Hiking distance: 1.5-mile loop
Hiking time: 45 minutes
Configuration: loop with spur trail to overlook
Elevation gain: 200 feet
Difficulty: easy
Exposure: exposed hills and shaded canyon
Dogs: allowed
Maps: U.S.G.S. Beverly Hills and Van Nuys · N.P.S. Franklin Canyon Site
Franklin Canyon Park Nature Trails map

Upper Franklin Canyon Park is home to the Sooky Goldman Nature Center and the William O. Douglas Outdoor Classroom, providing educational programs to the public and local schools. The Blinderman Trail is adjacent to the nature center. The path traverses the canyon slopes through chaparral, strolls along stream-fed side canyons with meadows, and climbs to overlooks of Franklin Canyon Lake and the entire canyon oasis.

To the trailhead

From Sunset Boulevard in Beverly Hills, head north on Beverly Drive for 0.6 miles. At the fork, go left on Beverly Drive, where the main road continues as Coldwater Canyon Drive. Continue 0.8 miles and curve right onto Franklin Canyon Drive. Drive 1.8 miles, winding through Franklin Canyon Park, to the large William O. Douglas Outdoor Classroom and Sooky Goldman Nature Center parking lot on the right.

From the Ventura Freeway/Highway 101 in Studio City, exit on Coldwater Canyon Drive. Head 2.5 miles south to the intersection with Mulholland Drive by the Coldwater Canyon Park/TreePeople Park. Make a 90-degree right turn onto Franklin Canyon Drive. Continue 0.7 miles to the William O. Douglas Outdoor Classroom and Sooky Goldman Nature Center parking lot on the left.

The hike

Cross the wooden bridge to the information board. The left fork is a northbound connector trail to Coldwater Canyon Park (Hikes 63 and 64). Bear right and wind up the hill to the Sooky Goldman Nature Center. Walk through the courtyard to the back (east) side of the buildings and the posted Blinderman Trail. Twenty yards up the footpath is a trail fork. The left fork leads through walnut groves to a maintenance road. Head right and traverse the hillside, curving left to a trail split. Take the left fork and climb up the hillside to an overlook of Franklin Lake. Continue uphill to the ridge, with views down the entire length of Franklin Canyon. The ridge path leads to additional observation points.

Return to the main trail, and continue on the south fork to the canyon floor by "geology rock." Bear left on the dirt road, passing Wild Pond on the right to a 4-way junction. (En route, a short side path loops around the pond to Sycamore Meadow.) Bear left and climb steps up the hillside. The undulating path crosses a wooden bridge and returns to the canyon floor at a T-junction. The left fork leads 100 yards to a large grassy flat with towering redwoods at the park boundary. The right fork returns to the 4-way junction. Take the left fork and climb the hill through a eucalyptus grove. Curve right to the park road by Franklin Canyon Lake. Follow the one-way road to the right, returning to the trailhead parking lot. ■

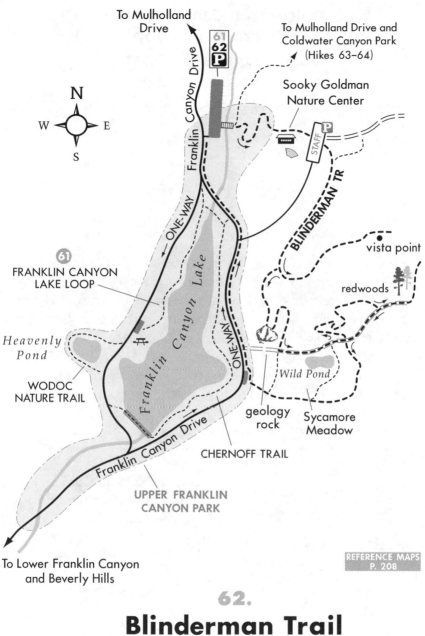

To Mulholland
Drive

To Mulholland Drive and
Coldwater Canyon Park
(Hikes 63–64)

61
62 P

Sooky Goldman
Nature Center

N
W E
S

STAFF P

Franklin Canyon Drive

ONE-WAY

BLINDERMAN TR

vista point

61

FRANKLIN CANYON
LAKE LOOP

Franklin Canyon Lake

redwoods

*Heavenly
Pond*

ONE-WAY

WODOC
NATURE TRAIL

Wild Pond

geology
rock

Sycamore
Meadow

Franklin Canyon Drive

CHERNOFF TRAIL

UPPER FRANKLIN
CANYON PARK

REFERENCE MAPS
P. 208

To Lower Franklin Canyon
and Beverly Hills

62.

Blinderman Trail
UPPER FRANKLIN CANYON PARK
CROSS MOUNTAIN PARK SYSTEM

63. Coldwater Canyon Park— Wilacre Park Loop

CROSS MOUNTAIN PARK SYSTEM

12601 Mulholland Drive · Beverly Hills

Hiking distance: 2.7-mile loop
Hiking time: 1.5 hours
Configuration: loop (partially on residential streets)
Elevation gain: 500 feet
Difficulty: easy
Exposure: exposed slopes and shaded canyon
Dogs: allowed
Maps: U.S.G.S. Van Nuys
Trails Illustrated Santa Monica Mountains Nat'l Rec Area

Coldwater Canyon Park (44 acres) is home to TreePeople Park, a non-profit educational facility known for planting more than a million trees. TreePeople, which maintains and improves Coldwater Canyon Park, includes a tree nursery, fruit orchard, organic garden, and the Magic Forest Nature Trail. The adjacent Wilacre Park is formerly the estate of silent film star Will Acres. The 128–acre greenbelt in Studio City contains chaparral-covered ridges and wooded canyons surrounded by residential homes. This loop hike crosses Coldwater Canyon Park and Wilacre Park, offering panoramic views of the San Fernando Valley.

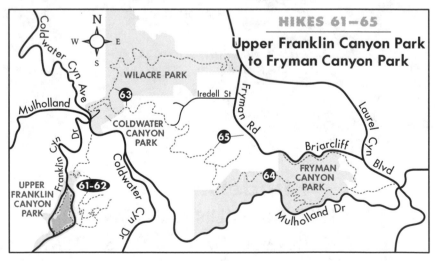

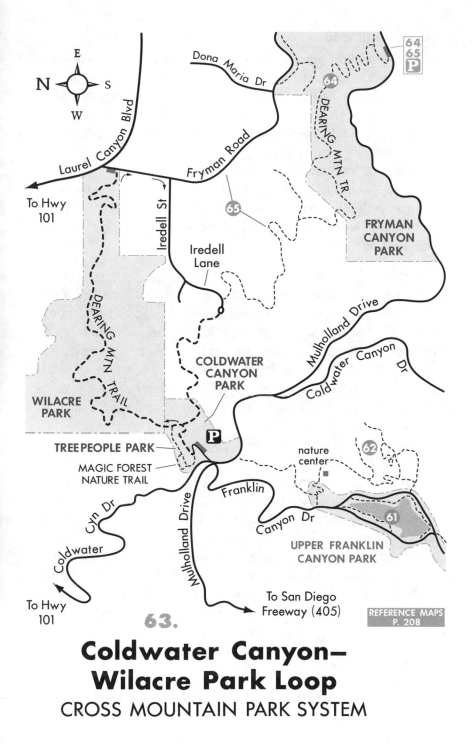

N E S W

Dona Maria Dr

Laurel Canyon Blvd

Fryman Road

To Hwy 101

Iredell St

Iredell Lane

64 65 P

64

DEARING MTN TR

65

FRYMAN CANYON PARK

DEARING MTN TRAIL

Mulholland Drive

Coldwater Canyon Dr

WILACRE PARK

COLDWATER CANYON PARK

P

TREEPEOPLE PARK

MAGIC FOREST NATURE TRAIL

Coldwater Cyn Dr

Coldwater

To Hwy 101

Mulholland Drive

Franklin Canyon Dr

nature center

62

61

UPPER FRANKLIN CANYON PARK

To San Diego Freeway (405)

63.

REFERENCE MAPS P. 208

Coldwater Canyon– Wilacre Park Loop
CROSS MOUNTAIN PARK SYSTEM

To the trailhead

From Sunset Boulevard in Beverly Hills, head north on Beverly Drive for 0.6 miles. At the fork, go right onto Coldwater Canyon Drive. Continue 3 miles to an intersection with Mulholland Drive. Go to the left, staying on Coldwater Canyon Drive, and drive 0.4 miles to the posted Coldwater Canyon/TreePeople Park on the right. Turn right into the parking area.

From the Ventura Freeway/Highway 101 in Studio City, exit on Coldwater Canyon Drive. Head 2.5 miles south to the intersection with Mulholland Drive. The posted Coldwater Canyon/TreePeople Park entrance is on the left (east) side of the intersection.

The hike

From the information kiosk at the far end of the parking area, bear left on the nature trail, and head 30 yards to a junction. Cut back sharply to the right, and follow the wide path on an easy downhill grade to the second hillside level. Switchback to the left and descend to the third level and a junction with the Dearing Mountain Trail. Begin the loop to the left, gaining elevation while crossing the head of Iredell Canyon. Cross a small saddle and curve around the hillside to sweeping bird's-eye views of the valley. Continue on a slow but steady descent with wide curves. Along the way, the trail becomes a narrow, paved path, winding through cypress and pine tree groves. The trail ends at the Wilacre Park trailhead on Fryman Road at 1.5 miles. For a loop hike, follow Fryman Road 0.15 miles to the right to Iredell Street. Bear right and walk a half mile through a residential area, curving left onto Iredell Lane to the cul-de-sac at the end of the street. (The trail to Fryman Canyon—Hike 64—is to the left, shortly before the cul-de-sac.) Pick up the posted Dearing Mountain Trail, and ascend the hillside along the open space boundary. Make a wide right curve, completing the loop. Return to the left and stroll through the Magic Forest Nature Trail. ■

64. Dearing Mountain Trail
Fryman Canyon Park to TreePeople Park
CROSS MOUNTAIN PARK SYSTEM

Hiking distance: 5 miles round trip
Hiking time: 2.5 hours
Configuration: out-and-back or loop on residential streets
Elevation gain: 500 feet
Difficulty: moderate
Exposure: exposed slopes and shaded canyon
Dogs: allowed
Maps: U.S.G.S. Beverly Hills and Van Nuys
Trails Illustrated Santa Monica Mountains Nat'l Rec Area

Fryman Canyon Park, which encompasses more than 120 acres, sits on a north-facing hillside bordering Mulholland Drive. At the trailhead, the Nancy Hoover Pohl Overlook (formerly known as the Fryman Canyon Overlook) provides views across the wooded canyon to the San Fernando Valley, Santa Susana Mountains, and the San Gabriel Mountains. This hike on the Dearing Mountain Trail descends into the canyon from the overlook, connecting Fryman Canyon Park with Coldwater Canyon Park and Wilacre Park.

To the trailhead

From Sunset Boulevard in Beverly Hills, head north on Beverly Drive for 0.6 miles. At the fork, go right onto Coldwater Canyon Drive. Continue 3 miles to an intersection with Mulholland Drive. Turn right on Mulholland Drive, and go 2 miles to the posted Fryman Canyon Park entrance on the left. Turn left into the parking lot.

From the Ventura Freeway/Highway 101 in Studio City, exit on Laurel Canyon Boulevard. Head 2.8 miles south to the intersection with Mulholland Drive. Turn right on Mulholland Drive, and drive 0.8 miles to the posted Fryman Canyon Park entrance on the right.

The hike

To the left of the trailhead, steps lead up to the Pohl (Fryman Canyon) Overlook. The posted Dearing Mountain Trail descends to a junction a short distance ahead (also known as the Betty B. Dearing Trail). Bear left and zigzag down seven switchbacks into Fryman Canyon. Follow the contours of the hillside, and make a horseshoe right bend across a spring-fed drainage. Pass remnants of a few old cars, and continue on the canyon wall to a T-junction. Take the left fork and stroll through a mature grove of oak and eucalyptus trees. Cross a stream in a ravine and bear left. Cross another drainage by a huge sandstone outcrop, and pass an overlook of a few showcase homes. Curve right on a footpath and traverse the sloping hillside. Descend steps and emerge on Iredell Lane at 2 miles. Bear left for 0.1 mile to the cul-de-sac. Pick up the posted Dearing Mountain Trail, and ascend the hillside for a half mile to a junction. Bear left and stroll through the Magic Forest Nature Trail, or ascend the steps to the park headquarters and an educational facility at TreePeople Park.

To return to the trailhead, there are three hiking options. Return along the same route for the shortest option. Continue with Hike 63 for a loop through Wilacre Park. Or, loop back through residential areas utilizing Iredell Street and Fryman Road—reference Hike 65. ■

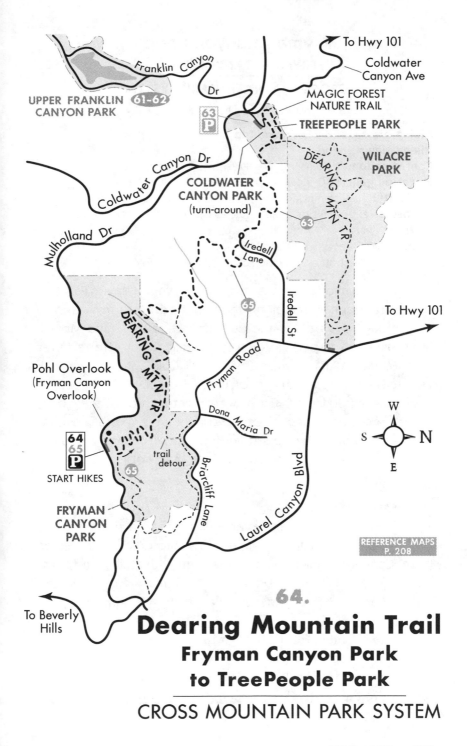

Franklin Canyon

UPPER FRANKLIN
CANYON PARK 61-62

To Hwy 101
Coldwater
Canyon Ave

Dr

MAGIC FOREST
NATURE TRAIL

63
P

TREEPEOPLE PARK

Coldwater Canyon Dr

DEARING MTN TR

WILACRE
PARK

COLDWATER
CANYON PARK
(turn-around)

Mulholland Dr

Iredell
Lane

63

Iredell St

65

To Hwy 101

DEARING MTN TR

Pohl Overlook
(Fryman Canyon
Overlook)

Fryman Road

64
65
P

Dona Maria Dr

trail
detour

START HIKES

65

Briarcliff Lane

Laurel Canyon Blvd

W
S ⊕ N
E

FRYMAN
CANYON
PARK

REFERENCE MAPS
P. 208

To Beverly
Hills

64.
Dearing Mountain Trail
Fryman Canyon Park
to TreePeople Park

CROSS MOUNTAIN PARK SYSTEM

65. Fryman Canyon Loop

FRYMAN CANYON PARK

CROSS MOUNTAIN PARK SYSTEM

8401 Mulholland Drive · Studio City

Hiking distance: 4 miles round trip
Hiking time: 2 hours
Configuration: loop (partially on residential streets)
Elevation gain: 500 feet
Difficulty: easy to moderate
Exposure: exposed slopes and shaded canyon
Dogs: allowed
Maps: U.S.G.S. Beverly Hills and Van Nuys
   Trails Illustrated Santa Monica Mountains Nat'l Rec Area

The Fryman Canyon Loop passes through Fryman Canyon Park and a quiet residential area along the park border, forming a loop hike through this park at the eastern end of the Santa Monica Mountains. Several parks in this area are collectively referred to as Cross Mountain Park: Fryman Canyon Park, Coldwater Canyon Park, Wilacre Park, and Franklin Canyon Park. (Hikes 60—65 are located within these parklands.) The mountain paths through the 1,000-acre park system cross ridges, wind through chaparral-covered hillsides, and meander up stream-fed canyons. All of the parks are connected with hiking paths, offering many opportunities for extended hiking.

To the trailhead

From Sunset Boulevard in Beverly Hills, head north on Beverly Drive for 0.6 miles. At the fork, go right onto Coldwater Canyon Drive. Continue 3 miles to an intersection with Mulholland Drive. Turn right on Mulholland Drive, and go 2 miles to the posted Fryman Canyon Park entrance on the left. Turn left into the parking lot.

From the Ventura Freeway/Highway 101 in Studio City, exit on Laurel Canyon Boulevard. Head 2.8 miles south to the intersection with Mulholland Drive. Turn right on Mulholland Drive, and drive 0.8 miles to the posted Fryman Canyon Park entrance on the right.

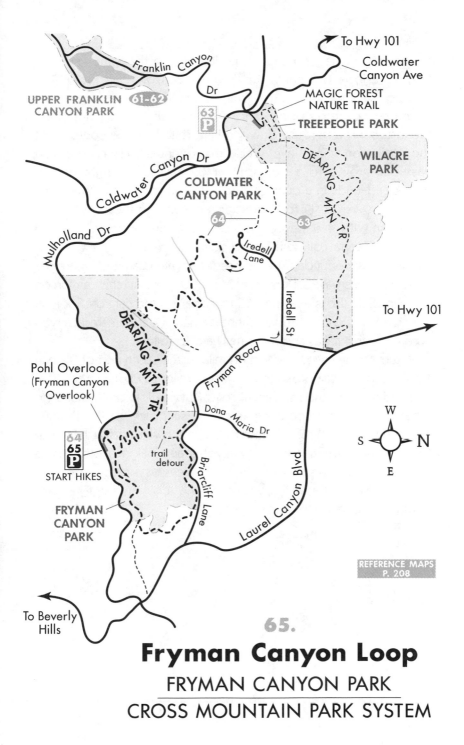

Fryman Canyon Loop
FRYMAN CANYON PARK
CROSS MOUNTAIN PARK SYSTEM

To Hwy 101
Coldwater Canyon Ave

Franklin Canyon

UPPER FRANKLIN CANYON PARK 61-62

Dr

63 P

MAGIC FOREST NATURE TRAIL
TREEPEOPLE PARK

WILACRE PARK

DEARING MTN TR

Coldwater Canyon Dr

COLDWATER CANYON PARK

64

63

Mulholland Dr

Iredell Lane

Iredell St

To Hwy 101

DEARING MTN TR

Pohl Overlook
(Fryman Canyon Overlook)

Fryman Road

Dona Maria Dr

64
65 P
START HIKES

trail detour

Briarcliff Lane

Laurel Canyon Blvd

W
S — N
E

FRYMAN CANYON PARK

REFERENCE MAPS
P. 208

To Beverly Hills

65.

The hike

To the left of the trailhead, steps lead up to the Nancy Hoover Pohl Overlook (formerly the Fryman Canyon Overlook). The posted Dearing Mountain Trail gradually descends on the chaparral-covered slope. A short distance ahead is a junction on the left, our return route. Stay straight, following the contours of the hillside on a near-level grade that overlooks Fryman Canyon. Pass oak groves to a trail split at 0.4 miles. The right (upper trail) dead-ends in a quarter mile near Laurel Canyon Boulevard. Take the lower (left) fork, dropping down into the canyon to a T-junction with an unpaved road behind a row of homes fronted on Briarcliff Lane. Follow the road downhill to the left for 0.3 miles along the park boundary to the base of Fryman Canyon, where the road becomes paved. Detour left for 100 yards up the canyon on the footpath. Cross a ravine and meander up the canyon floor on the tree-shaded path. Curving right is a narrow, stream-fed canyon where the trail fades and becomes hard to follow.

Return to the road. Bear left 0.1 mile to the south end of Fryman Road. Follow Fryman Road to the left 0.4 miles to Iredell Street. Bear left and walk up the residential road, curving left on Iredell Lane. One hundred yards before the cul-de-sac, pick up the Dearing Mountain Trail on the left. Climb the steps and wind through Fryman Canyon under the shade of eucalyptus and oak groves. Cross a spring-fed drainage, and steadily climb seven switchbacks to the head of Fryman Canyon, completing the loop at the T-junction. Return to the trailhead on the right. ■

66. Dixie Canyon Park

South end of Dixie Canyon Place · Sherman Oaks

Hiking distance: 0.7-mile loop
Hiking time: 30 minutes
Configuration: loop
Elevation gain: 300 feet
Difficulty: very easy
Exposure: shaded canyon
Dogs: allowed
Maps: U.S.G.S. Van Nuys
　　　　 Santa Monica Mountains Recreational Topo Map

Dixie Canyon Park is a small, 20-acre, heavily wooded canyon overlooking the San Fernando Valley in Sherman Oaks. The open space was donated to the Santa Monica Mountains Conservancy by actor/director Warren Beatty in 1986. Tucked into the north slope of the Santa Monica Mountains, the shaded canyon is rich with California black walnut and coast live oak, with an understory of mushrooms, ferns, fungus, and poison oak. A perennial stream flows through the heart of the parkland. A short hiking-only loop trail winds through the canyon along both sides of the stream.

To the trailhead

From the Ventura Freeway/Highway 101 in Sherman Oaks, exit on Woodman Avenue. Drive a half mile south to Ventura Boulevard. Turn left and continue 0.4 miles to Dixie Canyon Avenue. Turn right and go 0.7 miles south to Dixie Canyon Place. Veer left on Dixie Canyon Place and go 0.2 miles up the narrow road to the signed trailhead at the end of the cul-de-sac. Park along the side of the road.

The hike

Walk to the end of the cul-de-sac, and pass the trailhead sign. Climb the concrete steps and cross to the east side of the stream. Follow the lush, narrow canyon upstream. Recross the drainage on the second bridge. At the third crossing is a bridge and a junction. Begin the loop on the right fork and head up the hillside. Traverse the west canyon wall on the serpentine path. At 0.3 miles, cross the waterway and loop back on the east side of the canyon. Weave down the hillside with the aid of four switchbacks, completing the loop at the third bridge. ■

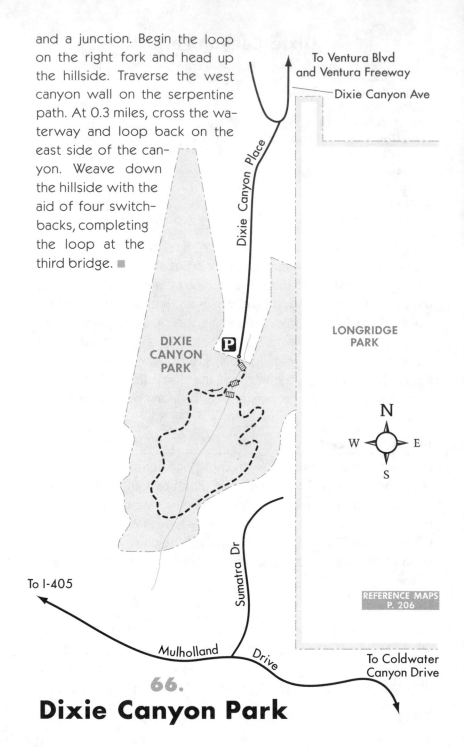

To Ventura Blvd and Ventura Freeway

Dixie Canyon Ave

Dixie Canyon Place

DIXIE CANYON PARK

P

LONGRIDGE PARK

N
W E
S

To I-405

Sumatra Dr

REFERENCE MAPS
P. 206

Mulholland Drive

To Coldwater Canyon Drive

66.
Dixie Canyon Park

67. Getty View Trail

SEPULVEDA PASS OPEN SPACE

405 Freeway · Bel Air

Hiking distance: 3.6 miles round trip
Hiking time: 2 hours
Configuration: out-and-back
Elevation gain: 600 feet
Difficulty: easy to moderate
Exposure: exposed slopes and ridge
Dogs: allowed
Maps: U.S.G.S. Beverly Hills
       Santa Monica Mountains Conservancy map

The Getty View Trail in Bel Air ascends the steep hillside from Sepulveda Pass to Sepulveda Fire Road, an unpaved road on the ridgeline. A three-quarter mile trail climbs through chaparral and pockets of live oak and toyon, providing access to a section of the 376-acre Sepulveda Pass Open Space. The ridge-top trail overlooks Hoag Canyon, with sweeping vistas of the Getty Center Museum, West Los Angeles, Santa Monica, and the Pacific Ocean.

To the trailhead

Heading northbound from Los Angeles on the San Diego Freeway/Interstate 405, take the Getty Center Drive exit. Turn left (north) 0.1 mile to the trailhead parking lot on the right, just before crossing under the freeway.

Heading southbound from the San Fernando Valley on the San Diego Freeway/Interstate 405, take the Getty Center Drive exit. Turn left (south) and cross under the freeway to the trailhead parking lot, immediately on the left.

The hike

From the trailhead map, bear left (north) on the signed trail, and head up the side canyon past sycamore trees. Switchbacks lead up the chaparral-covered hillside east of Sepulveda Pass. The views improve with every step. Switchbacks make the eleva-tion gain easier. At 0.6 miles, the trail reaches the ridge and a T-junction with the Sepulveda Fire Road.

Bear left on the ridge-hugging dirt road above the deep and undeveloped Hoag Canyon. A footpath parallels the road on the west, gaining elevation to an incredible overlook by an isolated oak tree. The footpath parallels the cliffs and rejoins the fire road.

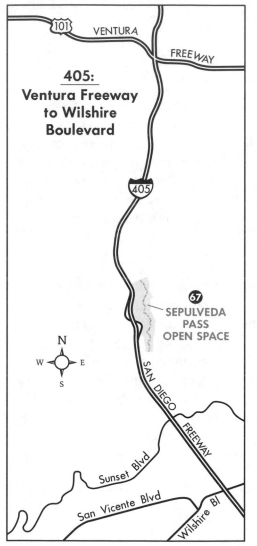

A short distance ahead, a second side path on the left parallels the road to additional overlooks before re-joining the road again. At 0.4 miles, the pave-ment begins at a gated residential area.

Return south, back to the Getty View Trail junction. Continue south on the fire road while descending along the ridge. An undulat-ing footpath parallels the east side of the road, overlooking Hoag Canyon. At 0.7 miles the fire road ends at Casiano Road in Bel Air Estates, where views open up across West Los Angeles. Return along the same route. ▪

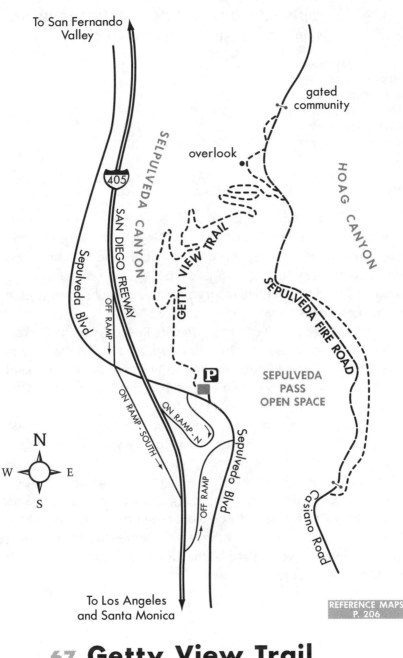

To San Fernando Valley

gated community

overlook

SELPULVEDA CANYON

SAN DIEGO FREEWAY

405

Sepulveda Blvd

OFF RAMP

HOAG CANYON

GETTY VIEW TRAIL

SEPULVEDA FIRE ROAD

ON RAMP - SOUTH

ON RAMP - N

P

SEPULVEDA PASS OPEN SPACE

Sepulveda Blvd

OFF RAMP

N
W E
S

Casiano Road

To Los Angeles and Santa Monica

REFERENCE MAPS P. 206

67. Getty View Trail
SEPULVEDA PASS OPEN SPACE

68. Sepulveda Basin Wildlife Reserve
SEPULVEDA BASIN RECREATION AREA

Hiking distance: 1.2-mile loop
Hiking time: 45 minutes
Configuration: loop
Elevation gain: level
Difficulty: easy
Exposure: exposed
Dogs: not allowed in the wildlife reserve
      (but allowed on all other trails in the recreation area)
Maps: U.S.G.S. Van Nuys · U.S. Army Corps of Engineers map

The Sepulveda Basin Recreation Area is a 2,097-acre flood control basin at the junction of the San Diego (405) Freeway and the Ventura (101) Freeway. The expansive parkland contains three golf courses, two parks, two lakes, ball fields, tennis courts, a Japanese garden, a wildlife reserve, and the only unpaved stretch of the Los Angeles River.

The 225-acre Sepulveda Basin Wildlife Reserve (within the recreation area) is an oasis for migratory waterfowl and shorebirds. The reserve is considered among the finest refuges of its kind within a major urban area in the United States. The restored natural habitat also serves as a living laboratory for wildlife. The lush habitat has oak savannah, sycamores, coastal live oaks, and valley oaks. A lake within the reserve is fed by year-round Haskell Creek, a tributary of the Los Angeles River. The lake contains an 11-acre island which serves as a nesting and resting ground for a variety of birds (including herons, egrets, pelicans, cormorants, and geese). Cottonwood trees were planted on the bird refuge island. A paved path with shaded and secluded wildlife-viewing areas follows the west edge of the lake, while a natural dirt path skirts the east side of the lake.

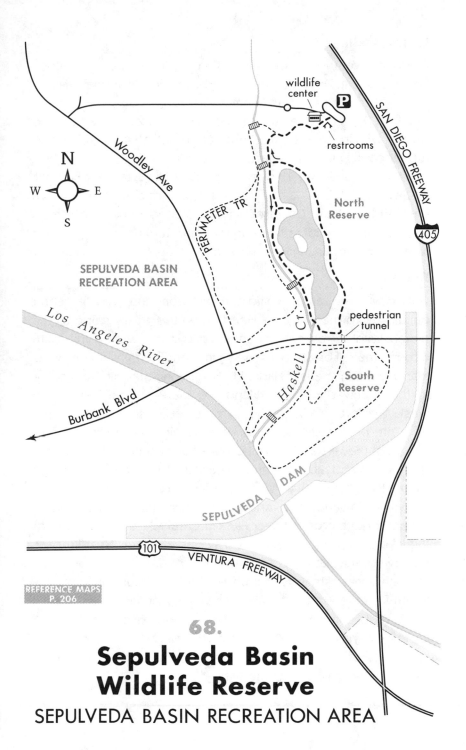

wildlife center

P

restrooms

SAN DIEGO FREEWAY

Woodley Ave

N
W E
S

PERIMETER TR

North Reserve

405

SEPULVEDA BASIN RECREATION AREA

Los Angeles River

Haskell Cr.

pedestrian tunnel

Burbank Blvd

South Reserve

SEPULVEDA DAM

SEPULVEDA

101

VENTURA FREEWAY

REFERENCE MAPS
P. 206

68.
Sepulveda Basin
Wildlife Reserve
SEPULVEDA BASIN RECREATION AREA

To the trailhead

From the Ventura Freeway (101) in Encino, take the Balboa Boulevard exit. Drive one block north to Burbank Boulevard and turn right (east). Continue 1.7 miles east to Woodley Avenue and turn left. Drive 0.7 miles to the second park access road (signed for the wildlife area) on the right. Turn right and go a half mile to the far parking lot on the left.

From the San Diego Freeway (405) in Van Nuys, take the Burbank Boulevard exit. Drive a half mile west to Woodley Avenue. Turn right and continue 0.7 miles to the second park access road (signed for the wildlife area) on the right. Turn right and go a half mile to the far parking lot on the left.

The hike

Walk down the ramp behind the restroom and wildlife center building onto the dirt path. Head down the grassy slope to the signed wildlife reserve entrance. Follow the wide path south through the tall brush to a 4-way junction. The right fork crosses a bridge over perennial Haskell Creek, linking the wildlife reserve to the Sepulveda Basin parkland and the Perimeter Trail to the west. The left fork leads 50 yards to a lakeside viewing area with interpretive signage. Stay on the main trail straight ahead— between the lake and Haskell Creek—to another trail on the left. This side path leads 75 yards to another lake overlook and a view of the bird refuge island. Continue along the west side of the lake to a series of overlooks and information panels, plus a second bridge crossing over Haskell Creek. At the south end of the lake is the outlet stream feeding Haskell Creek. Near Burbank Boulevard, the path veers left to a junction. The right fork goes through a pedestrian tunnel under Burbank Boulevard into the South Reserve. (In the South Reserve, the path follows Haskell Creek to its confluence with the Los Angeles River.) For this hike, go left, staying in the North Reserve. Follow the undeveloped east edge of the lake, completing the loop at the first bridge. Return to the trailhead on the right. ▪

69. Lake Balboa

ANTHONY C. BEILENSON PARK

SEPULVEDA BASIN RECREATION AREA

6300 Balboa Boulevard, Encino

Hiking distance: 1.3-mile loop
Hiking time: 45 minutes
Configuration: loop
Elevation gain: level
Difficulty: very easy
Exposure: exposed
Dogs: allowed in park but not allowed to swim
Maps: U.S.G.S. Van Nuys

Anthony C. Beilenson Park (formerly Balboa Park) is an 80-acre park within the 2,097-acre Sepulveda Basin Recreation Area. The centerpiece of Beilenson Park is 27-acre Lake Balboa, an amoeba-shaped, manmade lake. The popular lake has a 1.3-mile walking path that circles the perimeter. The Lake Balboa Hiking Trail attracts walkers, joggers, bikers, dog owners, fishing enthusiasts, and birders. This is not a wilderness hike, but rather a scenic and pastoral urban respite.

To the trailhead

From the Ventura Freeway (101) in Encino, take the Balboa Boulevard exit. Drive 0.7 miles north on Balboa Boulevard to the signed Anthony Beilenson Park and Lake Balboa entrance on the right. Turn right into the park and go 0.4 miles to the parking lot on the left. Parking is also available along the road in dirt pullouts.

The hike

Walk to the shore of Lake Balboa and the Lake Balboa Hiking Trail. Follow the paved path to the right along the edge of the lake, walking counter-clockwise. Cross a bridge over the lake's outlet stream, and pass the boat dock and boat access ramp. Continue up the lake's east shore while marveling at the vast variety of birds. On the north shore, pass a beautiful manmade cascade. Curve south to views across the length of Lake Balboa. Complete the loop at the south end of the lake. ■

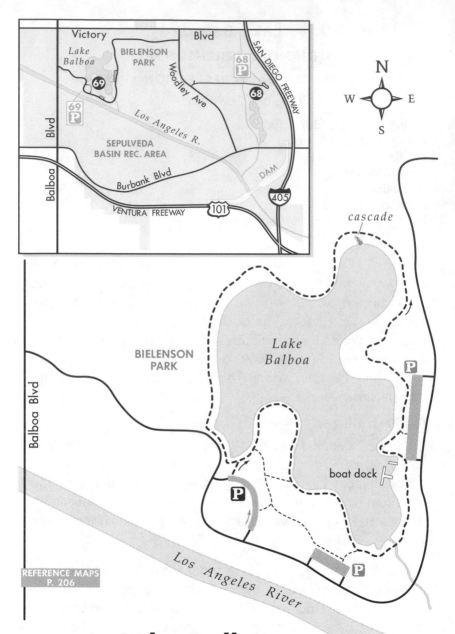

cascade

Lake
Balboa

BIELENSON
PARK

boat dock

REFERENCE MAPS
P. 206

Los Angeles River

Balboa Blvd

Map inset labels:

Victory   Blvd

Lake
Balboa

BIELENSON
PARK

Woodley Ave

SAN DIEGO FREEWAY

68 P

68

69 P

Blvd

Balboa

Los Angeles R.

SEPULVEDA
BASIN REC. AREA

Burbank Blvd

DAM

405

VENTURA FREEWAY   101

N
W   E
S

69. Lake Balboa

ANTHONY C. BEILENSON PARK
SEPULVEDA BASIN RECREATION AREA

70. San Vicente Mountain Park and Nike site

from Mulholland Scenic Overlook and Dirt Mulholland

17500 Mulholland Drive · Encino

Hiking distance: 2 miles round trip
Hiking time: 1 hour
Configuration: out-and-back
Elevation gain: 300 feet
Difficulty: easy
Exposure: exposed ridge
Dogs: allowed
Maps: U.S.G.S. Conoga Park · Topanga State Park map
　　　　Tom Harrison Maps: Topanga State Park Trail map

San Vicente Mountain Park was a former Nike Missile Control Site. From 1956 through 1968, this Cold War sentry post was utilized to guard Los Angeles from Soviet attacks. The site contained radar towers atop the 1,950-foot peak to neutralize Soviet planes. The radar would guide missiles launched from the Sepulveda Basin below to destroy any invading aircraft.

The 10-acre mountaintop park sits at the head of Mandeville Canyon nearly 2,000 feet above the city. It is now home to a self-guided interpretive center with information panels, a radar tower, guard shack, picnic areas, and a variety of overlooks. This hike begins at the Mulholland Scenic Overlook, then follows "Dirt" Mulholland, an unpaved portion of the famous ridge road, to San Vicente Mountain Park. The scenic parkway corridor, constructed in 1924, offers spectacular panoramic vistas across the San Fernando Valley and the Los Angeles Basin to the ocean.

San Vicente Mountain Park can also be accessed from the west via Dirt Mulholland and from the south via the Westridge Fire Road (Hike 72).

To the trailhead

Heading northbound from Los Angeles on the San Diego Freeway/ Interstate 405, exit on Mulholland Drive. Turn right and drive 0.3 miles to Mulholland Drive. Turn left and follow the scenic winding road 2 miles to the end of the paved road by Encino Hills Drive on the right. Curve left on Dirt Mulholland and park.

Heading southbound from the San Fernando Valley on the San Diego Freeway/Interstate 405, exit on Mulholland Drive. Turn left and drive 0.4 miles to Mulholland Drive. Turn left and follow the winding road 2 miles to the end of the paved road by Encino Hills Drive on the right. Curve left on Dirt Mulholland and park.

The hike

From the overlook of the San Fernando Valley, walk up unpaved Dirt Mulholland. Curve to the southern slope and a view towards Los Angeles, then return to the sweeping valley vistas that span to the San Gabriel Mountains and the Santa Susana Mountains. Continue on a gentle incline above the Encino Reservoir to a fork at the top of Mandeville Canyon at one mile. Dirt Mulholland continues straight ahead for one mile to Caballero Canyon and Tarzana Fire Road, 3.1 miles ahead (Hike 84).

For this hike, bear left into San Vicente Mountain Park, the former Cold War sentry post. At the 1,950-foot rim above Mandeville Canyon, stairs lead up to an overlook platform with expansive views. The 360-degree vistas stretch from the San Gabriel Mountains and Burbank, across the Los Angeles Basin to the sea, and across the San Fernando Valley from the Santa Susana Mountains to the Santa Monica Mountains. Explore the former helicopter platform and tower platform while savoring the views from the overlooks. Return by retracing your steps back along Dirt Mulholland. ■

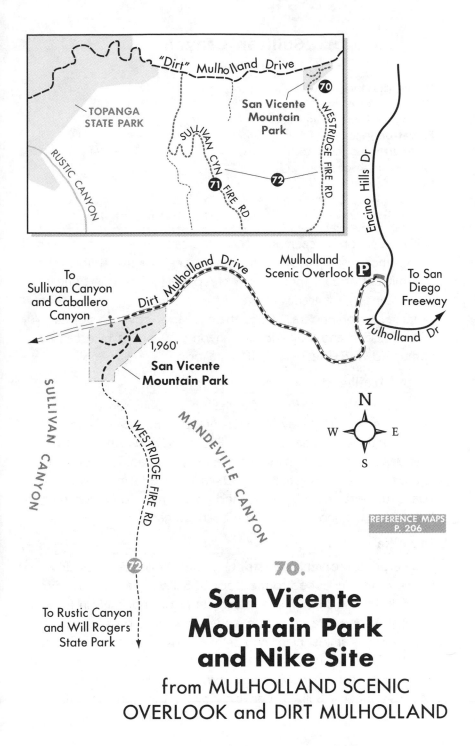

"Dirt" Mulholland Drive

TOPANGA
STATE PARK

RUSTIC CANYON

San Vicente
Mountain
Park

SULLIVAN CYN FIRE RD

WESTRIDGE FIRE RD

70

71

72

Mulholland Drive

To
Sullivan Canyon
and Caballero
Canyon

Dirt Mulholland Drive

Mulholland
Scenic Overlook

P

To San
Diego
Freeway

Mulholland Dr

1,960'

San Vicente
Mountain Park

SULLIVAN CANYON

WESTRIDGE FIRE RD

MANDEVILLE CANYON

Encino Hills Dr

N
W   E
S

REFERENCE MAPS
P. 206

72

To Rustic Canyon
and Will Rogers
State Park

70.
San Vicente Mountain Park and Nike Site
from MULHOLLAND SCENIC OVERLOOK and DIRT MULHOLLAND

71. Sullivan Canyon
Brentwood

Hiking distance: 8.6 miles round trip
Hiking time: 4 hours
Configuration: out-and-back
Elevation gain: 1,200 feet
Difficulty: moderate to strenuous
Exposure: shaded canyon
Dogs: allowed
Maps: U.S.G.S. Topanga · Topanga State Park map
Tom Harrison Maps: Topanga State Park Trail map

Sullivan Canyon is a secluded steam-fed canyon with huge stands of sycamore, oak, willow, and walnut trees. The trail follows the intermittent stream through the steep-walled canyon beneath a rich canopy of green foliage. After meandering up the long, pristine canyon, the trail climbs the chaparral-covered slopes to Sullivan Ridge and magnificent canyon views. This hike can be combined with Hike 72 for a 10-mile loop.

To the trailhead

From Santa Monica, drive 1.6 miles northbound on the Pacific Coast Highway/Highway 1 to Chautauqua Boulevard and turn right. Continue 0.9 miles to Sunset Boulevard and turn right. Drive 2.8 miles and turn left on Mandeville Canyon Road. Turn left again at the first street—Westridge Road—and drive 1.2 miles to Bayliss Road. Turn left on Bayliss Road, and go 0.3 miles to Queensferry Road. Turn left and park near the trailhead gate.

The hike

Step around the vehicle-restricting gate. Walk 0.2 miles down the paved service road to the floor of Sullivan Canyon. Head to the right up the serene, sylvan canyon floor under a lush forest canopy. At one mile, cross a seasonal stream and pass sandstone outcroppings amidst high and narrow canyon walls. At 3.5 miles, Sullivan Canyon curves right (northeast) while the trail curves left (northwest) up a narrow side canyon. Climb the west canyon wall overlooking Sullivan Canyon. Follow the contours of the

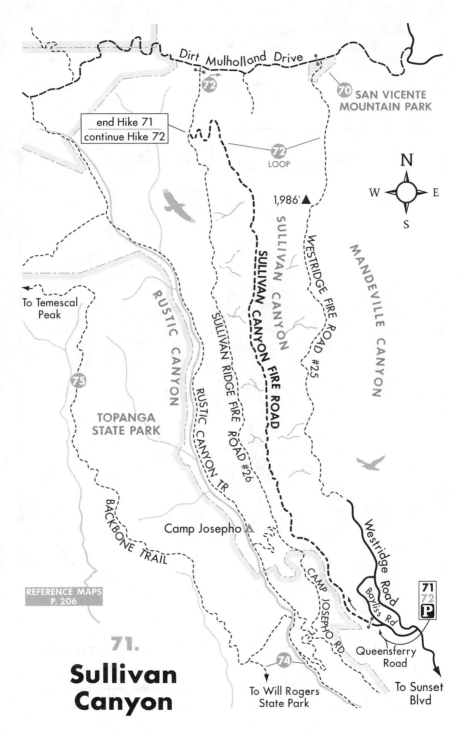

Dirt Mulholland Drive

72

70 SAN VICENTE
MOUNTAIN PARK

end Hike 71
continue Hike 72

72
LOOP

1,986' ▲

SULLIVAN CANYON

SULLIVAN CANYON FIRE ROAD

WESTRIDGE FIRE ROAD #25

MANDEVILLE CANYON

N
W E
S

To Temescal
Peak

RUSTIC CANYON

SULLIVAN RIDGE FIRE ROAD #26

RUSTIC CANYON TR

75

TOPANGA
STATE PARK

BACKBONE TRAIL

Camp Josepho ▲

REFERENCE MAPS
P. 206

CAMP JOSEPHO RD

Westridge Road

Bayliss Rd

71
72
P

Queensferry
Road

74

To Will Rogers
State Park

To Sunset
Blvd

71.

Sullivan
Canyon

mountain up to the ridge and a T-junction with the Sullivan Ridge Fire Road at 4.3 miles. This is the turn-around spot. Return back down Sullivan Canyon along the same route.

To hike a 10-mile loop, bear right (north) up to Dirt Mulholland, and continue with Hike 72. ■

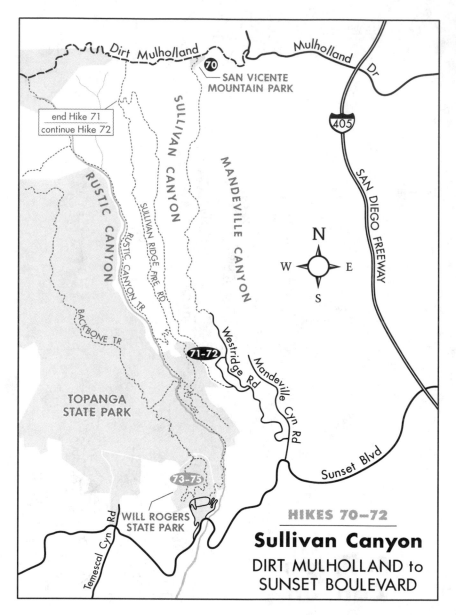

72. Sullivan Canyon—
Westridge Fire Road Loop
Brentwood

Hiking distance: 10-mile loop
Hiking time: 5 hours
Configuration: loop
Elevation gain: 1,300 feet
Difficulty: strenuous
Exposure: shaded canyon and exposed ridge
Dogs: allowed
Maps: U.S.G.S. Topanga and Conoga Park · Topanga State Park map
Tom Harrison Maps: Topanga State Park Trail map

This canyon-to-ridge loop hike follows the forested canyon floor of Sullivan Canyon, climbs the chaparral-covered slopes to Sullivan Ridge, then returns back on the ridge along the Westridge Fire Road. En route, the trail follows Dirt Mulholland Drive a short distance, an unimproved road along the ridge overlooking the west end of Los Angeles, the San Fernando Valley, and the Encino Reservoir. (Dirt Mulholland is the unpaved portion of Mulholland Drive.) At the top end of the loop is San Vicente Mountain Park, formerly a Nike Missile Control Site. The old military outpost was active from 1956 through 1968. The 10-acre park includes a self-guided interpretive center with descriptions of its former life (see Hike 70). From the park, the trail descends on the Westridge Fire Road, a hiking and biking route straddling the ridgeline between Sullivan Canyon and Mandeville Canyon.

To the trailhead

From Santa Monica, drive 1.6 miles northbound on the Pacific Coast Highway/Highway 1 to Chautauqua Boulevard and turn right. Continue 0.9 miles to Sunset Boulevard and turn right. Drive 2.8 miles and turn left on Mandeville Canyon Road. Turn left again at the first street—Westridge Road—and drive 1.2 miles to Bayliss Road. Turn left on Bayliss Road, and go 0.3 miles to Queensferry Road. Turn left and park near the trailhead gate.

The hike

Step around the vehicle-restricting gate. Walk 0.2 miles down the paved service road to the floor of Sullivan Canyon. Head to the right up the serene, sylvan canyon floor under a lush forest canopy. At one mile, cross a seasonal stream and pass sandstone outcroppings amidst high and narrow canyon walls. At 3.5 miles, Sullivan Canyon curves right (northeast) while the trail curves left (northwest) up a narrow side canyon. Climb the west canyon wall overlooking Sullivan Canyon. Follow the contours of the mountain up to the ridge and a T-junction with the Sullivan Ridge Fire Road, the turn-around point for Hike 71.

Bear right and head north on the ridge between Rustic Canyon and Sullivan Canyon, reaching Dirt Mulholland at a half mile. Walk around the gate and follow Dirt Mulholland to the right for 0.8 miles, overlooking the Encino Reservoir and the San Fernando Valley. Pass another gate and bear right into San Vicente Mountain Park, the defunct missile silo site. Walk up the paved road and through the park, passing picnic areas and vista overlooks. Take the Westridge Fire Road (also known as Sullivan Ridge East) along the narrow ridge that divides Sullivan and Mandeville Canyons. Follow the ridge south to the high point of the hike at 1,986 feet. Gradually descend along the contours of the ridge, overlooking Sullivan Canyon, Rustic Canyon, the west ridge of Temescal Canyon, and the Los Angeles basin. The fire road continues along the ridge until exiting at Westridge Road. Walk a half mile down Westridge Road, and turn right on Bayliss Road. Walk another half mile to Queensferry Road and turn right, returning to the trailhead. ▩

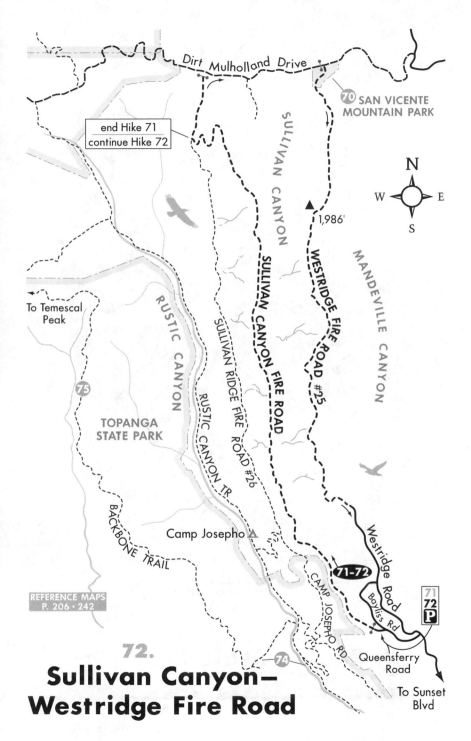

end Hike 71
continue Hike 72

Dirt Mulholland Drive

70 SAN VICENTE MOUNTAIN PARK

SULLIVAN CANYON

1,986'

N
W • E
S

MANDEVILLE CANYON

SULLIVAN CANYON FIRE ROAD

WESTRIDGE FIRE ROAD #25

To Temescal Peak

RUSTIC CANYON

SULLIVAN RIDGE FIRE ROAD #26

75

TOPANGA STATE PARK

RUSTIC CANYON TR

BACKBONE TRAIL

Camp Josepho △

REFERENCE MAPS P. 206 • 242

Westridge Road

71-72

Bayliss Rd

71 **72** **P**

CAMP JOSEPHO RD

74

Queensferry Road

To Sunset Blvd

72.
Sullivan Canyon— Westridge Fire Road

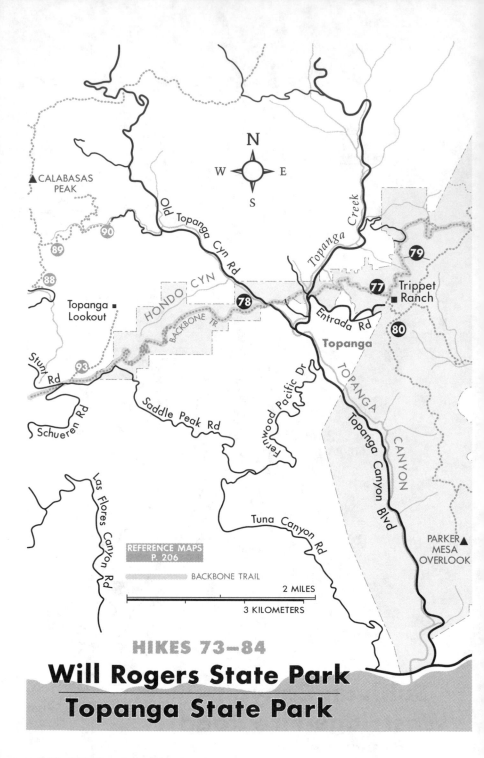

CALABASAS
PEAK

Old Topanga Cyn Rd

90

89

88

Topanga
Lookout

HONDO CYN

BACKBONE TR

93

Stunt Rd

Schueren Rd

Saddle Peak Rd

Las Flores Canyon Rd

Fernwood Pacific Dr

Tuna Canyon Rd

Topanga Creek

79

77 Trippet
Ranch

Entrada Rd

78

80

Topanga

TOPANGA CANYON

Topanga Canyon Blvd

PARKER
MESA
OVERLOOK

REFERENCE MAPS
P. 206

BACKBONE TRAIL

2 MILES
3 KILOMETERS

HIKES 73-84
Will Rogers State Park
Topanga State Park

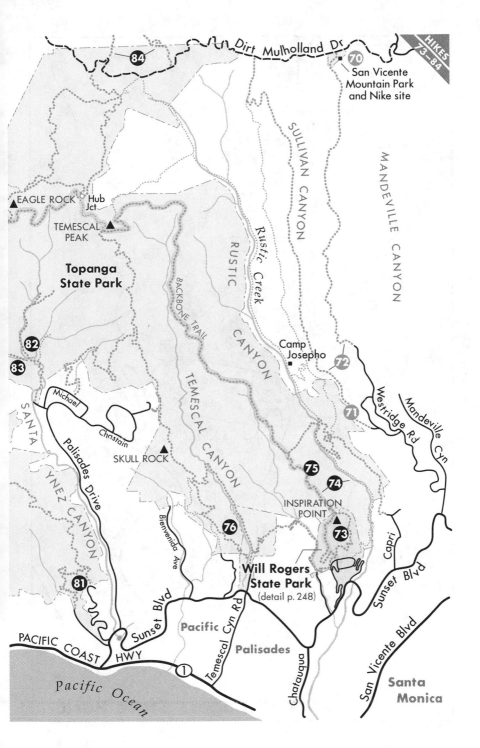

Dirt Mulholland Dr

San Vicente
Mountain Park
and Nike site

SULLIVAN CANYON

MANDEVILLE CANYON

EAGLE ROCK Hub Jct

TEMESCAL PEAK

Topanga State Park

RUSTIC CANYON

Rustic Creek

BACKBONE TRAIL

Camp Josepho

Michael

Chastain

TEMESCAL CANYON

SKULL ROCK

Westridge Rd

Mandeville Cyn

SANTA YNEZ CANYON

Palisades Drive

Bienvenida Ave

INSPIRATION POINT

Capri

Will Rogers State Park
(detail p. 248)

Sunset Blvd

Sunset Blvd

San Vicente Blvd

PACIFIC COAST HWY

Pacific Cyn Rd

Temescal Cyn Rd

Pacific
Palisades

Chatauqua

Santa Monica

1

Pacific Ocean

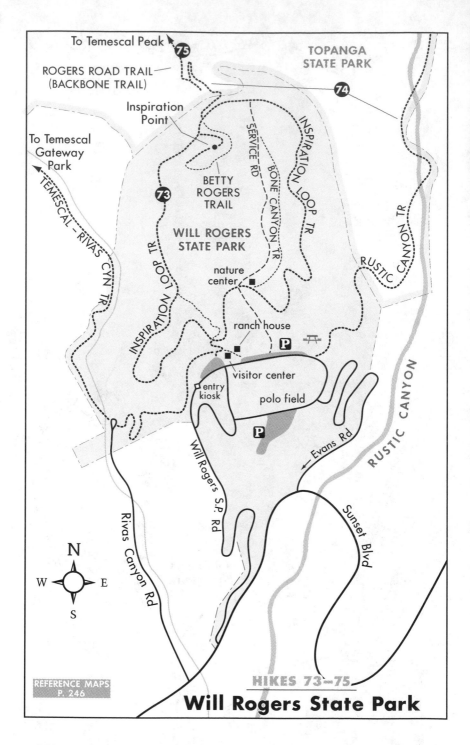

To Temescal Peak

ROGERS ROAD TRAIL
(BACKBONE TRAIL)

Inspiration
Point

To Temescal
Gateway
Park

TEMESCAL – RIVAS CYN TR

BETTY
ROGERS
TRAIL

WILL ROGERS
STATE PARK

INSPIRATION LOOP TR

SERVICE RD

BONE CANYON TR

INSPIRATION LOOP TR

TOPANGA
STATE PARK

RUSTIC
CANYON
TR

RUSTIC

nature
center

ranch house

visitor center

entry
kiosk

polo field

RUSTIC CANYON

Will Rogers S.P. Rd

Evans Rd

Rivas Canyon Rd

Sunset Blvd

N
W E
S

REFERENCE MAPS
P. 246

HIKES 73–75

Will Rogers State Park

73. Inspiration Loop Trail to Inspiration Point

WILL ROGERS STATE HISTORIC PARK

1501 Will Rogers State Park Road · Pacific Palisades
Open 8 a.m.—5 p.m. daily

Hiking distance: 2-mile loop
Hiking time: 1 hour
Configuration: loop
Elevation gain: 300 feet
Difficulty: easy
Exposure: exposed
Dogs: allowed
Maps: U.S.G.S. Topanga · Topanga State Park map
Tom Harrison Maps: Topanga State Park Trail Map

Will Rogers State Historic Park is a 186-acre retreat in the hills above Santa Monica. The land was set aside as a state park in 1944. Within the parkland are picnic grounds, horse riding stables, and trails with spectacular views. Tours of Will Rogers' 31-room ranch home are offered daily.

At the upper reaches of the park is Inspiration Point, a broad, flat knoll overlooking the beautiful park grounds and the rugged mountain canyons and ridges. The expansive views from the 751-foot overlook extend from downtown Los Angeles to Santa Monica and across Santa Monica Bay to Palos Verdes. Inspiration Point Loop Trail, designed by Rogers himself, is a two-mile trail that climbs the undeveloped hillside behind the ranch to Inspiration Point. The top of the loop connects with the eastern terminus of the Backbone Trail, which crosses the spine of the Santa Monica Mountains for 69 miles to Point Mugu State Park. For longer hiking options, take the Backbone Trail to Rustic Canyon (Hike 74) or Temescal Peak (Hike 75).

To the trailhead

From Santa Monica, drive 1.6 miles northbound on the Pacific Coast Highway/Highway 1 to Chautauqua Boulevard. Turn right and continue 0.9 miles to Sunset Boulevard. Turn right again. Drive 0.5 miles and turn left at Will Rogers State Park Road. The parking area is 0.7 miles ahead on the left, just past the entrance station. Another parking lot is a short distance farther, on the left by the visitor center. A parking fee is required.

The hike

Begin the hike from the visitor center and Will Rogers' home, built in 1928. Head west (left) past the tennis courts and the Temescal-Rivas Canyon Trail to a dirt fire road—the Inspiration Loop Trail. Head uphill on the gentle slope, with views across coastal Los Angeles to Palos Verdes and Catalina Island. Climb the ridge to the north above Rivas Canyon, with additional views across the mountainous backcountry, to a junction at 0.8 miles. The left fork begins the first segment of the Backbone Trail on the Rogers Road Trail (Hike 74). Detour 0.1 mile to the right to Inspiration Point, an overlook on a flat-topped knoll. After resting and savoring the views of the entire state park, Santa Monica Bay, and the greater Los Angeles area, return to the junction.

Take the fork that is now on your right (northeast). Pass the beginning of the Backbone Trail on the left by an information kiosk. Stay on the main trail and continue northeast. Descend to the south, overlooking the polo field at the base of the hill. Walk through a eucalyptus-lined lane, returning to the well-maintained park grounds and visitor center. ▪

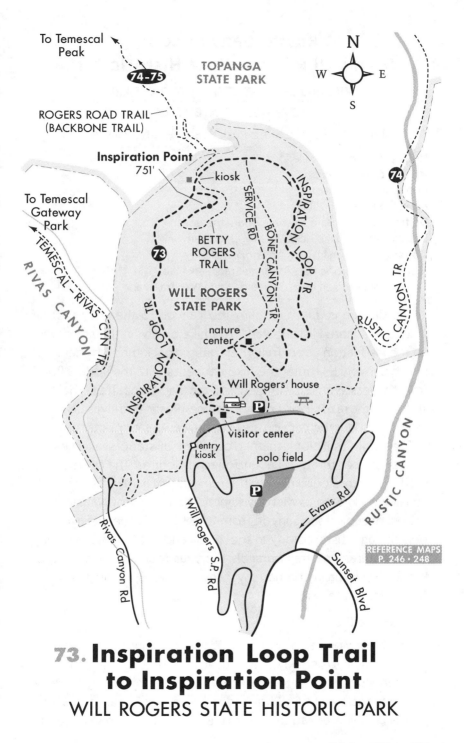

To Temescal
Peak

74-75

TOPANGA
STATE PARK

N
W   E
S

ROGERS ROAD TRAIL
(BACKBONE TRAIL)

Inspiration Point
751'

kiosk

74

INSPIRATION LOOP TR

SERVICE RD

BONE CANYON TR

To Temescal
Gateway
Park

TEMESCAL-RIVAS CYN TR

RIVAS CANYON

73

BETTY
ROGERS
TRAIL

RUSTIC CANYON TR

WILL ROGERS
STATE PARK

nature
center

INSPIRATION LOOP TR

Will Rogers' house

P

P

entry
kiosk

visitor center

polo field

RUSTIC CANYON

Evans Rd

REFERENCE MAPS
P. 246 · 248

Rivas Canyon Rd

Will Rogers S.P. Rd

Sunset Blvd

73. Inspiration Loop Trail
to Inspiration Point
WILL ROGERS STATE HISTORIC PARK

74. Rustic Canyon Loop
from Will Rogers State Historic Park

WILL ROGERS STATE HISTORIC PARK
TOPANGA STATE PARK

1501 Will Rogers State Park Road · Pacific Palisades

Hiking distance: 5-mile loop
Hiking time: 3 hours
Configuration: loop
Elevation gain: 1,000 feet
Difficulty: moderate to somewhat strenuous
Exposure: exposed ridge and forested canyon
Dogs: allowed on Inspiration Loop Trail only
Maps: U.S.G.S. Topanga · Topanga State Park map
Tom Harrison Maps: Topanga State Park Trail Map

Rustic Canyon is a lush, stream-fed canyon to the northeast of Will Rogers State Historic Park. This hike begins in the state park on the Inspiration Loop Trail, then returns back through secluded Rustic Canyon. En route, the hike connects with the Rogers Road Trail, the easternmost segment of the Backbone Trail. The trail straddles the razor-point ridge between Rustic and Rivas Canyons. From the ridge, the canyon and ocean views are spectacular.

The return trail along the narrow floor of steep-walled Rustic Canyon passes three old abandoned structures. The dilapidated, graffiti-covered buildings are the remnants of a 50-acre pro-Nazi compound known as Murphy Ranch. The colony of Nazi sympathizers occupied the canyon from 1933 to 1945. The enclave later became an artists' colony in the 1950s and 1960s. After passing the structures, the trail parallels the year-round watercourse of Rustic Creek through a narrow canyon before looping back to Will Rogers State Park.

To the trailhead

From Santa Monica, drive 1.6 miles northbound on the Pacific Coast Highway/Highway 1 to Chautauqua Boulevard. Turn right and continue 0.9 miles to Sunset Boulevard. Turn right again. Drive 0.5 miles and turn left at Will Rogers State Park Road. The parking area is 0.7 miles ahead on the left, just past the entrance station.

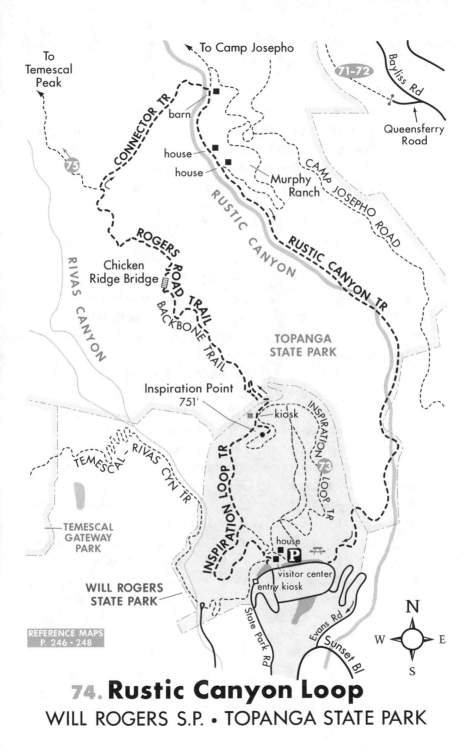

To Temescal Peak

To Camp Josepho

71-72

Bayliss Rd

Queensferry Road

CONNECTOR TR

barn

house

house

75

Murphy Ranch

CAMP JOSEPHO ROAD

RUSTIC CANYON

RUSTIC CANYON TR

ROGERS ROAD TRAIL

Chicken Ridge Bridge

BACKBONE TRAIL

RIVAS CANYON

TOPANGA STATE PARK

Inspiration Point 751'

kiosk

INSPIRATION LOOP TR

TEMESCAL - RIVAS CYN TR

73

INSPIRATION LOOP TR

TEMESCAL GATEWAY PARK

house

P

visitor center

entry kiosk

WILL ROGERS STATE PARK

State Park Rd

Evans Rd

Sunset Bl

N W E S

REFERENCE MAPS P. 246 • 248

74. Rustic Canyon Loop
WILL ROGERS S.P. • TOPANGA STATE PARK

Another parking lot is a short distance farther, on the left by the visitor center. A parking fee is required.

The hike

Begin the hike from the visitor center and Will Rogers' home, built in 1928. Head west (left) past the tennis courts and the Temescal-Rivas Canyon Trail to a dirt fire road—the Inspiration Loop Trail. Head uphill on the gentle uphill grade with views across coastal Los Angeles to Palos Verdes and Catalina Island. At 0.8 miles is a junction and additional views across the mountainous back-country. Detour 0.1 mile straight ahead to Inspiration Point, with sweeping vistas across Los Angeles.

Return to the junction and head 70 yards north to Rogers Road Trail, the beginning of the Backbone Trail. Head up the footpath, entering Topanga State Park. (Dogs are not allowed on the trail after this point.) Climb north on the ridge between Rivas Canyon and Rustic Canyon. At 1.5 miles, cross Chicken Ridge Bridge and follow the steep, knife-edged slope at an elevation of 1,125 feet. At just under 2 miles is a junction on a saddle. The main trail continues along the ridge and leads to Temescal Peak (Hike 75).

For this hike, leave the Backbone Trail and steeply descend into Rustic Canyon on the right, dropping nearly 700 feet in a half mile. At the canyon floor, cross Rustic Creek to the Rustic Canyon Trail by a fenced barn, once part of Anatol Josepho's ranch. The left fork leads up canyon to Camp Josepho, a Boy Scout camp (named after Anatol Josepho, a friend of Will Rogers). Head down canyon to the right, and stroll through the dense forest among pine, eucalyptus, oak, bay laurel, spruce, and towering sycamore trees. Pass an amazing two-story metal building with rusted metal parts scattered around it and an abandoned concrete house with arches, used as a power-generator building. The entire house is covered inside and out with colorful graffiti and murals. Both buildings were part of the Murphy Ranch complex.

The vertical rock-walled canyon narrows, and the path crisscrosses Rustic Creek in the dense forest. Pass an old flood-control dam built in the early 1900s. The canyon widens and curves uphill to the polo field across from Will Rogers' home, completing the loop. ▪

75. Temescal Peak
from Will Rogers State Historic Park

WILL ROGERS STATE HISTORIC PARK
TOPANGA STATE PARK

1501 Will Rogers State Park Road · Pacific Palisades

Hiking distance: 14 miles round trip
Hiking time: 7.5 hours
Configuration: out-and-back
Elevation gain: 1,650 feet
Difficulty: strenuous
Exposure: exposed with shady pockets
Dogs: not allowed after first mile
Maps: U.S.G.S. Topanga · Topanga State Park map
Tom Harrison Maps: Topanga State Park Trail Map
Will Rogers State Historic Park map

Temescal Peak, rising to a height of 2,126 feet, is the highest peak in Topanga State Park. The peak separates the watersheds of Rustic Canyon, Santa Ynez Canyon, and Temescal Canyon. Atop the peak is a small mound of rocks, a survey benchmark, and a metal post. From the unadorned peak, the sweeping vistas extend north to the Los Padres National Forest, east to the San Gabriel Mountains, south to the Pacific Ocean and Catalina Island, and west across the seemingly endless ridges of the Santa Monica Mountains.

Temescal Peak is accessible from several approaches. This route begins from Will Rogers State Historic Park and follows a ridge northwest between Temescal Canyon and Rustic Canyon, two stream-fed drainages. From Will Rogers State Park, the trail heads into Topanga State Park on the Rogers Road Trail, the easternmost segment of the 69-mile-long Backbone Trail. The trail follows the steep ridge nearly all the way to Temescal Peak. Throughout the hike are wide-angle panoramas of the Santa Monica Mountains stretching across Los Angeles and the San Fernando Valley.

Other accesses to the peak are from the south in Pacific Palisades (Temescal Ridge Trail), from the west at Trippet Ranch (Hike 78), and from the north off of Dirt Mulholland.

To the trailhead

From Santa Monica, drive 1.6 miles northbound on the Pacific Coast Highway/Highway 1 to Chautauqua Boulevard. Turn right and continue 0.9 miles to Sunset Boulevard. Turn right again. Drive 0.5 miles and turn left at Will Rogers State Park Road. The parking area is 0.7 miles ahead on the left, just past the entrance station. Another parking lot is a short distance farther, on the left by the visitor center. A parking fee is required.

REFERENCE MAPS
P. 246 · 248

75. Temescal Peak
from Will Rogers State Historic Park
WILL ROGERS STATE HISTORIC PARK
TOPANGA STATE PARK

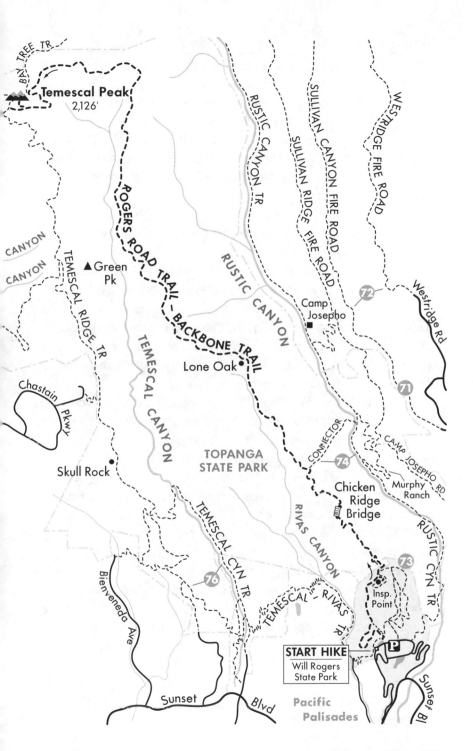

BAY TREE TR.

Temescal Peak
2,126'

ROGERS ROAD TRAIL — BACKBONE TRAIL

RUSTIC CANYON TR.

SULLIVAN CANYON FIRE ROAD

SULLIVAN RIDGE FIRE ROAD

WESTRIDGE FIRE ROAD

CANYON

CANYON

TEMESCAL RIDGE TR.

▲Green Pk

RUSTIC CANYON

Camp Josepho

72

Westridge Rd

71

Lone Oak

TEMESCAL CANYON

Chastain Pkwy

Skull Rock

TOPANGA STATE PARK

CONNECTOR

74

CAMP JOSEPHO RD.

Murphy Ranch

Chicken Ridge Bridge

RUSTIC CYN TR.

RIVAS CANYON

TEMESCAL CYN TR.

76

Bienveneda Ave

73

Insp. Point

TEMESCAL – RIVAS TR.

START HIKE
Will Rogers
State Park

P

Sunset Bl.

Sunset   Blvd

Pacific Palisades

The hike

Begin the hike from the visitor center and Will Rogers' home, built in 1928. Head west (left) past the tennis courts and the Temescal-Rivas Canyon Trail to a dirt fire road—the Inspiration Loop Trail. Head uphill on the gentle uphill grade with views across coastal Los Angeles to Palos Verdes and Catalina Island. At 0.8 miles is a junction and additional views across the mountainous back-country. Detour 0.1 mile straight ahead to Inspiration Point, with sweeping vistas across Los Angeles.

Return to the junction and head 70 yards north to Rogers Road Trail, the beginning of the Backbone Trail. Head up the footpath, leaving Will Rogers State Park, and enter Topanga State Park. (Dogs are not allowed on the trail after this point.) Climb north on the ridge between Rivas Canyon and Rustic Canyon. At 1.5 miles, cross Chicken Ridge Bridge and follow the steep, knife-edged slope at an elevation of 1,125 feet. Climb to additional views into forested Rustic Canyon and Sullivan Canyon to the right. At just under 2 miles is a junction on a saddle. To the right is the connector trail into Rustic Canyon—Hike 74.

Stay on the main Rogers Road Trail to the left. Descend along the east wall of Temescal Canyon to Lone Oak, a massive coast live oak tree with five trunks. The tree sits on a flat with northern views towards the Los Padres National Forest. Veer left and meander through a corridor under a tree-shaded canopy. Weave through the quiet of the backcountry as the trail dips and rises. From 1,900 feet above the city, the views extend across Tarzana, Woodland Hills, and the entire San Fernando Valley. Bear left and cross the head of the canyon. Traverse the north-facing slope to a posted junction with the Bay Tree Trail at 6.3 miles. Stay to the left towards the signed Hub Junction. Wind along the mountainous contours 0.6 miles to the Temescal Ridge Trail. Just shy of this junction, a side path climbs the hill up to Temescal Peak, the 2,126-foot summit of the hike. After enjoying the 360-degree vistas, return along the same trail.

From Temescal Peak, the Backbone Trail connects to the Temescal Ridge Trail, which heads south to Temescal Gateway Park and Sunset Boulevard (Hike 76) and north to Hub Junction and Eagle Rock (Hike 78). ▪

76. Temescal Canyon Loop

TEMESCAL GATEWAY PARK • TOPANGA STATE PARK

15601 Sunset Boulevard · Pacific Palisades

Hiking distance: 4.2-mile loop
Hiking time: 2 hours
Configuration: loop with half-mile spur to Skull Rock
Elevation gain: 1,000 feet
Difficulty: moderate to somewhat strenuous
Exposure: exposed ridge and forested canyon
Dogs: not allowed
Maps: U.S.G.S. Topanga · Topanga State Park map
Tom Harrison Maps: Topanga State Park Trail map

Temescal Canyon is a creek-fed canyon within Topanga State Park that is shaded by oaks, maples, and sycamores. This canyon-to-ridgetop loop hike climbs the hillside cliffs on the west side of the canyon and follows the ridge, offering far-reaching views of Los Angeles and the Pacific coastline. The return route drops into the tree-shaded canyon to a footbridge at the seasonal Temescal Canyon Falls, framed by huge volcanic rocks. The trail begins at Temescal Gateway Park, a 141-acre oasis in the hills above Pacific Palisades. En route, a short spur trail leads to Skull Rock, a weather-carved formation resembling a human skull.

To the trailhead

From Santa Monica, drive 2 miles northbound on the Pacific Coast Highway/Highway 1 to Temescal Canyon Road. Turn right and drive 1.3 miles to the end of Temescal Canyon Road, crossing Sunset Boulevard en route. Park in the Temescal Gateway parking lot at the conference and retreat center. A parking fee is required.

The hike

Walk up the paved road, staying to the left at a road split that is just past the Temescal Camp Store. Continue 25 yards to a signed junction on the left. Leave the road and begin the loop to the left on the Temescal Ridge Trail. Climb steps and zigzag up the scrubby west canyon wall, entering Topanga State Park at 0.3

miles. Short switchbacks continue uphill to the open ridge, with sweeping views of Santa Ynez Canyon, Pacific Palisades, Santa Monica, and the entire Santa Monica Bay. Pass the signed Leacock Trail on the left, a neighborhood connector path. Continue up the ridge overlooking Temescal Canyon to a junction with the Bienvenida Trail at 1.6 miles. En route are a series of coastal over-looks. The Bienvenida Trail leads one mile downhill to Bienvenida Avenue in Pacific Palisades. Walk 70 yards straight ahead to the posted Temescal Canyon Trail on the right. The right fork drops into the canyon—the return route. To visit Skull Rock, detour left and continue a half mile uphill to the wind-sculpted rock. En route are inland vistas across the Los Angeles Basin.

After viewing the carved sandstone formation, return to the junction with the Temescal Canyon Trail. Take the Temescal Canyon Trail (now on the left/east) and steeply descend into the densely wooded canyon. At the canyon floor is a wooden footbridge over the creek in the rock grotto just below Temescal Canyon Falls. The trail parallels the creek downstream along the east canyon wall. At the canyon floor, wind through the park-lands under groves of eucalyptus, sycamore, willow, and coastal oak, back to the trailhead. ▪

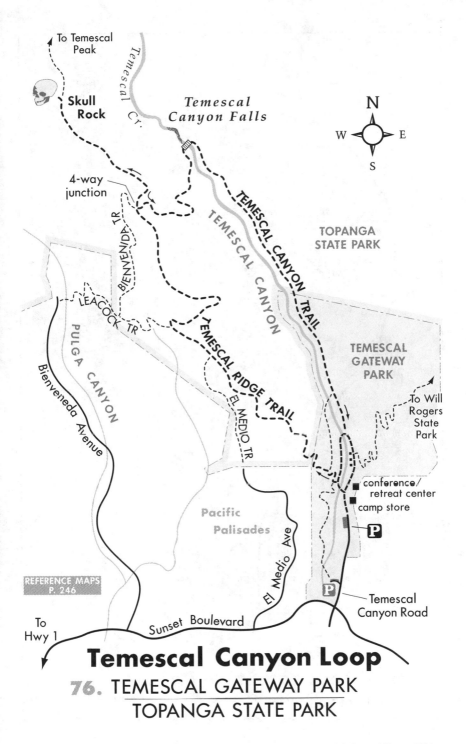

To Temescal
Peak

Skull
Rock

Temescal Cr.

Temescal Canyon Falls

*Temescal
Canyon Falls*

N
W   E
S

4-way
junction

BIENVENIDA TR

TEMESCAL CANYON TRAIL

TEMESCAL CANYON

TOPANGA
STATE PARK

LEACOCK TR

PULGA CANYON

TEMESCAL RIDGE TRAIL

TEMESCAL
GATEWAY
PARK

Bienveneda Avenue

EL MEDIO TR

To Will
Rogers
State
Park

Pacific
Palisades

El Medio Ave

conference/
retreat center

camp store

P

REFERENCE MAPS
P. 246

P

Temescal
Canyon Road

To
Hwy 1

Sunset Boulevard

Temescal Canyon Loop
76. TEMESCAL GATEWAY PARK
TOPANGA STATE PARK

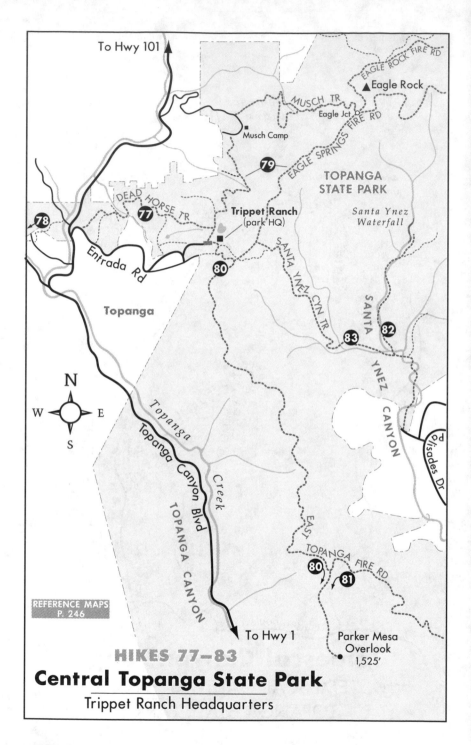

To Hwy 101

EAGLE ROCK FIRE RD

▲ Eagle Rock

MUSCH TR

Eagle Jct

EAGLE SPRINGS FIRE RD

■ Musch Camp

79

TOPANGA
STATE PARK

*Santa Ynez
Waterfall*

DEAD HORSE TR

77

Trippet Ranch
(park HQ)

SANTA YNEZ CYN TR

78

Entrada Rd

80

SANTA YNEZ CANYON

Topanga

83

82

N
W ✦ E
S

Topanga

Topanga Canyon Blvd

Creek

TOPANGA CANYON

Old Palisades Dr

EAST TOPANGA FIRE RD

80

81

REFERENCE MAPS
P. 246

To Hwy 1

Parker Mesa
Overlook
• 1,525'

HIKES 77–83
Central Topanga State Park
Trippet Ranch Headquarters

Topanga State Park

Topanga State Park is located adjacent to the unincorporated town of Topanga in western Los Angeles County. The state park is entirely within the city of Los Angeles, making it the world's largest municipal wildland. The 11,525-acre park is bordered by Topanga Canyon on the west and the rugged Rustic Canyon on the east. Between Topanga Canyon and Rustic Canyon are two other major drainages—Temescal Canyon and Santa Ynez Canyon. At the head of Temescal Canyon lies Temescal Peak, the highest peak in the park at 2,126 feet.

The park contains a wide variety of habitats, including open grasslands; stream-fed canyons with riparian forests; live oak woodlands; bay laurel, walnut, and sycamore groves; and coastal sage scrub. Scattered throughout the landscape are boulder-studded ridges, dramatic sandstone cliffs, caves, waterfalls, earthquake faults, marine fossils, and volcanic intrusions. Overlooks, such as Parker Mesa Overlook and Eagle Rock, offer spectacular ocean-to-mountain vistas.

Trippet Ranch, the park headquarters, is located on an old homestead from the 1890s. The 80-acre homestead is currently the main entrance into Topanga State Park and a popular staging area for accessing the trails. At the ranch is a nature center, pond, shaded picnic areas, and trailheads. Another popular access point into the park is the Reseda Boulevard trailhead, northwest of Trippet Ranch at the north boundary.

The sprawling state park wildland has a complex network of more than 36 miles of hiking, mountain biking, and equestrian trails. The trail system is a combination of wide fire roads, single-track trails, and informal footpaths. An unpaved portion of Mulholland Drive (Dirt Mulholland) runs through the north end of the park. Nearly 15 miles of the Backbone Trail traverse through the heart of the park, beginning at the trail's easternmost trailhead at Will Rogers State Park.

Note: Dogs are not allowed in the state park.

77. Dead Horse Trail from Trippet Ranch

TOPANGA STATE PARK

20825 Entrada Road · Topanga

Hiking distance: 2.5 miles round trip
Hiking time: 1.5 hours
Configuration: out-and-back
Elevation gain: 400 feet
Difficulty: easy
Exposure: mixed sun and shade
Dogs: not allowed
Maps: U.S.G.S. Topanga · Topanga State Park map
Tom Harrison Maps: Topanga State Park Trail map

Topanga State Park covers more than 11,500 acres at the west end of Los Angeles County. It has been designated as the world's largest wildland within the boundaries of a major city. Within the park are 36 miles of trails through open grasslands, chaparral, and oak woodlands. The Dead Horse Trail begins at Trippet Ranch, the park headquarters and visitor center. The diverse trail crosses rolling grasslands, enters a riparian forest, and descends into a streamside oak forest. The path crosses a rustic wooden bridge over Trippet Creek in a rocky grotto. The Dead Horse Trail is a segment of the 69-mile Backbone Trail.

To the trailhead

From Santa Monica, drive 4 miles northbound on the Pacific Coast Highway/Highway 1 to Topanga Canyon Boulevard and turn right. Continue 4.6 miles to Entrada Road on the right and turn right again. Drive 0.7 miles and turn left, following the state park signs. Turn left again in 0.3 miles into the parking lot.

From the Ventura Freeway/Highway 101 in Woodland Hills, exit on Topanga Canyon Boulevard, and drive 7.6 miles south to Entrada Road. Turn left and follow the posted state park signs to the Trippet Ranch parking lot.

The hike

Take the signed Musch Trail for 50 yards, heading north to a pond on the right. The Dead Horse Trail heads left (west) across from the pond. The footpath parallels a wood rail fence, rolling grass-lands, and an oak woodland. At a half mile is a trail split. Take the right fork along the contours of the ridge. Descend into a shady riparian forest of bay and sycamore trees. A wooden bridge crosses the rocky streambed of Trippet Creek in a narrow draw. After crossing, steps lead up to a junction. Take the middle fork downhill to a trail split. Bear right and loop around to the lower parking lot near Topanga Canyon Boulevard. Return by retracing your steps.

The Backbone Trail continues west across from Topanga Canyon Boulevard. This short, 0.7-mile section of trail connects to the Hondo Canyon Trail—Hike 78. ■

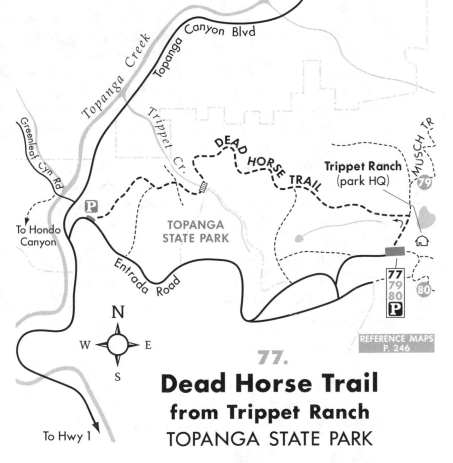

77.
Dead Horse Trail
from Trippet Ranch
TOPANGA STATE PARK

78. Hondo Canyon Trail
Old Topanga Canyon Road to Lois Ewen Overlook
TOPANGA STATE PARK
20825 Entrada Road · Topanga

Hiking distance: 8.6 miles round trip (plus optional 2-mile side trip)
Hiking time: 5 hours
Configuration: out-and-back
Elevation gain: 1,450 feet
Difficulty: moderate to strenuous
Exposure: an equal mix of tree-shaded areas and open slopes
Dogs: not allowed (but many 4-legged friends have been known to enjoy this trail)
Maps: U.S.G.S. Topanga and Malibu Beach · Topanga State Park map
　　　Tom Harrison Maps: Topanga State Park Trail Map

The Hondo Canyon Trail, a section of the Backbone Trail, climbs from the stream-fed canyon floor of Old Topanga Canyon to the Lois Ewen Overlook atop the Santa Monica Mountains at Stunt Road. From the summit are northern views across Cold Creek Canyon Preserve and Calabasas Peak to the San Fernando Valley. The sweeping southern views overlook Las Flores Canyon to the expansive Santa Monica Bay. The trail climbs the south wall of Hondo Canyon through majestic live oaks, California bays, and tall chaparral while passing massive sedimentary rock formations. At the top, the Fossil Ridge Trail passes an exceptional display of sea shell fossils embedded in the exposed rock, including clams, snails, and sand dollars.

This hike can also be started from the Lois Ewen Overlook, but it is more pleasant to first walk up from Old Topanga Canyon, then make the descent on the return.

To the trailhead

From Santa Monica, drive 4 miles northbound on the Pacific Coast Highway/Highway 1 to Topanga Canyon Boulevard and turn right. Continue 4.2 miles to Old Topanga Canyon Road on the left (west), just north of the town of Topanga. Turn left and drive 0.4 miles to the posted trailhead and a narrow dirt pullout on the left.

From the Ventura Freeway/Highway 101 in Woodland Hills, exit on Topanga Canyon Boulevard. Drive 8 miles south to Old Topanga Canyon Road on the right (west). Turn right and continue 0.4 miles to the posted trailhead and a narrow dirt pullout on the left.

The hike

Pass the trailhead sign and descend to Old Topanga Creek. Rock-hop over the creek, ascend steps, and walk through a meadow. Enter the lush, live oak forest in a side drainage, and follow the left side of the watercourse. Cross to the north side of the stream, passing through meadows with sandstone outcroppings. Climb up the rolling meadow to a rocky perch with sweeping views. Weave along the contour of the hills, overlooking layers of mountains and canyons. Climb the south wall of Hondo Canyon, zigzagging past conglomerate rock formations. The views span across the Santa Monica Mountains to the San Fernando Valley and Los Padres National Forest. At 3.7 miles, the path reaches a junction by Saddle Peak Road at the head of Hondo Canyon.

Bear right on the Fossil Ridge Trail, and head up to coastal views that span down Las Flores Canyon to Santa Monica Bay and Catalina Island. Parallel Saddle Peak Road, passing an endless display of sea shell fossils embedded in the sedimentary rock. Reach the Topanga Ridge Motorway at 4.3 miles. The right fork leads 0.9 miles to the Topanga Fire Lookout (Hike 93). The left fork ends at a three-way road junction with Saddle Peak Road, Schueren Road, and Stunt Road at the Lois Ewen Overlook. The Saddle Peak Trail begins across the road (the continuation of the Backbone Trail). Return by retracing your steps.

To trail to the Topanga Fire Lookout may be hiked as an optional 2-mile sidetrip. To head up to the lookout, take the paved Topanga Ridge Motorway northeast, following the ridge high above Cold Creek Canyon. At the road split, the paved right fork leads to a radar tower. Stay to the left on the wide, unpaved path to the graffiti-covered concrete foundation, which is all that remains of the lookout tower. It is one mile to the lookout tower, with an additional 200 feet in elevation. ■

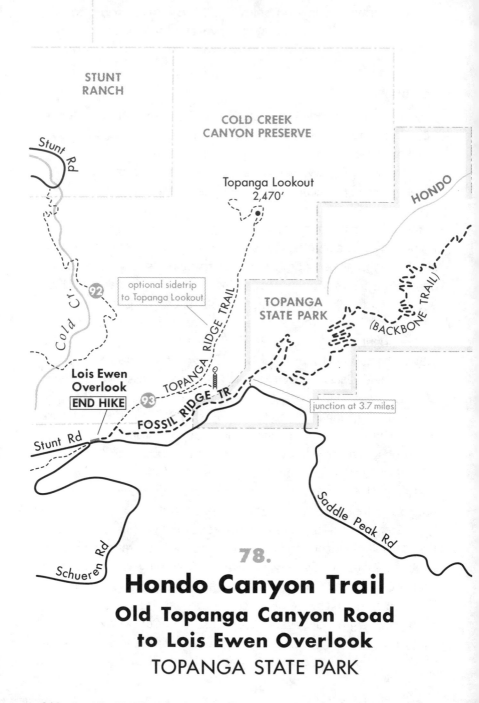

STUNT
RANCH

COLD CREEK
CANYON PRESERVE

Stunt Rd

Topanga Lookout
2,470'

HONDO

92

optional sidetrip
to Topanga Lookout

Cold Cr

TOPANGA RIDGE TRAIL

TOPANGA
STATE PARK

(BACKBONE TRAIL)

Lois Ewen
Overlook
END HIKE

93

TOPANGA RIDGE TR

FOSSIL RIDGE TR

junction at 3.7 miles

Stunt Rd

Saddle Peak Rd

Schueren Rd

78.
Hondo Canyon Trail
Old Topanga Canyon Road
to Lois Ewen Overlook
TOPANGA STATE PARK

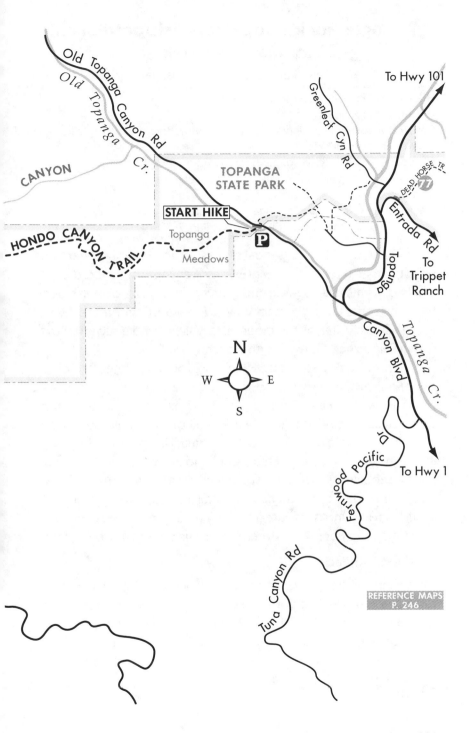

Old Topanga Canyon Rd

Old Topanga Cr.

CANYON

Greenleaf Cyn Rd

To Hwy 101

TOPANGA
STATE PARK

DEAD HORSE TR.

77

START HIKE

Topanga
Meadows

P

HONDO CANYON TRAIL

Entrada Rd

To
Trippet
Ranch

Topanga

Canyon Blvd

Topanga Cr.

N

W · E

S

Fernwood Dr

Pacific

To Hwy 1

Tuna Canyon Rd

REFERENCE MAPS
P. 246

79. Eagle Rock Loop from Trippet Ranch

TOPANGA STATE PARK

20825 Entrada Road · Topanga

Hiking distance: 8-mile loop
Hiking time: 4 hours
Configuration: figure-eight double loop with short spur to Eagle Rock
Elevation gain: 800 feet
Difficulty: moderate to somewhat strenuous
Exposure: exposed hills and forested pockets
Dogs: not allowed
Maps: U.S.G.S. Topanga · Topanga State Park map
Tom Harrison Maps: Topanga State Park Trail Map

Eagle Rock is a massive sandstone outcrop towering over the landscape at the head of Santa Ynez Canyon. The layered crag, pocked with small caves from water erosion, is a popular destination for its unobstructed views. From a perch on the 1,957-foot rock are vistas of the mountains, valleys, and a superb view down Santa Ynez Canyon to the ocean.

This hike begins at Trippet Ranch in Topanga State Park by a bucolic picnic area with a pond and a one-mile nature trail. The hike follows the Eagle Springs Fire Road through grasslands and oak groves up to Eagle Rock. After a short scramble up to the summit, the hike circles around the formation past Hub Junction (a 4-way junction by Temescal Peak) and Eagle Springs (a natural spring seeping out of the sandstone). The hike returns on the Musch Trail. The footpath meanders through lush vegetation that includes ferns, moss-covered rocks, and sycamore, oak and bay trees, making a couple of stream crossings back to Trippet Ranch.

To the trailhead

From Santa Monica, drive 4 miles northbound on the Pacific Coast Highway/Highway 1 to Topanga Canyon Boulevard and turn right. Continue 4.6 miles to Entrada Road on the right and turn right again. Drive 0.7 miles and turn left, following the state park signs. Turn left again and go 0.3 miles into the Topanga State Park parking lot. A parking fee is required.

From the Ventura Freeway/Highway 101 in Woodland Hills, exit on Topanga Canyon Boulevard. Drive 7.6 miles south to Entrada Road. Turn left and follow the posted state park signs to the Trippet Ranch parking lot.

The hike

Walk to the end of the parking lot by the grassy picnic area and weathered live oaks. Follow the trail uphill a short distance to a posted junction. The East Topanga Fire Road (Hike 80) bends right. Bear left on the Eagle Springs Fire Road, and pass the Santa Ynez Canyon Trail (Hike 83) on the right at a half mile. Continue uphill on the ridge road to the Musch Trail on the left—the return route—and a road split at 1.5 miles. Veer left on the Eagle Rock Fire Road, reaching the north slope of prominent Eagle Rock as the road crests. Leave the trail to the right to explore the tilted formation with sculptured caves and hollows. Scramble up the gorgeous monolith for great views down Santa Ynez Canyon to the Pacific.

Back on the Eagle Rock Fire Road, continue east, passing the Garapito Trail on the left. Climb the slope with views across the San Fernando Valley. Top the hill to westward views across Los Angeles to the ocean. Descend to Hub Junction, a 4-way cross-roads with a map kiosk at 3 miles. The Temescal Ridge Fire Road, the middle right trail, leads 0.7 miles to Temescal Peak and 4.8 miles to Temescal Gateway Park at the mouth of the canyon (Hike 76). To the left, the Temescal Ridge Fire Road leads to Dirt Mulholland and Reseda Boulevard in Tarzana. (South of Hub Junction, the Temescal Ridge Fire Road is called the Temescal Ridge Trail.)

For this hike, make a sharp right back onto the Eagle Springs Fire Road. Descend 1.3 miles, now skirting under the south side of Eagle Rock, to a posted fork with the Musch Trail on the right. (En route, a short side path on the right leads to Eagle Springs, a trickling spring in the sandstone bedrock under a sycamore and oak glen.)

Take the Musch Trail, leaving the fire road, and wind down into a verdant valley. Cross a couple of ravines through lush riparian vegetation and woodlands of oak, sycamore, and bay laurel. One mile down is a junction with Musch Camp at the former Musch Ranch. Follow the trail sign, crossing a meadow. Wind down to a junction with the Dead Horse Trail (Hike 77). Continue straight, passing a pond on the left and crossing an earthen dam to the main Topanga State Park parking lot at Trippet Ranch. ■

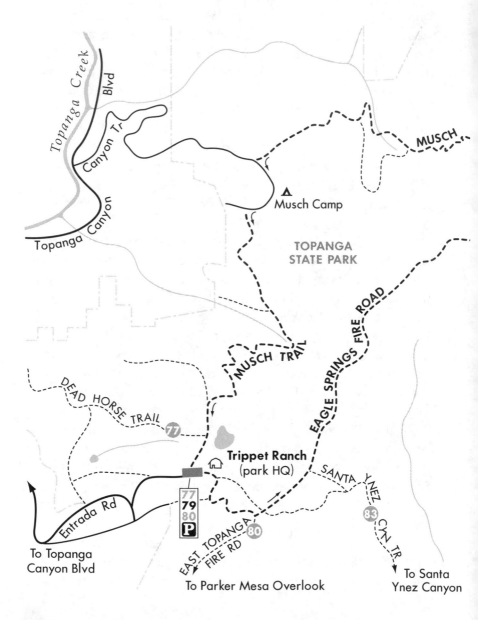

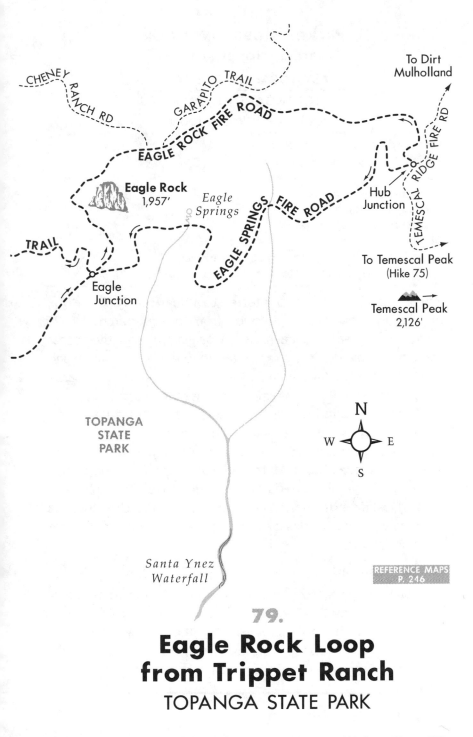

CHENEY RANCH RD

GARAPITO TRAIL

EAGLE ROCK FIRE ROAD

To Dirt
Mulholland

TEMESCAL RIDGE FIRE RD

Eagle Rock
1,957'

*Eagle
Springs*

EAGLE SPRINGS FIRE ROAD

Hub
Junction

TRAIL

Eagle
Junction

To Temescal Peak
(Hike 75)

Temescal Peak
2,126'

N
W   E
S

TOPANGA
STATE
PARK

*Santa Ynez
Waterfall*

REFERENCE MAPS
P. 246

79.

Eagle Rock Loop
from Trippet Ranch
TOPANGA STATE PARK

80. Parker Mesa Overlook
from Trippet Ranch

EAST TOPANGA FIRE ROAD
TOPANGA STATE PARK
20825 Entrada Road · Topanga

Hiking distance: 6 miles round trip
Hiking time: 3 hours
Configuration: out-and-back
Elevation gain: 800 feet
Difficulty: moderate
Exposure: exposed ridge
Dogs: not allowed
Maps: U.S.G.S. Topanga · Topanga State Park map
　　　　 Tom Harrison Maps: Topanga State Park Trail map

Parker Mesa Overlook (also referred to as the Topanga Overlook, or simply *the overlook*) is an oceanfront lookout perched 1,525 feet above the Pacific Ocean. East Topanga Fire Road, the access route to the overlook, is a restricted road that travels north and south through Topanga State Park from Trippet Ranch (the park's headquarters) to Paseo Miramar off Sunset Boulevard.

Parker Mesa Overlook can be accessed from three trailheads: from the north via this trailhead at Trippet Ranch and from the south via the Los Liones trailhead or the Paseo Miramar trailhead in Pacific Palisades (Hike 81). The fire road follows the ridge high above Topanga Canyon and Santa Ynez Canyon, passing enormous slabs of sandstone and numerous ravines that drop into the canyons along both sides of the ridge. Throughout the hike are spectacular vistas in every direction.

To the trailhead

From Santa Monica, drive 4 miles northbound on the Pacific Coast Highway/Highway 1 to Topanga Canyon Boulevard and turn right. Continue 4.6 miles to Entrada Road on the right and turn right again. Drive 0.7 miles and turn left, following the posted state park signs. Turn left again at 0.3 miles into the Topanga State Park parking lot.

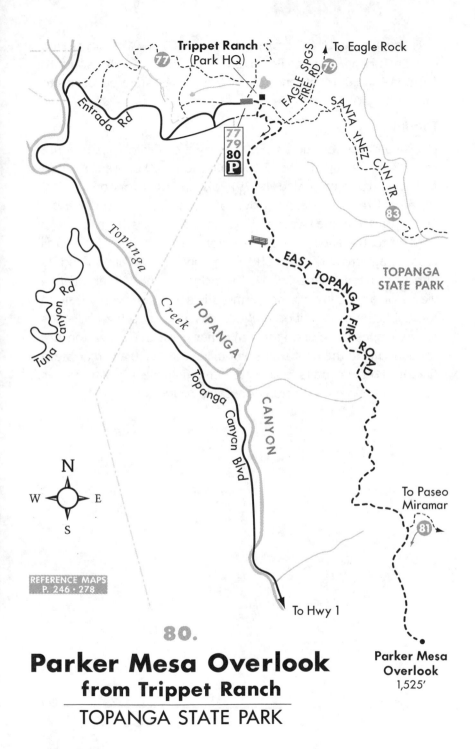

Trippet Ranch
(Park HQ)

To Eagle Rock

Entrada Rd

EAGLE SPGS FIRE RD

SANTA YNEZ CYN TR

77
79
80
P

77

79

83

Topanga Creek

TOPANGA

EAST TOPANGA FIRE ROAD

TOPANGA
STATE PARK

Tuna Canyon Rd

Topanga Canyon Blvd

CANYON

N
W   E
S

To Paseo
Miramar

81

REFERENCE MAPS
P. 246 · 278

To Hwy 1

Parker Mesa
Overlook
1,525'

80.

Parker Mesa Overlook
from Trippet Ranch
TOPANGA STATE PARK

From the Ventura Freeway/Highway 101 in Woodland Hills, exit on Topanga Canyon Boulevard, and drive 7.6 miles south to Entrada Road. Turn left and follow the posted state park signs to the parking lot.

The hike

Head southeast on the signed trail towards Eagle Rock to a fire road. Bear left up the road to a junction at 0.2 miles. The left fork leads to Eagle Rock (Hike 79). Take the right fork on the East Topanga Fire Road past a grove of coastal oaks. Continue up-hill to a ridge and a bench with panoramic views from Topanga Canyon to the Pacific Ocean. A short distance ahead, the trail crosses a narrow ridge overlooking Santa Ynez Canyon and its tilted sandstone slabs. Follow the ridge south, with alternating views of both canyons. At 2.5 miles is a junction with a trail on the right. The main trail on the left (east) leads to the trailheads at Los Liones Drive and Paseo Miramar (Hike 81). Leave the fire road, and take the right trail a half mile south to the Parker Mesa Overlook at the trail's end. After enjoying the fantastic views, return to Trippet Ranch along the same route. ▪

81. Parker Mesa Overlook
from Paseo Miramar in Pacific Palisades
EAST TOPANGA FIRE ROAD
TOPANGA STATE PARK
Paseo Miramar trailhead · Pacific Palisades

Hiking distance: 5.5 miles round trip
Hiking time: 2.5 hours
Configuration: out-and-back
Elevation gain: 1,200 feet
Difficulty: moderate to somewhat strenuous
Exposure: exposed ridge
Dogs: not allowed
Maps: U.S.G.S. Topanga · Topanga State Park map
　　　　Tom Harrison Maps: Topanga State Park Trail map

Parker Mesa Overlook sits on a wide ridge overlooking the Santa Monica Bay from an elevation of 1,525 feet. From the ocean-front knoll are expansive 360-degree views, extending from the bay to Palos Verdes. The East Topanga Fire Road is a 4.6-mile vehicle-restricted road that connects the community of Pacific Palisades with Trippet Ranch in Topanga State Park. The unpaved road climbs northeast on the high ridge between Santa Ynez Canyon and Los Liones Canyon, all within Topanga State Park. This hike begins from the upper end of Paseo Miramar in Pacific Palisades and follows the lower two miles of the fire road to the Parker Mesa Overlook. Throughout the hike are amazing panoramas of the ocean, city, and mountains.

To the trailhead

From Santa Monica, drive 3 miles northbound on the Pacific Coast Highway/Highway 1 to Sunset Boulevard. Turn right and drive 0.3 miles to Paseo Miramar. Turn left on Paseo Miramar, and drive 1.2 miles to the trailhead at the end of the road. Park alongside the curb on the west side of the street.

The hike

From the north end of Paseo Miramar, pass the trailhead gate and enter Topanga State Park. Hike north on the dirt fire road along the ridge, overlooking Santa Ynez Canyon, Pacific Palisades, and Santa Monica. Bend left to a junction with the Los Liones Trail on the left at 0.2 miles. (The trail leads 1.6 miles downhill to the trailhead at the north end of Los Liones Drive.) Continue straight ahead, staying on the East Topanga Fire Road. Traverse the hillside above Santa Ynez Canyon to a junction at 2 miles. The main road leads 2.7 miles to Trippet Ranch (Hike 80) and 4 miles to Eagle Rock (Hike 79). Instead, leave the fire road and take the trail to the left. Walk a half mile south to the Parker Mesa Overlook at the end of the trail. From the bald knoll are great vistas overlooking the ocean and coastline. After savoring the views, return along the same route. ■

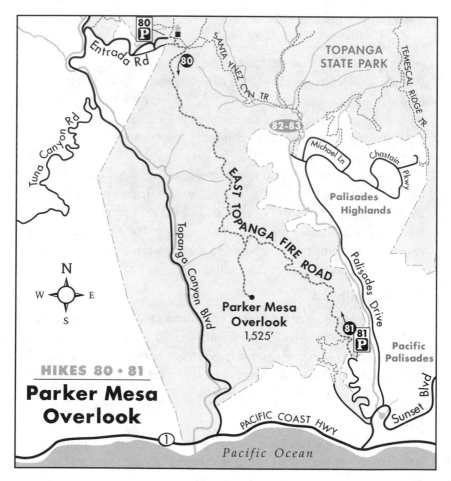

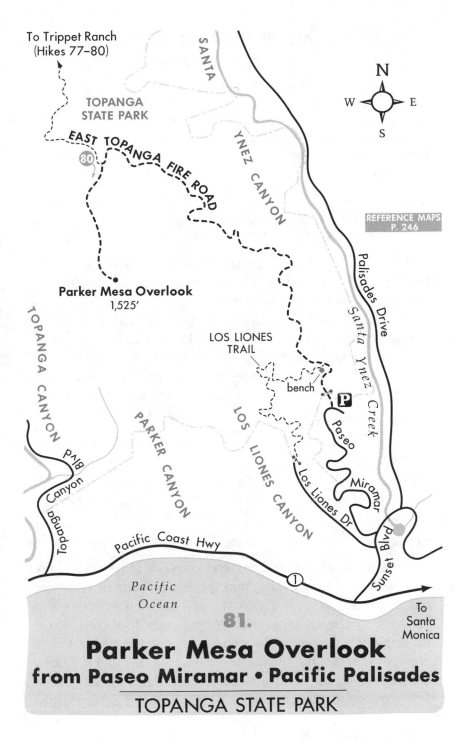

To Trippet Ranch
(Hikes 77–80)

TOPANGA
STATE PARK

EAST TOPANGA FIRE ROAD

80

SANTA

YNEZ CANYON

REFERENCE MAPS
P. 246

Palisades Drive

Parker Mesa Overlook
1,525'

Santa Ynez Creek

LOS LIONES
TRAIL

bench

P

Paseo

TOPANGA CANYON

PARKER CANYON

LOS LIONES CANYON

Los Liones Dr

Miramar

Topanga Canyon Blvd

Pacific Coast Hwy

1

Sunset Blvd

Pacific
Ocean

N
W   E
S

81.

To
Santa
Monica

Parker Mesa Overlook
from Paseo Miramar • Pacific Palisades
TOPANGA STATE PARK

82. Santa Ynez Canyon Falls

TOPANGA STATE PARK

Pacific Palisades trailhead

Hiking distance: 2.7 miles round trip
Hiking time: 1.5 hours
Configuration: out-and-back
Elevation gain: 300 feet
Difficulty: easy
Exposure: forested
Dogs: not allowed
Maps: U.S.G.S. Topanga · Topanga State Park map
     Tom Harrison Maps: Topanga State Park Trail Map

Santa Ynez Canyon Falls is a 25-foot cataract within Topanga State Park. The waterfall pours out of a channel in the sandstone rock into a pool. The falls is tucked into a narrow, steep-walled branch of the main canyon in a peaceful grotto surrounded by mossy sandstone cliffs and fern-lined pools. The trail to the falls winds through the natural sanctuary on the forested floor of Santa Ynez Canyon. Along the way are a series of stream crossings, magnificent sandstone formations, and lush riparian vegetation.

To the trailhead

From Santa Monica, drive 3 miles northbound on the Pacific Coast Highway/Highway 1 to Sunset Boulevard. Turn right and drive 0.4 miles to Palisades Drive. Turn left and continue 2.4 miles to Vereda de la Montura on the left. Turn left and park at the end of the road 0.1 mile ahead.

The hike

Pass the trailhead gate and descend steps to Santa Ynez Creek. Follow the east bank of the creek under the shade of sycamore and oak trees. Cross stepping stones over a side stream and continue up canyon. Cross the seasonal creek four consecutive times under a canopy of sycamores, passing sandstone formations with caves. After the fourth crossing is a trail split at Quarry Canyon, named for an abandoned limestone quarry. Stay to the left, crossing to the west side of the creek and a posted trail split at a half mile. The left fork leads 1.5 miles to Trippet Ranch (Hike 83).

Bear right on the Waterfall Trail, and cross to the east side of the creek. Follow the watercourse, crossing four more times as the steep-walled canyon tightly narrows. Work your way up the canyon, passing a jumble of boulders, cave-pocked sandstone formations, and ledges. Boulder-hop up the fern-lined rock grotto to the waterfall at the end of the box canyon. Just before reaching the falls, a path on the right climbs the east canyon wall to an over-look of the canyon. ■

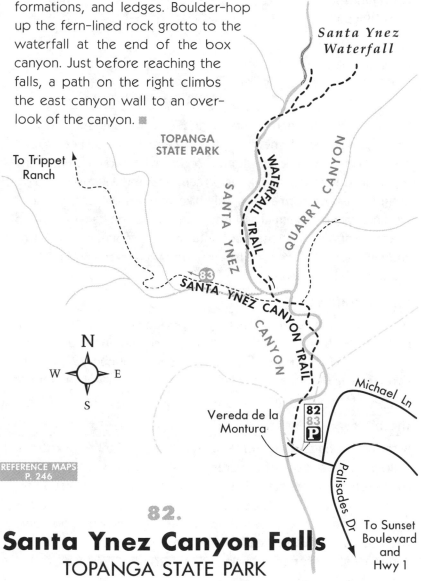

82.
Santa Ynez Canyon Falls
TOPANGA STATE PARK

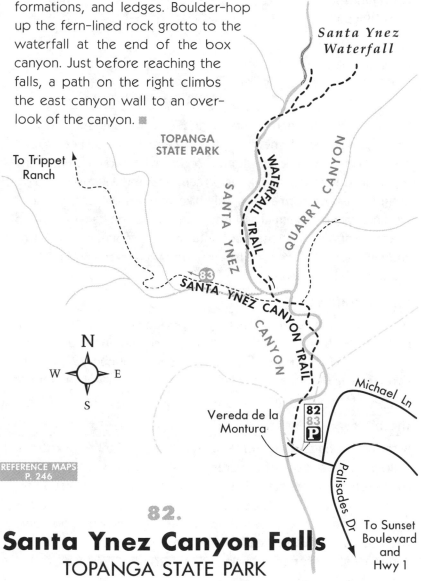
REFERENCE MAPS
P. 246

83. Santa Ynez Canyon to Trippet Ranch

TOPANGA STATE PARK
Pacific Palisades trailhead

Hiking distance: 4 miles round trip
Hiking time: 2 hours
Configuration: out-and-back
Elevation gain: 800 feet
Difficulty: moderate
Exposure: forested and exposed ridge
Dogs: not allowed
Maps: U.S.G.S. Topanga · Topanga State Park map
　　　　Tom Harrison Maps: Topanga State Park Trail Map

Santa Ynez Canyon runs north and south from the heart of Topanga State Park beneath Eagle Rock and Temescal Peak to the Pacific Highlands. The lush stream-fed canyon and natural sanctuary is filled with oaks, willows, sycamores, bay laurels, and towering sandstone formations. This hike follows the canyon floor with numerous stream crossings, then climbs the canyon wall to spectacular vistas across the Santa Monica Mountains. The trail ends at Trippet Ranch by a tree-shaded picnic area and pond at the park's headquarters.

To the trailhead

From Santa Monica, drive 3 miles northbound on the Pacific Coast Highway/Highway 1 to Sunset Boulevard. Turn right and drive 0.4 miles to Palisades Drive. Turn left and continue 2.4 miles to Vereda de la Montura on the left. Turn left and park at the end of the road 0.1 mile ahead.

The hike

Pass the trailhead gate and descend steps to Santa Ynez Creek. Follow the east bank of the creek under the shade of sycamore and oak trees. Cross stepping stones over a side stream and continue up canyon. Cross the seasonal creek four consecutive times under a canopy of sycamores while passing sandstone boulders with caves. After the fourth crossing is a trail split at Quarry Canyon, named for an abandoned limestone quarry. Stay to the

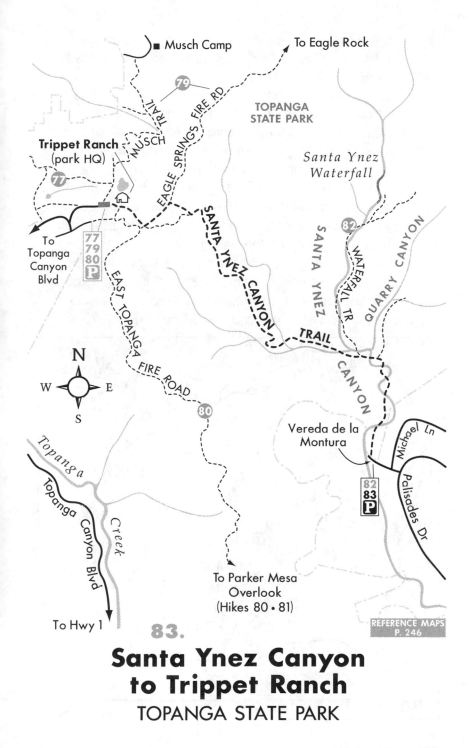

Musch Camp

To Eagle Rock

79

MUSCH TRAIL

EAGLE SPRINGS FIRE RD

TOPANGA
STATE PARK

*Santa Ynez
Waterfall*

Trippet Ranch
(park HQ)

77

To
Topanga
Canyon
Blvd

77
79
80
P

EAST TOPANGA

FIRE ROAD

80

SANTA YNEZ CANYON

TRAIL

SANTA YNEZ

CANYON

82

WATERFALL TR

QUARRY CANYON

N
W   E
S

Vereda de la
Montura

Michael Ln

82
83
P

Palisades Dr

Topanga

Topanga Canyon Blvd

Creek

To Parker Mesa
Overlook
(Hikes 80 • 81)

To Hwy 1

83.
Santa Ynez Canyon
to Trippet Ranch
TOPANGA STATE PARK

left, crossing to the west side of the creek and a posted trail split at a half mile. The right fork leads 0.8 miles to Santa Ynez Falls (Hike 82).

Stay to the left and wind through the lush riparian habitat, following the ephemeral stream. Cross to the north side of the stream and head up canyon. Ascend the hillside to the exposed, chaparral-covered slopes with dense stands of ceanothus, chamise, sumac, and toyon. From the hillside are 360-degree views of the mountainous backcountry Follow the slab-rock path on the ridge between two canyons feeding Santa Ynez Creek. Continue gaining altitude on the ridge, with a view of Temescal Peak at the head of the canyon to the right. Pass a posted trail on the left that cuts across to the East Topanga Fire Road. Walk straight ahead 150 yards to a junction with the Eagle Springs Fire Road at 2 miles. The left fork leads to Trippet Ranch and a picnic area. The right fork leads to Eagle Rock and Hub Junction (Hike 79). ▰

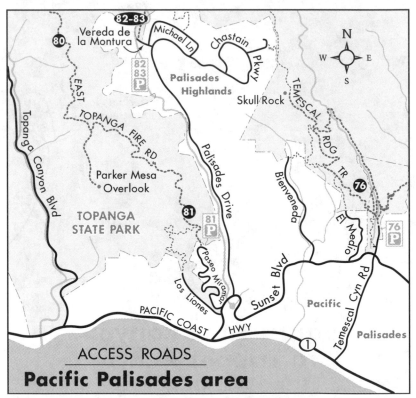

84. Caballero Canyon—
Dirt Mulholland Loop
MARVIN BRAUDE MULHOLLAND GATEWAY PARK
3600 Reseda Boulevard · Tarzana

Hiking distance: 3.7-mile loop
Hiking time: 2 hours
Configuration: loop (partially on paved road)
Elevation gain: 600 feet
Difficulty: easy to moderate
Exposure: exposed
Dogs: allowed
Maps: U.S.G.S. Conoga Park · Topanga State Park map
   Tom Harrison Maps: Topanga State Park Trail map

Caballero Canyon runs into the north border of Topanga State Park from Marvin Braude Mulholland Gateway Park. The grassy hillside park with picnic sites lies adjacent to Tarzana in the San Fernando Valley. From the north slope of the Santa Monica Mountains, this loop trail connects with an unpaved section of Mulholland Drive (commonly referred to as Dirt Mulholland). The hike follows the ridge and returns down Caballero Canyon through sycamore and willow groves along a seasonal streambed.

The trailhead is a popular link to Dirt Mulholland and is a key entry point into the northern part of Topanga State Park.

To the trailhead

From the Ventura Freeway/Highway 101 in Tarzana, exit on Reseda Boulevard. Drive 3.4 miles south into Marvin Braude Mulholland Gateway Park, and park at the end of the road. Inside the park gate is a white line painted across the road. Parking is free north of the white line, located 0.2 miles away from the trailhead. A parking fee is required south of the white line.

The hike

From the south end of Reseda Boulevard, take the gated Tarzana Fire Road, an unpaved fire road, up the hill into Topanga State Park. Pass a second vehicle gate, reaching Dirt Mulholland at 0.2 miles on a U-bend in the road. Bear left on the wide road, and follow the ridge across the head of Caballero Canyon, curving south then east. From the ridge are southern views into Temescal and Rustic Canyons and northern views into Caballero Canyon. At 0.7 miles, pass the Bent Arrow Trail, a connector trail to the Temescal Ridge Fire Road, and continue along the ridge. Just before the road curves left around a prominent hill known as Farmer Ridge, watch for the Caballero Canyon Trail on the left at 1.1 miles.

Bear left and descend down the east flank of the canyon. Wind downhill to the canyon floor dotted with sycamore trees and coastal sage scrub. Head north, parallel to an intermittent stream, and meander through the canyon to Reseda Boulevard at the old Caballero Canyon trailhead. Bear left and follow landscaped Reseda Boulevard above Caballero Canyon for 1.2 miles, back to the trailhead. ■

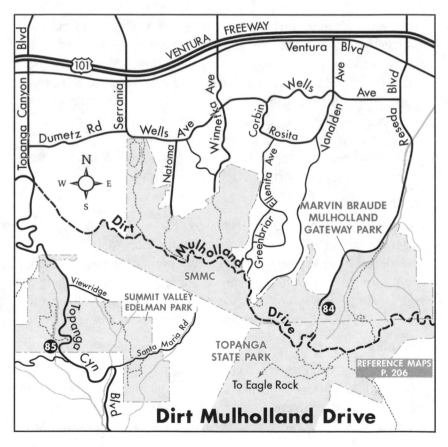

Dirt Mulholland Drive

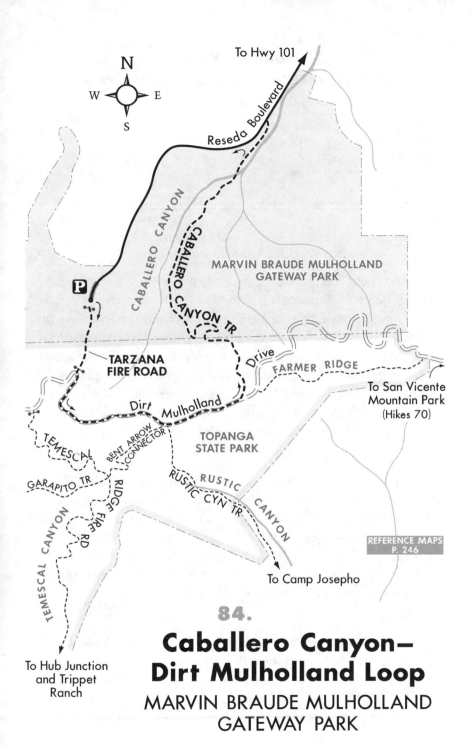

To Hwy 101

Reseda Boulevard

CABALLERO CANYON

CABALLERO CANYON TR

MARVIN BRAUDE MULHOLLAND
GATEWAY PARK

P

**TARZANA
FIRE ROAD**

Drive

FARMER RIDGE

To San Vicente
Mountain Park
(Hikes 70)

Dirt Mulholland

TEMESCAL

BENT ARROW
CONNECTOR

**TOPANGA
STATE PARK**

GARAPITO TR

RIDGE FIRE RD

RUSTIC CYN TR

RUSTIC CANYON

REFERENCE MAPS
P. 246

TEMESCAL CANYON

To Camp Josepho

To Hub Junction
and Trippet
Ranch

N
W   E
S

84.
Caballero Canyon–
Dirt Mulholland Loop
MARVIN BRAUDE MULHOLLAND
GATEWAY PARK

85. Summit Valley
SUMMIT VALLEY · EDMUND D. EDELMAN PARK
Topanga Canyon Boulevard · Topanga

Hiking distance: 2 miles round trip
Hiking time: 1 hour
Configuration: loop
Elevation gain: 300 feet
Difficulty: easy
Exposure: shaded canyon bottom and exposed ridge
Dogs: allowed
Maps: U.S.G.S. Conoga Park · Topanga State Park map
      Tom Harrison Maps: Topanga State Park Trail map

Edmund D. Edelman Park is located in bowl-shaped Summit Valley at the head of Topanga Canyon. The 1,500-foot ridge at the north end of this 652-acre park separates rural Topanga Canyon from the urban San Fernando Valley. The park's wildlife corridor includes oak woodlands, mixed chaparral communities, native grasslands, and the headwaters of Topanga Creek. The network of trails is open to hikers, bikers, and equestrians. This hike loops through two valleys, crosses the gently rolling hills, and parallels the headwaters of Topanga Creek.

To the trailhead

From Santa Monica, drive 4 miles northbound on the Pacific Coast Highway/Highway 1 to Topanga Canyon Boulevard and turn right. Continue 8.2 miles to the signed Summit Valley/Edmund D. Edelman parking area on the left (west).

From the Ventura Freeway/Highway 101 in Woodland Hills, exit on Topanga Canyon Boulevard, and drive 4 miles south to the parking area on the right (west).

The hike

Head west past the trailhead gate, and descend into the forested stream-fed draw, crossing the headwaters of Topanga Creek. At 0.2 miles is a five-way junction. Take the far right trail—the Summit Valley Canyon Trail—to begin the loop. Head north along the canyon floor, parallel to the seasonal Topanga Creek on the right. At one mile, just before descending into a eucalyptus grove, the unsigned Summit Valley Loop Trail bears left. Take this trail as it zigzags up the hillside towards the south. Traverse the edge of the hill to a ridge and a junction. (For a shorter hike, the left fork returns to the five-way junction along the ridge.) Take the middle fork straight ahead, and descend into the next drainage. The trail curves south, returning down the draw to the five-way junction. ■

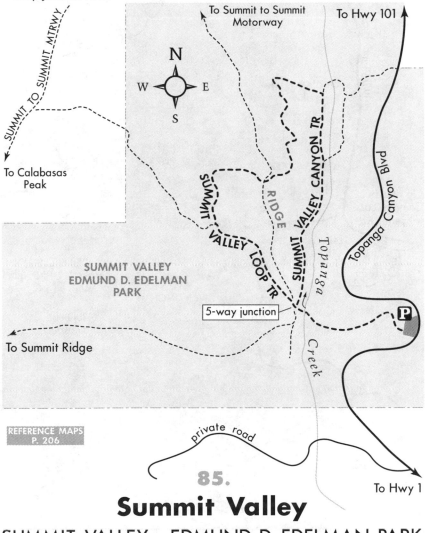

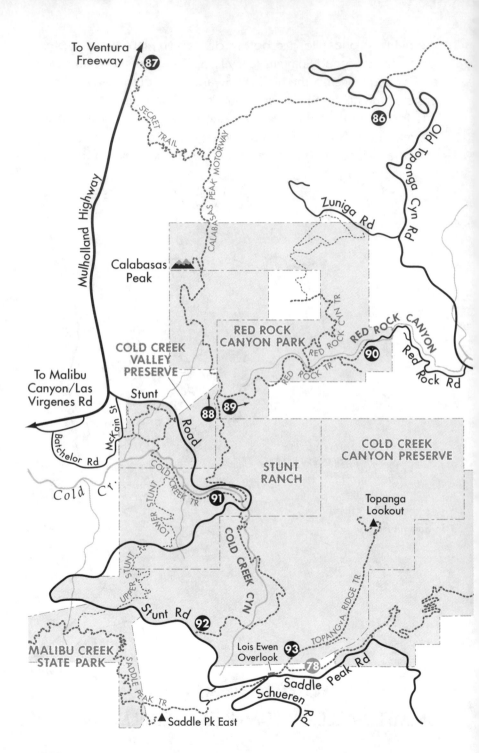

To Ventura Freeway

87

SECRET TRAIL

Mulholland Highway

86

Pid Canga Cyn Rd

Zuniga Rd

CALABASAS PEAK MOTORWAY

Calabasas Peak

RED ROCK CANYON PARK

RED ROCK CANYON

RED ROCK CYN TR

RED ROCK TR

90

Red Rock Rd

COLD CREEK VALLEY PRESERVE

To Malibu Canyon/Las Virgenes Rd

Stunt

88 89

Road

McKain St

Batchelor Rd

COLD CREEK CANYON PRESERVE

Cold Cr.

COLD CREEK TR

LOWER STUNT

STUNT RANCH

Topanga Lookout

91

COLD CREEK CYN

UPPER STUNT

Stunt Rd

92

TOPANGA RIDGE TR

93

Lois Ewen Overlook

78

Saddle Peak Rd

MALIBU CREEK STATE PARK

SADDLE PEAK TR

Schueren Rd

Saddle Pk East

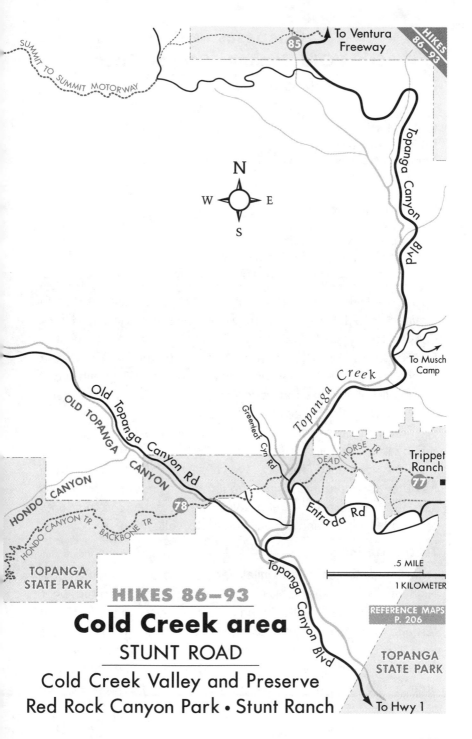

To Ventura Freeway

85

SUMMIT TO SUMMIT MOTORWAY

N
W · E
S

Topanga Canyon Blvd

To Musch Camp

Topanga Creek

Greenleaf Cyn Rd

Old Topanga Canyon Rd

OLD TOPANGA CANYON

DEAD HORSE TR

Trippet Ranch

77

HONDO CANYON

HONDO CANYON TR · BACKBONE TR

78

Entrada Rd

.5 MILE

1 KILOMETER

TOPANGA STATE PARK

Topanga Canyon Blvd

REFERENCE MAPS
P. 206

TOPANGA STATE PARK

To Hwy 1

HIKES 86–93
Cold Creek area
STUNT ROAD
Cold Creek Valley and Preserve
Red Rock Canyon Park • Stunt Ranch

86. Calabasas Peak
from Old Topanga Canyon Road
Calabasas Peak Motorway
Calabasas · Malibu

Hiking distance: 5 miles round trip
Hiking time: 2.5 hours
Configuration: out-and-back
Elevation gain: 700 feet
Difficulty: moderate
Exposure: exposed
Dogs: allowed
Maps: U.S.G.S. Malibu Beach
Tom Harrison Maps: Topanga State Park Trail Map
Tom Harrison Maps: Malibu Creek State Park Trail Map

Calabasas Peak is perched high above the city of Calabasas at an elevation of 2,163 feet. From the summit are views into Red Rock Canyon to the east, Cold Creek Canyon to the south, and the San Fernando Valley to the north. Access to the peak is via the Calabasas Peak Motorway, an unpaved fire road. The gated dirt road follows a ridge between Old Topanga Canyon Road and Stunt Road by Cold Creek Canyon Preserve.

Three routes lead to the rounded peak. This hike ascends to the peak along the fire road from Old Topanga Canyon Road from the northeast. (The next two hikes climb to the peak from its other access routes.) Throughout the hike are weather-carved sandstone outcroppings and sweeping vistas across the Santa Monica Mountains and the San Fernando Valley.

To the trailhead

From Santa Monica, drive 4 miles northbound on the Pacific Coast Highway/Highway 1 to Topanga Canyon Boulevard and turn right. Continue 4.2 miles to Old Topanga Canyon Road on the left. Turn left and drive 4.1 miles up Old Topanga Canyon Road to Calabasas Peak Motorway on the left, across from the Summit to Summit Motorway. Turn left and continue 140 yards to a wide parking area on the left. (En route, the road passes the posted trailhead

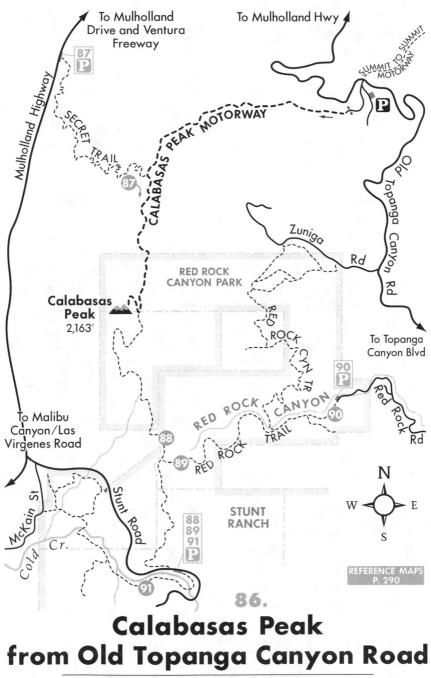

To Mulholland Drive and Ventura Freeway

To Mulholland Hwy

SUMMIT TO SUMMIT MOTORWAY

Mulholland Highway

87 P

SECRET TRAIL

CALABASAS PEAK MOTORWAY

87

P

PIO

Topanga Canyon Rd

Zuniga Rd

RED ROCK CANYON PARK

Calabasas Peak 2,163'

RED ROCK CYN TR

To Topanga Canyon Blvd

To Malibu Canyon/Las Virgenes Road

RED ROCK CANYON TRAIL

90 P

90

Red Rock Rd

88

89

RED ROCK TRAIL

McKain St

Cold Cr.

Stunt Road

88 89 91 P

STUNT RANCH

91

N
W   E
S

REFERENCE MAPS P. 290

86.

Calabasas Peak
from Old Topanga Canyon Road

Calabasas Peak Motorway

on the right.) Limited parking is also available in narrow pullouts on the left (southwest) side of Old Topanga Canyon Road.

From the Ventura Freeway/Highway 101 in Woodland Hills, exit on Topanga Canyon Boulevard. Drive 1.3 miles south to Mulholland Drive. Turn right and continue 2.2 miles to Old Topanga Canyon Road on the left. (En route, veer left onto Mulholland Highway.) Turn left on Old Topanga Canyon Road, and drive 1.5 miles to Calabasas Peak Motorway on the right, across from the Summit to Summit Motorway. Turn right and go 140 yards to a wide parking area on the left, passing the signed trailhead on the right. Limited parking is also available in narrow pullouts on the left (southwest) side of Old Topanga Canyon Road.

The hike

From the parking area, walk 60 yards down the paved road to the signed access trail on the left. From Old Topanga Canyon Road, walk 80 yards up the paved road to the signed access trail on the right.

Walk up the slope on the footpath 0.1 mile to a T-junction with the Calabasas Peak Motorway, a dirt fire road. The right fork leads a short distance to a home on private land. Bear left and head west. From the trail are exceptional views of the San Fernando Valley and the interior of the Santa Monica Mountains. Climb the first hill, then descend on the rolling ridge. Steadily climb the second slope, with continuing vistas across the valley to the Los Padres National Forest and the San Gabriel Mountains. At the top of the slope, Calabasas Peak comes into full view. Curve left and head south towards the peak.

At 1.6 miles, pass the signed Calabasas–Cold Creek (Secret) Trail (Hike 87) on the right. Continue up the road 0.9 miles, with alternating east and west views. Just before the crest of the road, a footpath to the summit veers sharply to the right. The main Calabasas Peak Motorway continues straight, leading 1.7 miles down to Stunt Road (Hike 88). Leave the fire road and switchback to the right. Follow the ridge 0.2 miles, bending left to the 2,163-foot summit on a small, exposed knoll. At the peak is a rock cairn, survey pin, and 360-degree vistas. ∎

87. Calabasas Peak from Mulholland Highway
Calabasas-Cold Creek (Secret) Trail
Calabasas · Malibu

Hiking distance: 4.6 miles round trip
Hiking time: 2.5 hours
Configuration: out-and-back
Elevation gain: 700 feet
Difficulty: moderate
Exposure: exposed with shaded pockets
Dogs: allowed
Maps: U.S.G.S. Malibu Beach
　　　　 Tom Harrison Maps: Malibu Creek State Park Trail Map

The Calabasas-Cold Creek Trail (also known as the Secret Trail) is a multi-use trail that winds up the mountain from Mulholland Highway to the Calabasas Peak Motorway. Ascending from the northwest, the 1.5-mile connector path weaves through grasslands, chaparral, oak woodland, riparian willow, and volcanic rock formations. This hike leads through this diverse area to the 2,163-foot summit of Calabasas Peak. The trail offers outstanding vistas into Red Rock Canyon, Cold Creek Canyon, Old Topanga Canyon, and across the San Fernando Valley to the San Gabriel Mountains. En route, the trail passes multi-colored sandstone formations, winds through shaded ravines with scrub oak groves, and climbs chaparral-covered slopes to the ridge.

To the trailhead

From Santa Monica, drive 12 miles northbound on the Pacific Coast Highway/Highway 1 to Malibu Canyon Road. Turn right and drive 6.5 miles to Mulholland Highway. Turn right and continue 5.8 miles to the signed trailhead on the right. Park in the pullouts alongside the road.

From the Ventura Freeway/Highway 101 in Calabasas, exit on Las Virgenes Road. Head 3.1 miles south to Mulholland Highway. Turn left and continue 5.8 miles to the signed trailhead on the right. Park in the pullouts alongside the road.

The hike

Pass the trailhead sign and climb the mountain slope. Enter a forest of mature oak trees, then return to the open grassy hillside. Weave along the foothills and enter an oak forest again. Cross a stream and continue above and parallel to Mulholland Highway. Curve left, away from the road, and leave the forest. Steadily head upward to great mountain views. Top a ridge to a close-up view of Calabasas Peak. Drop down into a canyon with eroded sandstone outcroppings. Walk over slab rock and cross the canyon. Climb the south canyon wall, walking among additional weather-carved rock formations. At 1.5 miles, the trail ends at a T-junction with the Calabasas Peak Motorway. The left fork leads 1.4 miles to Old Topanga Canyon Road (Hike 86).

To ascend Calabasas Peak, bear right on the dirt fire road and head south. From the trail are expansive views across the mountains to the ocean. Follow the serpentine path uphill, with alternating east and west views. Just before the crest of the road, a footpath to the summit veers sharply to the right. The Calabasas Peak Motorway continues straight, leading 1.7 miles down to Stunt Road (Hike 88). Leave the fire road and switchback to the right. Follow the ridge 0.2 miles, bending left to the 2,163-foot summit in a low thicket of chaparral. At the peak is a rock cairn, survey pin, and 360-degree vistas. ■

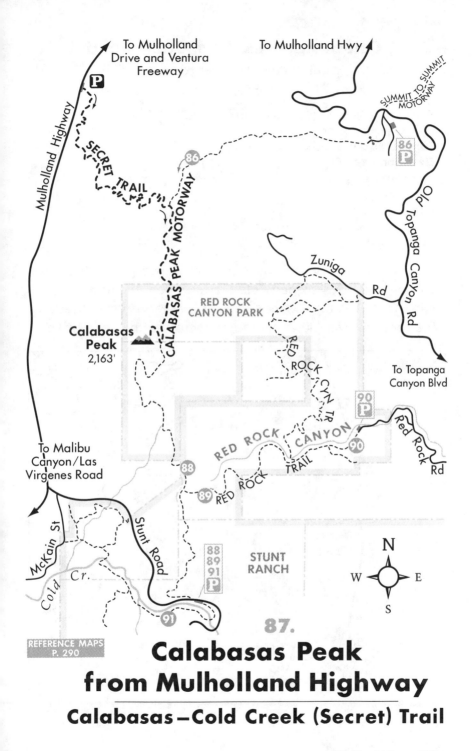

To Mulholland Drive and Ventura Freeway

P

To Mulholland Hwy

Mulholland Highway

SUMMIT TO SUMMIT MOTORWAY

SECRET TRAIL

86

P10

Topanga Canyon Rd

86 **P**

CALABASAS PEAK MOTORWAY

Zuniga

Rd

Calabasas Peak 2,163'

RED ROCK CANYON PARK

RED ROCK CYN TR

To Topanga Canyon Blvd

90 **P**

To Malibu Canyon/Las Virgenes Road

RED ROCK

CANYON

TRAIL

90

Red Rock Rd

88

89

RED ROCK

McKain St

Stunt Road

88
89
91
P

STUNT RANCH

Cold Cr.

91

N
W E
S

REFERENCE MAPS P. 290

87.

Calabasas Peak
from Mulholland Highway
Calabasas–Cold Creek (Secret) Trail

88. Calabasas Peak from Stunt Road
Calabasas Peak Motorway
Calabasas · Malibu

Hiking distance: 4 miles round trip
Hiking time: 2 hours
Configuration: out-and-back
Elevation gain: 900 feet
Difficulty: easy to moderate
Exposure: exposed
Dogs: allowed
Maps: U.S.G.S. Malibu Beach · Topanga State Park map
      Tom Harrison Maps: Malibu Creek State Park Trail map

Calabasas Peak towers over Red Rock Canyon, Old Topanga Canyon, and bowl-shaped Cold Creek Canyon. The route to the 2,163-foot peak follows the Calabasas Peak Motorway, a graded fire road. The vehicle-restricted road crosses the head of Red

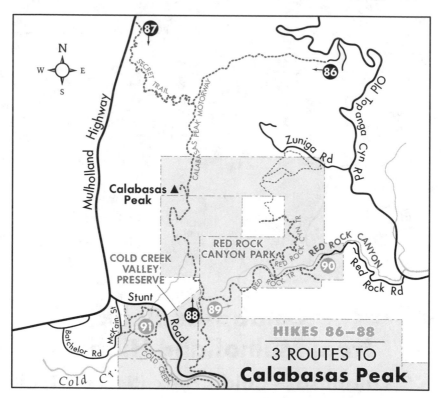

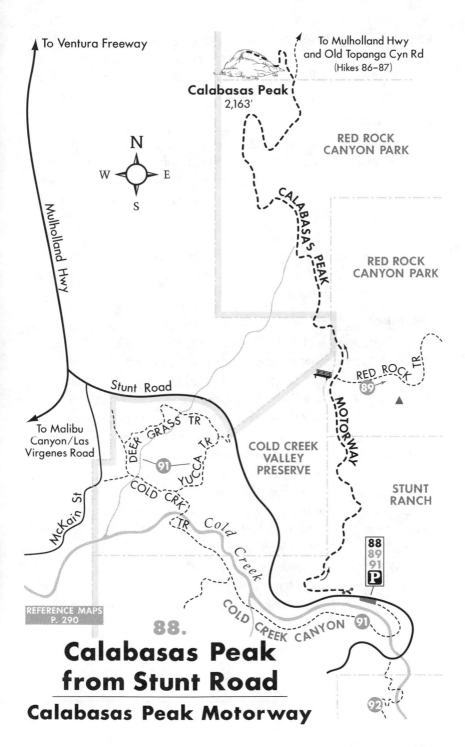

To Ventura Freeway

To Mulholland Hwy
and Old Topanga Cyn Rd
(Hikes 86–87)

Calabasas Peak
2,163'

RED ROCK
CANYON PARK

RED ROCK
CANYON PARK

N
W   E
S

Mulholland Hwy

CALABASAS PEAK

RED ROCK TR

Stunt Road

89

To Malibu
Canyon/Las
Virgenes Road

DEER GRASS TR

YUCCA TR

91

COLD CRK

COLD CREEK
VALLEY
PRESERVE

MOTORWAY

STUNT
RANCH

McKain St

TR

Cold Creek

88
89
91
P

REFERENCE MAPS
P. 290

COLD CREEK CANYON

91

88.

Calabasas Peak
from Stunt Road
Calabasas Peak Motorway

92

Rock Canyon past magnificent geological formations, including large, weathered sandstone outcroppings and tilted sandstone slabs with long ribs. Along the trail are spectacular 360-degree vistas into the surrounding canyons and the San Fernando Valley.

To the trailhead

From Santa Monica, drive 12 miles northbound on the Pacific Coast Highway/Highway 1 to Malibu Canyon Road. Turn right and drive 6.5 miles to Mulholland Highway. Turn right and continue 4 miles to Stunt Road. Turn right again and drive one mile to the pullout on the right.

From the Ventura Freeway/Highway 101 in Calabasas, exit on Las Virgenes Road. Head 3 miles south to Mulholland Highway. Turn left and go 4 miles to Stunt Road. Turn right and drive one mile to the pullout on the right.

The hike

Cross Stunt Road and walk 20 yards downhill to the trailhead on the right. Walk up the unpaved fire road past the gate. The trail zigzags up the mountain to a junction at 0.7 miles on a saddle at the head of Red Rock Canyon. The right fork heads into Red Rock Canyon (Hike 89). Continue straight ahead to the north along the cliff's edge, passing large eroded sandstone slabs while over-looking Red Rock Canyon. As Calabasas Peak comes into view, the trail curves sharply to the right, circling the peak along an eastern ridge. From the ridge are views into Old Topanga Canyon to the northeast. Just past the crest of the road, a narrow foot-path veers off to the left. Follow the ridge 0.2 miles, bending left to the rounded 2,163-foot summit. At the chaparral-covered peak is a rock cairn, survey pin, and 360-degree vistas.

The Calabasas Peak Motorway continues 2.5 miles north to Old Topanga Canyon Road (Hike 86) and Mulholland Highway (Hike 87). ■

89. Red Rock Canyon
from Calabasas Peak Motorway

COLD CREEK—RED ROCK CANYON
Calabasas · Malibu

Hiking distance: 4 miles round trip
Hiking time: 2 hours
Configuration: out-and-back
Elevation gain: 700 feet
Difficulty: easy
Exposure: exposed
Dogs: allowed
Maps: U.S.G.S. Malibu Beach
      Tom Harrison Maps: Malibu Creek State Park Trail map
      Tom Harrison Maps: Topanga State Park Trail map

Red Rock Canyon is a beautiful, multicolored canyon that looks similar to the canyons in the southwest. Huge weather-sculpted red sandstone formations and conglomerate rocks dominate a landscape that is dotted with oaks and sycamores. Shell fossils can be spotted in the eroded rocks, shallow caves, overhangs, and arches. The riparian canyon is a wildlife corridor connecting Topanga State Park and Malibu Creek State Park. The trail follows the first portion of the Calabasas Peak Motorway—a graded fire road—to the head of Red Rock Canyon.

To the trailhead

From Santa Monica, drive 12 miles northbound on the Pacific Coast Highway/Highway 1 to Malibu Canyon Road. Turn right and drive 6.5 miles to Mulholland Highway. Turn right and continue 4 miles to Stunt Road. Turn right again and drive one mile to the pullout on the right.

From the Ventura Freeway/Highway 101 in Calabasas, exit on Las Virgenes Road. Head 3 miles south to Mulholland Highway. Turn left and go 4 miles to Stunt Road. Turn right and drive one mile to the pullout on the right.

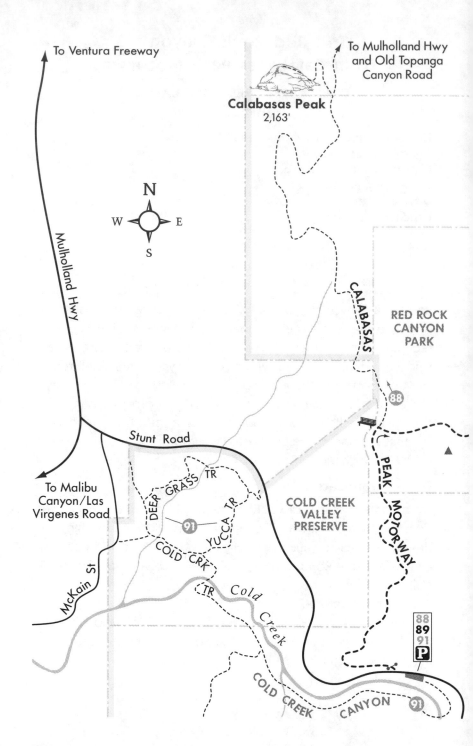

To Ventura Freeway

To Mulholland Hwy
and Old Topanga
Canyon Road

Calabasas Peak
2,163'

N
W — E
S

Mulholland Hwy

CALABASAS

RED ROCK
CANYON
PARK

Stunt Road

To Malibu
Canyon/Las
Virgenes Road

DEER GRASS TR

YUCCA TR

91

COLD CRK

TR

McKain St

Cold Creek

COLD CREEK
VALLEY
PRESERVE

PEAK MOTORWAY

88

88
89
91
P

COLD CREEK CANYON

91

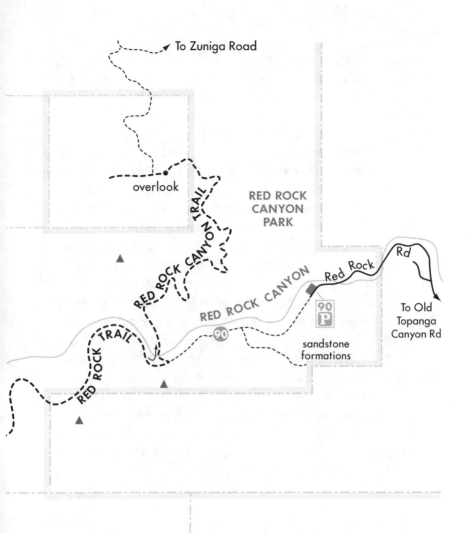

To Zuniga Road

overlook

RED ROCK
CANYON
PARK

RED ROCK CANYON TRAIL

Red Rock Rd

To Old
Topanga
Canyon Rd

RED ROCK CANYON

RED ROCK TRAIL

90
P

90

sandstone
formations

STUNT RANCH

REFERENCE MAPS
P. 290

89.
Red Rock Canyon
from Calabasas Peak Motorway
COLD CREEK–RED ROCK CANYON

The hike

Cross Stunt Road and walk 20 yards downhill to the trailhead on the right. Walk up the unpaved fire road past the gate. The trail zigzags up the mountain to a junction at 0.7 miles on a saddle at the head of Red Rock Canyon. The trail straight ahead to the north leads to Calabasas Peak (Hike 88).

Take the right fork to the east, and descend into Red Rock Canyon. Continue downhill, skirting the base of the imposing rock walls. At 1.4 miles, the dirt road reaches a posted junction in an oak grove beneath towering sandstone rock. The road continues a half mile straight ahead to Red Rock Road (Hike 90). For this hike, take the footpath to the left. Cross a small stream and walk up wooden steps to the base of additional formations. Curve up the draw, crossing a seasonal stream to 360-degree vistas of the rock formations and surrounding mountains. With every step, new formations and different angles of the gorgeous rocks come into view. Climb the spine of the mountain while being frequently distracted by the visuals. The maintained trail ends among sandstone rocks that sit atop a 1,500-foot knoll on the north rim. Fifty yards beyond the knoll is a fork. The left branch climbs to another knoll, then the path narrows and is overgrown with vegetation. The right fork descends into an adjoining canyon to the north, with an additional display of red rock outcrops. The path to the north ends at Zuniga Road. ▪

90. Red Rock Canyon from Red Rock Road

RED ROCK CANYON PARK
Calabasas · Malibu

Hiking distance: 2.4 miles round trip
Hiking time: 1.5 hours
Configuration: out-and-back
Elevation gain: 500 feet
Difficulty: easy to moderate
Exposure: shaded canyon bottom and exposed hillside
Dogs: allowed
Maps: U.S.G.S. Malibu Beach
       Tom Harrison Maps: Malibu Creek State Park Trail map
       Tom Harrison Maps: Topanga State Park Trail map

Red Rock Canyon is a picturesque, riparian gorge with sculptured red sandstone formations and conglomerate rocks. The uplifted and tilted outcroppings are a visual treat. The narrow canyon bottom is rich with sycamore and oak trees, creating a stunning contrast of red rocks rising out of the lush green surroundings. The canyon, adjacent to Calabasas Peak, is a wildlife corridor linking Topanga State Park with Malibu Creek State Park.

Red Rock Canyon can be accessed from the west via the Calabasas Peak Motorway off of Stunt Road (Hike 89) and from the east via Red Rock Road off of Old Topanga Canyon Road (this hike). The trail begins on a fire road along the cool canyon floor beneath the towering weather-carved monoliths. The hike climbs the north canyon wall to additional formations and overlooks.

To the trailhead

From Santa Monica, drive 4 miles northbound on the Pacific Coast Highway/Highway 1 to Topanga Canyon Boulevard and turn right. Continue 4.2 miles to Old Topanga Canyon Road on the left. Turn left and drive 1.8 miles up Old Topanga Canyon Road to Red Rock Road on the left. Turn left and drive 0.8 miles on the narrow, winding road to the trailhead and parking area at the end of the road. A parking fee is required.

From the Ventura Freeway/Highway 101 in Woodland Hills, exit on Topanga Canyon Boulevard. Drive 8 miles south to Old Topanga Canyon Road on the right. Turn right and continue 1.8 miles up Old Topanga Canyon Road to Red Rock Road on the left. Turn left and drive 0.8 miles on the narrow, winding road to the trailhead and parking area at the end of the road. A parking fee is required.

The hike

Walk past the trailhead gate and follow the south side of Red Rock Canyon. Wind along the old dirt road besides chaparral, oaks, and sycamores among a magnificent display of cavernous red rock formations and walls of weather-sculpted conglomerates. A short side path on the left detours to massive sandstone formations with weather-carved caves and overhangs. At a half mile, the dirt road reaches a posted junction in an oak grove beneath towering sandstone rock. The road continues 0.8 miles straight ahead to the Calabasas Peak Motorway (Hike 89).

For this hike, take the footpath to the right. Cross a small stream and walk up wooden steps to the base of additional formations. Curve up the draw, crossing a seasonal stream to 360-degree vistas of the rock formations and surrounding mountains. With every step, new formations and different angles of the gorgeous rocks come into view. Climb the spine of the mountain while being frequently distracted by the visuals. The maintained trail ends among sandstone rock atop a 1,500-foot knoll on the north rim. Fifty yards beyond the knoll is a fork. The left branch climbs to another knoll, then the path narrows and is overgrown with vegetation. The right fork descends into an adjoining canyon to the north with an additional display of red rock outcrops. The path to the north ends at Zuniga Road. ▨

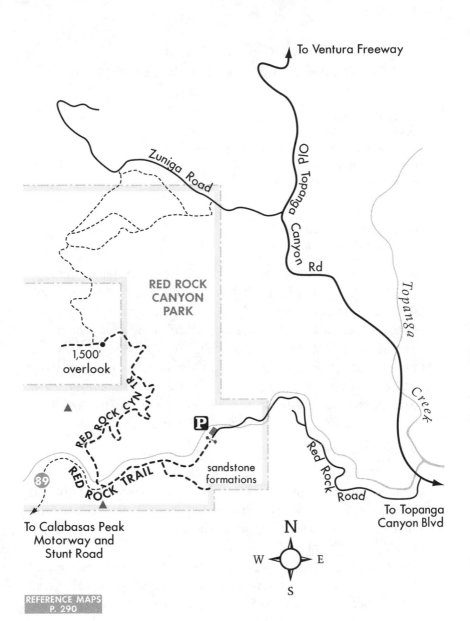

To Ventura Freeway

Zuniga Road

Old Topanga Canyon Rd

Topanga Creek

RED ROCK
CANYON
PARK

1,500'
overlook

RED ROCK CYN TR

P

RED ROCK TRAIL

sandstone
formations

Red Rock Road

89

To Calabasas Peak
Motorway and
Stunt Road

To Topanga
Canyon Blvd

N
W   E
S

REFERENCE MAPS
P. 290

90.
Red Rock Canyon
from Red Rock Road
RED ROCK CANYON PARK

91. Cold Creek Trail

STUNT RANCH—COLD CREEK VALLEY PRESERVE

Calabasas · Malibu

Hiking distance: 2.5 miles round trip
Hiking time: 1.5 hours
Configuration: out-and-back with loop
Elevation gain: 300 feet
Difficulty: easy
Exposure: exposed
Dogs: allowed
Maps: U.S.G.S. Malibu Beach
   Tom Harrison Maps: Malibu Creek State Park Trail map

The Cold Creek Valley Preserve sits in a shallow bowl among craggy sandstone peaks. It is home to a wide assortment of flowers and plant communities. Perennial Cold Creek flows through the valley preserve and Cold Creek Canyon. It is one of the few year-round streams in the Santa Monica Mountains. The Cold Creek Trail leads to the 57-acre preserve, parallel to the creek. The trail meanders through riparian woodlands and a gently rolling grass meadow. En route, the trail crosses the creek three times and traverses the hillside under the shade of oaks and sycamores.

To the trailhead

From Santa Monica, drive 12 miles northbound on the Pacific Coast Highway/Highway 1 to Malibu Canyon Road. Turn right and drive 6.5 miles to Mulholland Highway. Turn right and continue 4 miles to Stunt Road. Turn right again and drive one mile to the pullout on the right.

From the Ventura Freeway/Highway 101 in Calabasas, exit on Las Virgenes Road. Head 3 miles south to Mulholland Highway. Turn left and go 4 miles to Stunt Road. Turn right and drive one mile to the pullout on the right.

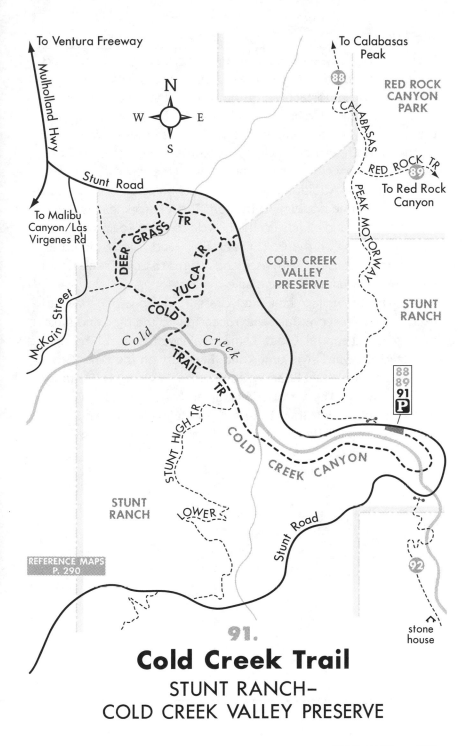

To Ventura Freeway

To Calabasas Peak

Mulholland Hwy

Stunt Road

88

RED ROCK CANYON PARK

CALABASAS

To Malibu Canyon/Las Virgenes Rd

DEER GRASS TR

YUCCA TR

RED ROCK TR

89

To Red Rock Canyon

PEAK MOTORWAY

McKain Street

COLD

COLD CREEK VALLEY PRESERVE

STUNT RANCH

Cold Creek

TRAIL TR

88
89
91
P

COLD CREEK CANYON

STUNT HIGH TR

STUNT RANCH

LOWER

Stunt Road

92

REFERENCE MAPS
P. 290

stone house

91.
Cold Creek Trail
STUNT RANCH–
COLD CREEK VALLEY PRESERVE

The hike

Take the trail southeast for a short distance, parallel to Stunt Road. Curve right and cross Cold Creek. Just after crossing, watch for Native American mortar holes ground into the sandstone rocks on the right. Chumash Indians originally lived in this area and formed these holes while grinding acorns. Follow the creek downstream on the Cold Creek Trail, and head into the oak-shaded corridor. Cross a tributary stream to a junction with the Lower Stunt High Trail on the left. Additional ancient mortar holes can be spotted on the sandstone boulder to the left. The left fork leaves the riparian canopy and climbs up the hillside to Stunt Road. Continue straight—staying on the Cold Creek Trail—and follow the creek. Walk northwest as the path rises and returns to Cold Creek. Cross the creek to a junction at one mile.

Begin the half-mile Yucca-Deer Grass Trail loop within the Cold Creek Valley Preserve. Take the Yucca Trail to the right and stroll through the chaparral. Cross a small drainage to a fork. The right fork leads 30 yards to Stunt Road. Bear left on the Deer Grass Trail, and parallel Stunt Road through a meadow. Cross a tributary of Cold Creek and curve left. Climb up and over a hill to a junction with the Cold Creek Trail. The right fork leads to McKain Street. Go left and complete the loop at 1.5 miles. Stay to the right and retrace your steps. ▪

92. Cold Creek Canyon Preserve
Calabasas · Malibu

A free access permit is required from
The Mountains Restoration Trust: (818) 591-1701
www.mountainstrust.org

Hiking distance: 3.3 miles round trip
Hiking time: 1.5 hours
Configuration: out-and-back
Elevation gain: 800 feet
Difficulty: easy to moderate
Exposure: a mix of exposed slope and shaded streamside habitat
Dogs: not allowed
Maps: U.S.G.S. Malibu Beach
　　　　Tom Harrison Maps: Malibu Creek State Park Trail map
　　　　Tom Harrison Maps: Topanga State Park Trail map

Cold Creek Canyon is a pristine, bowl-shaped canyon nestled on the steep north slope behind Saddle Peak (northeast of Malibu). Cold Creek, a perennial stream and major upland tributary of Malibu Creek, flows through the preserve. The Cold Creek watershed is among the most biologically diverse ecosystems in the Santa Monica Mountains. It supports manzanita, chaparral, coast live oak, sycamore woodlands, riparian streamside habitats (including orchids), a variety of ferns, phacelia, cattails, red shank, and Humboldt lily. The 1,100-acre nature preserve is owned by the Mountains Restoration Trust, a non-profit land trust created to protect and enhance the natural resources of the Santa Monica Mountains. To protect the fragile resources of the preserve, a free access permit is requested (see contact information above).

Cold Creek Canyon has high ridges, a steep slope, magnificent sandstone formations, rocky grottoes, waterfalls, and canyon views. The headwaters of Cold Creek originate within the preserve, rising from springs and cascading down canyon. This hike winds down the north-facing watershed through lush streamside vegetation and jungle-like ferns, passing cascades and small waterfalls. The trail weaves through the natural basin in an idyllic setting under oak, maple, sycamore, and bay woodlands. Watch for the remains of a 1900s-era homesteader house, hand-carved into the giant split sandstone boulders.

To the trailhead

From Santa Monica, drive 12 northbound on the Pacific Coast Highway/Highway 1 to Malibu Canyon Road and turn right. Drive 6.5 miles to Mulholland Highway. Turn right and continue 4 miles to Stunt Road. Turn right and drive 3.3 miles to the Cold Creek parking pullout on the left by a chain-link fence. Park off road on the shoulder.

From the Ventura Freeway/Highway 101 in Calabasas, exit on Las Virgenes Road. Head 3 miles south to Mulholland Highway. Turn left and continue 4 miles to Stunt Road. Turn right and drive 3.3 miles to the Cold Creek parking pullout on the left.

The hike

Walk through the gate in the chain-link fence, and head east through the tall chaparral. The trail leads gradually downhill along the contours of the hillside and across a wooden bridge over Cold Creek at 0.6 miles. Pass moss-covered rocks and a rusty classic Dodge truck as you make your way into the lush vegetation and open oak woodland of the canyon floor. Cross Cold Creek again and continue past large sandstone boulders to the remains of gold miner Herman Hethke's stone house. Several switchbacks lead downhill across side streams and past small waterfalls. At 1.6 miles, the path reaches the locked lower gate at Stunt Road. Return by retracing your steps up canyon. ∎

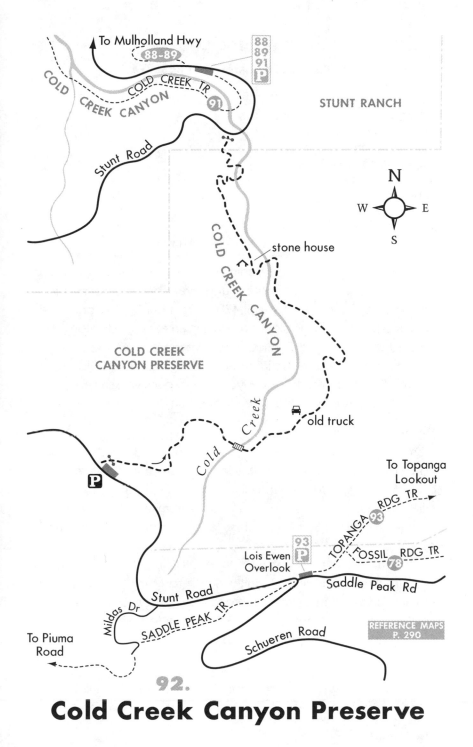

To Mulholland Hwy

88-89

88
89
91
P

COLD CREEK TR

91

STUNT RANCH

COLD CREEK CANYON

Stunt Road

N

W — E

S

COLD CREEK CANYON

stone house

COLD CREEK
CANYON PRESERVE

Cold Creek

old truck

P

To Topanga
Lookout

TOPANGA RDG TR

93

FOSSIL RDG TR

78

Lois Ewen
Overlook

93
P

Saddle Peak Rd

Stunt Road

Mildas Dr

SADDLE PEAK TR

Schueren Road

To Piuma
Road

REFERENCE MAPS
P. 290

92.
Cold Creek Canyon Preserve

93. Topanga Fire Lookout
COLD CREEK CANYON PRESERVE
Calabasas · Malibu

Hiking distance: 2 miles round trip
Hiking time: 1 hour
Configuration: out-and-back
Elevation gain: 200 feet
Difficulty: easy
Exposure: exposed
Dogs: allowed
Maps: U.S.G.S. Malibu Beach
      Tom Harrison Maps: Topanga State Park Trail map

The Topanga Fire Lookout, ironically, was destroyed in a 1970 fire. All that remains is a large multi-level concrete foundation perched at the edge of the 2,470-foot mountain. A one-mile fire road leads to the lookout, following an easy grade along the east ridge of the Cold Creek Canyon Preserve. From the foundation are spectacular views into Old Topanga Canyon, Cold Creek Canyon Preserve, Red Rock Canyon, the expansive San Fernando Valley to Los Angeles, and Santa Monica Bay.

To the trailhead

From Santa Monica, drive 12 miles northbound on the Pacific Coast Highway/Highway 1 to Malibu Canyon Road. Turn right and drive 6.5 miles to Mulholland Highway. Turn right and continue 4 miles to Stunt Road. Turn right and drive 4 miles up the winding road to the end of Stunt Road. Turn left on Saddle Peak Road, and park in the pullout on the left.

From the Ventura Freeway/Highway 101 in Calabasas, exit on Las Virgenes Road. Head 3.1 miles south to Mulholland Highway. Turn left and go 4 miles to Stunt Road. Turn right and drive 4 miles up the road to the end of Stunt Road. Turn left on Saddle Peak Road, and park in the pullout on the left.

The hike

From the parking pullout (the Lois Ewen Overlook), walk to the gated service road. Head northeast on the paved road—the

Topanga Ridge Trail. Follow the ridge high above Cold Creek Canyon. Calabasas Peak (Hikes 86—88) can be seen to the north. Pass the Fossil Ridge Trail on the right (a section of the Backbone Trail) to a road split at a quarter mile. The paved right fork leads to a radar tower. Stay to the left on the wide, unpaved path and continue gradually uphill. At one mile is a graffiti-covered concrete foundation on a buttress, the site of the abandoned fire lookout. From the old lookout foundation on the mountain's edge is a view into Hondo Canyon, Red Rock Canyon, Old Topanga Canyon, the Cold Creek drainage, and across sections of Los Angeles. Miles beyond, the views span across the San Fernando Valley to the Santa Susana Mountains. ■

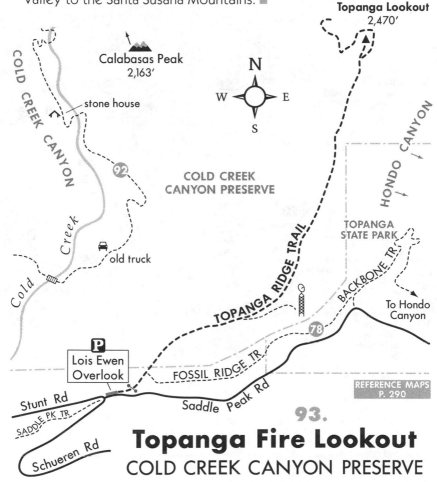

COLD CREEK CANYON

Calabasas Peak
2,163'

stone house

N
W ← → E
S

COLD CREEK
CANYON PRESERVE

Topanga Lookout
2,470'

HONDO CANYON

TOPANGA
STATE PARK

Creek

old truck

Cold

TOPANGA RIDGE TRAIL

BACKBONE TR.

To Hondo
Canyon

P
Lois Ewen
Overlook

FOSSIL RIDGE TR.

Stunt Rd

SADDLE PK. TR.

Saddle Peak Rd

Schueren Rd

REFERENCE MAPS
P. 290

93.
Topanga Fire Lookout
COLD CREEK CANYON PRESERVE

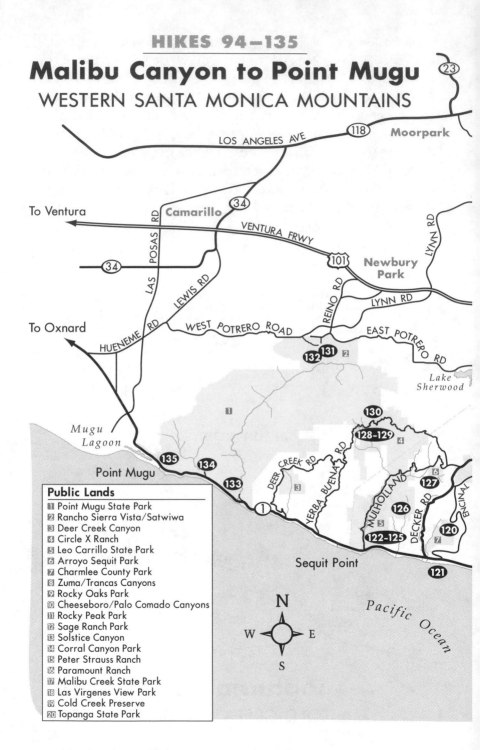

Malibu Canyon to Point Mugu
WESTERN SANTA MONICA MOUNTAINS

LOS ANGELES AVE

118

Moorpark

To Ventura

RD

Camarillo

34

VENTURA FRWY

LAS POSAS

34

101

Newbury
Park

LEWIS RD

REINO RD

LYNN RD

LYNN RD

To Oxnard

HUENEME RD

WEST POTRERO ROAD

EAST POTRERO RD

132 131 2

Lake
Sherwood

Mugu
Lagoon

130

128-129

4

135

134

DEER CREEK RD

YERBA BUENA RD

MULHOLLAND

DECKER RD

ENCINAL

133

Point Mugu

3

1

5

127

126

120

7

122-125

Sequit Point

121

Public Lands

1 Point Mugu State Park
2 Rancho Sierra Vista/Satwiwa
3 Deer Creek Canyon
4 Circle X Ranch
5 Leo Carrillo State Park
6 Arroyo Sequit Park
7 Charmlee County Park
8 Zuma/Trancas Canyons
9 Rocky Oaks Park
10 Cheeseboro/Palo Comado Canyons
11 Rocky Peak Park
12 Sage Ranch Park
13 Solstice Canyon
14 Corral Canyon Park
15 Peter Strauss Ranch
16 Paramount Ranch
17 Malibu Creek State Park
18 Las Virgenes View Park
19 Cold Creek Preserve
20 Topanga State Park

N
W · E
S

Pacific Ocean

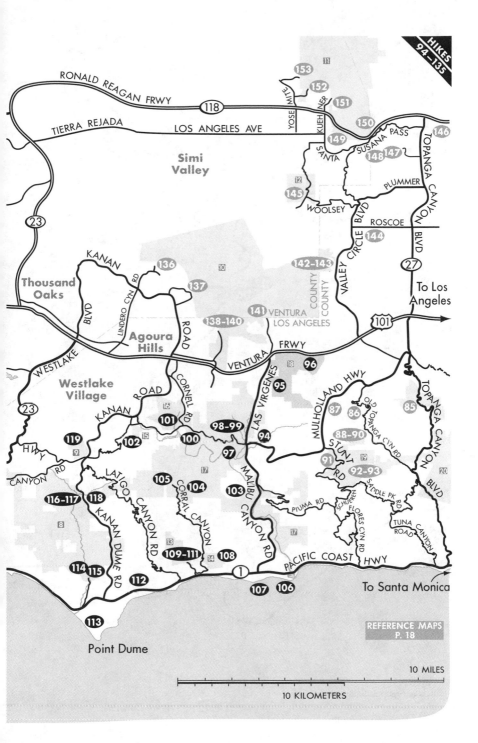

RONALD REAGAN FRWY

118

TIERRA REJADA — LOS ANGELES AVE

Simi Valley

23

Thousand Oaks

KANAN

136

137

138-140

Agoura Hills

WESTLAKE

Westlake Village

23

ROAD

CORNELL RD

KANAN

119

102

101

100

98-99

94

97

LINDERO CYN RD

BLVD

10

ROAD

141 VENTURA LOS ANGELES

VENTURA FRWY

101

142-143

COUNTY COUNTY

VALLEY CIRCLE BLVD

144

ROSCOE

27

To Los Angeles

PLUMMER

WOOLSEY

145

12

SANTA

149

148 147

SUSANA PASS

150

151

152

153

YOSEMITE

KUEHNER

11

146

TOPANGA CANYON BLVD

18

96

95

MULHOLLAND HWY

87

86

OLD TOPANGA CYN RD

85

TOPANGA CANYON BLVD

88-90

STUNT

91

92-93

RD

19

SADDLE PK RD

20

116-117

118

LATIGO CANYON RD

CORRAL CANYON RD

105

104

103

109-111

108

MALIBU CANYON RD

PIUMA RD

SCHUEREN

FLORES CYN RD

TUNA CANYON ROAD

17

17

HWY

9

CANYON RD

8

15

16

13

14

114

115

112

KANAN DUME RD

113

Point Dume

PACIFIC COAST HWY

1

107

106

To Santa Monica

REFERENCE MAPS P. 18

10 MILES

10 KILOMETERS

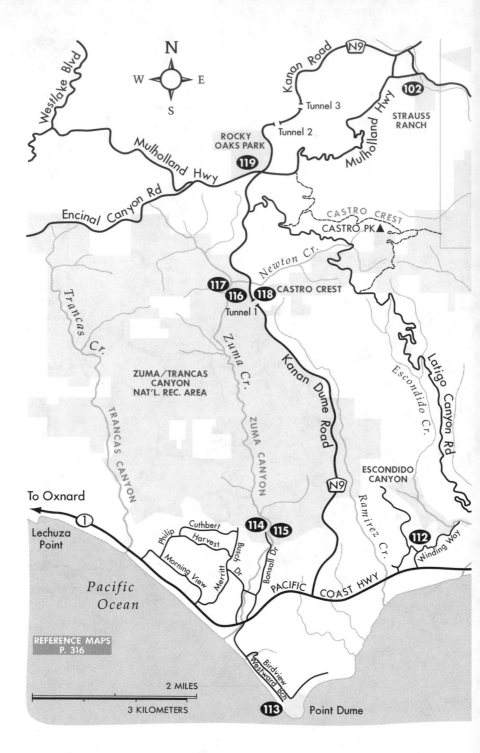

N

W   E

S

Westlake Blvd

Kanan Road

N9

Mulholland Hwy

STRAUSS RANCH

102

Tunnel 3

Tunnel 2

ROCKY OAKS PARK

119

Encinal Canyon Rd

CASTRO CREST

CASTRO PK▲

Newton Cr.

117

116

118 CASTRO CREST

Tunnel 1

Trancas Cr.

Zuma Cr.

ZUMA/TRANCAS CANYON NAT'L. REC. AREA

ZUMA CANYON

Kanan Dume Road

Escondido Cr.

Latigo Canyon Rd

TRANCAS CANYON

N9

ESCONDIDO CANYON

To Oxnard

1

Lechuza Point

Cuthbert

Philip

Harvest

Busch Dr.

Bonsall Dr.

114 115

Ramirez Cr.

112

Winding Way

Morning View

Merritt

Pacific Ocean

PACIFIC COAST HWY

REFERENCE MAPS P. 316

2 MILES

3 KILOMETERS

Birdview

Westward Bch

113 Point Dume

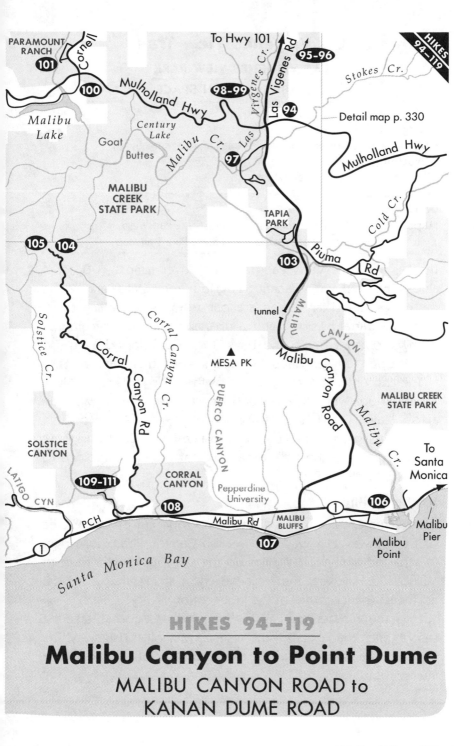

PARAMOUNT
RANCH
101

Cornell

100

Mulholland Hwy

To Hwy 101

Las Virgenes Cr.

Las Vigenes Rd

95-96

Stokes Cr.

HIKES
94-119

98-99

94

Detail map p. 330

*Malibu
Lake*

*Century
Lake*

Goat
Buttes

Malibu Cr.

Las

97

Mulholland Hwy

Cold Cr.

**MALIBU
CREEK
STATE PARK**

TAPIA
PARK

103

Piuma Rd

105 **104**

tunnel

MALIBU

CANYON

Solstice Cr.

Corral Canyon Cr.

▲
MESA PK

Malibu

Canyon Road

Malibu Cr.

**MALIBU CREEK
STATE PARK**

Corral Canyon Rd

PUERCO CANYON

To
Santa
Monica

**SOLSTICE
CANYON**

109-111

CORRAL
CANYON

Pepperdine
University

106

LATIGO CYN

108

1

Malibu Rd

MALIBU
BLUFFS

1

Malibu
Pier

PCH

1

107

Malibu
Point

Santa Monica Bay

HIKES 94-119

Malibu Canyon to Point Dume

MALIBU CANYON ROAD to
KANAN DUME ROAD

94. Las Virgenes View Trail
LAS VIRGENES VIEW PARK
CALABASAS OPEN SPACE

Hiking distance: 4.8 miles round trip
Hiking time: 2.5 hours
Configuration: out-and-back with small loop at summit
Elevation gain: 450 feet
Difficulty: easy to moderate
Exposure: exposed hillside with shaded pockets of oak
Dogs: allowed
Maps: U.S.G.S. Malibu Beach · Malibu Creek State Park Map
Tom Harrison Maps: Malibu Creek State Park Trail Map

The Las Virgenes View Park stretches over almost 700 acres, across the road and adjacent to Malibu Creek State Park. Within the park's varied landscape are oak woodlands, rolling grasslands, chaparral hillsides, and a riparian zone with sycamores, willows, cottonwoods, and bays. The undeveloped multi-use park is open to hikers, mountain bikers, equestrians, and dogs.

The Las Virgenes View Trail climbs the rolling hills to an 1,100-foot overlook with sweeping 360-degree vistas. The views span across Malibu Creek State Park, Goat Buttes, Lady Face Mountain, Stokes Canyon, Saddle Peak, Castro Peak, and Calabasas Peak. The trailhead is a short distance north of the main entrance to Malibu Creek State Park.

To the trailhead

From Santa Monica, drive 12 miles northbound on the Pacific Coast Highway/Highway 1 to Malibu Canyon Road. Turn right (north) and continue 6.7 miles up the winding canyon road to Mulholland Highway. The trailhead and parking area is on the northeast (right) corner of the intersection.

From the Ventura Freeway/Highway 101 in Calabasas, take the Las Virgenes Road exit. Drive 3.1 miles to Mulholland Highway. The trailhead and parking area is on the northeast (left) corner of the intersection.

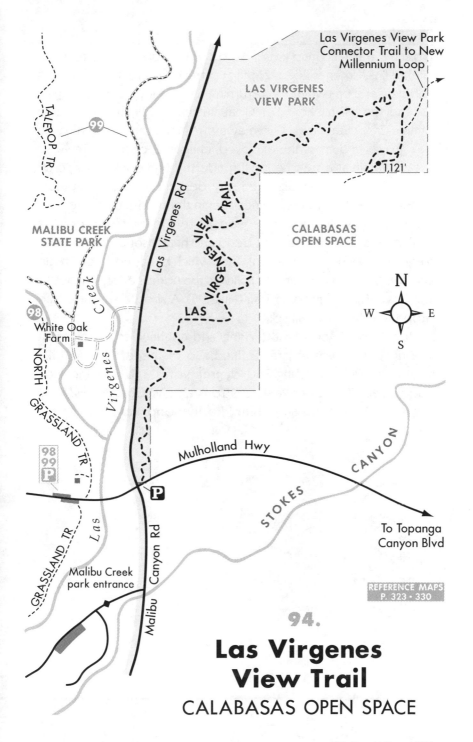

Las Virgenes View Park
Connector Trail to New
Millennium Loop

LAS VIRGENES
VIEW PARK

TALEPOP TR

99

MALIBU CREEK
STATE PARK

Creek

Las Virgenes Rd

VIEW TRAIL

LAS VIRGENES

CALABASAS
OPEN SPACE

1,121'

LAS

98

White Oak
Farm

Virgenes

NORTH

GRASSLAND TR

N
W   E
S

98
99
P

Mulholland Hwy

CANYON

GRASSLAND TR

Las

STOKES

Malibu Canyon Rd

P

To Topanga
Canyon Blvd

Malibu Creek
park entrance

REFERENCE MAPS
P. 323 - 330

94.

Las Virgenes
View Trail
CALABASAS OPEN SPACE

The hike

From the trailhead map kiosk, head up the slope, above and parallel to Las Virgenes Road. Zigzag up the hill on four switchbacks and descend on two more, returning to Las Virgenes Road. Again ascend the hill to views of Goat Buttes and Phantom Ridge in Malibu Creek State Park. Curve away from the road. Walk through oak groves and cross the exposed, chaparral-clad hills. Traverse the mountain at a steady uphill grade through pockets of scrub oak and oak woodlands. Gradually descend again, losing most of the elevation that was gained. Begin the third ascent, weaving up the south wall of a side canyon. At two miles, the serpentine path makes a horseshoe right bend and heads south. Pass the Las Virgenes View Park Connector Trail, which heads north on an old dirt road. The connector trail follows the ridgeline for 1.5 miles to the New Millennium Loop Trail (Hike 95). A short distance ahead, atop the ridge, is a trail split.

Begin a small loop to the right, and continue to a T-junction. The right fork ends at private land. Go to the left to the 1,121-foot peak with sweeping 360-degree vistas. The views include Saddle Peak, Calabasas Peak, Castro Peak, and Goat Buttes. From the summit, descend and complete the loop. Return along the same trail. ▪

95. New Millennium Loop Trail

LAS VIRGENES VIEW PARK
CALABASAS—COLD CREEK TRAIL SYSTEM

Hiking distance: 12.2-mile loop
Hiking time: 7 hours
Configuration: loop
Elevation gain: 1,000 feet
Difficulty: strenuous
Exposure: exposed with forested sections
Dogs: allowed
Maps: U.S.G.S. Calabasas and Malibu Beach
      Tom Harrison Maps: Malibu Creek State Park Trail Map

The New Millennium Loop Trail is a magnificent, dog-friendly, multi-use trail that is open to hikers, bikers, and equestrians. The trail is located in Las Virgenes View Park in the mountains east

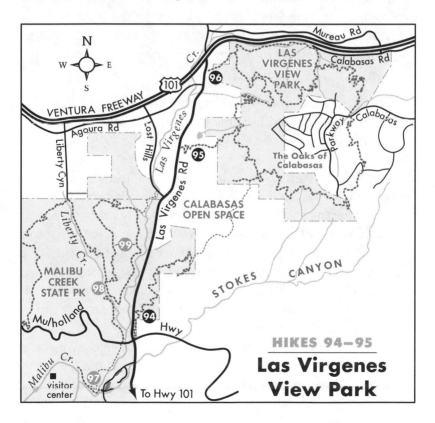

HIKES 94–95

Las Virgenes
View Park

of Las Virgenes Road and south of the Ventura Freeway. This 9.8-mile loop, part of the extensive Calabasas–Cold Creek Trail System, follows chaparral-covered ridges, forested canyons, riparian waterways, rolling grasslands, oak woodlands, and scenic overlooks. The trail also traverses the perimeter of "The Oaks of Calabasas" subdivision, an affluent hillside neighborhood. This hike begins on the Bark Park Trail, a 1.2-mile connector path that begins from Las Virgenes Road.

To the trailhead

From the Ventura Freeway/Highway 101 in Calabasas, exit on Las Virgenes Road. Drive 0.9 miles south to Bark Park on the left. (It is directly across from Arthur Wright Middle School.) Turn left into the parking lot and park.

From Santa Monica, drive 12 miles northbound on the Pacific Coast Highway/Highway 1 to Malibu Canyon Road. Turn right (north) and continue 9.1 miles to Bark Park on the right. (It is 2.4 miles past Mulholland Highway and directly across from Arthur Wright Middle School.) Turn right into the parking lot and park.

The hike

From the north end of Bark Park, by the trailhead kiosk, head up the signed Bark Park Trail. Skirt the fenced off-leash dog area, and weave up the slope at an easy grade. Pass the Las Virgenes Water District reservoir on the left. Continue up the side canyon to a bowl of tree-dotted rolling hills. At 1.2 miles, the trail ends at a T-junction with the New Millennium Loop Trail. Begin the loop to the right, heading southeast. Views immediately open up across the Santa Monica Mountain Range. Traverse the open slopes to an unsigned fork by a fence. The right fork detours 0.2 miles to a 1,300-foot knoll with 360-degree vistas. This side path, the Las Virgenes View Park Connector Trail, continues south on an old dirt road. The trail follows the ridgeline for 1.5 miles to the top of the Las Virgenes View Trail (Hike 94).

Continue on the main loop trail. Follow the ridge downhill and wind into the canyon. Cross a stream and head up the west canyon wall. Follow the mountain contours, dropping in and out of a

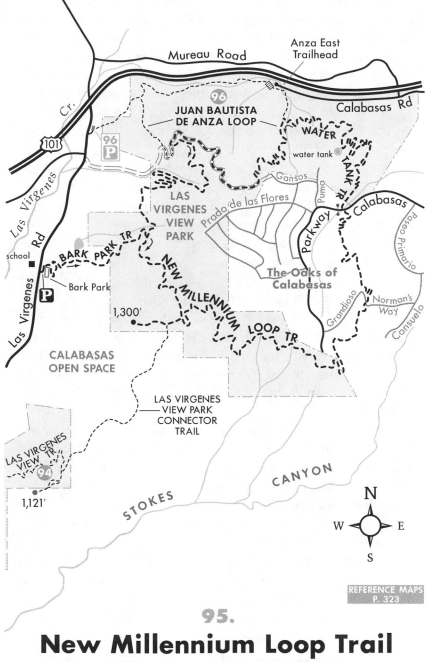

95.
New Millennium Loop Trail
LAS VIRGENES VIEW PARK

few drainages. A series of short switchbacks lead up to a ridge that overlooks some mega-size homes. Traverse the ridge and descend into the canyon to the east. The footpath crosses a couple of wood footbridges over drainages descending from the steep hillside. Cross a road within "The Oaks of Calabasas" subdivision, then wind through the hills above the homes. Gradually descend along five switchbacks to the west end of Parkway Calabasas. On the left is the entrance gate of the exclusive subdivision, a development of 550 mini-mansions dotting the Calabasas Hills.

Cross the road and pick up the signed Water Tank Trail. Drop into the canyon and cross over the drainage. Traverse the exposed canyon slope, steadily gaining elevation. Pass a perpetually dripping rock grotto on the left. Zigzag up seven switchbacks to the top of the mountain by a water tank on the left. Curve right and descend, with far-reaching views of the Santa Monica Mountains. Walk through a pocket of oaks, then zipper down the hill to the canyon floor in an oak grove. Cross a wooden bridge over the seasonal creek, and head up the west canyon slope. Climb over the hill and drop into the next drainage to the west. Continue downhill to the stream-fed canyon bottom. Rock-hop across the stream to a junction at 6 miles. The right fork leads 0.2 miles to the Juan Bautista de Anza East Trailhead at the end of Calabasas Road.

Bear left on the Juan Bautista de Anza Loop Trail, and wind up to the ridge. Head downhill into the canyon to the west, and traverse the east canyon wall to a utility road. Go to the right on the old dirt road. Cross the head of the canyon, and descend to a signed junction at 9 miles. The right fork leads 0.8 miles to the Juan Bautista de Anza West Trailhead (Hike 96). Bear left on the New Millennium Loop Trail. Weave along the mountain contours to a stream in a picturesque grotto. Follow the willow-lined stream past an old man-made rock fountain and pool. Continue downhill through a forested canopy. Ascend the hill with the aid of four switchbacks, and meander through the rolling hills to a signed junction, completing the loop at 11.2 miles. Bear right on the Bark Park Trail, and return to the trailhead. ▪

96. Juan Bautista de Anza Loop

LAS VIRGENES VIEW PARK

CALABASAS—COLD CREEK TRAIL SYSTEM

Hiking distance: 4.4-mile loop
Hiking time: 2.5 hours
Configuration: loop
Elevation gain: 500 feet
Difficulty: easy to moderate
Exposure: open slopes with forested pockets
Dogs: allowed
Maps: U.S.G.S. Calabasas
  Tom Harrison Maps: Malibu Creek State Park Trail Map

The Anza Trail is a portion of the Juan Bautista de Anza National Historic Trail, an old missionary trail from San Diego to San Francisco. The trail represents the route taken in 1775—76, when de Anza led approximately 200 colonists, 100 soldiers, and 1,000 head of livestock from what is now Mexico to form a colony in what is now San Francisco. Most of the historic route is on private property, but some segments of the trail are still located on public parklands, such as this one. The 1.4-mile multi-use trail runs between the western end of Calabasas Road and Las Virgenes Road near the Ventura Freeway. Information panels along the way describe the history and significance. This hike begins on the historic trail and forms a loop with a mixture of single-track and dirt roads. The loop crosses through wetlands, lush canyons, oak woodlands, rolling hills, and open ridges with great mountain views.

To the trailhead

From the Ventura Freeway/Highway 101 in Calabasas, exit on Las Virgenes Road. Drive 0.1 mile south to the turnoff on the left. Turn left and continue 0.1 mile uphill to the posted trailhead and parking area at the end of the dirt road.

The hike

Pass the trailhead kiosk and walk up the canyon to the east. At 0.3 miles is a posted junction. Begin the loop straight ahead on the left fork, hiking clockwise. Traverse the hillside past mature oaks, then curve left and descend. Parallel the south side of Highway 101, dropping into a lush draw. Pass through the slightly swampy area among willows and bay laurel as the path fades in and out. Cross the north side of the stream and return to the distinct trail. Continue east to The Old Road, a small segment of the original El Camino Real, dating back to the early 20th century. Walk 30 yards to the left on the 100-year-old section of pavement, and pick up the footpath again on the right. Rock-hop over the stream and follow the undulating grassy path to a trail on the right at 1.4 miles. The junction is just shy of the Anza East trailhead by a rock pillar commemorating Juan Bautista de Anza. His expedition camped here on February 22, 1776, en route to what is now San Francisco. Bear right and cross the creek on a wooden bridge. Recross the creek to an asphalt road. To the left is Calabasas Road and the Juan Bautista de Anza East Trailhead.

Take the right fork and enter the oak-dotted canyon. Traverse the west canyon slope 0.2 miles on the footpath to a junction with the Water Tank Trail on the left. Continue straight on the Anza Loop Trail, and wind up to the ridge. Head downhill into the canyon to the west, and traverse the east canyon wall to a utility road. Go to the right and take the old dirt road. Cross the head of the canyon, and descend to a signed junction with the New Millennium Trail on the left at 3.4 miles. Stay on the Anza Loop Trail straight ahead. Descend on the serpentine dirt road 300 yards to the "trail" sign on the right in a horseshoe left bend. Bear right and go to the north through the rolling, oak-dotted hills, completing the loop at the head of the canyon. Return to the trailhead 0.3 miles to the left. ■

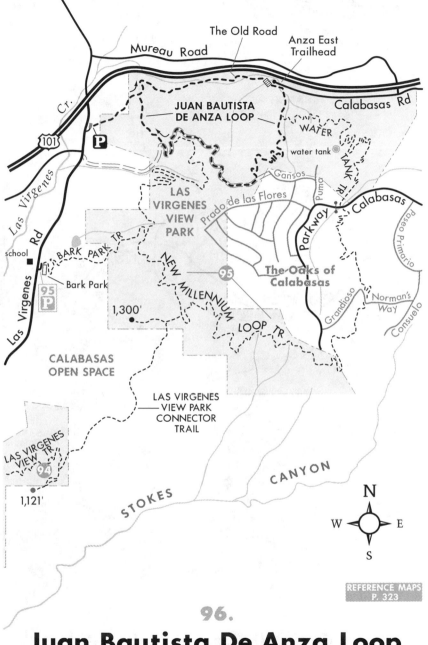

The Old Road
Mureau Road
Anza East Trailhead
Cr.
JUAN BAUTISTA DE ANZA LOOP
Calabasas Rd
101
WATER
P
water tank
TANK TR
Gansos
Las Virgenes
LAS VIRGENES VIEW PARK
Prado de las Flores
Puma
Calabasas
Paseo Primario
BARK PARK TR
Parkway
school
NEW
95
The Oaks of Calabasas
Bark Park
MILLENNIUM
Grandioso
Norman's Way
95
P
1,300'
LOOP TR
Consuelo
CALABASAS OPEN SPACE
LAS VIRGENES VIEW PARK CONNECTOR TRAIL
LAS VIRGENES VIEW TR
94
CANYON
1,121'
STOKES
N
W   E
S

REFERENCE MAPS
P. 323

96.

Juan Bautista De Anza Loop
LAS VIRGENES VIEW PARK

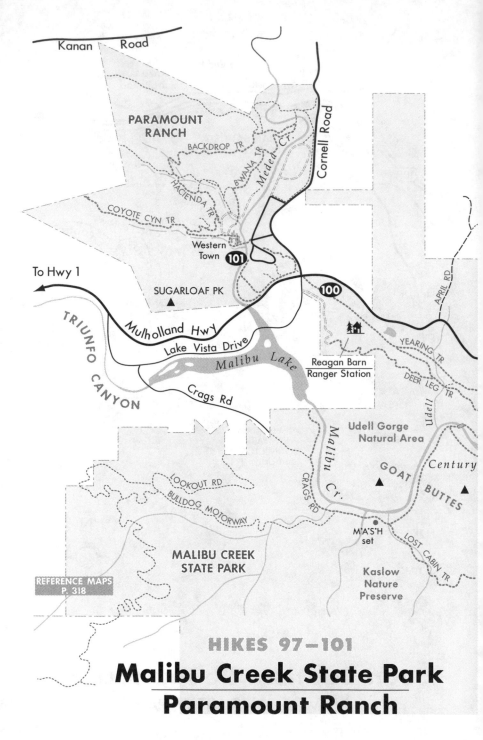

Kanan Road

PARAMOUNT RANCH

BACKDROP TR

Meden CT.

BWANA TR

Cornell Road

HACIENDA TR

COYOTE CYN TR

Western Town **101**

To Hwy 1

SUGARLOAF PK ▲

100

TRIUNFO CANYON

Mulholland Hwy

Lake Vista Drive

Malibu Lake

Reagan Barn
Ranger Station

YEARING TR

APRIL RD

Crags Rd

DEER LEG TR

Udell

Malibu Cr.

Udell Gorge
Natural Area

GOAT ▲

Century

CRAGS RD

BUTTES ▲

LOOKOUT RD

BULLDOG MOTORWAY

M*A*S*H
set

LOST CABIN TR

MALIBU CREEK
STATE PARK

Kaslow
Nature
Preserve

REFERENCE MAPS
P. 318

HIKES 97–101

Malibu Creek State Park
Paramount Ranch

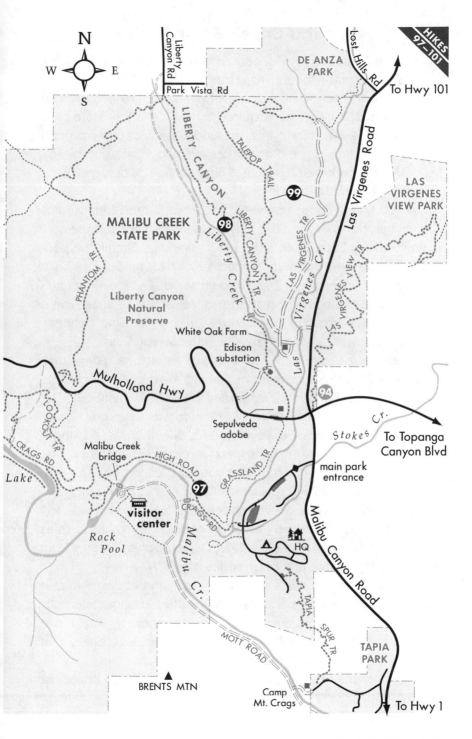

N
W E
S

Liberty Canyon Rd
Park Vista Rd

Lost Hills Rd

To Hwy 101

DE ANZA PARK

LIBERTY CANYON

TALEPOP TRAIL

99

LAS VIRGENES VIEW PARK

MALIBU CREEK STATE PARK

LIBERTY CANYON TR.

Liberty Creek

98

LAS VIRGENES TR.

LAS VIRGENES VIEW TR.

Las Virgenes Cr.

Las Virgenes Road

PHANTOM TR.

Liberty Canyon Natural Preserve

White Oak Farm

Edison substation

Mulholland Hwy

Sepulveda adobe

94

Stokes Cr.

To Topanga Canyon Blvd

LOOKOUT TR.

CRAGS TR.

Malibu Creek bridge

HIGH ROAD

GRASSLAND TR.

main park entrance

Lake

visitor center

Rock Pool

CRAGS RD.

97

Malibu Cr.

△ 🏕 HQ

Malibu Canyon Road

TAPIA TR.

SPUR TR.

MOTT ROAD

△ BRENTS MTN

Camp Mt. Crags

TAPIA PARK

To Hwy 1

Malibu Creek State Park

Malibu Creek State Park, located in the central section of the Santa Monica Mountains, stretches over 10,000 acres of rugged, diverse terrain. It is one of the mountain range's premier state parks. The land was acquired by the California state park system in 1974. Previous to this, the land was divided into parcels belonging to Bob Hope, Ronald Reagan, and 20th Century Fox. Although the park is still used as a filming site, it is primarily used for day-hiking and picnicking.

Malibu Creek, the principal watercourse in the Santa Monica Mountains, flows through the park from Malibu Lake. It is the only stream-channel that bisects the mountain range. Within the park, Malibu Creek was dammed around 1900 to form Century Lake. The river continues over 13 miles down Malibu Canyon and enters the ocean at Malibu Lagoon at Surfrider Beach. Malibu Canyon is the chief pass-through in the Santa Monica Mountains, connecting the inland valley at Calabasas with the Malibu Coast.

Malibu Creek State Park has a mix of sandstone, conglomerate, and volcanic rock formations that include picturesque buttes, deep gorges, prominent cliffs, vertical peaks, and rocky outcroppings. The diverse plant habitats include coastal sage scrub, chaparral, rolling grasslands, broad meadows, oak savannas, sycamore woodlands, freshwater marshes, and streamside vegetation. The state park is also home to three natural preserves: 1,920-acre Kaslow Preserve, 730-acre Liberty Canyon, and 300-acre Udell Gorge. Amenities include a visitor center and a campground.

The park was the filming location of notable movies such as *Butch Cassidy and the Sundance Kid*, *Daniel Boone*, *Tarzan*, *Planet of the Apes*, and the television series *M*A*S*H*.

More than twenty miles of hiking, biking, and equestrian trails crisscross the park. The trail system includes streamside strolls, paths through canyons and valleys to natural preserves, movie and historic sites, and high ridges with spectacular scenery that spans from the ocean to the mountains,.

The main entrance into the park is on Malibu Canyon Road, just south of Mulholland Highway.

97. Rock Pool, Century Lake, Udell Gorge Preserve and M*A*S*H Site

MALIBU CREEK STATE PARK

1925 Las Virgenes Road · Calabasas

Hiking distance: 8.3 miles round trip
Hiking time: 4.5 hours
Configuration: out-and-back plus three spur trails
Elevation gain: 400 feet
Difficulty: moderate
Exposure: a mix of exposed hills and shaded forest
Dogs: not allowed
Maps: U.S.G.S. Malibu Beach and Point Dume
Tom Harrison Maps: Malibu Creek State Park Trail Map
Malibu Creek State Park Map

The Santa Monica Mountains are bisected near their center by Malibu Creek. It is the only creek that cuts entirely through the mountain range from north to south. The year-round stream flows more than 13 miles, beginning from its headwaters in Westlake Village to Santa Monica Bay at Malibu Lagoon. Along the way, it meanders through Malibu Creek State Park and down Malibu Canyon to the ocean. The Malibu Creek watershed, the largest in the range, drains over 100 miles of land from the southern Simi Hills and western San Fernando Valley.

This premier hike begins from the main entrance road to Malibu Creek State Park and follows Malibu Creek through the heart of the state park to Malibu Lake, passing a series of scenic landmarks and man-made features. The creek and trail weave along Goat Buttes, the two picturesque volcanic peaks rising from the center of the park. At the base of the buttes are Century Lake and Rock Pool. Century Lake was formed in 1901 when a dam was built at the mouth of a gorge by members of the Crags Country Club. The 20-acre, man-made lake was used for fishing, sailing, and duck hunting. Since that time, the reservoir has silted up and become a pastoral, 7-acre freshwater marsh. Rock Pool is a natural lake dammed by volcanic boulders. The pool sits in a deep gorge in Triunfo Canyon and is framed by massive vertical cliffs

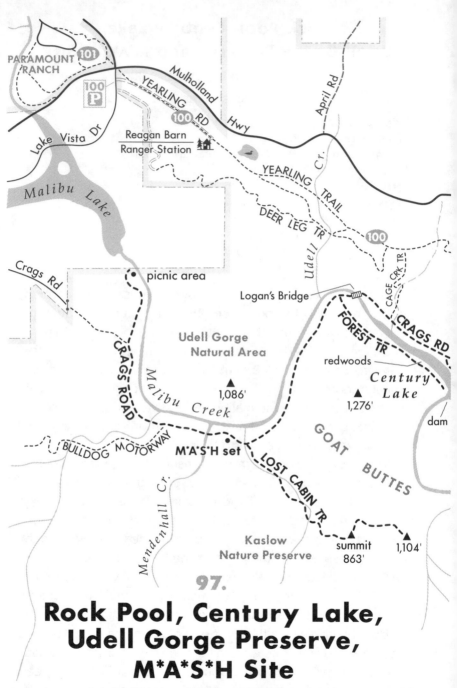

97.
Rock Pool, Century Lake, Udell Gorge Preserve, M*A*S*H Site
MALIBU CREEK STATE PARK

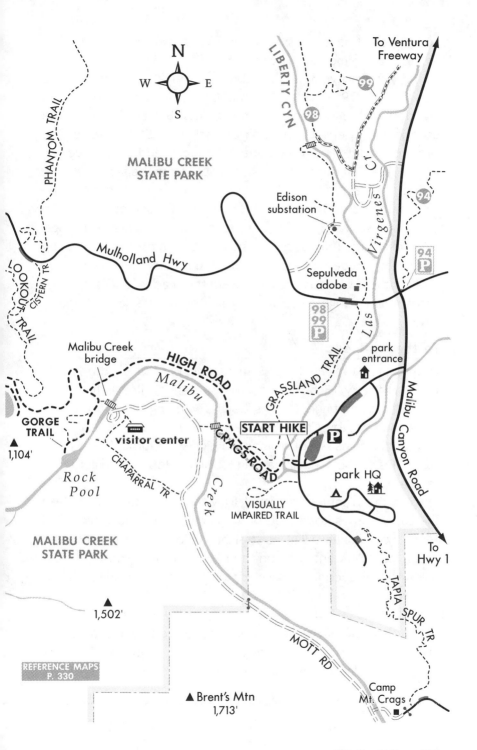

N
W E
S

LIBERTY CYN

To Ventura
Freeway

99

98

MALIBU CREEK
STATE PARK

Edison
substation

Virgenes Cr.

94

PHANTOM TRAIL

Mulholland Hwy

LOOKOUT TRAIL

CISTERN TR

94
P

Sepulveda
adobe

Las

98
99
P

Malibu Creek
bridge

HIGH ROAD

Malibu

GORGE
TRAIL

GRASSLAND TRAIL

park
entrance

1,104'

visitor center

START HIKE

CRAGS ROAD

P

CHAPARRAL TR

Creek

Malibu Canyon Road

Rock
Pool

VISUALLY
IMPAIRED TRAIL

park HQ

MALIBU CREEK
STATE PARK

To
Hwy 1

1,502'

MOTT RD

TAPIA SPUR TR

REFERENCE MAPS
P. 330

▲ Brent's Mtn
1,713'

Camp
Mt. Crags

and groves of bays and sycamores. The *Tarzan* movies and *South Pacific* were filmed at this site.

The well-known *M*A*S*H* television series was filmed in the park from 1972 to 1983. The *M*A*S*H* site sits in a gorgeous meadow in Triunfo Canyon beneath Goat Buttes. The area was used in the opening sequence of each *M*A*S*H* episode. The production sets are gone, but a rusted jeep and ambulance still remain. The film site is very recognizable from the series.

The trail passes through two of the park's three natural pre-serves. The Udell Gorge Natural Preserve (300 acres) and Kaslow Natural Preserve (1,920 acres) protects rare plants and volca-nic formations. The Kaslow Preserve is also a protected nesting ground for golden eagles. En route, the hike detours to an over-look on the Lost Cabin Trail at the southern edge of Goat Buttes and strolls through a redwood grove on the banks of Century Lake.

To the trailhead

From Santa Monica, drive 12 miles northbound on the Pacific Coast Highway/Highway 1 to Malibu Canyon Road. Turn right (north) and continue 6 miles up the winding canyon road to the signed Malibu Creek State Park entrance on the left. (It is located 0.2 miles shy of Mulholland Highway.) Turn left and drive 0.35 miles to the second parking lot on the left. A parking fee is required.

From the Ventura Freeway/Highway 101 in Calabasas, take the Las Virgenes Road exit. Drive 3.1 miles south to Mulholland Highway. Continue 0.2 miles straight ahead to the signed Malibu Creek State Park entrance on the right. Turn right and drive 0.35 miles to the second parking lot on the left. A parking fee is required.

FREE ROADSIDE PARKING ALTERNATIVE: Park west of the intersec-tion of Malibu Canyon Road/Las Virgenes Road and Mulholland Highway in the pullouts along Mulholland Highway. Take the posted Grassland Trail (a footpath) south 0.7 miles to Crags Road.

The hike

Cross the park road to the posted trailhead. Take Crags Road, crossing over Las Virgenes Creek. The paved road turns to a narrower dirt road. Pass the signed Grassland Trail on the right, a 0.7-mile connector trail from Mulholland Highway. Continue straight, following the north bank of Malibu Creek while enjoying the great views of Goat Buttes. Stroll through overhanging oak groves with picture-perfect views to a posted junction. Detour left towards the visitor center. Walk 60 yards to a trail on the right, just before the Malibu Creek Bridge (which leads to the visitor center).

Veer right on the Gorge Trail and go another 100 yards to a picnic area. The dirt road bends to the right and climbs to the top of the rock formations. Continue straight, staying on the canyon bottom among the deeply eroded rock formations with caves. Follow the west (right) side of the canyon to Rock Pool by a massive, rock-walled gorge.

Return to Crags Road and continue a half mile west to a footpath on the left. Take the path into a lush, shaded canopy with ferns and moss-covered boulders. The short path ends at the dam overlooking Century Lake by another steep-walled gorge.

Return to Crags Road and head northwest along the narrow lake, passing the Lookout Trail and Cage Creek Trail on the right. Stroll through the meadow surrounded by mountains. Cross Logan's Bridge over Malibu Creek. (The bridge was named after the 1998 film *Logan's Run*, which was filmed here.) Walk 75 yards to the signed Forest Trail on the left, where Crags Road becomes a footpath. Detour to the left on the half-mile-long trail along the backside of Century Lake. Walk east through the oak-rimmed meadow. Enter the forest, skirting the south edge of the meadow. The shaded path passes towering redwood trees planted in the 1920s by Crag's Country Club members, and a series of weather-etched volcanic boulders. Follow the south edge of Century Lake, passing more redwoods, to the end of the fern-lined trail at the concrete dam and another view into the vertical-walled gorge beneath Goat Buttes.

Return to Crags Road and continue up the forested canyon. Follow the perimeter of the Udell Gorge Natural Preserve between Malibu Creek and the steep rock wall of Goat Buttes on the left and a dense isolated forest on the right. At the southeast corner of the wetland, where the canyon widens, is a posted junction with the Lost Cabin Trail on the left, just shy of the M*A*S*H* site. For now, detour left and head south into the Kaslow Natural Preserve, a nesting area for golden eagles. Cross a stream and meander up the isolated side valley along the southern base of Goat Buttes. Cross the stream two more times while walking beneath the gorgeous rock cliffs and pock-marked outcrops. Climb to a 700-foot saddle at the head of the canyon. Curve left and go downhill to the posted end of the trail and the site of the lost cabin, although no remnants remain. The spot is located just before a branch of Malibu Creek in a deep gorge between Century Lake and Rock Pool.

Return to Crags Road. Bear left and enter the M*A*S*H site in a meadow framed by the prominent Goat Buttes. Walk around the famous flat surrounded by mountains. Meander among the vehicle props, abandoned after filming, and an unlocked shed with artifacts and photographs from the TV series. Detour left up the slope to the old helicopter landing area on a perch overlooking the site. After perusing the area, cross Mendenhall Creek and continue through oak-filled Triunfo Canyon to a posted junction with the Bulldog Motorway on the left. This dirt road leads 3.4 miles to Castro Crest, high above Solstice Canyon. Continue straight on Crags Road, and cross another stream to a fork 0.2 miles ahead. Crags Road veers left and leads 0.3 miles to the park boundary and onto residential Crags Road, located 0.7 miles from Lake Vista Drive. Instead, veer right and pass rock-lined pools and massive outcrops to the park boundary, just short of the Malibu Lake Dam. The fenced private land halts access. On the right is a quiet picnic area. Return along the same route. ▪

98. Liberty Canyon Natural Preserve
MALIBU CREEK STATE PARK
Calabasas

Hiking distance: 4 miles round trip
Hiking time: 2 hours
Configuration: out-and-back
Elevation gain: 100 feet
Difficulty: easy
Exposure: exposed
Dogs: not allowed
Maps: U.S.G.S. Malibu Beach and Calabasas · Malibu Creek State Park map
Tom Harrison Maps: Malibu Creek State Park Trail map

Liberty Canyon Natural Preserve is one of three natural preserves in Malibu Creek State Park. The preserve is home to a rare stand of California valley oaks. This hike begins just north of the main park entrance. The path crosses the rolling grassland at the V-shaped merging of Liberty Canyon and Las Virgenes Canyon. After crossing a bridge that spans Liberty Creek, the route follows the Liberty Canyon Trail, a fire road that parallels the east side of the creek. The trail gently climbs through oak woodlands to the head of the canyon, where there are views of the surrounding hills. En route, the trail connects with the Talepop Trail (Hike 99) and the Phantom Trail.

To the trailhead

From Santa Monica, drive 12 miles northbound on the Pacific Coast Highway/Highway 1 to Malibu Canyon Road. Turn right (north) and continue 6.5 miles up the winding canyon road to Mulholland Highway. Turn left and park 0.1 mile ahead in the parking pullouts on either side of the road.

From the Ventura Freeway/Highway 101, take the Las Virgenes Road exit. Drive 3.1 miles south to Mulholland Highway. Turn right and park 0.1 mile ahead in the parking pullouts.

The hike

Take the signed North Grassland Trail and head north. Pass the Sepulveda Adobe, a historic white adobe house built by pioneer homesteader Pedro Sepulveda in 1863. Cross the rolling grass-lands at the convergence of Liberty Canyon and Las Virgenes Canyon. Loop around the west side of the Edison substation. Continue north past oak trees, bearing right at a trail split. Cross a footbridge over Liberty Creek by a small waterfall and pools to a signed T-junction. Head left on the Liberty Canyon Trail, passing a junction at one mile with the Talepop Trail (Hike 99). Continue straight ahead, climbing the hillside through an oak grove over-looking the canyon, then return to the canyon bottom. The trail ends at the head of the canyon by Park Vista Road and Liberty Canyon Road. The Phantom Trail heads southwest through the meadow to the left. Return along the same trail. ▄

99. Talepop Trail—Las Virgenes Loop
MALIBU CREEK STATE PARK
Calabasas

Hiking distance: 4.8-mile loop
Hiking time: 2.5 hours
Configuration: loop
Elevation gain: 450 feet
Difficulty: moderate
Exposure: exposed hills and open canyon bottom
Dogs: not allowed
Maps: U.S.G.S. Malibu Beach and Calabasas · Malibu Creek State Park map
    Tom Harrison Maps: Malibu Creek State Park Trail map

The Talepop-Las Virgenes Loop is on the north end of Malibu Creek State Park in the 730-acre Liberty Canyon Natural Preserve. This loop climbs a grassy ridge between two stream-fed canyons—Liberty Canyon and Las Virgenes Canyon. Both creeks are tributaries of Malibu Creek, the largest watershed in the Santa Monica Mountains. The hike climbs up the ridge on the Talepop Trail, named for a Chumash Indian village that once inhabited the area. From the ridgeline are views into Liberty Canyon and Malibu Canyon. The return route descends into Las Virgenes Canyon along the Las Virgenes Trail. The trail parallels the creek, passing through open meadows surrounded by the oak-studded hills.

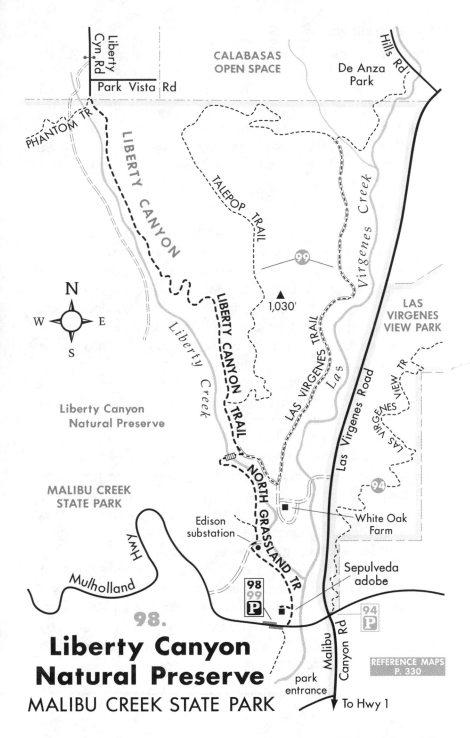

Liberty Cyn Rd

Park Vista Rd

PHANTOM TR

CALABASAS OPEN SPACE

De Anza Park

Hills Rd

LIBERTY CANYON

TALEPOP TRAIL

Liberty Creek

99

▲ 1,030'

Las Virgenes Creek

LAS VIRGENES VIEW PARK

N
W E
S

Liberty Canyon Natural Preserve

LIBERTY CANYON TRAIL

LAS VIRGENES TRAIL

Las

LAS VIRGENES VIEW TR

MALIBU CREEK STATE PARK

NORTH GRASSLAND TR

Las Virgenes Road

Edison substation

White Oak Farm

94

Mulholland Hwy

98 99 P

Sepulveda adobe

94 P

98.
Liberty Canyon
Natural Preserve
MALIBU CREEK STATE PARK

park entrance

Malibu Canyon Rd

REFERENCE MAPS P. 330

▼ To Hwy 1

To the trailhead

From Santa Monica, drive 12 miles northbound on the Pacific Coast Highway/Highway 1 to Malibu Canyon Road. Turn right and continue 6.5 miles up this beautiful, winding canyon road to Mulholland Highway. Turn left and park 0.1 mile ahead in the parking pullouts on either side of the road.

From the Ventura Freeway/Highway 101, take the Las Virgenes Road exit. Drive 3.1 miles south to Mulholland Highway. Turn right and park 0.1 mile ahead in the parking pullouts.

The hike

Take the signed North Grassland Trail, and head north across the rolling meadow. Pass the Sepulveda Adobe, a historic white adobe house built by pioneer homesteader Pedro Sepulveda in 1863. Loop around an Edison substation as Liberty Canyon and Las Virgenes Canyon separate into a V-shape. Continue north past oak trees, bearing right at a trail split. Cross a footbridge over Liberty Creek by a small waterfall and pools to a signed T-junction.

Take the left fork on the Liberty Canyon Trail, beginning the loop. At one mile is a posted junction with the Talepop Trail on the right. Head right (east) on the Talepop Trail, winding up the west canyon wall a half mile to the ridge. Follow the grassy ridge north to the 1,030-foot summit, overlooking Liberty Canyon on the west and Las Virgenes Canyon on the east. At the northern park boundary, bear right and descend down the hillside. Switchbacks lead to the Las Virgenes Canyon floor by Las Virgenes Creek and a junction at 2.75 miles. The left fork crosses the creek and leads 0.3 miles to De Anza Park.

Take the right fork—the Las Virgenes Trail—along the west side of the creek. As you approach White Oak Farm at the lower end of the loop (a private residence), take the signed Liberty Canyon Trail to the right. A short distance ahead is the junction by the bridge, completing the loop. Bear left on the North Grassland Trail, cross the bridge, and retrace your steps. ■

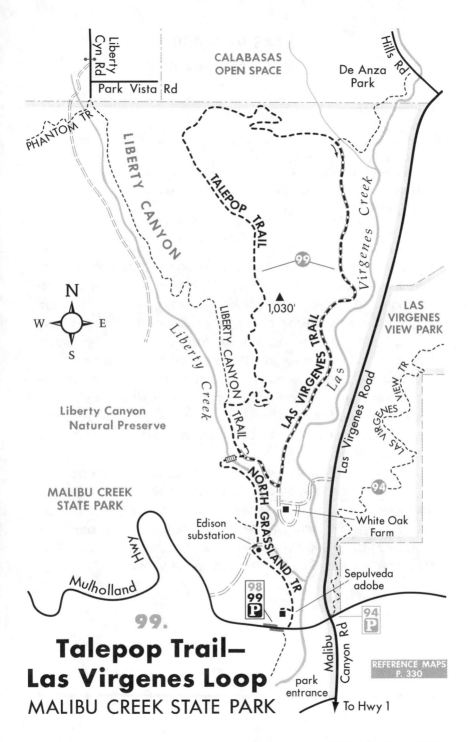

CALABASAS OPEN SPACE

De Anza Park

Liberty Cyn Rd

Park Vista Rd

PHANTOM TR

LIBERTY CANYON

TALEPOP TRAIL

99

1,030'

Virgenes Creek

LAS VIRGENES VIEW PARK

LIBERTY CANYON TRAIL

LAS VIRGENES TRAIL

Liberty Creek

Las

N
W E
S

Liberty Canyon
Natural Preserve

LAS VIRGENES VIEW TR

MALIBU CREEK
STATE PARK

NORTH GRASSLAND TR

Las Virgenes Road

94

Edison
substation

White Oak
Farm

Mulholland Hwy

98
99
P

Sepulveda
adobe

94
P

99.

Malibu Canyon Rd

REFERENCE MAPS
P. 330

Talepop Trail—
Las Virgenes Loop
MALIBU CREEK STATE PARK

park
entrance

To Hwy 1

100. Reagan Ranch

MALIBU CREEK STATE PARK
Calabasas

Hiking distance: 5.2 miles round trip
Hiking time: 3.5 hours
Configuration: double loop with optional spur trail
Elevation gain: 700 feet
Difficulty: easy to somewhat moderate
Exposure: exposed meadow with forested hillsides
Dogs: not allowed
Maps: U.S.G.S. Malibu Beach · Malibu Creek State Park map
      Tom Harrison Maps: Malibu Creek State Park Trail map

Reagan Ranch encompasses 305 acres on the northwest corner of Malibu Creek State Park. From 1951 through 1966, it was a second home to former President Ronald Reagan, who raised thoroughbred horses on the ranch. Originally named Yearling Row Ranch, it was sold by the Reagans to pay his campaign debts from the 1966 California governor's campaign. The original barn and stables, currently used as a park maintenance facility, are located in an open meadow at the junction of Mulholland Highway and Cornell Road. A network of trails, once used as horse riding trails by the Reagans, connects the ranch to the heart of Malibu Creek State Park.

This hike, the Yearling–Deer Leg Loop, leads to a duck pond, a large rolling meadow, an oak woodland, stream crossings, and the Reagan barn. There are vistas of the surrounding tree-dotted hills and jagged mountains. The Lake Vista Trail, an optional spur trail, leads to an 1,102-foot overlook of Malibu Lake, Sugarloaf Mountain (in Paramount Ranch), and Medea Valley.

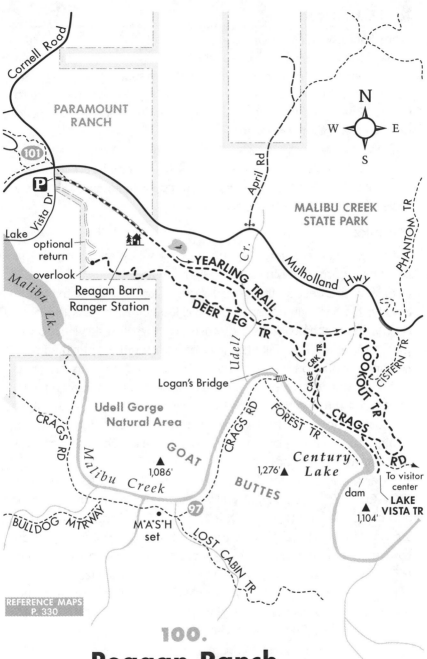

Cornell Road

PARAMOUNT
RANCH

N
W E
S

101

P

Lake
Vista Dr

April Rd

MALIBU CREEK
STATE PARK

PHANTOM TR

optional
return

overlook

Malibu Lk.

Cr.

YEARLING TRAIL

Mulholland Hwy

Reagan Barn
Ranger Station

DEER LEG
TR

Udell

CAGE CRK TR

LOOKOUT TR

CISTERN TR

Logan's Bridge

Udell Gorge
Natural Area

CRAGS RD

CRAGS RD

FOREST TR

CRAGS

RD

To visitor
center

GOAT

Malibu Creek

1,086'

1,276'

Century
Lake

dam

LAKE
VISTA TR

BUTTES

1,104'

BULLDOG MTRWAY

97

M·A·S·H
set

LOST CABIN TR

REFERENCE MAPS
P. 330

100.
Reagan Ranch
MALIBU CREEK STATE PARK

To the trailhead

From Santa Monica, drive 12 miles northbound on the Pacific Coast Highway/Highway 1 to Malibu Canyon Road. Turn right (north) and continue 6.5 miles up this beautiful winding canyon road to Mulholland Highway. Turn left and drive 3.2 miles to Cornell Road. Turn left again and immediately park along the road wherever a spot is available.

From the Ventura Freeway/Highway 101 in Agoura Hills, exit on Kanan Road. Drive south 0.4 miles to Cornell Road. Turn left and continue 2.2 miles to the intersection of Mulholland Highway. Cross and park along the road.

The hike

Enter the ranch at a gateway through the white rail fence on the southeast corner of Mulholland Highway and Cornell Road. Walk a quarter mile east on the paved Yearling Road, lined with stately eucalyptus and oak trees, to the old Reagan Barn. Pass the barn, corral, and ranch buildings (now used by the park service) to the posted Yearling Trail. Take the footpath down the open meadow, passing a pond on the left. Continue to a Y-fork with the Deer Leg Trail, our return route. Stay to the left on the Yearling Trail, continuing through the valley floor. Pass a side path on the right that drops down to Udell Creek and the Deer Leg Trail. Continue straight to a trail split on a minor ridge at the east end of both the Yearling Trail and Deer Leg Trail.

Veer left and descend on the Lookout Trail to a fork with the Cage Creek Trail. Begin what will be another loop on the left fork and climb the hill, staying on the Lookout Trail. Drop into another stream-fed drainage. Weave through the forested side canyon to a fork with the Cistern Trail, a connector trail to Mulholland Highway. Stay to the right on the Lookout Trail. Descend to a T-junction with Crags Road while overlooking Century Lake and the volcanic Goat Buttes. Bear right on the dirt road 100 yards to a side road on the left that leads a short distance to the dam and overlook of Century Lake. The site is in a shaded canopy with ferns and mossy boulders by a steep-walled gorge. After enjoying the area, return to Crags Road and head northwest to the Cage Creek Trail on the right. Bear right on the footpath, crossing Cage Creek twice. Head up the narrow canyon and climb the west canyon wall, completing the 1.4-mile loop at the Lookout Trail.

Bear left and return to the junction on the ridge with the Yearling Trail and Deer Leg Trail. Now take the Deer leg Trail to the left and top the slope. Make a U-bend and descend into the forest. Cross a small stream, and pass the Yearling connector path on the right to Udell Creek, a tributary of Malibu Creek. Hop over ephemeral Udell Creek to a picnic area with stone fire pits. In the early 1960s, these barbecue pits were used by the Reagans for entertaining friends, actors, and political figures.

Watch for the unsigned Lake Vista Trail, a distinct footpath on the left by a picnic site. To overlook Malibu Lake, detour left on the footpath. Climb through the shade of oak trees, oak scrub, and tall brush while overlooking Reagan ranch through the foliage. At 0.7 miles, the trail reaches a ridge with a brush-obscured view of Malibu Lake. Veer right and drop down 0.1 mile to a clearing and overlook by a power pole, where there is a great view of Malibu Lake, Sugarloaf Mountain, and the Medea Valley.

From here are two options. For a quick half-mile return, take the unpaved utility road and wind down the hill into a meadow. Veer left along the park boundary to the trailhead at Mulholland Highway and Cornell Road. Or, to continue on the Deer Leg Trail, returning 0.8 miles down the Lake Vista Trail to the picnic area and the Deer Leg Trail. Go to the left and continue 0.3 miles northwest under a canopy of massive oaks, completing the second loop at the Yearling Trail. Return past the pond and ranch buildings to the trailhead. ■

101. Paramount Ranch
2813 Cornell Road · Agoura Hills

Hiking distance: 2.75 miles round trip
Hiking time: 1.5 hours
Configuration: two small loops and out-and-back spur trail
Elevation gain: 400 feet
Difficulty: easy
Exposure: exposed
Dogs: allowed
Maps: U.S.G.S. Point Dume · N.P.S. Paramount Ranch Site map
Tom Harrison Maps: Malibu Creek State Park Trail map

Paramount Ranch lies adjacent to the northwest end of Malibu Creek State Park. The parkland has a diverse landscape filled with oak savannahs, chaparral-covered hillsides, canyons, creekside thickets, rolling grasslands, and prominent Sugarloaf Peak. The historic 326-acre ranch has been a motion picture filming site for hundreds of movies and television shows, including *Dr. Quinn, Medicine Woman*; *Have Gun Will Travel*; *The Cisco Kid*; *Gunsmoke*; *The Rifleman*; and *Tom Sawyer*.

This hike takes in two short loop trails within the ranch that represent the diverse terrain. The Medea Creek Trail and Run Trail parallel Medea Creek (a tributary of Malibu Creek) through a riparian zone with willow thickets. The creek flows south through the length of Paramount Ranch into Malibu Lake. The trail loops around an 860-foot hill near Sugarloaf Peak. The second loop follows the Coyote Canyon Trail up a ravine, climbing a chaparral-clad slope to a panorama of the ranch and an overlook of the mountains to the west. To reach the trail, the route leads through the streets of the realistic-looking Western Town movie set with false store fronts, saloons, and hotels.

To the trailhead

From Santa Monica, drive 12 miles northbound on the Pacific Coast Highway/Highway 1 to Malibu Canyon Road. Turn right (north) and continue 6.5 miles to Mulholland Highway. Turn left and drive 3.2 miles to Cornell Road. Turn right and drive 0.4 miles to the Paramount Ranch entrance on the left. Turn left and continue 0.2 miles to the parking area.

From the Ventura Freeway/Highway 101 in Agoura Hills, exit on Kanan Road. Head 0.4 miles south to Cornell Road and turn left. Drive 1.8 miles to the ranch entrance on the right (west).

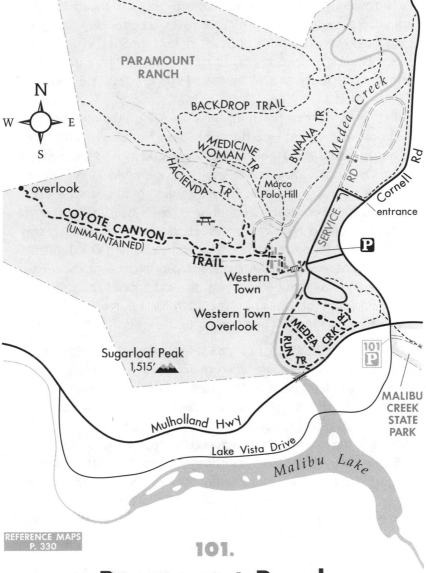

101.
Paramount Ranch

The hike

MEDEA CREEK AND RUN TRAILS · 1–MILE LOOP: From the parking area, head south on the service road. Parallel Medea Creek to a Y-fork. Begin the loop on the right fork, entering an oak and bay laurel forest. Follow Medea Creek on the right, with Sugarloaf Peak towering over the trail. A short distance ahead is a trail split. Detour on the right fork (Run Trail), continuing alongside the waterway. The path ends at private property under the Mulholland Highway bridge. Just before the bridge, a trail curves left and heads east to Mulholland Highway, 0.2 miles west of Cornell Road.

Return to the main junction, and continue on the Medea Creek Trail, now on the right. Head up the hillside, high above Mulholland Highway, to a trail on the left. Detour left 0.1 mile to the Western Town Overlook atop a minor knoll. There are views in every direction, including Western Town. Return to the Medea Creek Trail and proceed east. One hundred yards before the Cornell Road/Mulholland Highway intersection, veer sharply left, staying on the Medea Creek Trail. Descend steps and stroll through the shade of an oak forest to a Y-fork. Both forks are the Medea Creek Trail, and both paths end at the old asphalt road. The left fork remains in the trees as a footpath for a longer distance. At the road, go to the left and complete the loop.

COYOTE CANYON TRAIL · 1.75 MILES: Cross the bridge over Medea Creek, and walk through Western Town to the signed Coyote Canyon Trail. Head west up the small ravine to a junction. The left fork leads a half mile on an unmaintained trail to an overlook. The path ends at private property.

Back at the junction, continue on the loop and head northeast, following the ridgeline to another junction. The left fork leads a short distance to a picnic area. Stay to the right, continuing downward to a junction with the Hacienda Trail. Veer right, returning to the paved road by Western Town. Return through the town to the trailhead. ■

102. Peter Strauss Ranch

30000 Mulholland Highway at Troutdale Drive · Agoura Hills

Open Daily: 8 a.m.–5 p.m.

Hiking distance: 1-mile loop
Hiking time: 30 minutes
Configuration: loop
Elevation gain: 200 feet
Difficulty: easy
Exposure: mostly shaded hillside
Dogs: allowed
Maps: U.S.G.S. Point Dume · N.P.S. Peter Strauss Ranch Site map
Tom Harrison Maps: Malibu Creek State Park Trail map

Peter Strauss Ranch spreads across 65 acres in Agoura Hills along Mulholland Highway. Triunfo Creek, the main fork of Malibu Creek, flows year around through the ranch. Back in 1926, Harry Miller built a stone ranch house with a white banister, a stone

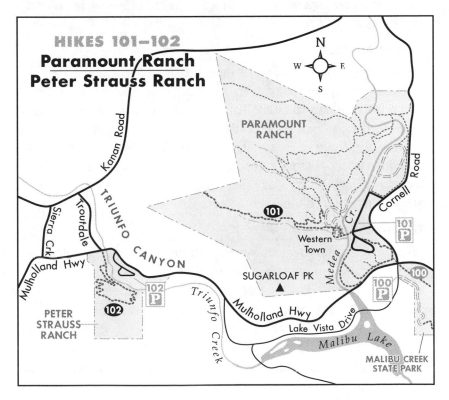

caretaker's cottage, a giant outdoor aviary, and lookout tower on the property. In the 1930s and 1940s, the ranch became an amusement park and children's summer camp. In the 1940s, a dam was built on Triunfo Creek, forming a lake. The lake was named Lake Enchanto and became a popular swimming, fishing, and boating site. By 1960, the ranch fell into disrepair. The dam washed out in a 1969 flood, and the lake ceased to exist. The ranch was abandoned in the early 1970s. In 1977, actor/producer Peter Strauss purchased the ranch and restored it to a pristine state. He sold it to the Santa Monica Mountains Conservancy in 1983 and the conservancy deeded it to the National Park Service in 1987.

This loop hike explores the stone structures, the outdoor aviary, the tree-shaded lawns along the banks of Triunfo Creek, and the forested hillside terraces. The lush hills are home to diverse habitats with eucalyptus, live oak, scrub oak, California bay, and sycamore groves, with a lush understory of ferns and poison oak.

To the trailhead

From Santa Monica, drive 12 miles northbound on the Pacific Coast Highway/Highway 1 to Malibu Canyon Road. Turn right and drive 6.5 miles to Mulholland Highway. Turn left and drive 5.1 miles to the park entrance on the left.

From the Ventura Freeway/Highway 101 in Agoura Hills, exit on Kanan Road. Head 3 miles south to Troutdale Drive. Turn left and drive 0.4 miles to Mulholland Highway. Turn left and immediately turn right into the Peter Strauss Park entrance.

The hike

Take the footpath towards Mulholland Highway and the entrance arch. Cross the bridge spanning Triunfo Creek, and enter the park on the service road to the left, across from Troutdale Drive. Head south past the amphitheater to the end of the service road by the old Lake Enchanto Dam. Stay to the left, parallel to Triunfo Creek. The forested Peter Strauss Trail traverses the hillside above the creek to a junction. Take the right fork up a series of switchbacks.

At the top, the trail levels out and heads west. At the west end, switchbacks zigzag down the slope. Pass small meadows and cross a wooden bridge to a junction. The right fork leads to a picnic area. The left fork completes the loop at the amphitheater and aviary. ■

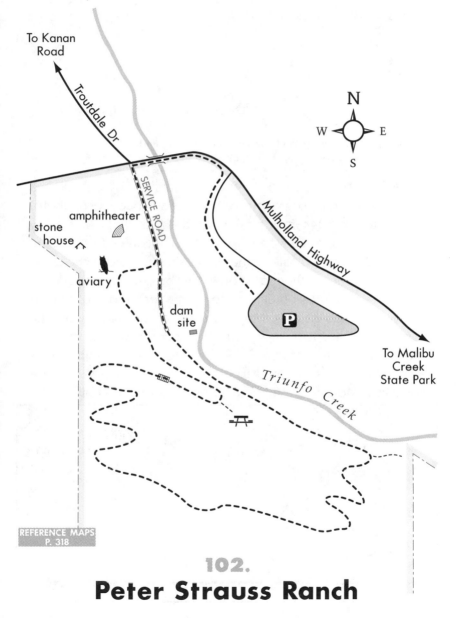

102.
Peter Strauss Ranch

103. Mesa Peak

MESA PEAK MOTORWAY from MALIBU CANYON

MALIBU CREEK STATE PARK

Calabasas · Malibu

Hiking distance: 5 miles round trip
Hiking time: 3 hours
Configuration: out-and-back
Elevation gain: 1,400 feet
Difficulty: moderate to strenuous
Exposure: exposed ridge
Dogs: not allowed (but many 4-legged friends have been known to enjoy this trail)
Maps: U.S.G.S. Malibu Beach · Malibu Creek State Park Map
Tom Harrison Maps: Malibu Creek State Park Trail Map

Mesa Peak sits on the oceanfront mountains just outside the southern boundary of Malibu Creek State Park (back cover photo). Access to the 1,844-foot peak is via the Mesa Peak Motorway, either from Corral Canyon (Hike 104) or this hike from Malibu Canyon. Both routes follow the mountain spine along the undeveloped upper, southern portion of Malibu Creek State Park.

This trail from Malibu Canyon follows a forested footpath up to the ridge, connecting with the exposed fire road. From the dramatic ridgetop are spectacular southern views across Santa Monica Bay from Point Dume to Palos Verdes and northern views across Malibu Creek State Park to the San Fernando Valley. The Mesa Peak Motorway is a segment of the Backbone Trail.

To the trailhead

From Santa Monica, drive 12 miles northbound on the Pacific Coast Highway/Highway 1 to Malibu Canyon Road. Turn right (north) and continue 4.7 miles up the winding canyon road to the paved but unsigned trailhead parking lot on the left. (The parking lot is located 0.1 mile south of the traffic signal at Piuma Road.)

From the Ventura Freeway/Highway 101 in Calabasas, take the Las Virgenes Road exit. Drive 5.1 miles to the Backbone Trail parking lot on the right. (The parking area is located 1.8 miles south of Mulholland Highway.)

The hike

Walk up the slope past the trailhead signs to a posted junction at 100 yards. The trail straight ahead meanders through the hills and dead-ends before reaching the deep gorge at Malibu Creek. Bear left on the Mesa Peak (Backbone) Trail. Wind up the hillside along the wooded canyon wall. At 0.6 miles, the footpath connects with the Mesa Peak Motorway, a dirt fire road. Make a U-shaped left bend around a rock formation. Continue uphill on the serpentine road. There are great views of Brents Mountain, the volcanic Goat Buttes, Malibu Creek State Park to the northwest, and an expanding view of Malibu Canyon. At just under 2 miles, on a sharp right bend, views open up to the Pacific Ocean. Follow the ridge, enjoying the 360-degree vistas, to a junction at 2.4 miles by metal posts, located 40 yards shy of a sharp right bend. The Mesa Peak Motorway (Backbone Trail) continues straight ahead.

Bear left, leaving the main road on the Puerco Motorway. Drop down and cross a saddle between Malibu Canyon and Corral Canyon. Pass through an open gate at the base of Mesa Peak, leaving Malibu Creek State Park. The dirt road curves around Mesa Peak and descends down Puerco Canyon to the Pacific Coast Highway at Puerco Beach. Rather than continue on the main road, a short but steep path at the base of Mesa Peak climbs to the 1,844-foot summit. From the summit are sweeping coastal views across Santa Monica Bay, from the north end at Point Dume to the southern end at Palos Verdes. Inland vistas expand across the layered mountain range. Return by retracing your steps. ∎

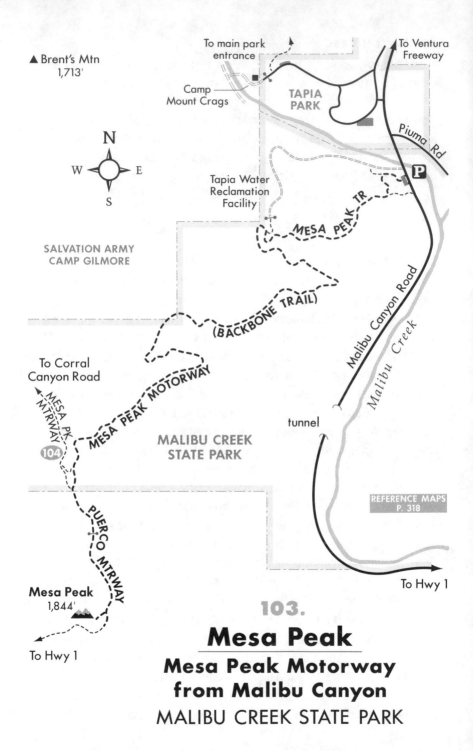

▲ Brent's Mtn
1,713'

To main park entrance

To Ventura Freeway

Camp Mount Crags

TAPIA PARK

Piuma Rd

P

N
W E
S

Tapia Water Reclamation Facility

MESA PEAK TR

SALVATION ARMY CAMP GILMORE

(BACKBONE TRAIL)

Malibu Canyon Road

Malibu Creek

To Corral Canyon Road

MESA PEAK MOTORWAY

MESA PK MTRWAY

104

MALIBU CREEK STATE PARK

tunnel

REFERENCE MAPS P. 318

PUERCO MTRWAY

Mesa Peak
1,844'

To Hwy 1

To Hwy 1

103.
Mesa Peak
Mesa Peak Motorway
from Malibu Canyon
MALIBU CREEK STATE PARK

104. Mesa Peak

MESA PEAK MOTORWAY from CORRAL CANYON

MALIBU CREEK STATE PARK

Malibu

Hiking distance: 6.6 miles round trip
Hiking time: 3 hours
Configuration: out-and-back
Elevation gain: 250 feet
Difficulty: moderate to somewhat strenuous
Exposure: exposed ridge
Dogs: not allowed (but many four-legged friends have been known
to enjoy this trail)
Maps: U.S.G.S. Point Dume and Malibu Beach
Tom Harrison Maps: Malibu Creek State Park Trail Map
Malibu Creek State Park Map

Mesa Peak sits on the oceanfront mountains just outside the southern boundary of Malibu Creek State Park. Access to the 1,844-foot peak is via the Mesa Peak Motorway, either from Malibu Canyon (Hike 103) or this hike from Corral Canyon by Castro Crest. Both routes follow the mountain spine along the undeveloped upper, southern portion of Malibu Creek State Park.

This hike from Corral Canyon begins in a garden of massive warped and weathered sandstone. Among the wind-eroded sedimentary rock are caves and stone arches that look like windows in the rock. The trail follows the exposed spine of the Santa Monica Mountains. The spectacular views include Santa Monica Bay in the south, from Point Dume to Palos Verdes, and northern views across Malibu Creek State Park to the San Fernando Valley. The Mesa Peak Motorway is a segment of the Backbone Trail.

To the trailhead

From Santa Monica, drive 14.5 miles northbound on the Pacific Coast Highway/Highway 1 to Corral Canyon Road. Turn right and wind 5.2 miles to the end of the paved road. Continue 0.1 mile on the dirt road to the trailhead parking area at the end of the road.

The only access to the trailhead is from the coast via Corral Canyon Road. The road is located 2.5 miles west of Malibu Canyon Road and 3.5 miles east of Kanan Dume Road.

The hike

From the east side of the parking area, take the posted trail east. Follow the dirt and sandstone slab path towards the gorgeous rock formations. Climb the slab rock and weave through the formations to a ridge. Climb the ridge to another amazing group of cave-riddled sandstone formations. Cross over and through the rock sculptures, then descend to the Mesa Peak Motorway at 0.4 miles. Stay to the left on the dirt road, part of the Backbone Trail. The views extend into the Kaslow Natural Preserve (a nesting ground for golden eagles), across Malibu Creek State Park

104.

Mesa Peak

Mesa Peak Motorway
from Corral Canyon
MALIBU CREEK STATE PARK

on the left and Corral Canyon and the Pacific Ocean on the right. Follow the undulating road, with alternating views of the San Fernando Valley and the coast. Make a long, but easy descent on the open ridge to a saddle while savoring the great views. Cross the saddle and head up the serpentine road. Descend to a trail split at 3 miles. The Mesa Peak Motorway (Backbone Trail) continues east 2.4 miles and ends at Malibu Creek Road (Hike 103).

To ascend Mesa Peak, bear right on the Puerco Motorway. Drop down and cross a saddle between Malibu Canyon and Corral Canyon. Pass through an open gate at the base of Mesa Peak, leaving Malibu Creek State Park. The dirt road curves around Mesa Peak and descends down Puerco Canyon to the Pacific Coast Highway at Puerco Beach. Rather than continue on the main road, a short but steep path at the base of Mesa Peak climbs to the 1,844-foot summit. From the summit are sweeping coastal views across Santa Monica Bay, from the northern end at Point Dume to the southern end at Palos Verdes. Inland vistas expand across the layered mountain range. Return by retracing your steps. ■

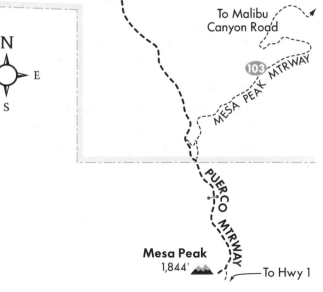

STATE PARK

(BACKBONE TRAIL)

N
W — E
S

CANYON

REFERENCE MAPS
P. 318

To Malibu
Canyon Road

103 MESA PEAK MTRWAY

PUERCO MTRWAY

Mesa Peak
1,844'

To Hwy 1

105. Castro Crest Trail from Corral Canyon Road

CASTRO CREST N.P.S.

Malibu

Hiking distance: 8.4 miles round trip
Hiking time: 4.5 hours
Configuration: out-and-back
Elevation gain: 600 feet
Difficulty: moderate to strenuous
Exposure: mostly forested
Dogs: allowed
Maps: U.S.G.S. Point Dume · Malibu Creek State Park Map
Tom Harrison Maps: Malibu Creek State Park Trail Map

The Castro Crest Trail, a portion of the Backbone Trail, weaves through upper Solstice Canyon and Newton Canyon to Latigo Canyon Road. This remote and isolated section of trail follows the canyon beneath Castro Crest, a jagged sandstone mountain stretching over two miles. The footpath descends to a lush riparian forest with oak and sycamore woodlands along the waterways in verdant Solstice Canyon. The trail then leads up to the drainage divide with Newton Canyon beneath the shadow of 2,824-foot Castro Peak, the fifth highest peak in the mountain range and easily identified by its radio towers. From the high ridges at both ends of the trail are panoramic views over the Santa Monica Range and across the ocean.

To the trailhead

From Santa Monica, drive 14.5 miles northbound on the Pacific Coast Highway/Highway 1 to Corral Canyon Road. Turn right and wind 5.2 miles to the end of the paved road. Continue 0.1 mile on the dirt road to the trailhead parking area at the end of the road.

The only access is from the coast via Corral Canyon Road. The road is located 2.5 miles west of Malibu Canyon Road and 3.5 miles east of Kanan Dume Road.

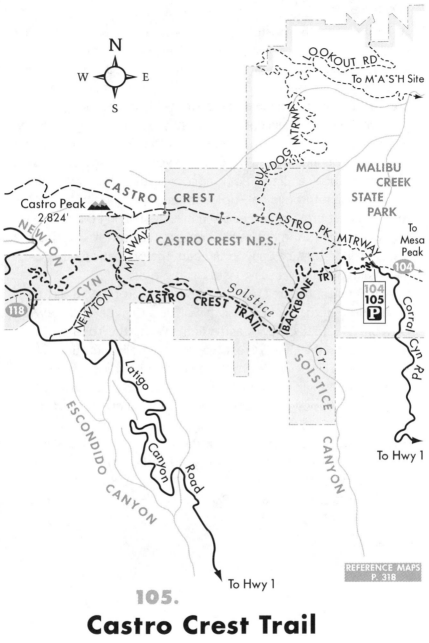

N
W   E
S

LOOKOUT RD
To M*A*S*H Site

BULLDOG MTRWAY

MALIBU
CREEK
STATE
PARK

CASTRO CREST

Castro Peak
2,824'

CASTRO PK MTRWAY

To
Mesa
Peak

NEWTON

CASTRO CREST N.P.S.

CYN

MTRWAY

104

104
105
P

NEWTON

CASTRO CREST TRAIL

Solstice

BACKBONE TR)

Corral Cyn Rd

118

Cr.

SOLSTICE

Latigo

SOLSTICE

CANYON

Canyon

ESCONDIDO CANYON

Road

To Hwy 1

REFERENCE MAPS
P. 318

To Hwy 1

105.

Castro Crest Trail
from Corral Canyon Road
CASTRO CREST N.P.S.

The hike

Head west on the posted Castro Crest Trail. Weave down the south-facing mountain slope into Solstice Canyon, overlooking the stream-fed canyons on the left that feed Solstice Creek. Towering above the trail to the north are the magnificent Castro Crest formations. Wind in and out of the shaded drainages while following the mountain contours. Gently descend to the canyon floor, crossing two seasonal streams. At the canyon bottom, veer right and continue west. Walk up canyon along the south side of Upper Solstice Creek. Rock-hop over the creek eight times while strolling through oak-dotted meadows and shaded glens. After the last crossing, ascend the hillside, leaving the lush riparian vegetation to the exposed scrub and chaparral. Traverse the south wall of Solstice Canyon beneath the dramatic Castro Crest mountains and far-reaching vistas to the east.

At 2.8 miles, the trail reaches Newton Motorway, a dirt road on a ridge at the head of both Solstice Canyon and Newton Canyon, 575 feet below Castro Peak. Cross the road and continue west on the Castro Crest (Backbone) Trail, contouring along the southern slope of Castro Peak. Follow the north canyon wall high above Newton Canyon. Top a hill to a coastal vista and a view of the Boney Mountains at Point Mugu State Park. Descend into Newton Canyon on a serpentine course. Enter the shady forest, and cross Newton Creek on the canyon floor. Ascend the slope and climb to Latigo Canyon Road and the trailhead parking area. The Newton Canyon Trail, a section of the Backbone Trail, is directly across Latigo Canyon Road (Hike 118). Return by retracing your route. ▩

106. Malibu Lagoon State Beach
MALIBU POINT
23200 Pacific Coast Highway · Malibu

Hiking distance: 1.5 miles round trip
Hiking time: 1 hour
Configuration: out-and-back
Elevation gain: level
Difficulty: easy
Exposure: exposed beachfront
Dogs: not allowed
Maps: U.S.G.S. Malibu Beach
Tom Harrison Maps: Malibu Creek State Park Trail map

Malibu Lagoon State Beach encompasses 167 acres in the heart of Malibu, with 22 acres of wetlands, a brackish lagoon at the mouth of perennial Malibu Creek, and nearly a mile of ocean frontage. The sand-barred lagoon, just off Malibu Point, is a resting and feeding estuary for more than 200 species of migrating and native birds on the Pacific Flyway. The state beach includes a museum; 35-acre Surfrider Beach, popularized by surfing movies in the 1950s and 1960s; and Malibu Pier, a 700-foot long pier in a cove called Kellers Shelter. The historic pier dates back to 1903 and was rebuilt in 1946. To the west of Malibu Point is the exclusive Malibu Colony gated community. Nature trails meander to the beach and around the lagoon.

To the trailhead

From Santa Monica, drive 11 miles northbound on the Pacific Coast Highway/Highway 1 to Cross Creek Road by the posted Malibu Lagoon State Beach turnoff. (The turnoff is 1.1 miles east/southbound of Malibu Canyon Road.) Turn left into the park, passing the entrance station to the parking lot. A parking fee is required.

The hike

Take the paved path from the south (ocean) side of the parking lot, crossing a series of bridges over the wetlands and lagoon. The path ends at the sandy beach on Malibu Point at the north end of Surfrider Beach. From here there are several walking options. Stroll south along Surfrider Beach to the Malibu Pier. Or, head north from Malibu Point along Malibu Beach in front of the Malibu Colony homes. (On this route, stay below the high-tide water line to avoid property owner hassles.) The third choice is to loop around the lagoon on the sandy beach.

Back at the trailhead, on the far end of the parking lot, a bridge crosses an arm of the lagoon on estuary trails to a junction. The right fork leads through tall brush to a small opening at the lagoon. The left fork winds through the brush under the Pacific Coast Highway to the main lagoon channel. ■

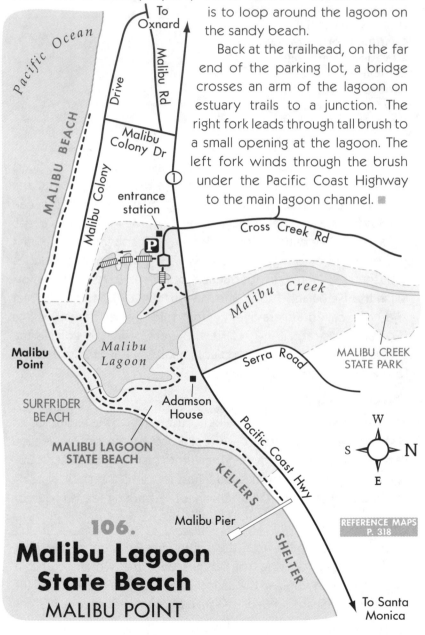

106.
Malibu Lagoon State Beach
MALIBU POINT

107. Malibu Bluffs

24250 Pacific Coast Highway · Malibu

Hiking distance: 2-mile loop
Hiking time: 1 hour
Configuration: loop
Elevation gain: 100 feet
Difficulty: easy
Exposure: exposed oceanfront
Dogs: allowed
Maps: U.S.G.S. Malibu Beach
       Tom Harrison Maps: Malibu Creek State Park Trail map

Malibu Bluffs Open Space comprises 84 acres on the bluffs between the Pacific Coast Highway and Malibu Road, directly opposite of Pepperdine University and Malibu Canyon Road. The 100-foot oceanside cliffs rise above Amarillo Beach and Puerco Beach and are covered with coastal sage scrub, willow scrub, and open grasslands. Five public stairways (which adjoin private property) lead down to the shoreline from the base of the bluffs. The open space is adjacent to Malibu Bluffs Community Park, a developed six-acre park with spacious lawns, baseball diamonds, soccer fields, picnic areas, a free parking lot, and a paved walkway lining the park's periphery. This hike begins from the expansive lawns in Malibu Bluffs Community Park. The hike forms an easy loop across the plateau that includes both coastal and mountain views.

To the trailhead

From Santa Monica, drive 12 miles northbound on the Pacific Coast Highway/Highway 1 to Malibu Canyon Road by Pepperdine University. Turn left into the posted Malibu Bluffs Community Park parking lot.

The hike

From the northwest corner of the parking lot, take the path closest to the Pacific Coast Highway and head west. Cross the meadow, passing a pocket of eucalyptus trees on the right, to a T-junction at the edge of deep Marie Canyon. The right fork exits the parkland to the Pacific Coast Highway, just east of John Tyler Drive. Bear left and follow the east rim of the canyon to the bluffs closest to the ocean. Curve left along the edge of the bluffs to a junction. The right fork descends to the oceanfront homes and coastal access stairways at Malibu Road. Bear left and cross the footbridge over a minor drainage to another junction. The right fork gradually climbs to a picnic area at the southwest corner of Malibu Bluffs Community Park. Take the left fork 100 yards, following the east side of the gully. Two switchbacks zig-zag up the hillside to great views of Pepperdine University and the Santa Monica Mountains. Continue to a trail fork. The left fork heads straight to the trailhead. Go to the right, climbing to a picnic area and paved path. Follow the blufftop path to the left and circle the park, passing the ball fields while overlooking Malibu Point (Hike 106). The path ends on the park road. Return along the road to the left. ■

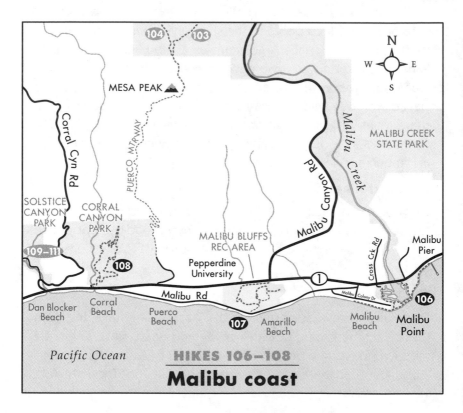

HIKES 106–108
Malibu coast

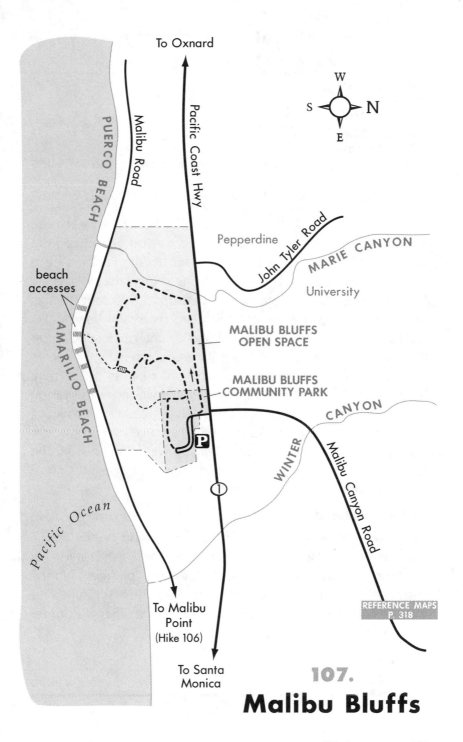

To Oxnard

W N S E

PUERCO BEACH

Malibu Road

Pacific Coast Hwy

Pepperdine

John Tyler Road

MARIE CANYON

University

beach
accesses

AMARILLO BEACH

MALIBU BLUFFS
OPEN SPACE

MALIBU BLUFFS
COMMUNITY PARK

CANYON

WINTER

Malibu Canyon Road

P

1

Pacific Ocean

To Malibu
Point
(Hike 106)

To Santa
Monica

REFERENCE MAPS
P. 318

107.
Malibu Bluffs

108. Corral Canyon Park
25623 Pacific Coast Highway · Malibu

Hiking distance: 2.5-mile loop
Hiking time: 1.5 hours
Configuration: loop
Elevation gain: 400 feet
Difficulty: easy
Exposure: mostly exposed hillside and some shaded canyon bottom
Dogs: allowed
Maps: U.S.G.S. Malibu Beach · Tom Harrison Maps: Malibu Creek State Park

Corral Canyon is an undeveloped, 2.5-mile watershed between Malibu Canyon and Latigo Canyon. The canyon stretches from the crest of the Santa Monica Mountains to the Pacific Ocean. Seasonal Corral Canyon Creek, which runs through the steep draw, forms in Malibu Creek State Park, then drops 2,500 feet through the rugged canyon before emptying into the sea at Dan Blocker State Beach. The area was once owned by entertainer Bob Hope. It has since become Corral Canyon Park, encompassing 340 acres.

This 2.5-mile loop trail travels through the center of the park. The well-maintained footpath climbs the east canyon slope on an ancient marine terrace with native bunch grasslands, providing wonderful ocean and mountain views. The trail climbs up through coastal sage scrub to the Puerco Canyon watershed divide. The return descends into the lush riparian canyon among alder, coast live oak, California sycamore, and willow trees.

To the trailhead

From Santa Monica, drive 13.8 miles northbound on the Pacific Coast Highway/Highway 1 to Malibu Seafood Fresh Fish Market on the right. Park along the side of the road for free or in the fee parking lot on the east side of the restaurant. The turnoff is located 1.8 miles past Malibu Canyon Road and 0.5 miles before Corral Canyon Road.

The hike

From the parking lot on the east side of the restaurant, walk to the signed trailhead. Immediately drop into a shaded riparian corridor under oaks, sycamores, and bays. Cross the creek and leave the lush vegetation to the exposed chaparral and veer left. Traverse the east slope of Corral Canyon to an unsigned fork. Begin the loop on the right fork, hiking counter-clockwise. Gently gain elevation to sweeping coastal and canyon views. Weave up the oceanfront hillside, with vistas stretching across Santa Monica Bay from Palos Verdes to Point Dume. Cut back to the left and continue climbing at a moderate grade on the east canyon wall. The path levels out, then begins to descend into the canyon with the aid of five switchbacks. Weave down canyon, passing the remains of an old home on the left with an intact chimney. Return to the creekside vegetation, completing the loop. ■

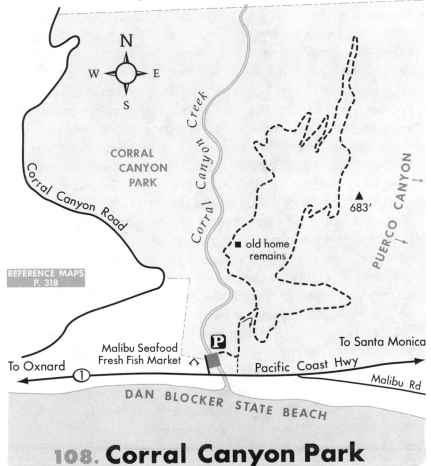

108. Corral Canyon Park

109. Rising Sun—Solstice Canyon Loop

SOLSTICE CANYON PARK

Corral Canyon Road · Malibu

Hiking distance: 3.6-mile loop
Hiking time: 2 hours
Configuration: loop
Elevation gain: 400 feet
Difficulty: easy to moderate
Exposure: exposed hills and shaded canyon
Dogs: allowed
Maps: U.S.G.S. Point Dume and Malibu Beach · N.P.S. Solstice Canyon map
      Tom Harrison Maps: Malibu Creek State Park Trail map

Solstice Canyon Park is a 550-acre park located along a coastal watershed between Malibu Canyon and Point Dume. Solstice Creek, a perennial stream, forms on the southern slope of Castro Crest to the north and flows down the coastal canyon, emptying into the ocean at Dan Blocker State Beach. A dense canopy of live oaks, white alders, California bay, walnut, giant sycamores, and a few rare coast redwoods shade the pastoral canyon.

The Solstice Canyon Trail follows the canyon floor along Solstice Creek to Tropical Terrace, the site of a 1950s ranch-style home that was destroyed by fire in 1982. Tropical Terrace is set along the creek in a jungle-like setting by a lush rock grotto. Within the grotto are cascades that tumble over huge sandstone boulders, rock-lined pools, and waterfalls. The house foundation, stone courtyard, giant fireplace, flagstone steps, and stone terraces still remain, surrounded by an exotic garden with palms, bamboo, philodendrons, birds-of-paradise, ivy-laced pines, banana trees, and maidenhair ferns.

This hike heads up to Tropical Terrace on the east wall of Solstice Canyon along the Rising Sun Trail, an undulating path that overlooks the lush canyon and the ocean. The hike returns along the canyon floor parallel to Solstice Creek through the shade of the forest. En route, the trail passes grassy meadows, picnic areas, and the Matthew Keller house, a river-rock structure that is claimed to be the oldest stone house in Malibu.

To the trailhead

From Santa Monica, drive 14.3 miles northbound on the Pacific Coast Highway/Highway 1 to Corral Canyon Road and turn right. (Corral Canyon Road is located 2.5 miles west of Malibu Canyon Road and 3.5 miles east of Kanan Dume Road.) Continue 0.2 miles to the gated entrance on the left. Turn left, entering the park, and drive 0.3 miles to the parking lot at road's end.

The hike

Hike north up the steps past the TRW trailhead sign. Wind up the hillside to a service road. Take the road uphill to the right to the TRW buildings, now home of the Santa Monica Mountains Conservancy. The Rising Sun Trail begins to the right of the second building. Long, wide switchbacks lead up to the east ridge of Solstice Canyon. Follow the ridge north towards the back of the canyon, and descend through lush vegetation. At the canyon floor, cross the creek to the ruins. Take the path upstream to the waterfalls and pools that are just past the terrace.

After exploring, return on the service road parallel to Solstice Creek. A half mile down canyon is the Keller House, a stone cottage built in 1865. Bear left at a road split, cross a wooden bridge, and return to the trailhead. ∎

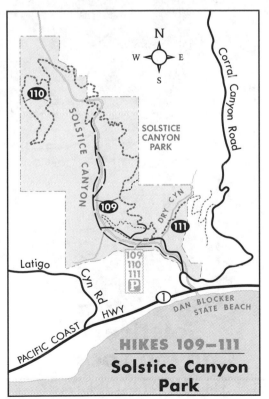

HIKES 109–111
Solstice Canyon Park

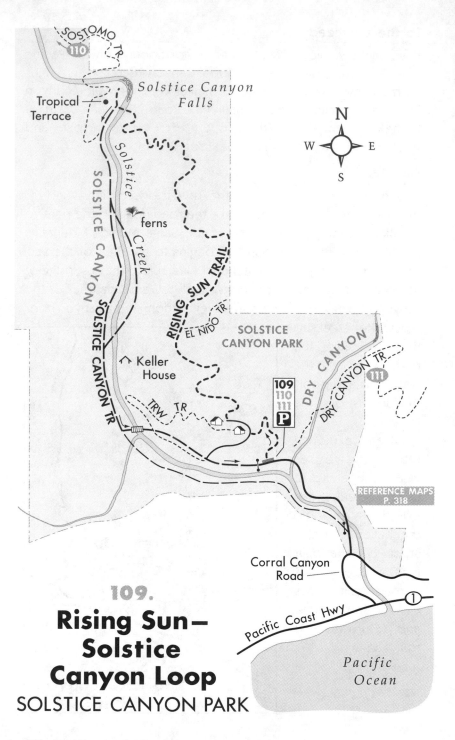

SOSTOMO TR.

110

Solstice Canyon
Falls

Tropical
Terrace

Solstice Canyon

Creek

SOLSTICE CANYON

SOLSTICE CANYON TR.

ferns

RISING SUN TRAIL

EL NIDO TR.

**SOLSTICE
CANYON PARK**

DRY CANYON

DRY CANYON TR.

111

Keller
House

TRW TR.

109
110
111
P

REFERENCE MAPS
P. 318

N
W   E
S

Corral Canyon
Road

Pacific Coast Hwy

1

*Pacific
Ocean*

109.
Rising Sun–
Solstice
Canyon Loop
SOLSTICE CANYON PARK

110. Sostomo—Deer Valley Loop

SOLSTICE CANYON PARK

Corral Canyon Road · Malibu

Hiking distance: 6.2 miles round trip
Hiking time: 3 hours
Configuration: out-and-back with loop
Elevation gain: 1,100 feet
Difficulty: moderate
Exposure: shaded canyon and exposed hills
Dogs: allowed
Maps: U.S.G.S. Point Dume · N.P.S. Solstice Canyon map
Tom Harrison Maps: Malibu Creek State Park Trail map

Solstice Canyon Park, formerly the 550-acre Roberts Ranch, was purchased by the Santa Monica Mountains Conservancy and transformed into public parkland. It was opened on June 21, 1988—the summer solstice. Five hiking, biking, and equestrian trails weave through the canyon park. This hike, the Sostomo-Deer Valley Loop, ascends the west wall of Solstice Canyon to a 1,200-foot grassy ridge at the preserve's north end. Sweeping vistas from the grassy flat above Point Dume extend across Santa Monica Bay. En route to the flat, the trail winds through chaparral and coastal sage, with stream crossings, oak woodlands, and grassy meadows. The Sostomo-Deer Valley Loop is accessed by the Solstice Canyon Trail (Hike 109), which follows Solstice Creek along the canyon floor through meadows, picnic areas, and groves of oak and walnut. The trail leads past the historic Keller House, a stone building dating back to 1865.

To the trailhead

From Santa Monica, drive 14.3 miles northbound on the Pacific Coast Highway/Highway 1 to Corral Canyon Road and turn right. (Corral Canyon Road is located 2.5 miles west of Malibu Canyon Road and 3.5 miles east of Kanan Dume Road.) Continue 0.2 miles to the gated entrance on the left. Turn left, entering the park, and drive 0.3 miles to the parking lot at road's end.

The hike

Take the posted Solstice Canyon Trail, and follow the paved road under sycamore trees alongside the creek. Cross a wood bridge to the west side of the creek at 0.2 miles. Continue up canyon past the historic Keller House. Just beyond the house is a trail split. The right fork leaves the main road and meanders through an oak grove, crossing the creek twice before rejoining the road. At 1.2 miles, just shy of Tropical Terrace, is the posted Sostomo Trail.

Bear left on the footpath and begin ascending the west canyon wall. Climb at a moderate grade to magnificent views of Solstice Canyon. Rock hop over the creek in a narrow gorge. Wind up the canyon wall, passing the remnants of a home and chimney. At the head of the canyon is a towering sedimentary rock monolith. The trail skirts the park boundary and curves left before reaching the spectacular outcropping. Cross the creek again, passing the shell of a sturdy rock house. Climb to a junction with the Deer Valley Loop. Begin the loop to the right, leading to an open, grassy flat where the trail levels off. At an unpaved road, bear left for 50 yards and return to the footpath on the left. The sweeping coastal views extend across Santa Monica Bay, including a bird's-eye view of Point Dume. Switchback sharply left at the trail sign, and return on the lower loop. The Rising Sun Trail (Hike 109) can be seen across the canyon. Complete the loop and return by retracing your steps. ▨

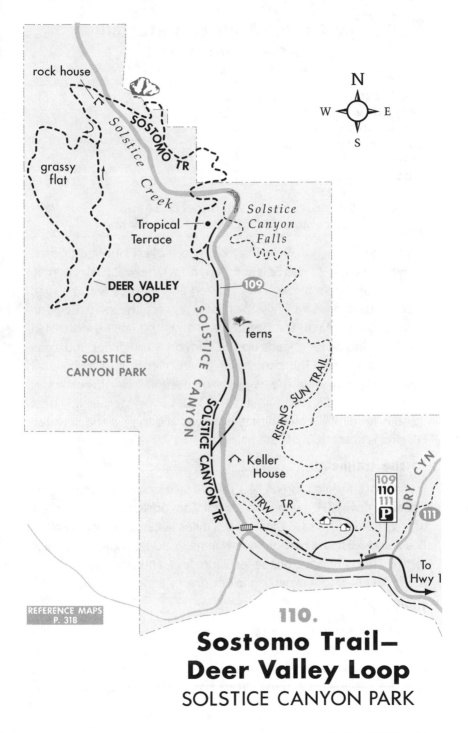

rock house

grassy flat

SOSTOMO TR

Solstice Creek

Tropical Terrace

Solstice Canyon Falls

DEER VALLEY LOOP

109

ferns

SOLSTICE CANYON PARK

SOLSTICE CANYON

SOLSTICE CANYON TR

RISING SUN TRAIL

Keller House

TRW TR

109
110
111
P

DRY CYN

111

To Hwy 1

N
W E
S

REFERENCE MAPS
P. 318

110.
Sostomo Trail—
Deer Valley Loop
SOLSTICE CANYON PARK

111. Dry Canyon Trail to waterfall
SOLSTICE CANYON PARK
Corral Canyon Road · Malibu

Hiking distance: 1.2 miles round trip
Hiking time: 30 minutes
Configuration: out-and-back
Elevation gain: 200 feet
Difficulty: easy
Exposure: shaded
Dogs: allowed
Maps: U.S.G.S. Malibu Beach · N.P.S. Solstice Canyon map
      Tom Harrison Maps: Malibu Creek State Park Trail map

Dry Canyon is a two-mile-long canyon tucked between Corral Canyon to the east and Solstice Canyon to the west. An intermittent stream flows through the canyon and merges with Solstice Creek, less than a half mile before it enters the ocean at Dan Blocker State Beach. The Dry Canyon Trail, the least used trail in Solstice Canyon Park, leads up the canyon through oak and sycamore woodlands. The path leads to an overlook of a seasonal, free-falling waterfall. The majority of the time, Dry Creek is dry, as the name implies. To witness the 150-foot waterfall, it is best to go after a rain. When the fall is active, the long, slender waterfall drops gracefully off the hillside cliffs.

To the trailhead

From Santa Monica, drive 14.3 miles northbound on the Pacific Coast Highway/Highway 1 to Corral Canyon Road and turn right. (Corral Canyon Road is located 2.5 miles west of Malibu Canyon Road and 3.5 miles east of Kanan Dume Road.) Continue 0.2 miles to the gated entrance on the left. Turn left, entering the park, and drive 0.3 miles to the parking lot at road's end.

The hike

From the parking area, hike 20 yards back down the road to the signed Dry Creek Trail on the left. Head north into the mouth of the side canyon. Pass through a grassy oak grove on the well-defined trail, parallel to Dry Creek. Cross the creek and gain elevation to the end of the maintained trail at 0.6 miles. Dry Canyon Falls, when active, can be seen across the narrow canyon on the left. This overlook is the turn-around spot.

To hike farther, the trail continues a short distance to the end of the canyon, where switchbacks lead up the canyon wall to Corral Canyon Road. Beyond the over-look, the trail is not maintained and becomes overgrown with brush. ■

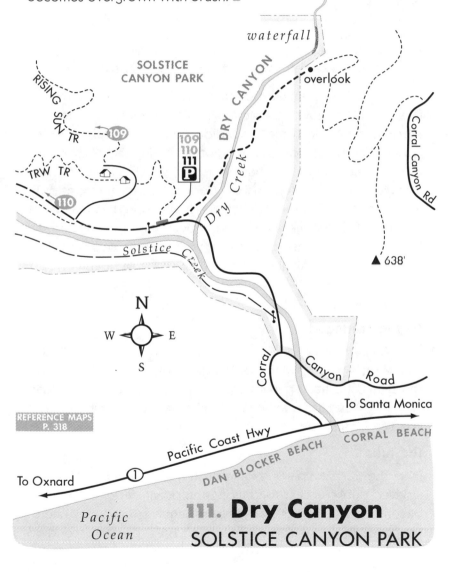

111. Dry Canyon
SOLSTICE CANYON PARK

112. Escondido Falls

ESCONDIDO CANYON NATURAL AREA

27200 Winding Way · Malibu

Hiking distance: 3.4 miles round trip
Hiking time: 2 hours
Configuration: out-and-back
Elevation gain: 300 feet
Difficulty: easy
Exposure: exposed road and shaded canyon
Dogs: allowed
Maps: U.S.G.S. Point Dume
　　　　 Tom Harrison Maps: Malibu Creek State Park Trail map

Escondido Falls is a multi-tiered 150-foot waterfall, the highest falls in the Santa Monica Mountains. The cataract sits deep in a box canyon within the Escondido Canyon Natural Area. The upper (larger) cascade can be spotted during the hike, but the trail ends at the base of the lower falls, which tumbles 60 feet off limestone cliffs into a shallow pool in a mossy fern grotto. To reach the upper falls requires actual climbing, using hands and feet.

The trail, a multi-use hiking and equestrian trail, winds up the lush canyon floor, criss-crossing the year-round creek. The sylvan path weaves through grassy flats in the shade of riparian woodlands to the waterfall and a pool. The hike begins on a winding, paved residential road.

To the trailhead

From Santa Monica, drive 16.5 miles northbound on the Pacific Coast Highway/Highway 1 to Winding Way East and turn right. The signed trailhead parking lot is on the left side of the road. (Winding Way East is located 4.5 miles west of Malibu Canyon Road and 1.3 miles east of Kanan Dume Road.)

The hike

From the trailhead parking lot, walk north up Winding Way East, a paved public-access road along the ocean-facing slope. Pass beautiful Malibu homes along the residential street to the end of the paved road at 0.8 miles. On the left is the posted Escondido

Canyon Trail, a dirt path. Bear left on the well-defined trail, crossing the meadow to the left. Drop down into Escondido Canyon and cross the creek. After crossing, take the left fork upstream. (The right fork leads a half mile towards Latigo Canyon.) Continue up the near-level canyon, following the creek through the forest. Cross the creek a few more times under magnificent coast live oaks and sycamores. At a half mile, the upper falls can be spotted at the back of the towering canyon wall. After the fifth creek crossing, lower Escondido Falls comes into view. Follow the east bank of the stream to the trail's end, located by a shallow pool surrounded by broken travertine rock, ferns, and moss at the base of the waterfall. Return by retracing your steps. ■

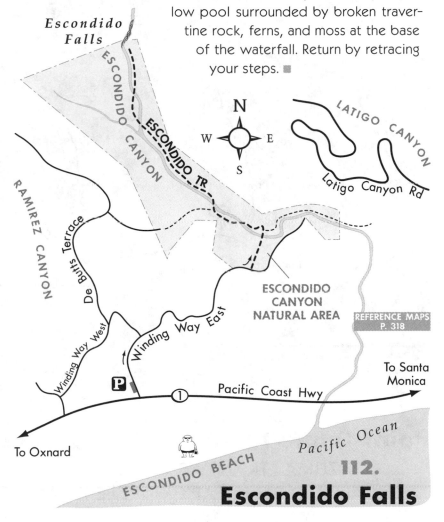

Escondido Falls

N

W —⊹— E

S

ESCONDIDO CANYON

ESCONDIDO TR.

LATIGO CANYON

Latigo Canyon Rd

RAMIREZ CANYON

De Butts Terrace

ESCONDIDO CANYON NATURAL AREA

REFERENCE MAPS P. 318

Winding Way West

Winding Way East

P

① Pacific Coast Hwy

To Santa Monica

To Oxnard

ESCONDIDO BEACH

Pacific Ocean

112.
Escondido Falls

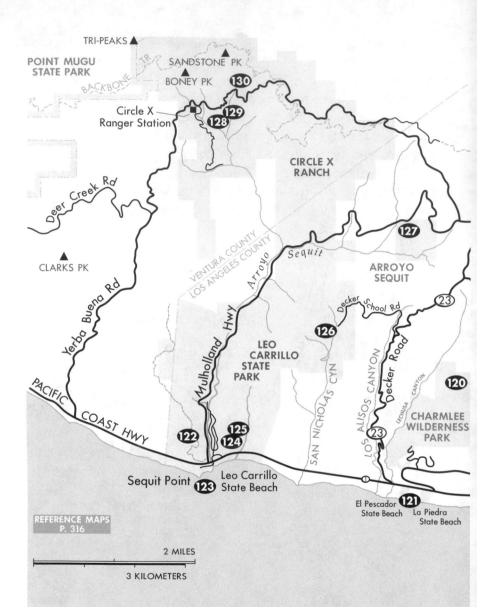

TRI-PEAKS ▲

POINT MUGU
STATE PARK

SANDSTONE PK ▲

BONEY PK ▲ **130**

BACKBONE TR

Circle X
Ranger Station

129

128

CIRCLE X
RANCH

Deer Creek Rd

CLARKS PK ▲

VENTURA COUNTY
LOS ANGELES COUNTY

Sequit

Arroyo

127

ARROYO
SEQUIT

Yerba Buena Rd

Mulholland Hwy

LEO
CARRILLO
STATE
PARK

Decker School Rd

126

23

PACIFIC

COAST HWY

SAN NICHOLAS CYN

LOS ALISOS CANYON

Decker Road

TECHUSA CANYON

120

CHARMLEE
WILDERNESS
PARK

122

125
124

23

Sequit Point
123

Leo Carrillo
State Beach

El Pescador
State Beach

La Piedra
State Beach

121

REFERENCE MAPS
P. 316

2 MILES

3 KILOMETERS

HIKES 113–130

Point Dume to Yerba Buena Road
ZUMA/TRANCAS CANYON
LEO CARRILLO STATE PARK • CIRCLE X RANCH

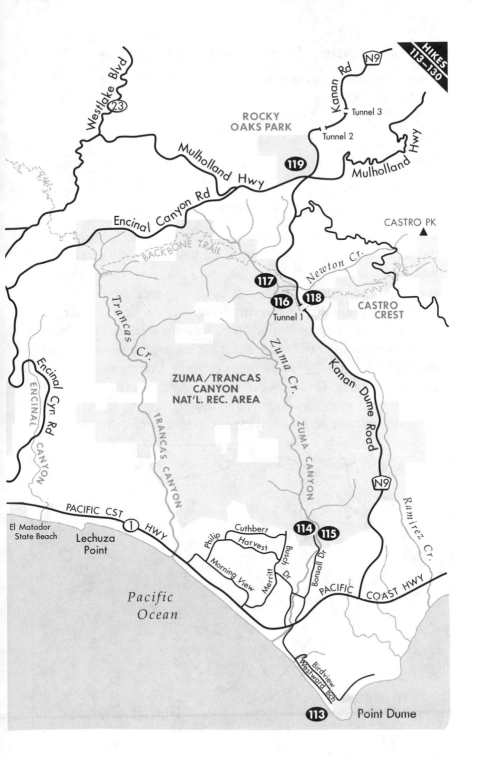

Westlake Blvd

23

Kanan Rd

N9

Tunnel 3

ROCKY
OAKS PARK

Mulholland Hwy

Tunnel 2

119

Mulholland Hwy

CASTRO PK ▲

Encinal Canyon Rd

BACKBONE TRAIL

Newton Cr.

117

116

118

Tunnel 1

CASTRO
CREST

Trancas Cr.

Zuma Cr.

Encinal Cyn Rd

ENCINAL CANYON

ZUMA/TRANCAS
CANYON
NAT'L. REC. AREA

TRANCAS CANYON

ZUMA CANYON

Kanan Dume Road

N9

Ramirez Cr.

PACIFIC CST

El Matador
State Beach

Lechuza
Point

1

HWY

Cuthbert

Philip

Harvest

Morning View

Merritt

Busch Dr

114

115

Bonsall Dr

PACIFIC COAST HWY

Pacific
Ocean

Birdview

Westward Bch

113

Point Dume

113. Point Dume Natural Preserve

Hiking distance: 1.5 miles round trip
Hiking time: 45 minutes
Configuration: several short out-and-back trails
Elevation gain: 200 feet
Difficulty: easy
Exposure: exposed
Dogs: not allowed
Maps: U.S.G.S. Point Dume
      Tom Harrison Maps: Zuma-Trancas Canyons Trail map

Point Dume Natural Preserve is a 35-acre blufftop preserve on the northwest end of Santa Monica Bay (front cover photo). Volcanic rock cliffs jut out to sea along a triangular-shaped headland that is surrounded by water on three sides. From the 203-foot perch at the tip of the promontory, views extend across Santa Monica Bay, from Point Mugu to Palos Verdes. From mid-December through March, the summit is among the finest sites to observe the migrating gray whales en route from the Bering Sea to Baja California. On the west side of the point is Point Dume State Beach, a popular swimming and sunbathing beach with a rocky shoreline and many tidepools to explore. To the east,

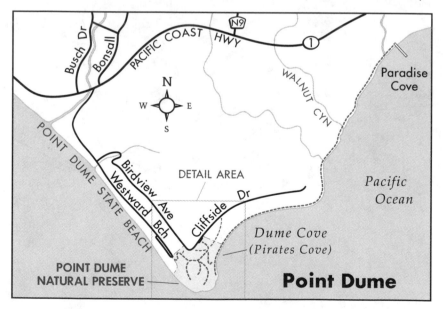

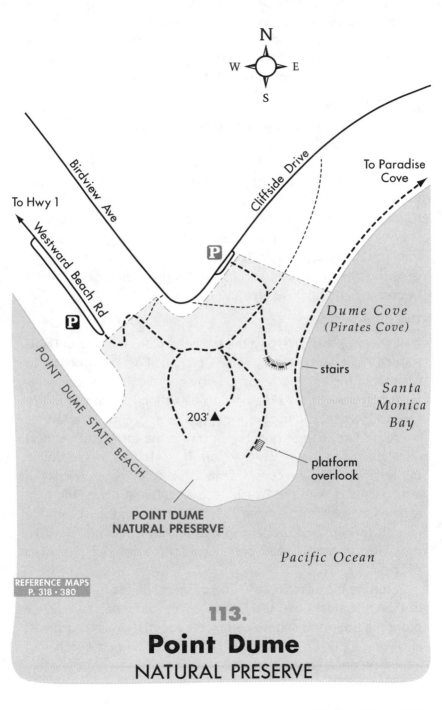

N
W E
S

To Paradise
Cove

Birdview Ave

Cliffside Drive

To Hwy 1

Westward Beach Rd

P

P

Dume Cove
(Pirates Cove)

stairs

Santa
Monica
Bay

203' ▲

platform
overlook

POINT DUME STATE BEACH

POINT DUME
NATURAL PRESERVE

Pacific Ocean

REFERENCE MAPS
P. 318 · 380

113.
Point Dume
NATURAL PRESERVE

tucked beneath the 200-foot sandstone cliffs, is Dume Cove (locally known as Pirates Cove), a secluded, unofficial clothing-optional beach between two rocky points. This hike climbs the ancient coastal bluffs through coastal scrub, grassland, and dunes to coastal overlooks and an oceanfront viewing platform.

To the trailhead

From Santa Monica, drive 20 miles northbound on the Pacific Coast Highway/Highway 1 to Westward Beach Road by Point Dume and turn left/oceanside. (Westward Beach Road is 0.9 miles west of Kanan Dume Road.) Turn left and drive 0.6 miles to the Point Dume State Beach entrance station. Continue 0.7 miles to the far south end of the parking lot. A parking fee is required.

For a second access point, just before reaching the beach entrance station, turn left on Birdview Avenue, and drive 1 mile to limited curbside parking spaces on the right. (Birdview Avenue becomes Cliffside Drive en route.)

The hike

Walk towards the cliffs, past the trailhead gate, at the Point Dume Natural Preserve boundary. Wind up the hill on the footpath to a junction. The left fork leads to Birdview Avenue in a residential neighborhood. Stay to the right to a second junction. The right fork follows the ridge to a rocky point and ends at a fenced overlook. Return to the junction and take the other fork. A short distance ahead is a 4-way junction. The left fork loops around the terraced flat with coastal sage scrub to Birdview Avenue; it also connects with the beach access to Dume Cove. The right fork leads uphill to the summit, 203 feet above the ocean. The middle fork follows a boardwalk to a platform overlook. From the platform, a sandy path continues a short distance around to the point.

Return to the beach access, and descend on the trail and stairs to Dume (Pirates) Cove at the base of the cliffs. At low tide, explore the tidepools and walk along the rocky shoreline northeast into Paradise Cove, a privately run, crescent-shaped beach with a small pier and concessions. ▪

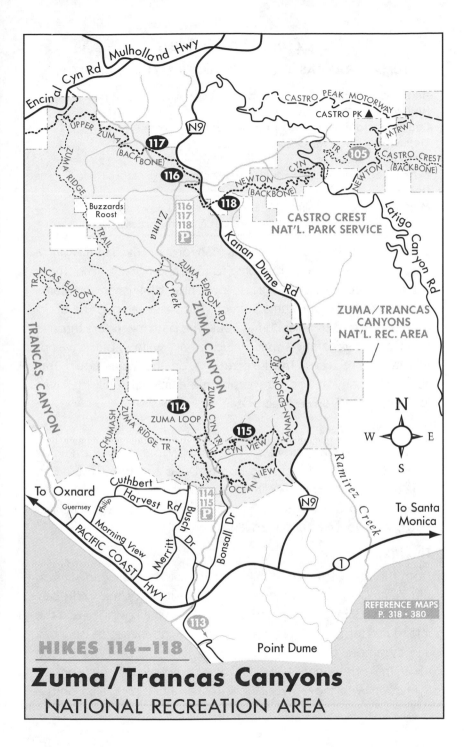

Mulholland Hwy

Encinal Cyn Rd

CASTRO PEAK MOTORWAY

CASTRO PK ▲

N9

UPPER ZUMA
(BACKBONE)

117

ZUMA RIDGE TRAIL

116

MTRWY

CASTRO CREST
(BACKBONE)

CYN TR

105

NEWTON
(BACKBONE)

NEWTON

Buzzards
Roost

Zuma

116
117
118
P

118

Kanan Dume Rd

CASTRO CREST
NAT'L. PARK SERVICE

Latigo Canyon Rd

TRANCAS EDISON

ZUMA EDISON RD

Creek

ZUMA CANYON

ZUMA/TRANCAS
CANYONS
NAT'L. REC. AREA

TRANCAS CANYON

CHUMASH

ZUMA RIDGE TR

114

ZUMA LOOP

ZUMA CYN TR

115

CYN VIEW

KANAN-EDISON RD

OCEAN VIEW

N

W ✦ E

S

Ramirez Creek

To Oxnard

Cuthbert

Guernsey

Philip

Harvest Rd

Morning View

Merritt

Busch Dr

114
115
P

Bonsall Dr

N9

To Santa
Monica

PACIFIC COAST HWY

113

Point Dume

1

REFERENCE MAPS
P. 318 • 380

HIKES 114–118

Zuma/Trancas Canyons
NATIONAL RECREATION AREA

114. Zuma Loop Trail

ZUMA/TRANCAS CANYONS: LOWER ZUMA CANYON

Hiking distance: 1.7-mile loop plus optional 1.4-mile spur trail
Hiking time: 1-2 hours
Configuration: loop plus optional spur trail
Elevation gain: 250-450 feet
Difficulty: easy
Exposure: partially shaded canyon bottom and exposed hillside
Dogs: allowed
Maps: U.S.G.S. Point Dume · N.P.S. Zuma-Trancas Canyons map
Tom Harrison Maps: Zuma-Trancas Canyons Trail map

Zuma Canyon is one of the few canyons in the Santa Monica Mountains that is accessible only to foot and horse traffic. There are no paved roads. This easy loop hike begins on the Zuma Canyon Trail in Lower Zuma Canyon. The trail heads up the drainage parallel to perennial Zuma Creek. The path meanders through lush riparian vegetation that includes oak, willow, black walnut, and sycamore trees. The hike returns on the Zuma Loop Trail above the canyon floor, traversing the east-facing hillside overlooking the canyon and the ocean.

To the trailhead

From Santa Monica, drive 21 miles northbound on the Pacific Coast Highway/Highway 1 to Bonsall Drive and turn right/north. (The turnoff is one mile west of Kanan Dume Road.) Continue one mile north to the trailhead parking area at road's end. The last 200 yards are on an unpaved lane.

The hike

From the end of the road, hike north past the trailhead sign on the Zuma Canyon Trail. Follow the west slope of the wide canyon wash 0.2 miles to a junction with the Zuma Loop Trail on the left, our return route. Begin the loop straight ahead, passing oak and sycamore trees. Continue past a junction with the Ocean View Trail on the right (Hike 115). Rock-hop over Zuma Creek to a junction with the Canyon View Trail at a half mile, also on the

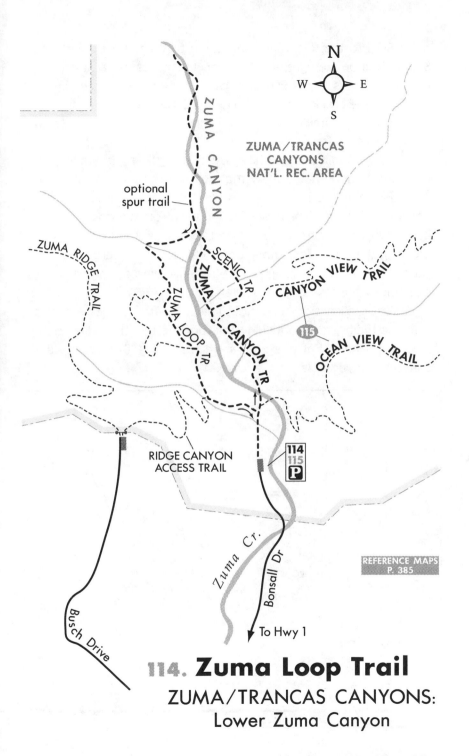

N
W   E
S

ZUMA/TRANCAS
CANYONS
NAT'L. REC. AREA

ZUMA CANYON

optional
spur trail

ZUMA RIDGE TRAIL

SCENIC TR

CANYON VIEW TRAIL

ZUMA

ZUMA LOOP TR

115

CANYON TR

OCEAN VIEW TRAIL

RIDGE CANYON
ACCESS TRAIL

114
115
P

Zuma Cr.

Bonsall Dr

REFERENCE MAPS
P. 385

Busch Drive

To Hwy 1

114. **Zuma Loop Trail**
ZUMA/TRANCAS CANYONS:
Lower Zuma Canyon

right. Stay to the left, remaining close to Zuma Creek. Pass the Scenic Trail on the right, a short loop that skirts the east canyon wall. Both paths merge 20 yards before the second creek crossing. Cross the creek and walk another 20 yards to a junction with the Zuma Loop Trail at 0.7 miles. The return route veers left on the Zuma Loop Trail.

To add 1.4 miles to the hike, detour to the right, staying on the Zuma Canyon Trail. Follow the west side of the drainage. The Zuma Ridge Trail can be seen to the west near the top of the canyon wall. (The Zuma Ridge Trail travels from the coast and up Zuma Ridge to Encinal Canyon Road.) Meander up Zuma Canyon, crossing the creek four more times. At the fourth crossing, the path fades. Beyond this point, the trail scrambles up the drainage among the sandstone boulders.

Back at the junction, take the Zuma Loop Trail to the west and traverse the hillside, continuing the loop. Follow the ridge south, staying to the left at three separate trail splits. Descend to the canyon floor, completing the loop. ∎

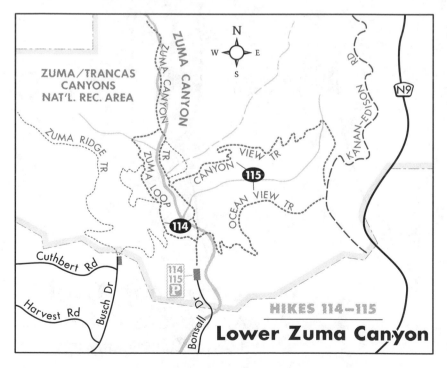

115. Ocean View—Canyon View Loop
ZUMA/TRANCAS CANYONS: Lower Zuma Canyon

Hiking distance: 3.1-mile loop
Hiking time: 1.5 hours
Configuration: loop
Elevation gain: 600 feet
Difficulty: easy to moderate
Exposure: partially shaded canyon bottom and exposed hillside
Dogs: allowed
Maps: U.S.G.S. Point Dume · N.P.S. Zuma-Trancas Canyons map
      Tom Harrison Maps: Zuma-Trancas Canyons Trail map

Lower Zuma Canyon remains a beautiful, natural stream-fed gorge with minimal development. The perennial stream makes its way down the canyon floor, reaching the ocean at the west end of Point Dume. The Ocean View Trail and Canyon View Trail form a loop through the chaparral-clad hillside along Zuma Canyon. The trail offers great vistas of Zuma Canyon and the ocean from the west-facing slope. This hike begins at the mouth of Zuma Canyon in a riparian wash dotted with sycamores, oaks, black walnut, willows, and laurel sumac bushes.

To the trailhead

From Santa Monica, drive 21 miles northbound on the Pacific Coast Highway/Highway 1 to Bonsall Drive and turn right/north. (The turnoff is one mile west of Kanan Dume Road.) Continue one mile north to the trailhead parking area at road's end. The last 200 yards are on an unpaved lane.

The hike

From the mouth of the canyon, head north up the canyon floor for 0.2 miles to a signed junction. The Zuma Loop Trail (Hike 114) curves left. Stay on the canyon bottom 30 yards to the posted Ocean View Trail. Bear right to begin the loop. Cross a rocky streambed and ascend the east canyon wall. Wind up the hillside to views of Point Dume and the ocean, reaching the ridge at 1.3 miles. At the summit are sweeping coastal views that extend (on clear days) to Palos

Verdes, Point Mugu, and Catalina. The Ocean View Trail ends at a T-junction, but the ocean views continue throughout the hike. Bear left 0.1 mile on the unpaved Kanan Edison Road to a junction with the Canyon View Trail. Curve left and follow the ridge across the head of the small side canyon. Weave down the hillside to the canyon floor and a junction at 2.6 miles. Bear left on the Zuma Canyon Trail and walk down canyon. Parallel the small stream past laurel sumac bushes and sycamore trees. Complete the loop and return to the trailhead. ■

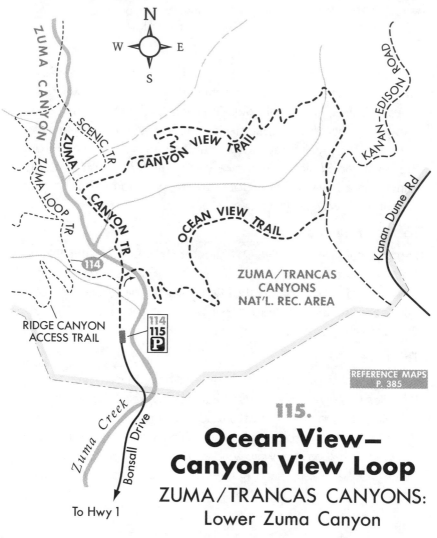

115.
Ocean View– Canyon View Loop
ZUMA/TRANCAS CANYONS:
Lower Zuma Canyon

116. Newton Canyon Falls

ZUMA/TRANCAS CANYONS: Upper Zuma Canyon

Hiking distance: 1.5 miles round trip
Hiking time: 1 hour
Configuration: out-and-back
Elevation gain: 200 feet
Difficulty: easy
Exposure: mostly shaded with some exposed areas
Dogs: allowed
Maps: U.S.G.S. Point Dume · N.P.S. Zuma-Trancas Canyons map
Tom Harrison Maps: Zuma-Trancas Canyons Trail map

Newton Canyon Falls is a 30-foot waterfall in a lush, thickly vegetated, water-worn grotto with mossy rocks, sandstone caves, and a tangle of vines. The hidden cataract on Newton Creek drops off a vertical limestone wall a short distance from the creek's confluence with Zuma Creek. At the base of the falls are large shaded boulders under a canopy of sycamores, bay laurel, and oaks. (The falls and creek may not be flowing if the season has been exceptionally dry.)

The hike begins on the first section of the Upper Zuma Canyon Trail—Hike 117—in the Zuma/Trancas Canyons area. The trail is a segment of the Backbone Trail that runs between Kanan Dume Road and Encinal Canyon.

To the trailhead

From Santa Monica, drive 18 miles northbound on the Pacific Coast Highway/Highway 1 to Kanan Dume Road (5.8 miles west of Malibu Canyon Road). Turn right and drive 4.4 miles north to the trailhead parking lot on the left (west). The parking lot is located just after the first tunnel (T-1).

From the Ventura Freeway/Highway 101 in Agoura Hills, exit on Kanan Road. Drive 7.9 miles south to the trailhead parking lot on the right (west). The parking lot is located just before entering the third tunnel (T-1). (Kanan Road becomes Kanan Dume Road south of Mulholland Highway.)

The hike

Hike west, away from Kanan Dume Road, on the signed Backbone Trail (the Upper Zuma Canyon Trail). The trail immediately begins its descent from the open chaparral into the shady canyon. After crossing the trickling Newton Creek, a side trail on the left leads 20 yards to sandstone rocks at the top of the falls. The main trail continues 100 yards downhill to a second cutoff trail on the left. Take this steep side path downhill through a forest of oaks, sycamores, and bay laurels to the creek, bearing to the left on the descent. Once at the creek, hike upstream along the path. Fifty yards up the narrow canyon is a lush grotto at the base of Newton Canyon Falls.

The main trail continues 1.9 miles northwest to the Zuma Ridge Trail, entering the rugged Zuma Canyon with its steep volcanic cliffs (Hike 117). Return by retracing your steps. ■

116.
Newton Canyon Falls
ZUMA/TRANCAS CANYONS:
Upper Zuma Canyon

117. Upper Zuma Canyon— Trancas Canyon
Kanan Dume Road to Encinal Canyon Road

ZUMA/TRANCAS CANYONS: Upper Zuma Canyon

Hiking distance: 9.6 miles round trip
Hiking time: 5 hours
Configuration: out-and-back
Elevation gain: 350 feet
Difficulty: moderate
Exposure: exposed hills and forested canyons
Dogs: allowed
Maps: U.S.G.S. Point Dume
　　　Tom Harrison Maps: Zuma-Trancas Canyons Trail Map

Zuma Canyon and Trancas Canyon are neighboring V-shaped canyons in the central portion of the Santa Monica Mountains. The steep gorges have cascading streams, weather-carved sandstone boulders, fern-lined pools, and jungle-like forests with oaks, bays, willows, and sycamores. The scenic canyons are located in the Zuma/Trancas Canyons area, managed by the National Park Service, and have remained natural and undisturbed.

This hike traverses the upper slopes of Zuma Canyon, climbs up to Zuma Ridge between the two canyons, and drops into Trancas Canyon. En route, the hike visits Newton Canyon Falls, Upper Zuma Falls, and Trancas Creek. The route utilizes the Upper Zuma Canyon Trail and the Trancas Canyon Trail, both sections of the Backbone Trail that connects Kanan Dume Road with Encinal Canyon Road. The two trails join atop Zuma Ridge.

To the trailhead

From Santa Monica, drive 18 miles northbound on the Pacific Coast Highway/Highway 1 to Kanan Dume Road (5.8 miles west of Malibu Canyon Road). Turn right and drive 4.4 miles north to the trailhead parking lot on the left (west). The parking lot is located just after the first tunnel (T-1).

From the Ventura Freeway/Highway 101 in Agoura Hills, take the Kanan Road exit. Drive 7.9 miles south to the trailhead parking

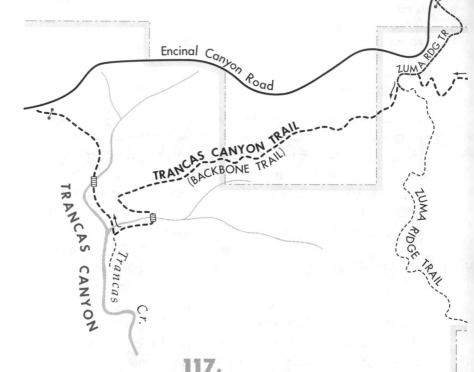

117.
Upper Zuma Canyon–
Trancas Canyon
Kanan Dume Road
to Encinal Canyon Road
ZUMA/TRANCAS CANYONS:
Upper Zuma Canyon

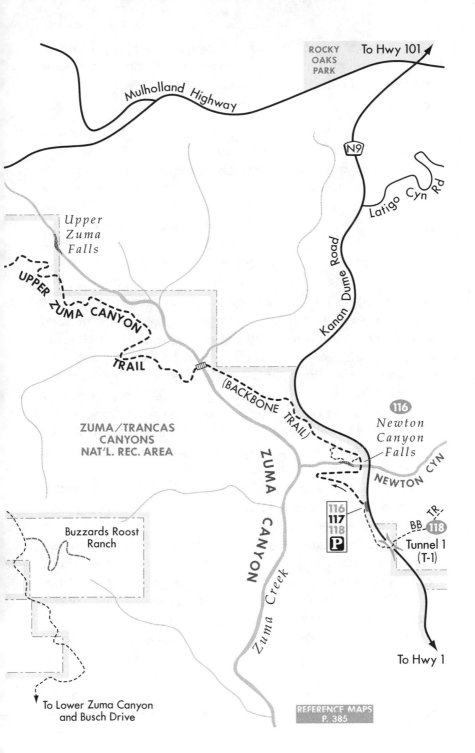

ROCKY
OAKS
PARK

To Hwy 101

Mulholland Highway

N9

Latigo Cyn Rd

Upper
Zuma
Falls

UPPER ZUMA CANYON

TRAIL

Kanan Dume Road

(BACKBONE TRAIL)

ZUMA/TRANCAS
CANYONS
NAT'L. REC. AREA

116
Newton
Canyon
Falls

NEWTON CYN

Buzzards Roost
Ranch

ZUMA CANYON

Zuma Creek

116
117
118
P

BB TR.
118

Tunnel 1
(T-1)

To Hwy 1

To Lower Zuma Canyon
and Busch Drive

REFERENCE MAPS
P. 385

lot on the right (west). The parking lot is located just before entering the third tunnel (T-1). (Kanan Road becomes Kanan Dume Road south of Mulholland Highway.)

The hike

Walk past the trailhead kiosk, and head west through the lush vegetation on the Backbone Trail (Upper Zuma Canyon Trail). Descend on the south wall of Upper Zuma Canyon. Switchback to the right and cross over to the north canyon wall. After crossing the trickling Newton Creek, two side paths on the left lead to Newton Canyon Falls. Continue on the rock-embedded path (the main trail) as the coastal views open down Zuma Canyon towards the ocean. Descend into the shade of a mixed forest with mature oaks to a bridge spanning Zuma Creek. Cross the bridge and parallel the waterway upstream. Climb to views of the surrounding mountains, then drop back into the forest and cross a feeder stream. Wind through the backcountry on the undulating path to a close-up view of Upper Zuma Falls as it flows down the face of a sandstone wall. Weave along the mountain contours to a posted T-junction with the Zuma Ridge Trail, a gated dirt road at 2.5 miles. The right fork leads 0.4 miles to the trailhead gate on Encinal Canyon Road. Bear left and follow the unpaved road 0.1 mile to a left U-bend. Mid-bend is a junction. The Zuma Ridge Trail (a fire road) continues down the ridge for 5.3 miles to Busch Drive by Zuma Beach.

Bear right on the Trancas Canyon Trail, continuing on another section of the Backbone Trail. Follow the ridge uphill, leaving Zuma Canyon. Descend and traverse the hillside into Trancas Canyon to the posted Backbone Trail sign. Veer left, staying on the Trancas Canyon Trail. Follow the gentle downward slope and switchback to the left, dropping deep into the lush canyon. Continue down to a tributary of Trancas Creek in a shaded forest. Cross a bridge over the tributary, and head down canyon through the oak forest to a fork at Trancas Creek. The left fork follows the creek about 100 feet and ends. Bear right and rock-hop over the creek. Climb the canyon wall, leaving the shade of the forest. Cross a bridge over the creek, and climb out of the canyon to the gated trailhead on Encinal Canyon Road. Return along the same route. ■

118. Newton Canyon
ZUMA/TRANCAS CANYONS • CASTRO CREST N.P.S.

Hiking distance: 4.6 miles round trip
Hiking time: 2.5 hours
Configuration: out-and-back
Elevation gain: 300 feet
Difficulty: easy to moderate
Exposure: shaded forest
Dogs: allowed
Maps: U.S.G.S. Point Dume • N.P.S. Zuma-Trancas Canyons map
       Tom Harrison Maps: Zuma-Trancas Canyons Trail map

The Newton Canyon Trail is a forested trail that runs through the Castro Crest National Park Service corridor, connecting Zuma/ Trancas Canyons Recreation Area to Malibu Creek State Park. This 2.3-mile-long path, part of the Backbone Trail, connects Kanan Dume Road by Tunnel 1 with Latigo Canyon Road beneath Castro Peak. The trail weaves through the oak-filled canyon with ocean views and seasonal stream crossings.

To the trailhead

From Santa Monica, drive 18 miles northbound on the Pacific Coast Highway/Highway 1 to Kanan Dume Road (5.8 miles west of Malibu Canyon Road). Turn right and drive 4.4 miles north to the trailhead parking lot on the left (west). The parking lot is located just after the first tunnel (T-1).

From the Ventura Freeway/Highway 101 in Agoura Hills, exit on Kanan Road. Drive 7.9 miles south to the trailhead parking lot on the right (west). The parking lot is located just before entering the third tunnel (T-1). (Kanan Road becomes Kanan Dume Road south of Mulholland Highway.)

The hike

The signed trail begins alongside Kanan Dume Road. Head south towards the ocean on the old fire road. Climb up to Tunnel 1 and cross over, high above Kanan Dume Road. After crossing, the road narrows to a footpath and enters a forested canopy. Slowly descend into Newton Canyon to Snakebite Ridge Road, a paved private road. Cross the road. Follow the serpentine path under the shade of oak and bay laurel trees, and climb to overlooks of the surrounding mountains. Continue winding along the mountainside and cross over to the north side of the canyon. Stroll through the lush, fern-filled forest. Zigzag up the north slope of Newton Canyon to a great westward view of the jagged ridgeline of the Boney Mountains. The trail exits on Latigo Canyon Road. Across the road is a trailhead parking lot.

To extend the hike, the trail continues on the Castro Crest Trail, a continuation of the Backbone Trail—Hike 105. The trail meanders through Newton Canyon and Solstice Canyon beneath Castro Crest to the north. The jagged sandstone mountain stretches for over two miles. The trail leads 4.2 miles to the upper end of Corral Canyon Road in Malibu Creek State Park. ■

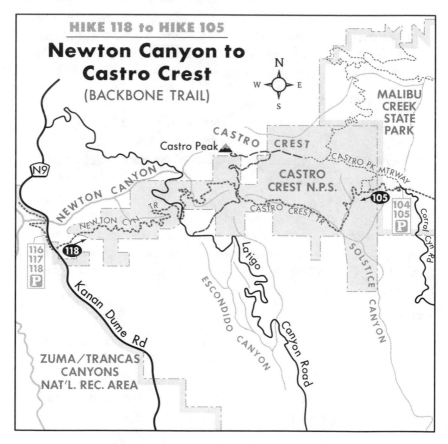

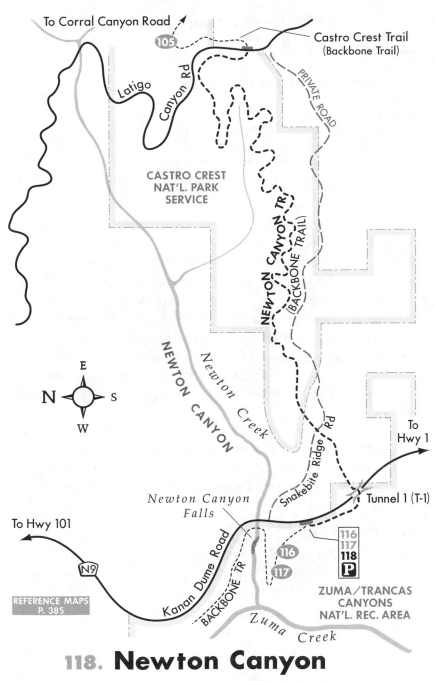

To Corral Canyon Road

105

Latigo Canyon Rd

Castro Crest Trail
(Backbone Trail)

PRIVATE ROAD

CASTRO CREST
NAT'L. PARK
SERVICE

NEWTON CANYON TR.
(BACKBONE TRAIL)

N E W T O N   C A N Y O N

Newton Creek

E
N — S
W

To
Hwy 1

Snakebite Ridge Rd

Newton Canyon
Falls

Tunnel 1 (T-1)

To Hwy 101

N9

REFERENCE MAPS
P. 385

Kanan Dume Road

BACKBONE TR

116

117

116
117
118
P

Zuma Creek

ZUMA/TRANCAS
CANYONS
NAT'L. REC. AREA

118. Newton Canyon

ZUMA/TRANCAS CANYONS • CASTRO CREST

119. Rocky Oaks Park

Hiking distance: 2-mile loop
Hiking time: 1 hour
Configuration: loop with optional connecting trails
Elevation gain: 200 feet
Difficulty: easy
Exposure: open slopes and forested pockets
Dogs: allowed
Maps: U.S.G.S. Point Dume · N.P.S. Rocky Oaks Site map
Tom Harrison Maps: Zuma-Trancas Canyons Trail map

Rocky Oaks Park was homesteaded in the early 1900s. Fifty years later, the remote site was developed into a working cattle ranch. A pond was built for watering the cattle, orchards were planted, and the grasslands were farmed. The ranching operation ended after the 1978 Kanan Fire swept through the area. In 1981, the pastoral 200-acre ranch was purchased by the National Park Service. The park has a diverse topography with rolling grasslands, chaparral-covered hills, volcanic rock formations, coastal live oak savannah, groves of Deodar cedar, willows, sycamores, and the former watering pond in a grassy meadow. A network of connecting trails weaves through the open space for several hiking options.

This hike forms an easy loop on the Rocky Oaks Trail, Overlook Trail, and Pond Trail. The hike meanders through the heart of the park, looping around the pond to picnic areas and to scenic overlooks of upper Zuma Canyon and the interior of the Santa Monica Mountains.

To the trailhead

From Santa Monica, drive 18 miles northbound on the Pacific Coast Highway/Highway 1 to Kanan Dume Road (5.8 miles west of Malibu Canyon Road). Turn right and drive 6.2 miles north to Mulholland Highway and turn left. Quickly turn right into the Rocky Oaks Park entrance and parking lot.

From the Ventura Freeway/Highway 101 in Agoura Hills, exit on Kanan Road. Drive 6.1 miles south to Mulholland Highway. Turn right and a quick right again into the park entrance.

The hike

Hike north past the rail fence to the Rocky Oaks Loop Trail, which heads in both directions. Take the left fork a short distance, passing old ranch ruins to a 4-way junction. Continue straight ahead on the middle path towards the Overlook Trail. Ascend the hillside overlooking the pond, and make a horseshoe left bend. Beyond the bend is the Overlook Trail. This is a short detour on the left to a scenic overlook with 360-degree panoramic views.

Back on the main trail, continue northeast around the ridge, slowly descending to the valley floor near Kanan Road. Bear sharply to the right, heading south to the Pond Trail junction. Both the left and right forks loop around the pond and rejoin at the south end. At the junction, go south and return to the Rocky Oaks Loop, then retrace your steps back to the trailhead. ■

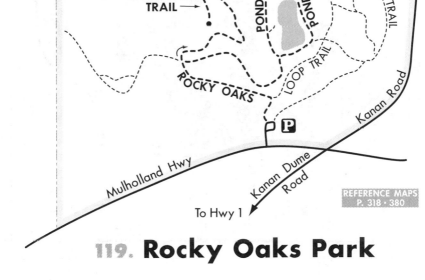

119. Rocky Oaks Park

120. Charmlee Wilderness Park

2577 S. Encinal Canyon Road
Open daily 8:00 a.m. to sunset

Hiking distance: 3-mile loop
Hiking time: 1.5 hours
Configuration: loop plus optional connecting trails
Elevation gain: 600 feet
Difficulty: easy
Exposure: exposed with forested pockets
Dogs: allowed
Maps: U.S.G.S. Triunfo Pass · City of Malibu-Charmlee Natural Area map
Tom Harrison Maps: Zuma-Trancas Canyons Trail map

Perched on oceanfront cliffs 1,300 feet above the sea, Charmlee Wilderness Park has a magnificent bird's-eye view of the Malibu coastline. The 532-acre wilderness park, sitting between Encinal Canyon and Lechusa Canyon, was once a cattle ranch. The land was purchased by Los Angeles County in 1968 and opened as

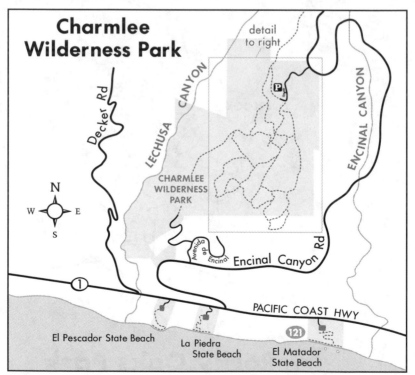

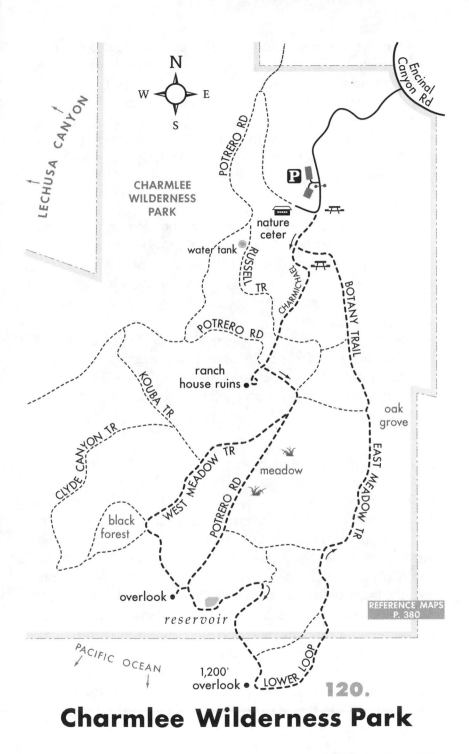

N
W · E
S

LECHUSA CANYON

Encinal Canyon Rd

CHARMLEE WILDERNESS PARK

POTRERO RD

P

nature ceter

water tank

RUSSELL TR

CHARMICHAEL

BOTANY TRAIL

POTRERO RD

ranch house ruins •

oak grove

KOUBA TR

EAST MEADOW TR

CLYDE CANYON TR

WEST MEADOW TR

POTRERO RD

meadow

black forest

REFERENCE MAPS P. 380

overlook •

reservoir

PACIFIC OCEAN

1,200' overlook •   LOWER LOOP

120.

Charmlee Wilderness Park

a park in 1981. Eight miles of interconnecting footpaths and old ranch roads weave through expansive mountain terrain with grassy meadows, oak and eucalyptus woodlands, mountain slopes, rocky ridges, sandstone formations, and 1,250-foot bluffs overlooking the sea. The park has picnic areas and a nature center with plant exhibits. This hike crosses the bluffs through meadows and forest groves to the old ranch reservoir and oceanfront overlooks.

To the trailhead

From Santa Monica, drive 23.2 miles northbound on the Pacific Coast Highway/Highway 1 to Encinal Canyon Road and turn right/ north. (Encinal Canyon Road is 11.2 miles west of Malibu Canyon Road.) Continue 3.7 miles to the park entrance on the left. Turn left and drive 0.2 miles on the park road to the parking lot. A parking fee is required.

From the Pacific Coast Highway/Highway 1 and Las Posas Road in southeast Oxnard, drive 14 miles southbound on the PCH to Encinal Canyon Road and turn left. Continue 3.7 miles to the Charmlee Park entrance on the left. Follow the park road 0.2 miles to the parking lot.

The hike

Hike past the information board and picnic area on the wide trail. Pass a second picnic area on the left in an oak grove, and continue uphill to a three-way trail split. The middle trail is a short detour leading to an overlook set among rock formations and the old ranch house foundation. Take the main trail to the left into the large grassy meadow. Two trails cross the meadow and rejoin at the south end—the main trail (Potrero Road) heads through the meadow while the right fork (West Meadow Trail) skirts the meadow's western edge. At the far end is an ocean overlook and a trail fork. Bear left past an old ranch reservoir, and pass two junctions to a 1,200-foot overlook on the right. Continue downhill, curving north through an oak grove to the unsigned Botany Trail, a narrow footpath on the right. The Botany Trail winds back to the picnic area and the trailhead. ■

121. El Pescador • La Piedra • El Matador State Beaches

ROBERT H. MEYER MEMORIAL STATE BEACH

Hiking distance: 2 miles round trip (total for all beaches)
Hiking time: 2 hours
Configuration: 3 out-and-back trails
Elevation gain: 100 feet for each hike
Difficulty: easy
Exposure: exposed beachfront coastline
Dogs: not allowed
Maps: U.S.G.S. Triunfo Pass and Point Dume

El Pescador, La Piedra, and El Matador State Beaches are three small oceanfront parks on the Malibu bluffs. Together they comprise the Robert H. Meyer Memorial State Beach. The three pocket beaches are within a one-mile stretch, bounded by rocky points. Each park contains a blufftop parking lot, a picnic area with overlooks, a pretty beach strand, and a trail down the 100-foot eroded cliffs to the shoreline. Of the three, El Matador Beach is the largest and most scenic, with large rock formations, arches, and caves.

To the trailhead

EL PESCADOR STATE BEACH: 32860 Pacific Coast Highway in Malibu. Heading northbound on the Pacific Coast Highway (Highway 1) from Santa Monica, drive 20 miles past Malibu Canyon Road and 6 miles past Kanan Dume Road to the posted turnoff on the left (oceanside).

From the Pacific Coast Highway (Highway 1) and Las Posas Road in southeast Oxnard, drive 13.4 miles southbound to the posted El Pescador State Beach on the right (oceanside). The turnoff is 2.3 miles south of Leo Carrillo State Beach and just south of Decker Road.

LA PIEDRA STATE PARK: 32628 Pacific Coast Highway in Malibu. The turn-off is 0.2 miles east (southbound) from El Pescador State Park.

EL MATADOR STATE PARK: 32215 Pacific Coast Highway in Malibu. The turn-off is 0.9 miles east (southbound) from El Pescador State Park.

The hike

EL PESCADOR STATE BEACH (10 acres): Walk across the grassy field to the bluffs. The path begins from the west side of the park. Descend the bluffs to the east, dropping onto the sandy beach. The small beach pocket is bordered on each end by blufftop homes.

LA PIEDRA STATE BEACH (9 acres): A side path by the picnic tables leads to an overlook on the edge of the 100-foot bluffs.

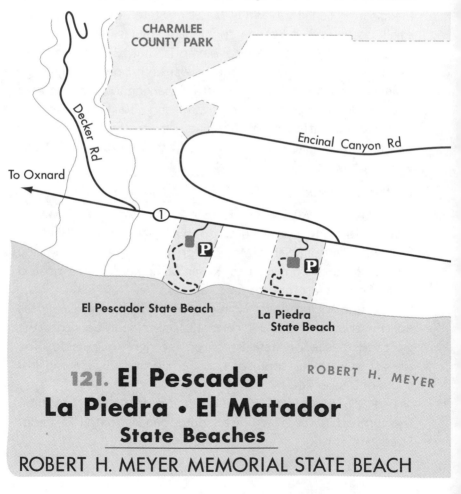

121. El Pescador La Piedra • El Matador State Beaches

ROBERT H. MEYER

ROBERT H. MEYER MEMORIAL STATE BEACH

The main trail begins at the upper west end of the parking lot. Drop down the sandstone cliffs through a draw to a long, narrow, sandy beach with a rocky west end. To the east, the beach ends at a home on the point at the base of the cliffs.

EL MATADOR STATE BEACH (18 acres): Walk towards the 100-foot bluffs to a picnic area overlooking the ocean and adjacent beachfront homes. Take the path to the left, looping clockwise down the eroding cliffs. Two sets of stairs lead down to the gorgeous beach with offshore rock outcroppings and caves. When the tide is right, water swirls through the caves and sea stack tunnels in the rock formations. To the east, beyond the state park boundary, are private homes. If strolling to the east, stay below the high-tide water line to avoid property owner hassles. ■

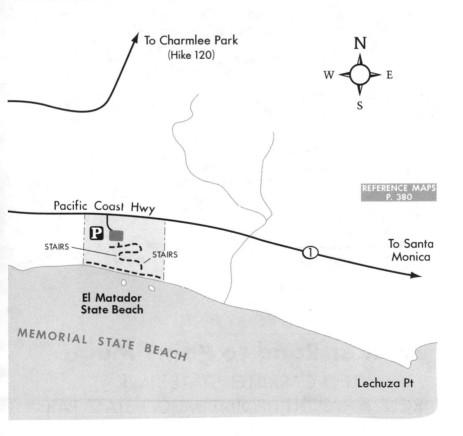

To Charmlee Park
(Hike 120)

N
W — E
S

REFERENCE MAPS
P. 380

Pacific Coast Hwy

P

STAIRS

STAIRS

1

To Santa
Monica

El Matador
State Beach

MEMORIAL STATE BEACH

Lechuza Pt

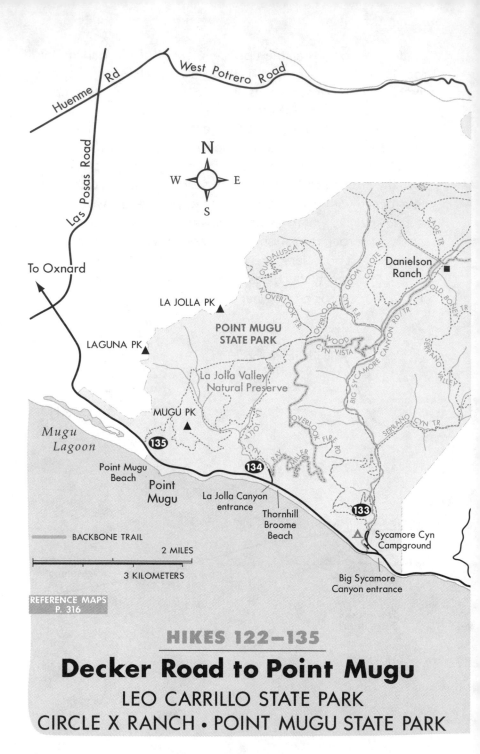

Huenme Rd

West Potrero Road

Las Posas Road

N
W · E
S

To Oxnard

LA JOLLA PK ▲

POINT MUGU
STATE PARK

LAGUNA PK ▲

La Jolla Valley
Natural Preserve

MUGU PK ▲

GUADALUSCA

N OVERLOOK FR

GOOM

COYOTE TR

OVERLOOK CYN FR

WOOD CYN VISTA

LA JOLLA CYN

OVERLOOK FIRE RD

RAY MILLER TR

BIG SYCAMORE CANYON RD/TR

SERRANO CYN TR

SERRANO VALLEY

OLD BONEY TR

SAGE TR

Danielson
Ranch

Mugu
Lagoon

135

Point Mugu
Beach

Point
Mugu

134

La Jolla Canyon
entrance

Thornhill
Broome
Beach

133

Sycamore Cyn
Campground

——— BACKBONE TRAIL

2 MILES

3 KILOMETERS

Big Sycamore
Canyon entrance

REFERENCE MAPS
P. 316

HIKES 122–135

Decker Road to Point Mugu
LEO CARRILLO STATE PARK
CIRCLE X RANCH • POINT MUGU STATE PARK

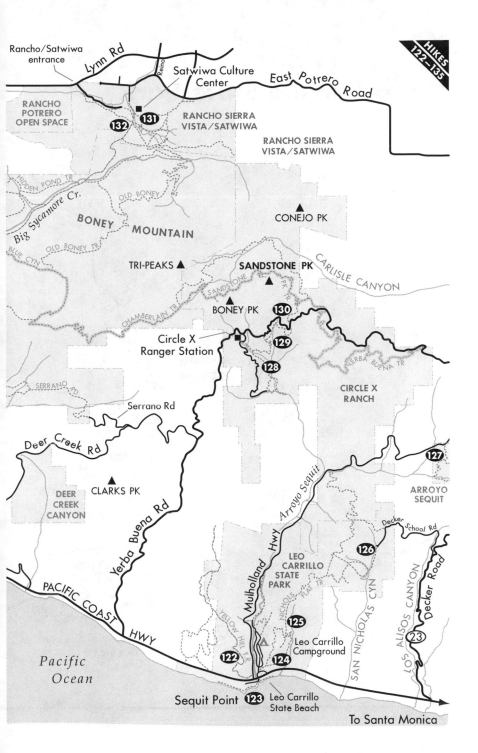

Rancho/Satwiwa
entrance

Lynn Rd

Reino

Satwiwa Culture
Center

East Potrero Road

RANCHO
POTRERO
OPEN SPACE

132 **131**

RANCHO SIERRA
VISTA/SATWIWA

RANCHO SIERRA
VISTA/SATWIWA

HIDDEN POND TR.

Big Sycamore Cr.

OLD BONEY

BONEY MOUNTAIN

OLD BONEY TR.

BLUE CYN

CONEJO PK ▲

CHAMBERLAIN TR.

TRI-PEAKS ▲

SANDSTONE PK

SANDSTONE PK TR.

▲

CARLISLE CANYON

BONEY PK ▲

130

Circle X
Ranger Station

129

128

YERBA BUENA TR.

SERRANO RD

Serrano Rd

CIRCLE X
RANCH

Deer Creek Rd

DEER
CREEK
CANYON

CLARKS PK ▲

Yerba Buena Rd

Arroyo Sequit

ARROYO
SEQUIT

127

Decker School Rd

PACIFIC COAST HWY

Mulholland Hwy

LEO
CARRILLO
STATE
PARK

NICHOLS FLAT TR.

126

SAN NICHOLAS CYN

LOS ALISOS CANYON

Decker Road

125

Leo Carrillo
Campground

23

*Pacific
Ocean*

YELLOW HILL FR.

122

124

Sequit Point **123**

Leo Carrillo
State Beach

To Santa Monica

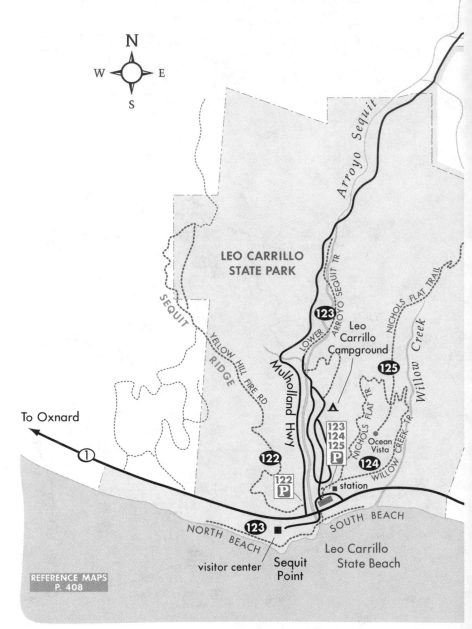

Leo Carrillo State Park

N **W** **E** **S**

LEO CARRILLO
STATE PARK

Arroyo Sequit

Nichols Flat Trail

Willow Creek

SEQUIT RIDGE

YELLOW HILL FIRE RD

Mulholland Hwy

LOWER ARROYO SEQUIT TR

123

Leo Carrillo Campground

125

NICHOLS FLAT TR

WILLOW CREEK TR

To Oxnard

1

123
124
125
P

Ocean Vista

124

122

122
P

station

123

NORTH BEACH

SOUTH BEACH

visitor center

Sequit Point

Leo Carrillo State Beach

REFERENCE MAPS
P. 408

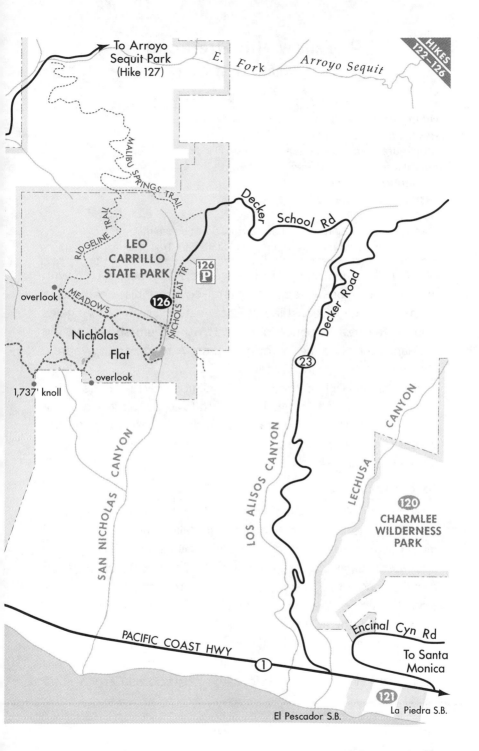

To Arroyo
Sequit Park
(Hike 127)

E. Fork   Arroyo Sequit

HIKES
122-126

Decker   School Rd

MALIBU SPRINGS TRAIL

RIDGELINE TRAIL

LEO
CARRILLO
STATE PARK

126
P

126

NICHOLS FLAT TR

Decker Road

overlook

MEADOWS

Nicholas
Flat

23

overlook

1,737' knoll

SAN NICHOLAS CANYON

LOS ALISOS CANYON

LECHUSA CANYON

120
CHARMLEE
WILDERNESS
PARK

Encinal Cyn Rd

To Santa
Monica

PACIFIC COAST HWY

1

121

El Pescador S.B.

La Piedra S.B.

122. Yellow Hill Fire Road
LEO CARRILLO STATE PARK
35000 W. Pacific Coast Hwy

Hiking distance: 5 miles round trip
Hiking time: 2.5 hours
Configuration: out-and-back with small loop
Elevation gain: 1,300 feet
Difficulty: moderate
Exposure: exposed
Dogs: not allowed
Maps: U.S.G.S. Triunfo Pass · Leo Carrillo State Beach map
Tom Harrison Maps: Point Mugu State Park Trail map

Leo Carrillo State Park is a picturesque 2,100-acre haven with mountain canyons, steep chaparral-covered hillsides, and a 1.5-mile stretch of coastline at the western tip of Los Angeles County. The area was once inhabited by the Chumash Indians. The parklands surround the lower end of the Arroyo Sequit, where it empties into the Pacific Ocean.

The Yellow Hill Fire Road steadily climbs a dirt road along the west side of the drainage. The trail follows Sequit Ridge in the backcountry hills, leaving the west side of the state park into Ventura County. En route are outstanding ocean views, including the four Channel Islands.

To the trailhead

Heading northbound on the Pacific Coast Highway/Highway 1 from Santa Monica, drive 14 miles past Malibu Canyon Road and 8 miles past Kanan Dume Road to Mulholland Highway. The highway is located 0.2 miles west of the Leo Carrillo State Beach entrance. Turn right and go 100 yards to the gated fire road on the left. Park along the side of the road. Parking is also available in Leo Carrillo State Park off the PCH.

From the Pacific Coast Highway/Highway 1 and Las Posas Road in southeast Oxnard, drive 10.8 miles southbound on the PCH to Mulholland Highway, just before the posted Leo Carrillo State

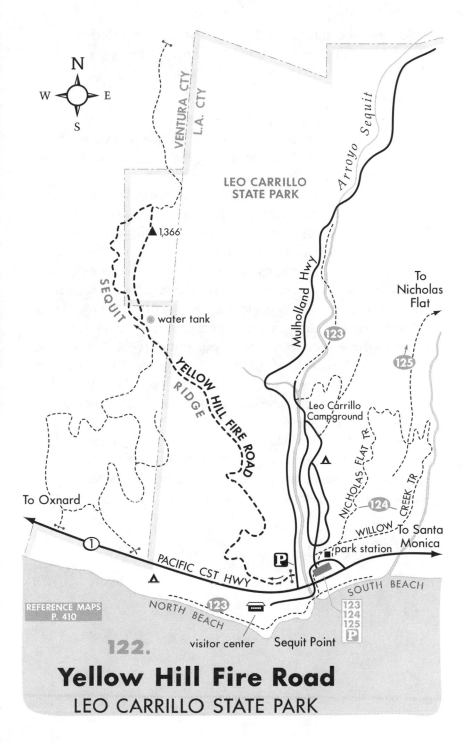

N
W E
S

VENTURA CTY
L.A. CTY

LEO CARRILLO
STATE PARK

Arroyo Sequit

▲ 1,366'

SEQUIT

● water tank

Mulholland Hwy

To
Nicholas
Flat

123

125

YELLOW HILL FIRE ROAD

RIDGE

Leo Carrillo
Campground

▲

NICHOLAS FLAT TR

CREEK TR

124

To Oxnard

WILLOW

To Santa
Monica

park station

P

1

PACIFIC CST HWY

▲

SOUTH BEACH

REFERENCE MAPS
P. 410

NORTH
BEACH

123

visitor center

Sequit Point

123
124
125
P

Beach entrance. Turn left and go 100 yards to the gated fire road on the left. Park along the side of the road. Parking is also available in Leo Carrillo State Park off the PCH.

The hike

Walk around the trailhead gate, and follow the old dirt road, passing prickly pear cactus. Coastal views quickly expand, from Point Dume to Point Mugu and across the ocean to the Channel Islands. The trail parallels the coast for 0.3 miles, then curves inland. Climb steadily up the ridge. Cross over a minor side canyon to a view of the sculptured land forms in the interior of Leo Carrillo State Park and the Arroyo Sequit drainage. At 1.4 miles, the encroaching vegetation narrows the winding road to a single track trail. Cross the county line and walk around a gate, continuing 300 yards ahead to a Y-fork. The left fork descends to the PCH. Stay to the right, below a water tank on the right. At 2 miles the road/trail makes a left bend. On the bend is a footpath veering up the knoll to the right, our return route. Stay on the main trail, curving around the west flank of the knoll. Near the ridge, the uphill grade eases, reaching a trail sign. Continue to the ridge 150 yards ahead, where there is an outstanding view of the Boney Mountain ridgeline.

Leave the road and return on the trail to the right, climbing up the north face of the knoll. Cross over the 1,366-foot summit, and descend along the ridge to the junction with the road at the water tank. Return along the same route. ▪

123. Lower Arroyo Sequit Trail and Sequit Point

LEO CARRILLO STATE PARK

35000 W. Pacific Coast Hwy

Hiking distance: 3 miles round trip
Hiking time: 1.5 hours
Configuration: two out-and-back trails
Elevation gain: 200 feet
Difficulty: easy
Exposure: shaded canyon; exposed beach
Dogs: not allowed
Maps: U.S.G.S. Triunfo Pass · Leo Carrillo State Beach map
   Tom Harrison Maps: Point Mugu State Park Trail map
   Tom Harrison Maps: Zuma-Trancas Canyons Trail map

Leo Carrillo State Park is a beautiful coastal park with a rocky shoreline, beaches, and tidepools where the Arroyo Sequit empties into the Pacific. Running inland along the drainage are shady backcountry trails. This hike offers both the rocky shoreline at Sequit Point and a cool retreat into the canyon drainage.

The first segment of the hike takes the Lower Arroyo Sequit Trail into the stream-fed canyon that is shaded with willow, sycamore, oak, and bay trees. The path ends in a deep, rock-walled canyon by large boulders and the trickling stream.

The second segment of the trail explores Sequit Point. The rocky bluff juts out from the shoreline at the south end of the park. The weather-carved point, which divides North Beach from South Beach, has sea caves, coves, ocean-sculpted arches, tidepools, and pocket beaches. A pedestrian tunnel under the Pacific Coast Highway connects South Beach (near the mouth of Arroyo Sequit) with the campground and the tree-shaded canyon. Many hours can be spent exploring the coastline.

To the trailhead

From Santa Monica, drive 26 miles northbound on the Pacific Coast Highway/Highway 1 to the posted Leo Carrillo State Beach entrance and turn right. (The state park is 14 miles west of Malibu Canyon Road and 8 miles west of Kanan Dume Road.) Park in the day-use parking lot. A parking fee is required.

From the Pacific Coast Highway/Highway 1 and Las Posas Road in southeast Oxnard, drive 11.1 miles southbound on the PCH to the posted Leo Carrillo State Beach entrance and turn left. Park in the day-use parking lot. A parking fee is required.

The hike

LOWER ARROYO SEQUIT TRAIL: From the parking area, hike north through the campground on the road past mature sycamores and oaks. Pass the amphitheater on the right to a gated road. Continue past the gate, crossing over the seasonal Arroyo Sequit to the end of the paved road. Take the footpath a hundred yards, and rock hop over the creek by a small grotto. Follow the path upstream along the east side of the creek. Recross the creek to the trail's end in a steep-walled box canyon with pools and large boulders.

Retrace your steps to the amphitheater, and now bear left on the footpath. Cross to the east side of the creek and head through the forest canopy. Switchbacks and two sets of wooden steps lead to a flat above the canyon. Descend back to the campground road, and continue back towards the coast.

SEQUIT POINT: To reach Sequit Point, take the paved path and walk through the tunnel under Highway 1 to the sandy beach. To the right (west), by the lifeguard station, are sandstone rock formations with caves, tunnels, a rock arch, tidepools, and a series of beach coves. After exploring the natural playground, return back to the parking lot. ▪

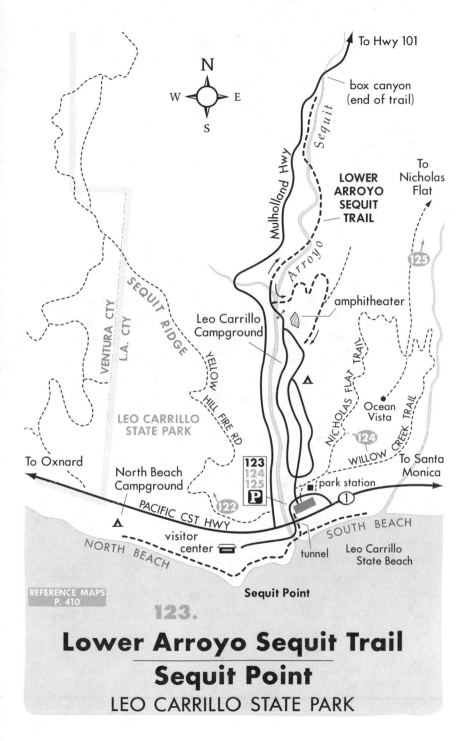

N
W E
S

To Hwy 101

box canyon
(end of trail)

Sequit

Mulholland Hwy

**LOWER
ARROYO
SEQUIT
TRAIL**

To
Nicholas
Flat

Arroyo

125

amphitheater

Leo Carrillo
Campground

VENTURA CTY
L.A. CTY

SEQUIT RIDGE

YELLOW HILL FIRE RD

NICHOLAS FLAT TRAIL

Ocean
Vista

WILLOW CREEK TRAIL

124

**LEO CARRILLO
STATE PARK**

To Oxnard

To Santa
Monica

North Beach
Campground

123
124
125
P

122

park station

1

PACIFIC CST HWY

SOUTH BEACH

NORTH BEACH

visitor
center

tunnel

Leo Carrillo
State Beach

REFERENCE MAPS
P. 410

Sequit Point

123.

Lower Arroyo Sequit Trail
Sequit Point
LEO CARRILLO STATE PARK

124. Ocean Vista
Willow Creek— Nicholas Flat Loop
LEO CARRILLO STATE PARK
35000 W. Pacific Coast Hwy

Hiking distance: 2.5-mile loop
Hiking time: 1.5 hours
Configuration: loop with spur trail to overlook
Elevation gain: 600 feet
Difficulty: easy to moderate
Exposure: mostly exposed with shaded pockets
Dogs: not allowed
Maps: U.S.G.S. Triunfo Pass · Leo Carrillo State Beach map
Tom Harrison Maps: Point Mugu State Park Trail map
Tom Harrison Maps: Zuma-Trancas Canyons Trail map

This loop hike in Leo Carrillo State Park leads to Ocean Vista, a 612-foot bald knoll with great views of the Malibu coastline and Point Dume. The Willow Creek Trail traverses the east-facing hillside up V-shaped Willow Creek Canyon to Ocean Vista at the north end of the loop. En route to the overlook, the trail leads through native grasslands and coastal sage scrub. The hike returns along the Nicholas Flat Trail, one of the few trails connecting the interior Santa Monica Mountains to the Pacific Ocean.

To the trailhead

From Santa Monica, drive 26 miles northbound on the Pacific Coast Highway/Highway 1 to the posted Leo Carrillo State Beach entrance and turn right. (The state park is 14 miles west of Malibu Canyon Road and 8 miles west of Kanan Dume Road.) Park in the day-use parking lot. A parking fee is required.

From the Pacific Coast Highway/Highway 1 and Las Posas Road in southeast Oxnard, drive 11.1 miles southbound on the PCH to the posted Leo Carrillo State Beach entrance and turn left. Park in the day-use parking lot. A parking fee is required.

The hike

The trailhead is 50 yards outside the park entrance station at the posted Camp 13 Trail on the left. Walk 50 yards on the footpath to the information kiosk and junction. The loop begins at this junction. Take the right fork—the Willow Creek Trail—up the hillside and parallel to the ocean, heading east. At a half mile the trail curves north, traversing the hillside while overlooking the arroyo and Willow Creek. Three switchbacks lead aggressively up to a saddle and a signed four-way junction with the Nicholas Flat Trail, which leads north to the upper reaches of the park (Hike 125). The left fork leads a quarter mile to Ocean Vista. After marveling at the views, return to the four-way junction and take the left (west) fork. Head downhill on the lower end of the Nicholas Flat Trail, returning to the trailhead along the grassy slopes above the park campground. ■

124.

Ocean Vista:
Willow Creek–
Nicholas Flat Loop
LEO CARRILLO STATE PARK

125. Nicholas Flat Trail
Nicholas Flat from the coast
LEO CARRILLO STATE PARK
35000 W. Pacific Coast Hwy

Hiking distance: 7.4 miles round trip
Hiking time: 4 hours
Configuration: out-and-back with 2 loops
Elevation gain: 1,700 feet
Difficulty: moderate to strenuous
Exposure: exposed hills and shady forest
Dogs: not allowed
Maps: U.S.G.S. Truinfo Pass · Leo Carrillo State Beach map
       Tom Harrison Maps: Zuma-Trancas Canyons Trail Map

The Nicholas Flat Trail, located entirely within Leo Carrillo State Park, is a 3.8-mile-long footpath that connects the interior mountains with the sea. The trail begins near the Pacific Coast Highway at the south end of the state park and climbs the oceanfront mountain to Nicholas Flat at the upper (north) end of the park. The flat is a large, grassy meadow dotted with oak forests and rock outcrops. A year-round pond lies on the south end of the flat, with mature oaks and picturesque sandstone rocks. From an elevation of 1,700 feet, the flat offers great mountain and coastal views. The trail also leads past Ocean Vista (a 612-foot overlook at the lower end of the park) and Vista Point (a 1,610-foot overlook at Nicholas Flat).

To the trailhead

From Santa Monica, drive 26 miles northbound on the Pacific Coast Highway/Highway 1 to the posted Leo Carrillo State Beach entrance and turn right. (The state park is 14 miles west of Malibu Canyon Road and 8 miles west of Kanan Dume Road.) Park in the day-use parking lot. A parking fee is required.

From the Pacific Coast Highway/Highway 1 and Las Posas Road in southeast Oxnard, drive 11.1 miles southbound on the PCH to the posted Leo Carrillo State Beach entrance and turn left. Park in the day-use parking lot. A parking fee is required.

The hike

The hike begins 50 yards outside the entrance station at the posted Camp 13 Trail on the left. Walk 50 yards on the footpath to the information kiosk and junction. The Willow Creek Trail curves around the hill to the right, our return route. Begin on the Nicholas Flat Trail to the left. Follow the east canyon slope above the campground while ascending through coastal scrub. At one mile, and over 500 feet in elevation, is a saddle and posted 4-way junction on a ridge overlooking Arroyo Sequit Canyon and Willow Creek Canyon. The trail straight ahead—the Willow Creek Trail—is the return route. To the right, the Ocean Vista Trail climbs a short distance to the 612-foot oceanfront knoll with 360-degree panoramas.

Back at the 4-way junction, continue north on the Nicholas Flat Trail. Follow the ridge inland, with continuous views into both canyons and across the ocean to the Channel Islands. At 2.2 miles, wind through tall, lush foliage in a shaded canopy to an unsigned junction. Detour 100 yards to the right to a 1,737-foot knoll with spectacular views of the Santa Monica Range and the Pacific Ocean. On the main trail, continue about 60 yards and veer right at a trail sign to a junction with the Ridgeline Trail at 2.7 miles.

Begin the loop and continue straight. A trail on the right leads to another overlook. Curve left around a vernal pool and drop into Nicholas Flat, a large grassy plateau dotted with oaks and surrounded by rolling hills. At 3.1 miles is a junction with the Meadow Trail to the left. Bear right and walk 25 yards to a Y-fork. Veer right to the pond. A side path to the right circles the pond to a grove of stately oaks and a beautiful rock formation. Continue on the main trail, walking through the meadow on the northwest side of the pond to a junction. The trail straight ahead leads to the trailhead at the end of Decker School Road (Hike 126). Take the left fork and complete the loop at the junction with the Meadow Trail. Walk straight ahead on the Meadow Trail to a T-junction with the Ridgeline Trail at 4.1 miles. The right fork leads to the Malibu Springs Trail. Bear left and weave through the forest to

Vista Point, overlooking Nicholas Flat. Continue to a junction with the Nicholas Flat Trail, completing the double loop at 4.7 miles.

Retrace your steps 1.7 miles (back towards the ocean) to the junction with the Willow Creek Trail at the lower end of the park. Take the Willow Creek Trail to the left. Descend on the west wall of secluded Willow Creek Canyon. Steadily loose elevation down three switchbacks. At the mouth of the canyon curve right. Parallel the Pacific Coast Highway, where there is a great view of Leo Carrillo State Beach. The 0.9-mile Willow Creek Trail ends at the trailhead kiosk. ■

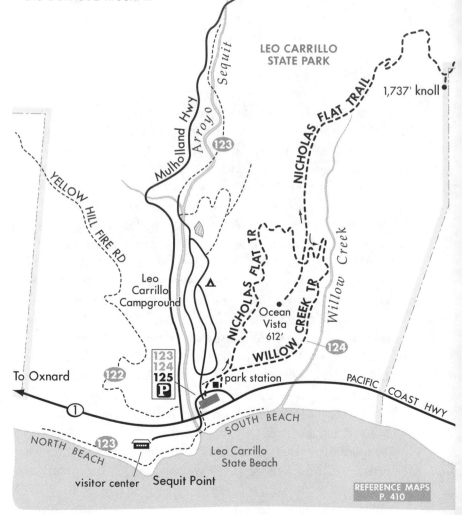

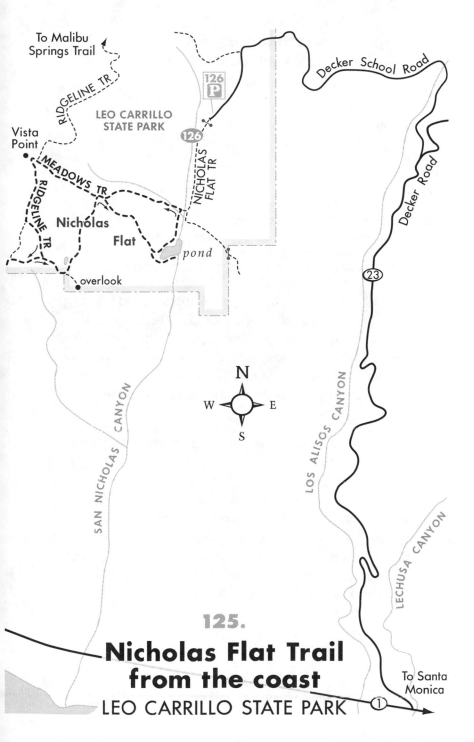

To Malibu
Springs Trail

RIDGELINE TR

LEO CARRILLO
STATE PARK

126 P

Vista
Point

MEADOWS TR

126

NICHOLAS
FLAT TR

RIDGELINE TR

Nicholas

Flat

pond

overlook

Decker School Road

Decker Road

23

N

W E

S

SAN NICHOLAS CANYON

LOS ALISOS CANYON

LECHUSA CANYON

125.

Nicholas Flat Trail
from the coast
LEO CARRILLO STATE PARK

To Santa
Monica

1

126. Nicholas Flat
LEO CARRILLO STATE PARK
Decker School Road

Hiking distance: 2.5-mile double loop
Hiking time: 1.5 hours
Configuration: double loop
Elevation gain: 100 feet
Difficulty: easy
Exposure: a mix of exposed meadows and shaded oak forest
Dogs: not allowed
Maps: U.S.G.S. Triunfo Pass · Leo Carrillo State Beach map
Tom Harrison Maps: Point Mugu State Park Trail map
Tom Harrison Maps: Zuma-Trancas Canyons Trail map

Nicholas Flat, in the upper reaches of Leo Carrillo State Park, is a grassy highland meadow with large oak trees, an old cattle pond, and sandstone outcroppings that lie 1,700 feet above the sea. This hike skirts around Nicholas Flat on old ranch roads. The easy hike offers spectacular views of the ocean, San Nicholas Canyon, and the surrounding mountains. The Nicholas Flat Trail may be hiked 3.8 miles downhill to the Pacific Ocean (see Hike 125).

To the trailhead

From Santa Monica, drive 23.8 miles northbound on the Pacific Coast Highway/Highway 1 to Decker Road and turn right. (Decker Road is 11.8 miles west of Malibu Canyon Road.) Continue 2.4 miles north to Decker School Road and turn left. Drive 1.5 miles to the road's end and park alongside the road.

From the Pacific Coast Highway/Highway 1 and Las Posas Road in southeast Oxnard, drive 13.3 miles southbound on the PCH to Decker Road and turn left. Continue 2.4 miles north to Decker School Road and turn left. Drive 1.5 miles to the road's end and park alongside the road.

The hike

Hike south past the gate and kiosk. Stay on the wide, oak-lined trail to a junction at 0.3 miles. Take the right fork, beginning the first loop. At 0.6 miles is another junction. Again take the right fork—the Meadows Trail. Continue to the Ridgeline Trail and an overlook, where there are great views into the canyons. Curve south to a junction with the Nicholas Flat Trail, leading to the coastline at the southern end of Leo Carrillo State Park. Take the Nicholas Flat Trail to the left, following the perimeter of the southern end of the flat. A trail on the right leads to another vista point. Complete the west loop at 1.8 miles. Take the trail to the right at two successive junctions to the pond. A side path to the right circles the pond to a grove of stately oaks and a beautiful rock formation. Return to the main trail and walk through the meadow along the northwest side of the pond to a junction, completing the east loop. Return to the trailhead. ■

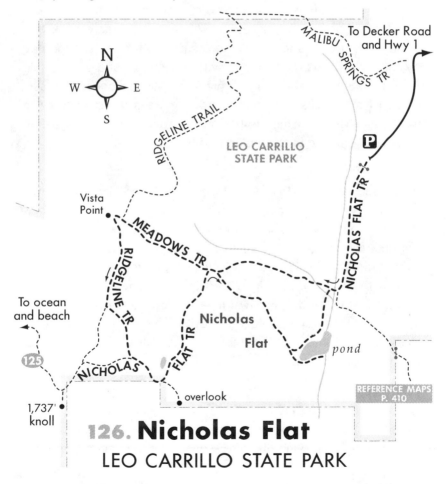

126. Nicholas Flat
LEO CARRILLO STATE PARK

127. Arroyo Sequit Park
34138 Mulholland Highway

Hiking distance: 2-mile loop
Hiking time: 1 hour
Configuration: loop
Elevation gain: 250 feet
Difficulty: easy
Exposure: mostly exposed with a few shaded areas
Dogs: allowed
Maps: U.S.G.S. Triunfo Pass
　　　　Tom Harrison Maps: Point Mugu State Park Trail map
　　　　Tom Harrison Maps: Zuma-Trancas Canyons Trail map

Arroyo Sequit Park was a ranch purchased by the Santa Monica Mountains Conservancy in 1985. Within the 155-acre park are open grassland meadows, picnic areas, and a small canyon cut by the East Fork Arroyo Sequit with oak groves and a waterfall. From the meadows are panoramic views of the ocean and surrounding mountains. This easy loop hike visits the diverse park habitats, crossing the meadows and dropping into the gorge that runs parallel to the East Fork Arroyo Sequit.

To the trailhead

From Santa Monica, drive 26.2 miles northbound on the Pacific Coast Highway/Highway 1 to Mulholland Highway and turn right. (Mulholland Highway is 14.2 miles west of Malibu Canyon Road.) Continue 5.5 miles up the canyon to the signed turnoff on the right at mailbox 34138. Turn right into the park entrance and park.

From the Pacific Coast Highway/Highway 1 and Las Posas Road in southeast Oxnard, drive 10.8 miles southbound on the PCH to Mulholland Highway. Turn left and drive 5.5 miles up the canyon to the signed turnoff on the right at mailbox 34138. Turn right into the entrance and park.

The hike

Head south on the park road past the gate, kiosk, and old ranch house. At 0.2 miles take the road to the left—past a barn, the astronomical observing site, a few coast live oaks, and the picnic area—to the footpath on the right. Leave the service road on the nature trail, heading south. Skirt the east edge of the meadow, with a great view of Boney Mountain to the northwest, then descend into a small canyon. Cross several seasonal tributaries of the Arroyo Sequit. Head west along the southern wall of the gorge, passing a waterfall on the left. Cross a wooden footbridge over the stream, and descend to the canyon floor. Continue west, cross the East Fork Arroyo Sequit, and begin the ascent out of the canyon to a junction. Continue on the right fork (straight ahead) up the hill. A series of switchbacks lead up the short but steep hill. Once at the top, cross the meadow to the road. Take the service road back to the parking area. ■

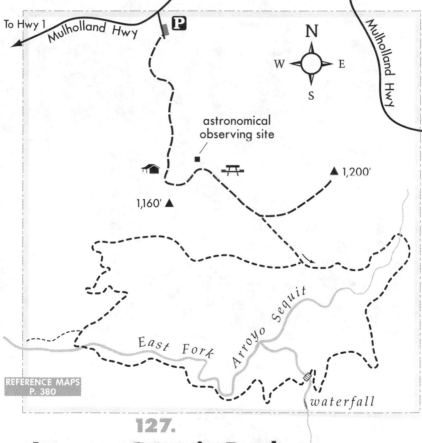

127.
Arroyo Sequit Park

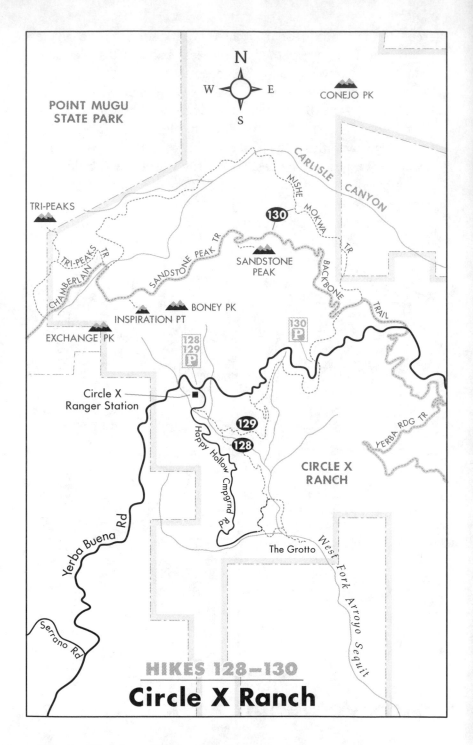

N
W E
S

POINT MUGU
STATE PARK

CONEJO PK

CARLISLE CANYON

TRI-PEAKS

TRI-PEAKS TR

MISHE MOKWA TR

130

SANDSTONE PEAK TR

SANDSTONE
PEAK

BACKBONE

CHAMBERLAIN

TRAIL

INSPIRATION PT

BONEY PK

130
P

EXCHANGE PK

128
129
P

Circle X
Ranger Station

129

128

Happy Hollow Cmpgrnd Rd

CIRCLE X
RANCH

YERBA RDG TR

Yerba Buena Rd

The Grotto

West Fork Arroyo Sequit

Serrano Rd

HIKES 128–130
Circle X Ranch

128. Grotto Trail
CIRCLE X RANCH
12896 Yerba Buena Road

Hiking distance: 3.5 miles round trip
Hiking time: 2 hours
Configuration: out-and-back with small loop
Elevation gain: 500 feet
Difficulty: easy to moderate
Exposure: mostly shaded canyon with some exposed hills
Dogs: allowed
Maps: U.S.G.S. Triunfo Pass · N.P.S. Circle X Ranch map
Tom Harrison Maps: Zuma-Trancas Canyons Trail map
Tom Harrison Maps: Point Mugu State Park Trail map

The Grotto Trail is located in the 1,655-acre Circle X Ranch, adjacent to the northeast end of Point Mugu State Park. Once a Boy Scout wilderness retreat, the Circle X Ranch is now part of the Santa Monica Mountains National Recreation Area. The scenic trail leads to The Grotto, a maze of large, volcanic boulders in a sheer, narrow gorge formed from landslides. The natural rock garden contains numerous caves, small waterfalls, and pools. The West Fork of the Arroyo Sequit flows through the caves and caverns of The Grotto, creating cascades and pools. En route, the path descends into a stream-cut gorge and passes Botsford Falls. The trail includes close-up vistas of the chiseled pinnacles of Boney Mountain and Sandstone Peak, the highest point in the Santa Monica Mountains at 3,111 feet.

To the trailhead

From the Pacific Coast Highway/Highway 1 in Santa Monica, drive 38 miles northbound to Yerba Buena Road and turn right. (Yerba Buena Road is 10.1 miles west of Kanan Dume Road and 2 miles west of Leo Carrillo State Beach.) Continue 5.3 miles up the winding road to the Circle X Ranger Station on the right. Park by the ranger station, or continue 0.2 miles downhill to the day-use parking area, located just past the posted Grotto Trailhead.

From the Pacific Coast Highway/Highway 1 and Las Posas Road in southeast Oxnard, drive 9 miles southbound to Yerba Buena

Road (3.3 miles past Big Sycamore Canyon) and turn left. Continue up Yerba Buena Road, following the directions above.

From the Ventura Freeway/Highway 101 in Thousand Oaks, exit on Westlake Boulevard (Highway 23). Drive 6.9 miles south on Westlake Boulevard, winding up the mountain road to Mulholland Highway at a stop sign. Turn right and go 0.4 miles to Little Sycamore Canyon Road. Turn right and drive 5.7 miles to the Circle X Ranger Station on the left. (At the county line, Little Sycamore Canyon Road becomes Yerba Buena Road.)

The hike

From the ranger station, walk 0.2 miles down the unpaved road to the posted Grotto Trailhead, located just before reaching the lower parking area. Pass the trail gate and follow the dirt road past a picnic area to another trail sign. Take the footpath downhill, heading south into the canyon among oaks, sycamores, and willows. Cross the West Fork Arroyo Sequit, and parallel the east side of the creek to a signed junction with the Canyon View Trail (Hike 129) on the left at 0.4 miles. Continue straight ahead on the left fork and recross the creek at 30-foot Botsford Falls.

After crossing, curve left and traverse the grassy meadow on a ridge. Great views extend down the gorge of volcanic and sandstone rock formations and up to jagged Boney Mountain and Sandstone Peak. Descend to the canyon floor, where the trail joins the gated Happy Hollow Campground Road at 1.2 miles. Follow the road to the left into a primitive campground. Cross the creek and pick up the Grotto Trail again. Head downstream to a bridge that crosses the creek into the Happy Hollow Campground. Instead of crossing the bridge, continue straight ahead, crossing the West Fork Arroyo Sequit by a pump house. Follow the east bank of the creek downstream in an oak woodland. After a few hundred feet, the path enters the sheer volcanic-rock walls of The Grotto, a sycamore-shaded cavern set among a jumble of massive boulders, small caves, cascades, small falls, pools, and ferns.

After exploring The Grotto, return to the bridge that accesses the Happy Hollow Campground. Cross the bridge and walk through the camp to the vehicle-restricted road. Bear right and follow the winding road. Rejoin the Grotto Trail on the left, completing the loop. Retrace your steps to the parking lot. ■

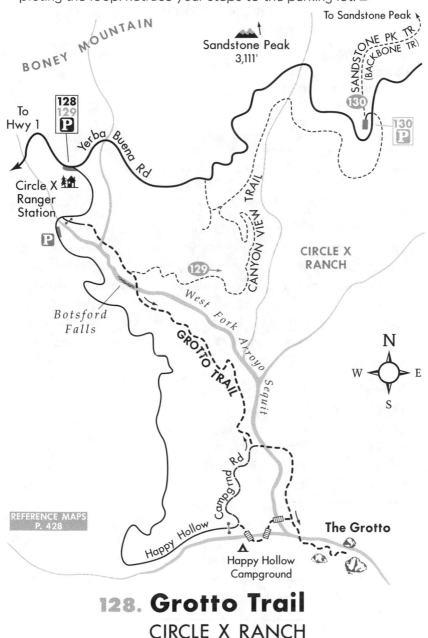

128. **Grotto Trail**
CIRCLE X RANCH

129. Canyon View— Yerba Buena Road Loop

CIRCLE X RANCH

12896 Yerba Buena Road

Hiking distance: 3.2-mile loop
Hiking time: 1.5 hours
Configuration: loop
Elevation gain: 500 feet
Difficulty: easy to moderate
Exposure: mostly exposed mountain slope with some shaded areas
Dogs: allowed
Maps: U.S.G.S. Triunfo Pass · N.P.S. Circle X Ranch map
    Tom Harrison Maps: Zuma-Trancas Canyons Trail map
    Tom Harrison Maps: Point Mugu State Park Trail map

Circle X Ranch, a former Boy Scout camp, sits below majestic Boney Mountain in the upper canyons of Arroyo Sequit. The Canyon View Trail traverses the brushy hillside of the deep, east-facing canyon. The panoramic views extend down the canyon to the Pacific Ocean. The northern views reach the jagged Boney Mountain ridge and the 3,111-foot Sandstone Peak, the highest peak in the Santa Monica Mountains. The trail connects the Grotto Trail (Hike 128) with the Sandstone Peak Trail (Hike 130).

To the trailhead

From the Pacific Coast Highway/Highway 1 in Santa Monica, drive 38 miles northbound to Yerba Buena Road and turn right. (Yerba Buena Road is 10.1 miles west of Kanan Dume Road and 2 miles west of Leo Carrillo State Beach.) Continue 5.3 miles up the winding road to the Circle X Ranger Station on the right. Park by the ranger station, or continue 0.2 miles downhill to the day-use parking area, located just past the posted Grotto Trailhead.

From the Pacific Coast Highway/Highway 1 and Las Posas Road in southeast Oxnard, drive 9 miles southbound to Yerba Buena Road (3.3 miles past Big Sycamore Canyon) and turn left. Continue 5.3 miles up the winding road to the Circle X Ranger

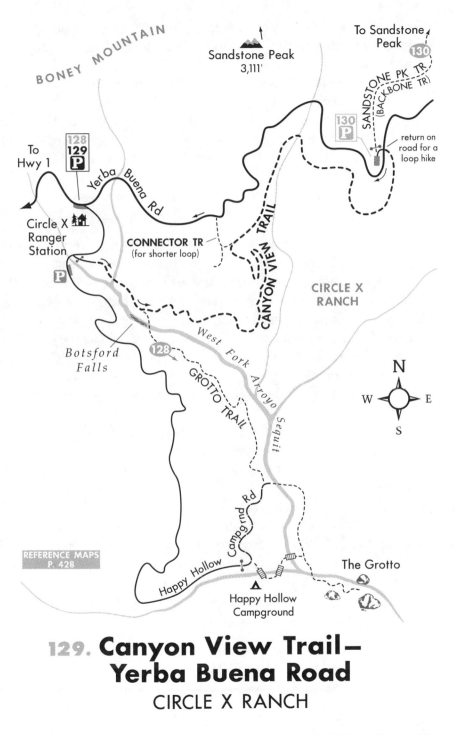

BONEY MOUNTAIN

Sandstone Peak
3,111'

To Sandstone
Peak

130

SANDSTONE PK. TR.
(BACKBONE TR.)

130 P

return on
road for a
loop hike

To
Hwy 1

128
129 P

Yerba Buena Rd

Circle X
Ranger
Station

P

CONNECTOR TR
(for shorter loop)

CANYON VIEW TRAIL

CIRCLE X
RANCH

*Botsford
Falls*

128

West Fork Arroyo Sequit

GROTTO TRAIL

N
W · E
S

Campgrnd Rd

REFERENCE MAPS
P. 428

Happy Hollow

The Grotto

Happy Hollow
Campground

129. **Canyon View Trail–
Yerba Buena Road**

CIRCLE X RANCH

Station on the right. Park by the ranger station, or continue 0.2 miles downhill to the day-use parking area, located just past the posted Grotto Trailhead.

From the Ventura Freeway/Highway 101 in Thousand Oaks, exit on Westlake Boulevard (Highway 23). Drive 6.9 miles south on Westlake Boulevard, winding up the mountain road to Mulholland Highway at a stop sign. Turn right and go 0.4 miles to Little Sycamore Canyon Road. Turn right and drive 5.7 miles to the Circle X Ranger Station on the left. (At the county line, Little Sycamore Canyon Road becomes Yerba Buena Road.)

The hike

From the ranger station, walk 0.2 miles down the unpaved road to the posted Grotto Trailhead, located just before reaching the lower parking area. Pass the trail gate and follow the dirt road past a picnic area to another trail sign. Take the footpath downhill, heading south into the canyon among oaks, sycamores, and willows. Cross the West Fork Arroyo Sequit, and parallel the east side of the creek to a signed junction with the Canyon View Trail on the left at 0.4 miles. (To see 30-foot Botsford Falls, detour 20 yards straight ahead. This trail continues downhill to The Grotto—Hike 128.)

From the junction, take the Canyon View Trail to the left (east). Traverse the canyon wall, following the contours of the mountain. Climb two switchbacks to a junction. For a shorter 1.5-mile loop, take the Connector Trail 100 yards to the left to Yerba Buena Road, and return 0.35 miles to the ranger station.

For this longer hike, stay to the right and cross a rocky wash. Head up the hillside to a south view that spans down canyon to the ocean and the Channel Islands and a north view of the Boney Mountain ridge. Continue to Yerba Buena Road, across from the Sandstone Peak (Backbone) Trail (Hike 130). For a loop hike, return to the left on Yerba Buena Road, and walk 1.1 mile back to the trailhead at the Circle X Ranger Station. ■

130. Sandstone Peak

Carlisle Canyon—Backbone Trail Loop

CIRCLE X RANCH

12896 Yerba Buena Road

Hiking distance: 6-mile loop (with optional 1.4-mile loop at west end)
Hiking time: 3—4 hours
Configuration: loop
Elevation gain: 1,100—1,250 feet
Difficulty: moderate to strenuous
Exposure: shaded canyon and exposed hillside
Dogs: allowed
Maps: U.S.G.S. Triunfo Pass · N.P.S. Circle X Ranch map
      Tom Harrison Maps: Point Mugu State Park Trail Map

Sandstone Peak, rising along Boney Ridge, stands as the highest point in the Santa Monica Mountains. Despite the name, Sandstone Peak is actually a mass of volcanic rock. From the 3,111-foot summit are far-reaching vistas that sprawl out as far as the eye can see, including the sweep of the mountain range, the Oxnard Plain, the Topatopa Mountains at Ojai, and the Pacific Ocean, which dominates the southern view. This loop through Circle X Ranch is a moderately strenuous, mid-range hike that offers amazing scenery, traveling from a shady canyon bottom up to the summit of Sandstone Peak.

The loop begins on the Mishe Mokwa Trail, dropping into Carlisle Canyon along Boney Mountain past weathered red volcanic formations. There are views of the sculpted crevices of Echo Cliffs and a forested streamside picnic area by a huge, split boulder known as Split Rock. The trail ascends out of the shaded canyon to join with the Sandstone Peak Trail, a segment of the Backbone Trail. The Sandstone Peak Trail climbs the east slope of Boney Mountain high above Carlisle Canyon to Sandstone Peak. Inspiration Point—another overlook along the spine of the mountain—lies a short distance to the west of the peak.

To the trailhead

From Santa Monica, drive 38 miles northbound on the Pacific Coast Highway/Highway 1 to Yerba Buena Road and turn right.

(Yerba Buena Road is 10.1 miles past Kanan Dume Road and 2 miles past Leo Carrillo State Beach.) Turn right and drive 5.3 miles up the winding road to the Circle X Ranger Station on the right. From the ranger station, continue 1 mile to the Sandstone Peak Trailhead parking lot on the left.

From the Pacific Coast Highway/Highway 1 and Las Posas Road in southeast Oxnard, drive 9 miles southbound to Yerba Buena Road and turn left. Continue up Yerba Buena Road, following the directions above.

From the Ventura Freeway/Highway 101 in Thousand Oaks, exit on Westlake Boulevard (Highway 23). Drive 6.9 miles south on Westlake Boulevard, winding up the mountain road to Mulholland Highway at a stop sign. Turn right and go 0.4 miles to Little Sycamore Canyon Road. Turn right and drive 4.7 miles to the Sandstone Peak Trailhead parking lot on the right. (At the county line, Little Sycamore Canyon Road becomes Yerba Buena Road.)

The hike

Pass the trailhead kiosk and take the Sandstone Peak Trail, a fire road. At 0.3 miles, leave the road and begin the loop, taking the signed Mishe Mokwa Connector Trail on the right. Continue 0.2 miles to a junction with the Mishe Mokwa Trail and take the left fork. Weave along the contour of the mountain, following the western wall of Carlisle Canyon. The canyon is rich with magnificent red rock sandstone formations. Echo Cliffs and Balanced Rock can be seen on the opposite wall of the canyon. At 1.3 miles, descend natural rock steps and cross a stream in a rock grotto. Descend deeper into Carlisle Canyon, shaded by oaks, bay laurel, and sycamores. Cross Carlisle Creek to Split Rock and a streamside picnic area under towering oaks at 1.9 miles. The cabin size volcanic boulder is split in two with a yard-wide access. Continue on the main trail along the floor of Carlisle Canyon on the north flank of Sandstone Peak. Veer left and head west, walking parallel to the stream through the shade of coast live oaks and sycamores. Cross the stream by weather-sculpted volcanic rocks. Gradually ascend out of Carlisle Canyon among a continuing display of outcroppings to a signed junction at 3.2

miles. The trail to the right leads to Tri-Peaks, while the Backbone Trail continues west into Big Sycamore Canyon. (See below for the optional hike to Tri-Peaks.)

Instead, bear left on the Sandstone Peak Trail (also the Backbone Trail), zigzagging up the slope towards Inspiration Peak. Pass a non-ending display of weather-carved outcrops to a junction. A short side path on the right leads up to the south-facing rocky overlook atop 2,800-foot Inspiration Peak. On the main trail, continue east about 0.7 miles to another junction at a spur trail to Sandstone Peak. Detour to the right 150 yards to the 3,111-foot peak. The side path climbs steps and rocks to the multi-colored outcroppings atop the peak.

After savoring the 360-degree views, return to the main trail. Descend over the next 1.3 miles on the rock-embedded path while enjoying the spectacular vistas and losing 1,000 feet in elevation. Complete the loop back at the Mishe Mokwa Connector Trail. From the junction, return 0.3 miles back to the trailhead on the fire road.

OPTIONAL TRI-PEAKS LOOP: Tri-Peaks lies directly west of Sandstone Peak. An optional 1.4-mile loop leads to the summit of the peak, offering more expansive views of the landscape.

At the far west end of the Mishe Mokwa Sandstone Peak loop is a signed junction. Take the trail that leads west and walk 30 yards to a Y-fork. The left fork (the Backbone Trail) descends to Big Sycamore Canyon in Point Mugu State Park. For this hike, go to the right on the Tri-Peaks Trail. Climb up the narrow, rocky path to a signed T-junction. The left fork is the return route. For now, detour right and loop around the hill to the rocky southern base of the massive formation. An unmaintained path weaves among the rocks (and includes some rock-scrambling) to the three-pointed summit. The commanding views range across the surrounding mountains, the Conejo Valley, and Thousand Oaks to the mountains beyond. After taking in the views, return to the junction and continue straight ahead at a near-level grade. Then drop down on the rocky path to a T-junction (the Chamberlain/Backbone Trail). Bear left and walk a half mile down canyon, parallel to a seasonal drainage, to complete the loop. ■

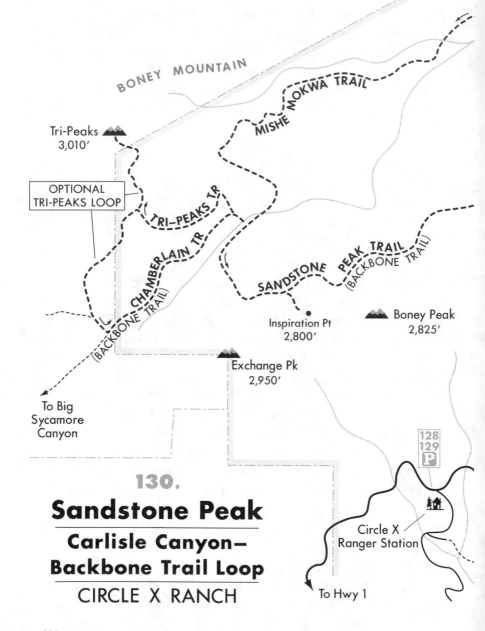

BONEY MOUNTAIN STATE WILDERNESS
POINT MUGU STATE PARK

BONEY MOUNTAIN

MISHE MOKWA TRAIL

Tri-Peaks
3,010'

OPTIONAL
TRI-PEAKS LOOP

TRI-PEAKS TR

CHAMBERLAIN TR

(BACKBONE TRAIL)

SANDSTONE PEAK TRAIL
(BACKBONE TRAIL)

Inspiration Pt
2,800'

Boney Peak
2,825'

Exchange Pk
2,950'

To Big
Sycamore
Canyon

128
129
P

Circle X
Ranger Station

130.

Sandstone Peak

Carlisle Canyon—
Backbone Trail Loop

CIRCLE X RANCH

To Hwy 1

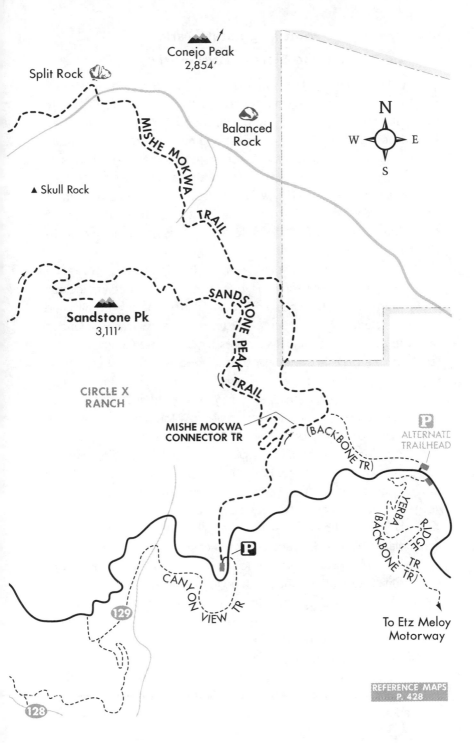

Conejo Peak
2,854'

Split Rock

Balanced
Rock

N
W ·◈· E
S

▲ Skull Rock

MISHE MOKWA

TRAIL

Sandstone Pk
3,111'

SANDSTONE PEAK TRAIL

CIRCLE X
RANCH

MISHE MOKWA
CONNECTOR TR

(BACKBONE TR)

P
ALTERNATE
TRAILHEAD

P

YERBA
(BACKBONE
TR)

RIDGE
TR
(BACKBONE TR)

CANYON VIEW TR

129

To Etz Meloy
Motorway

128

REFERENCE MAPS
P. 428

160 Great Hikes – **439**

Point Mugu State Park
Rancho Sierra Vista/Satwiwa

Point Mugu State Park lies at the west end of the Santa Monica Mountains in Ventura County, adjacent to the Pacific Ocean to the south, Newbury Park to the north, and Oxnard to the west. The 16,000-acre state park is the largest and most remote in the mountain range. The park is accessed from its north end directly through Rancho Sierra Vista/Satwiwa, a preserved parcel of land operated by the National Park Service. Weaving throughout are nearly 75 miles of hiking, biking, and equestrian trails. The trail system combines fire roads, paved service roads, single-track trails, and primitive paths. Hikes 131—135 are located here.

The sprawling parkland spans from the Pacific to the upper reaches of the Santa Monica Range. Five miles of ocean shoreline include rocky bluffs, sandy beaches, and rolling dunes. The rugged hills and uplands include two major creek-fed canyons and grass valleys dotted with oaks, walnuts, and sycamores. Big Sycamore Canyon runs the length of the park. It is a deep, tree-shaded, stream-fed canyon. A hiking trail (fire road) follows the canyon bottom for its entire length. Numerous connecting paths lead up to the high ridges to either side of the canyon. The Boney Mountain State Wilderness occupies the eastern portion of the park. The wilderness area, a 6,000-acre preserve, contains the jagged, rocky peaks of Boney Mountain, with pinnacles rising above 3,000 feet (the highest promontories of the Santa Monica Range). At the base of Boney Mountain is Serrano Valley, a gorgeous grassland marbled with slow-moving streams. The western side of the park is home to the La Jolla Valley Natural Preserve, a 600-acre upland valley with a rare native bunchgrass prairie.

Rancho Sierra Vista/Satwiwa is located at the northern boundary of Point Mugu State Park and the south edge of Newbury Park. The historical site is named for its two cultural legacies. For thousands of years it was the ancestral land of the Chumash and Gabrielino Indians. It later became a horse and cattle ranch named Rancho Sierra Vista. To reflect the Native American heritage, the Satwiwa Culture Center and Natural Area was established. A hub of hiking trails disperses from the center.

Dogs are not allowed in Point Mugu State Park. However, they are allowed in the Rancho Sierra Vista/Satwiwa section of the state land.

131. Old Boney Trail to Danielson Monument

BONEY MOUNTAIN STATE WILDERNESS and POINT MUGU STATE PARK

Hiking distance: 7.8 miles
Hiking time: 4 hours
Configuration: out-and-back with large loop
Elevation gain: 1,000 feet
Difficulty: moderate to strenuous
Exposure: a mix of shaded canyon and exposed grassland and hillsides
Dogs: allowed in Rancho Sierra Vista/Satwiwa but not allowed in Point Mugu State Park
Maps: U.S.G.S. Newbury Park · Point Mugu State Park map
Tom Harrison Maps: Point Mugu State Park Trail map

The Boney Mountain State Wilderness area occupies the eastern portion of Point Mugu State Park. The centerpiece of the preserved area is Boney Mountain, a rocky, jagged formation that rises 1,500 feet above Sycamore Canyon. The scenic mountain contains four of the highest peaks in the coastal Santa Monica Range, including well-known Sandstone Peak (Hike 130).

This hike begins in Rancho Sierra Vista/Satwiwa and loops through the wilderness area at the northern end of Point Mugu State Park. The route follows the Old Boney Trail in Upper Sycamore Canyon to the Danielson Monument, a stone monument with a metal arch honoring Richard Danielson. Danielson donated the ranch to the National Park Service for preservation as an open space. Near the monument is the old cabin site of Richard Danielson Jr., where a rock fireplace still remains. En route to the monument, the trail passes Sycamore Canyon Falls, a 70-foot cascade in a lush box canyon along the riparian corridor of Big Sycamore Creek. The hike weaves through open grassland, wooded forests, and a stream-fed canyon. Mountain overlooks offer close-up views of the sheer rock face of Boney Mountain.

To the trailhead

From Highway 101/Ventura Freeway in Newbury Park, exit on Wendy Drive. Drive 2 miles south to Lynn Road and turn right. Continue 1.7 miles to Via Goleta, the park entrance road. (En route, Lynn Road becomes West Potrero Road.) Turn left into the park and drive 0.7 miles to the main parking lot at the end of the road.

The hike

Take the posted trail past the restrooms a quarter mile to the service road at the Satwiwa Native American Indian Culture Center. Bear right on the road, entering Point Mugu State Park. As you approach the ridge overlooking Big Sycamore Canyon, take the Boney Mountain Trail to the left along the brink of the canyon. Climb a short hill, passing the Satwiwa Loop Trail on the left, and continue around to a ridge and a trail split. Take the right fork, descending down to the forested canyon floor and a junction with the Upper Sycamore Canyon Trail at 1.3 miles (the return route).

Begin the loop straight ahead under a canopy of oaks, sycamores, and bay laurel to a U-shaped right bend. Detour 100 yards to the left to seasonal Sycamore Canyon Falls in a rock-walled box canyon. Return to the Old Boney Trail, and continue up the hillside on the north flank of Boney Mountain to an overlook of Sycamore Canyon, the Oxnard Plain, and the Channel Islands. Inland views extend to the Los Padres National Forest. Steadily climb to a posted junction and views of the rounded rock formations of upper Boney Mountain. Detour 0.3 miles on the left fork, dropping down and crossing a seasonal drainage to the Danielson Monument at the end of the trail. To the right is the old cabin site with the remaining rock chimney and fireplace.

Return to the Old Boney Trail, and walk through the tall brush, gaining elevation while passing occasional overlooks that span from Point Mugu State Park to the Pacific Ocean. Gradually descend to a signed junction with the Fossil Trail at 4.4 miles. Straight ahead, the Old Boney Trail leads 2.1 miles to the Blue Canyon Trail, part of the Backbone Trail. (To the west, the Backbone Trail connects to the Danielson Ranch in Big Sycamore Canyon—Hike 132. To the east, the trail leads to Sandstone Peak—Hike 130.)

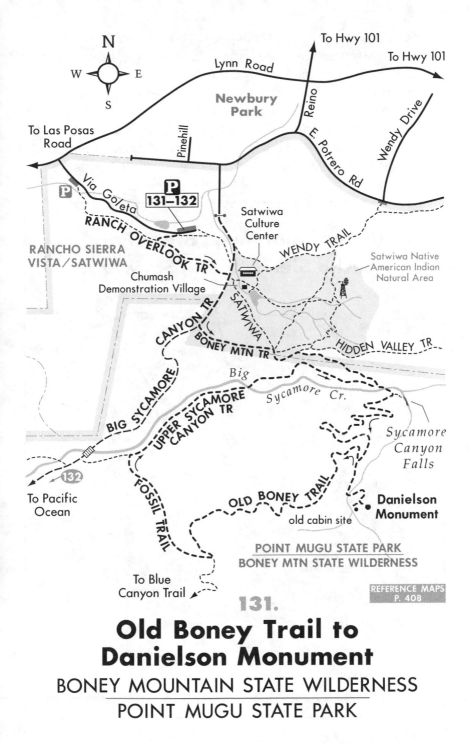

Old Boney Trail to Danielson Monument

BONEY MOUNTAIN STATE WILDERNESS
POINT MUGU STATE PARK

For this hike go to the right on the Fossil Trail, and descend into the stream-fed canyon. Follow the east canyon wall downstream, passing dozens of shell fossils embedded in the rock along the path. Near the bottom, enter an oak grove to a T-junction with the Upper Sycamore Canyon Trail. The left fork leads 0.1 mile to the Big Sycamore Canyon Fire Road/Trail. Bear right and head east upstream, following the upper canyon floor. Complete the loop at 6.5 miles, 0.2 miles shy of Sycamore Canyon Falls. Bear left and retrace your steps 1.3 miles back to the trailhead. ■

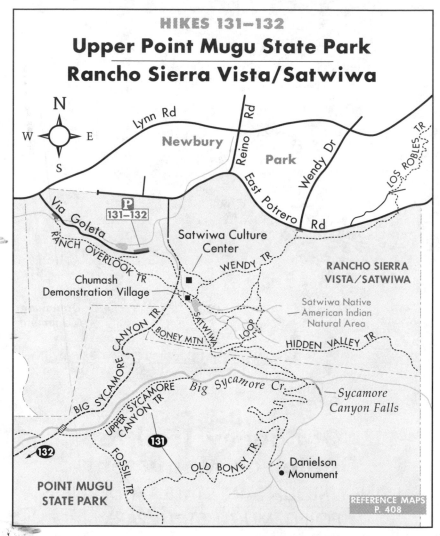

HIKES 131-132

Upper Point Mugu State Park
Rancho Sierra Vista/Satwiwa

132. Big Sycamore Canyon
Shuttle from Upper Trailhead to Lower Trailhead

Rancho Sierra Vista/Satwiwa
to Big Sycamore Canyon Trailhead at coast

POINT MUGU STATE PARK

Upper Trailhead: East Potrero Road in Newbury Park
Shuttle car (Lower Trailhead): West Pacific Coast Highway

Hiking distance: 8.4-mile one-way shuttle
Hiking time: 4.5 hours
Configuration: one-way shuttle
Elevation loss: 900 feet loss
Difficulty: moderate
Exposure: mostly shaded canyon with some exposed slope
Dogs: not allowed
Maps: U.S.G.S. Newbury Park, Camarillo and Point Mugu
      Tom Harrison Maps: Point Mugu State Park Trail map
      Point Mugu State Park map

With a shuttle car parked at the bottom of the canyon, this hike down the Big Sycamore Canyon Trail is a one-way, downhill, mountains-to-the-sea journey. The canyon was originally part of the Chumash Indian trade route. The trail, now a partially paved service road and fire road, connects Newbury Park at the Rancho Sierra Vista/Satwiwa site with the Sycamore Canyon Campground at the Pacific Ocean. The hike parallels Big Sycamore Creek through the heart of 15,000-acre Point Mugu State Park in a deep, wooded canyon under towering sycamores and oaks.

To the trailhead

From Highway 101/Ventura Freeway in Newbury Park, exit on Wendy Drive. Drive 2 miles south to Lynn Road and turn right. Continue 1.7 miles to Via Goleta, the park entrance road. (En route, Lynn Road becomes West Potrero Road.) Turn left into the park and drive 0.7 miles to the main parking lot at the end of the road.

Shuttle Car

From Santa Monica, drive 31 miles northbound on the Pacific Coast Highway/Highway 1 to the posted Big Sycamore Canyon

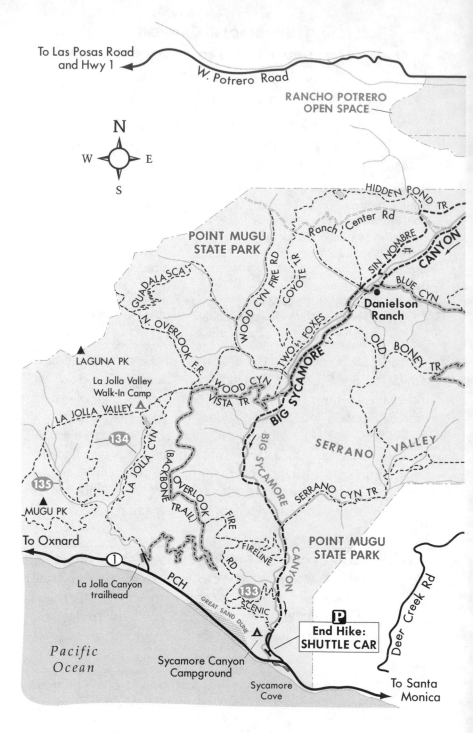

To Las Posas Road
and Hwy 1

W. Potrero Road

RANCHO POTRERO
OPEN SPACE

N
W E
S

HIDDEN POND TR

POINT MUGU
STATE PARK

Ranch Center Rd

SIN NOMBRE

CANYON

BLUE CYN

GUADALASCA

WOOD CYN FIRE RD

COYOTE TR

Danielson
Ranch

N. OVERLOOK FR

TWO FOXES

BIG SYCAMORE

OLD BONEY TR

LAGUNA PK

WOOD CYN
VISTA TR

La Jolla Valley
Walk-In Camp

LA JOLLA VALLEY

SERRANO VALLEY

LA JOLLA CYN

134

BIG SYCAMORE

135

(BACKBONE TRAIL)
OVERLOOK

SERRANO CYN TR

MUGU PK

FIRE RD

To Oxnard

1

FIRELINE RD

POINT MUGU
STATE PARK

CANYON

La Jolla Canyon
trailhead

PCH

133

SCENIC

GREAT SAND DUNE

Deer Creek Rd

Pacific
Ocean

P
End Hike:
SHUTTLE CAR

Sycamore Canyon
Campground

Sycamore
Cove

To Santa
Monica

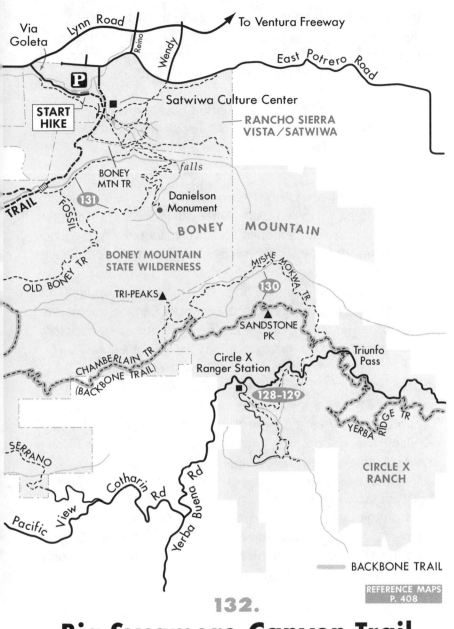

132.
Big Sycamore Canyon Trail
Shuttle from Upper Trailhead to Lower Trailhead
POINT MUGU STATE PARK

entrance on the right. (The trailhead entrance is 13.3 miles west of Kanan Dume Road in Malibu and 5.3 miles west of the well-marked Leo Carrillo State Beach.) Turn right and park in the day-use pay parking lot 0.1 mile ahead on the left. (Parking is free in the pullouts along the PCH.)

Heading southbound on the Pacific Coast Highway / Highway 1 from Las Posas Road in southeast Oxnard, drive 5.8 miles to the Point Mugu State Park entrance on the left.

The hike

Take the posted trail past the restrooms a quarter mile to the service road at the Satwiwa Native American Indian Cultural Center. Bear right on the road, entering Point Mugu State Park, to a junction with the Boney Mountain Trail on the left (Hike 131). Continue straight and begin the winding descent on the paved, vehicle-restricted road to the canyon floor. Cross a wooden bridge over Big Sycamore Creek to the Upper Sycamore Canyon Trail on the left and the Hidden Pond Trail on the right. This is an excellent single track alternative trail that rejoins the Big Sycamore Canyon Trail 1.7 miles down canyon. On the alternative Hidden Pond Trail, there is a split at 2.2 miles. Take the left fork (Sin Nombre Trail) to the Sycamore Camping and Picnic Area. At 3 miles is a signed "beach" path on the right, where the alternative trail rejoins the service road. Just past the junction is the Danielson Ranch. Past the ranch, the trail is unpaved.

Continue heading down canyon on the Big Sycamore Canyon Trail. Pass the Old Boney Trail on the left, the Wood Canyon Fire Road on the right, and the posted Wood Canyon Vista Trail on the right. (The Backbone Trail continues on the Wood Canyon Vista Trail.) Continue down the forested canyon under a canopy of sycamores and coast live oaks, passing the Serrano Canyon Trail on the left, the Overlook Fire Road on the right, and the Scenic Trail on the right. The trailhead gate appears shortly after the Scenic Trail. From the gate, the paved path leads through the campground to the shuttle car at the Big Sycamore Canyon trailhead. ■

133. Scenic Trail—
Overlook Fire Road Loop

POINT MUGU STATE PARK

9000 W. Pacific Coast Hwy

Hiking distance: 2-mile loop
Hiking time: 1 hour
Configuration: loop
Elevation gain: 900 feet
Difficulty: easy to moderate
Exposure: mostly exposed
Dogs: not allowed
Maps: U.S.G.S. Point Mugu · Point Mugu State Park map
 Tom Harrison Maps: Point Mugu State Park Trail map

The Scenic and Overlook Trails are located along the oceanfront mountains of Point Mugu State Park. The Overlook Fire Road, an unpaved, vehicle-restricted road, follows a high north/south-running ridgeline that separates Big Sycamore Canyon from La Jolla Valley. The Scenic Trail is a footpath that contours the ocean-front slope on a chaparral-covered ridge to panoramic over-looks of the Pacific. Both trails begin in the shade of Big Sycamore Canyon and form a loop on the west canyon slope.

To the trailhead

From Santa Monica, drive 31 miles northbound on the Pacific Coast Highway/Highway 1 to the posted Big Sycamore Canyon entrance on the right. (The trailhead entrance is 13.3 miles west of Kanan Dume Road in Malibu and 5.3 miles west of the well-marked Leo Carrillo State Beach.) Turn right and park in the day-use pay parking lot 0.1 mile ahead on the left. (Parking is free in the pullouts along the PCH.)

Heading southbound on the Pacific Coast Highway/Highway 1 from Las Posas Road in southeast Oxnard, drive 5.8 miles to the Big Sycamore Canyon entrance on the left.

The hike

From the parking area, walk up the road past the campground to the Big Sycamore Canyon trailhead gate. Continue up the unpaved road about 50 yards to the signed junction with the Scenic Trail. Take the trail to the left (west) across Big Sycamore Creek, and head up the wooden steps. Steadily gain elevation up an open, grassy hillside with views of Big Sycamore Canyon. At the saddle near the top of the hill is a trail split. The left fork leads a short distance to an oceanfront overlook. Continue up to several more viewpoints. Return back to the junction, and head north to a junction with the Overlook Fire Road. Take this service road downhill to the right, winding 0.9 miles back to the Big Sycamore Canyon floor. Near the bottom, five gentle switchbacks lead to the junction across the creek. Take the canyon trail to the right, leading 0.4 miles back to the trailhead gate. ∎

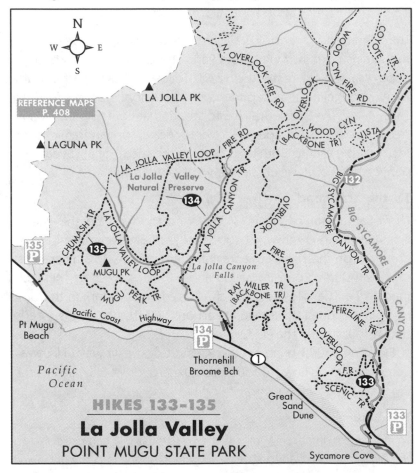

HIKES 133-135
La Jolla Valley
POINT MUGU STATE PARK

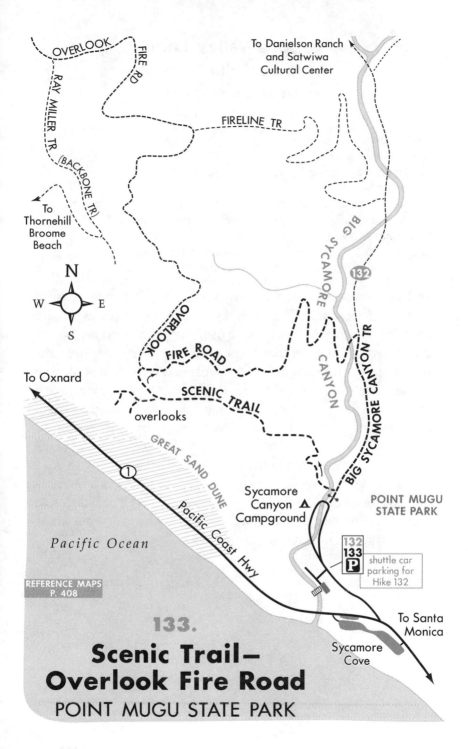

OVERLOOK

FIRE RD.

RAY MILLER TR. (BACKBONE TR)

To Danielson Ranch and Satwiwa Cultural Center

FIRELINE TR

To Thornehill Broome Beach

BIG SYCAMORE CANYON

132

N
W E
S

OVERLOOK FIRE ROAD

SCENIC TRAIL

BIG SYCAMORE CANYON TR

overlooks

To Oxnard

GREAT SAND DUNE

1

Pacific Coast Hwy

Pacific Ocean

Sycamore Canyon ▲ Campground

POINT MUGU STATE PARK

132
133 P shuttle car parking for Hike 132

REFERENCE MAPS P. 408

To Santa Monica

Sycamore Cove

133.
Scenic Trail–
Overlook Fire Road
POINT MUGU STATE PARK

134. La Jolla Valley Loop from La Jolla Canyon

POINT MUGU STATE PARK

W. Pacific Coast Hwy

Hiking distance: 6 miles
Hiking time: 3 hours
Configuration: out-and-back with large loop
Elevation gain: 750 feet
Difficulty: moderate to strenuous
Exposure: mostly exposed with some forested pockets
Dogs: not allowed
Maps: U.S.G.S. Point Mugu · Point Mugu State Park map
　　　　Tom Harrison Maps: Point Mugu State Park Trail map

La Jolla Canyon is a steep, narrow gorge with a perennial stream and a 15-foot waterfall. The rocky canyon is a gateway to the La Jolla Valley Natural Preserve, a 600-acre unspoiled landscape protecting the rare perennial native bunchgrass prairie. The natural preserve is tucked into the far west end of the Santa Monica Range within Point Mugu State Park. The 800-foot-high rolling grassland is rimmed by an arc of mountain ridges, including Mugu Peak, Laguna Peak, and La Jolla Peak, and is only accessible to foot traffic.

This hike climbs through the rock-walled canyon along La Jolla Creek, passing La Jolla Canyon Falls en route to the broad valley. The trail loops around the vast meadow, passing a seasonal tule and cattail-fringed pond, a walk-in campground, picnic areas, and coastal and mountain overlooks.

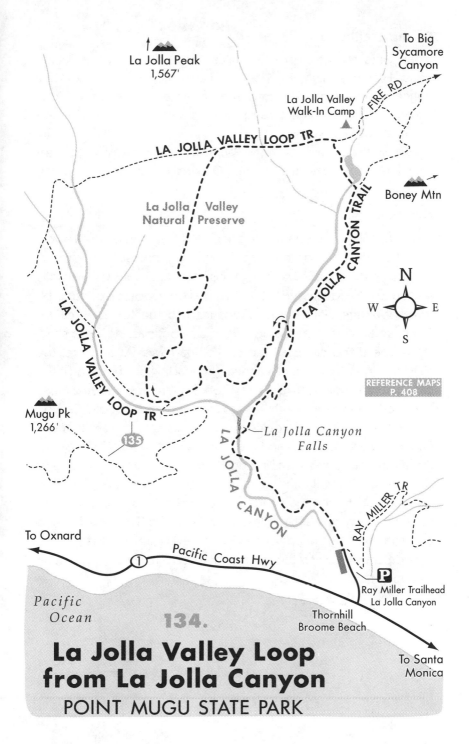

La Jolla Peak
1,567'

To Big
Sycamore
Canyon

La Jolla Valley
Walk-In Camp

FIRE RD

LA JOLLA VALLEY LOOP TR

LA JOLLA CANYON TRAIL

Boney Mtn

La Jolla Valley
Natural Preserve

N
W E
S

LA JOLLA VALLEY LOOP TR

REFERENCE MAPS
P. 408

Mugu Pk
1,266'

135

La Jolla Canyon
Falls

LA JOLLA CANYON

RAY MILLER TR

To Oxnard

Pacific Coast Hwy

1

P

Ray Miller Trailhead
La Jolla Canyon

Pacific
Ocean

134.

Thornhill
Broome Beach

To Santa
Monica

La Jolla Valley Loop
from La Jolla Canyon
POINT MUGU STATE PARK

To the trailhead

From Santa Monica, drive 33 miles northbound on the Pacific Coast Highway/Highway 1 to the posted La Jolla Canyon entrance on the right. (The trailhead entrance is 15 miles west of Kanan Dume Road in Malibu and 1.6 miles west of the well-marked Big Sycamore Canyon.)

Heading southbound on the Pacific Coast Highway/Highway 1 from Las Posas Road in southeast Oxnard, drive 4.2 miles to the La Jolla Canyon entrance on the left.

The hike

Take the La Jolla Canyon Trail at the end of the road by the vehicle gate. Follow the wide path up the canyon, crossing the stream several times. The third crossing is just below La Jolla Canyon Falls, a beautiful 15-foot waterfall with a shallow pool surrounded by large boulders. Natural rock steps lead to the top of the falls. Continue along the east side of the canyon, passing large sandstone rocks and caves as the canyon narrows. At a gorge, the trail sharply doubles back to the right, leading up the side of the canyon. At 1.2 miles, take the left fork towards Mugu Peak. Cross the stream and head southwest to a ridge above La Jolla Canyon and the ocean. The trail levels out and passes two trail junctions with the Mugu Peak Trail and the Chumash Trail (Hike 135). Stay to the right both times, heading north across the rolling grassland. At 2.7 miles the trail joins the wide La Jolla Valley Loop Trail/Fire Road—head to the right through upper La Jolla Valley. As you near the mountains of La Jolla Canyon, take the first cutoff trail to the right, skirting the edge of the pond and rejoining the La Jolla Canyon Trail. Head to the right, and go two miles down canyon, returning to the trailhead. ▪

135. Chumash Trail—Mugu Peak Loop

POINT MUGU STATE PARK

W. Pacific Coast Hwy

Hiking distance: 4.5-mile loop
Hiking time: 2.5 hours
Configuration: loop
Elevation gain: 1,100 feet
Difficulty: moderate to strenuous
Exposure: mostly exposed with some forested pockets
Dogs: not allowed
Maps: U.S.G.S. Point Mugu · Point Mugu State Park map
Tom Harrison Maps: Point Mugu State Park Trail map

The Chumash Trail is the westernmost trail in the Santa Monica Mountains. For centuries, this historic trail was a Chumash Indian route that connected their coastal village at Mugu Lagoon with La Jolla Valley atop the mountain. It is the steepest and most direct route to La Jolla Valley, an expansive, high-mountain valley within Point Mugu State Park. The oak-studded grassland rests 800 feet above the ocean at the foot of Mugu Peak. The high ridges of Laguna Peak, La Jolla Peak, and Mugu Peak curve around the west side of the rolling meadow.

This hike steeply ascends the oceanfront mountain on the west flank of Mugu Peak. The path climbs through giant coreopsis, yucca, and prickly pear cactus in full view of the Pacific Ocean, Mugu Lagoon, the adjoining wetlands, and the Oxnard Plain. From atop the mountain, the hike forms a loop on the west side of La Jolla Valley. The elevated Mugu Peak Trail circles the mountain slope below the twin peaks, offering sweeping mountain-to-coast vistas. A side path leads to the rounded, grassy summit of Mugu Peak.

To the trailhead

From Santa Monica, drive 35 miles northbound on the Pacific Coast Highway/Highway 1 to the large parking pullout on the right, across from the Navy Rifle Range and Mugu Lagoon. (The trailhead parking area is 16.8 miles west of Kanan Dume Road in Malibu and 3.5 miles west of the well-marked Big Sycamore Canyon.)

Heading southbound on the Pacific Coast Highway/Highway 1 from Las Posas Road in southeast Oxnard, drive 2.3 miles to the parking area on the left by the posted trailhead.

The hike

Begin climbing up the hillside covered in chaparral and cactus, gaining elevation with every step. At a half mile, the trail temporarily levels out on a plateau, where there are sweeping coastal views that include the Channel Islands. The steadily ascending trail gains 900 feet in 0.7 miles to a T-junction on a saddle. Begin the loop to the left, crossing over the saddle into the vast La Jolla Valley. The valley is surrounded by rounded mountain peaks, the jagged Boney Mountain ridge, and the surrealistic Navy radar towers atop Laguna Peak. Cross the open expanse to a posted junction with the La Jolla Valley Loop Trail at 1.2 miles.

Take the right fork and head southeast across the meadow on a slight downward slope. Drop into an oak woodland and cross a stream. Parallel the stream through a small draw to another junction. Take the right fork 100 yards to a path on the right by an old circular metal tank. Bear right on the Mugu Peak Trail and cross the creek. Traverse the hillside to the west edge of La Jolla Canyon. Follow the ridge south on the oceanfront cliffs. Wind along the south flank of Mugu Peak, following the contours of the mountain to a trail split on a saddle between the mountain's double peaks. The right fork ascends the grassy 1,266-foot summit. Continue hiking on the main trail along the steep hillside to the west side of the peak. Cross another saddle and complete the loop. Return down the mountain to the trailhead. ▪

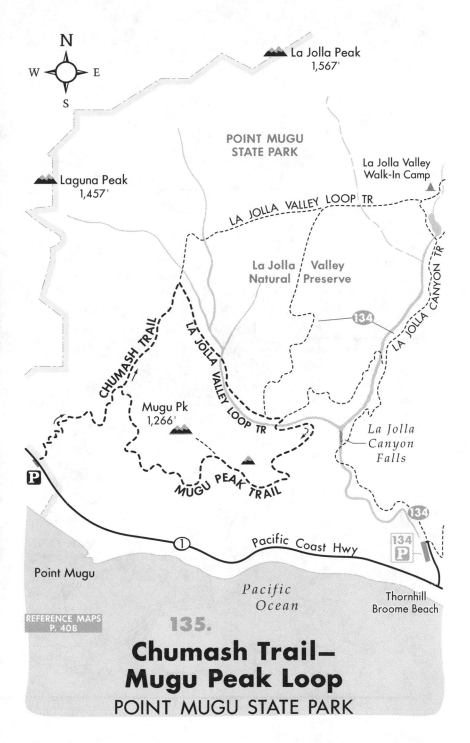

N

W   E

S

La Jolla Peak
1,567'

POINT MUGU
STATE PARK

La Jolla Valley
Walk-In Camp

Laguna Peak
1,457'

LA JOLLA VALLEY LOOP TR

La Jolla / Valley
Natural / Preserve

LA JOLLA CANYON TR

134

CHUMASH TRAIL

LA JOLLA VALLEY LOOP TR

Mugu Pk
1,266'

La Jolla
Canyon
Falls

MUGU PEAK TRAIL

P

134

134
P

1

Pacific Coast Hwy

Point Mugu

Pacific
Ocean

Thornhill
Broome Beach

REFERENCE MAPS
P. 408

135.

Chumash Trail–
Mugu Peak Loop
POINT MUGU STATE PARK

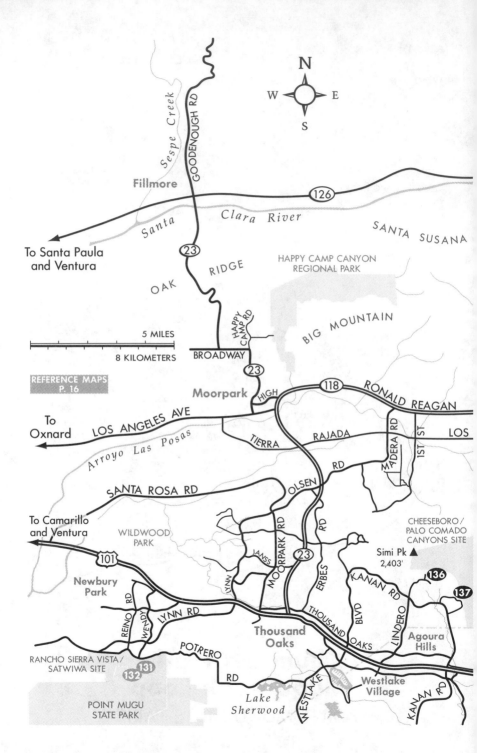

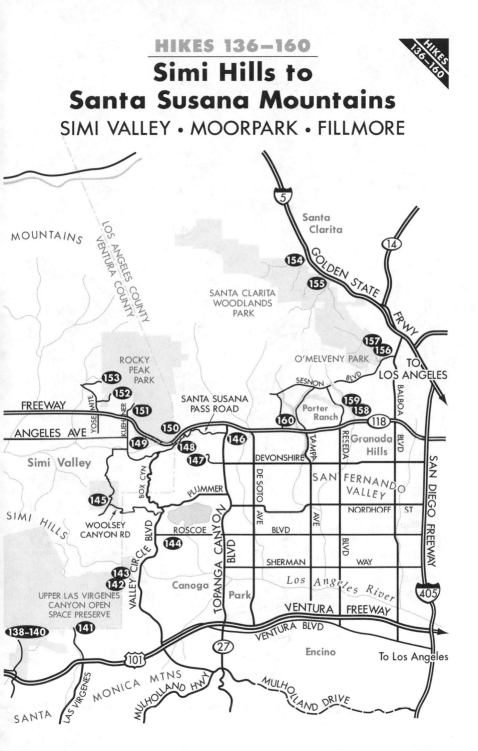

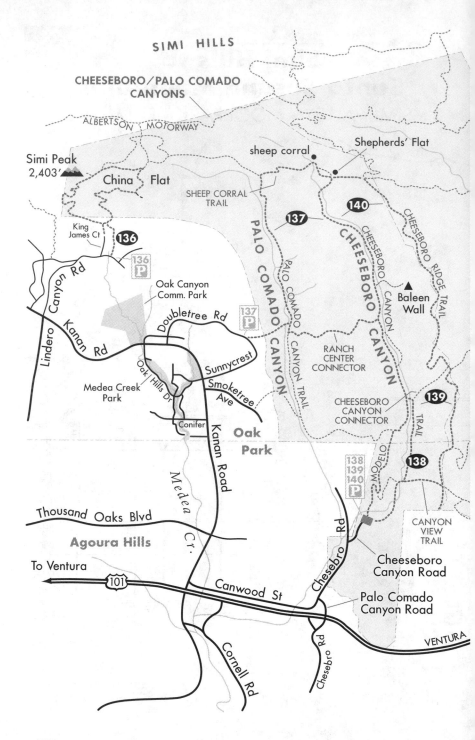

SIMI HILLS

CHEESEBORO/PALO COMADO
CANYONS

ALBERTSON MOTORWAY

Simi Peak
2,403'

China Flat

SHEEP CORRAL
TRAIL

sheep corral

Shepherds' Flat

140

137

King
James Ct

136

136 P

Oak Canyon
Comm. Park

Doubletree Rd

137 P

Sunnycrest

Smoketree
Ave

PALO COMADO CANYON

PALO COMADO CANYON TRAIL

CHEESEBORO CANYON

CHEESEBORO CANYON

Baleen
Wall

CHEESEBORO RIDGE TRAIL

RANCH
CENTER
CONNECTOR

CHEESEBORO
CANYON
CONNECTOR

139

TRAIL

Lindero Canyon Rd

Kanan Rd

Oak Hills Dr

Medea Creek
Park

Conifer

Oak
Park

Kanan Road

MODELO

**138
139
140 P**

138

Medea Cr.

Thousand Oaks Blvd

Agoura Hills

To Ventura

101

Canwood St

Chesebro Rd

CANYON
VIEW
TRAIL

Cheeseboro
Canyon Road

Palo Comado
Canyon Road

Cornell Rd

Chesebro Rd

VENTURA

Cheeseboro/Palo Comado Canyons
Upper Las Virgenes Canyon

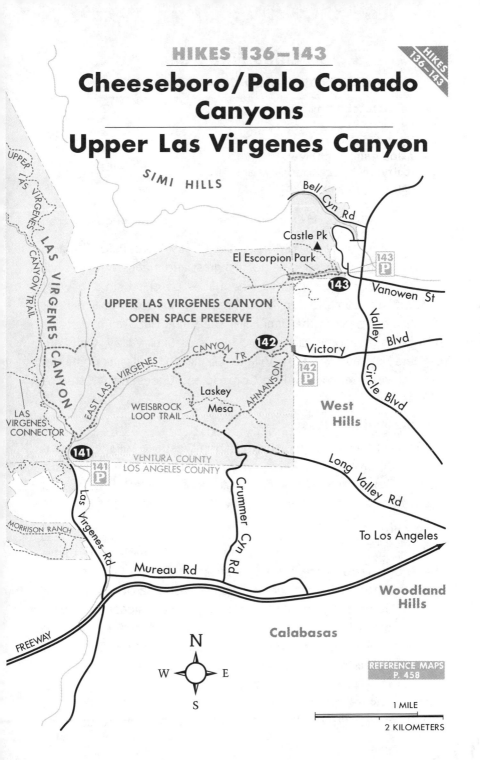

SIMI HILLS

Bell Cyn Rd

Castle Pk

El Escorpion Park

143

143 P

Vanowen St

UPPER LAS VIRGENES CANYON OPEN SPACE PRESERVE

UPPER LAS VIRGENES CANYON TRAIL

LAS VIRGENES CANYON

CANYON TR

142

142 P

Victory

Valley Blvd

EAST LAS VIRGENES

AHMANSON

Laskey Mesa

West Hills

Circle Blvd

WEISBROCK LOOP TRAIL

LAS VIRGENES CONNECTOR

141

141 P

VENTURA COUNTY
LOS ANGELES COUNTY

Long Valley Rd

MORRISON RANCH

Las Virgenes Rd

Crummer Cyn Rd

To Los Angeles

Mureau Rd

Woodland Hills

FREEWAY

Calabasas

N
W   E
S

1 MILE

2 KILOMETERS

136. China Flat Trail
CHEESEBORO/PALO COMADO CANYONS

Hiking distance: 4-mile loop
Hiking time: 2 hours
Configuration: loop
Elevation gain: 1,000 feet
Difficulty: moderate to somewhat strenuous
Exposure: mostly exposed
Dogs: allowed
Maps: U.S.G.S. Thousand Oaks · N.P.S. Cheeseboro/Palo Comado Canyons

China Flat, a newer addition to the Cheeseboro/Palo Comado Canyons site, is a high, oak-dotted grassland meadow with sedimentary rock outcroppings. The flat is perched on the west side of Palo Comado Canyon beneath the shadows of Simi Peak, the highest peak in the Simi Hills. The China Flat Trail is a steep hike with awesome, panoramic views of Simi Valley, Oak Park, Agoura Hills, and Westlake Village. Connector trails link China Flat to the upper reaches of Palo Comado and Cheeseboro Canyons (Hikes 137—140).

To the trailhead

From Ventura Freeway/Highway 101 in Westlake Village, exit on Lindero Canyon Road. Drive 4 miles north and park on Lindero Canyon Road by the China Flat Trailhead on the left. It is located between King James Court and Wembly Avenue.

The hike

Hike north past the trailhead sign towards the mountains. Climb the short, steep hill to where a trail from King James Court merges with the main trail. Continue around the east side of a large sandstone outcropping. The trail levels out and heads east, following the contour of the mountain base, to an unsigned junction. Take the left fork north, heading uphill towards the ridge. Once over the ridge, the trail meets another unsigned junction. Take the left fork and head west, with views overlooking the canyon. Proceed uphill along the ridgeline to a flat area and trail junction. The right fork leads back towards Palo Comado and Cheeseboro Canyons.

Take the left fork and descend to another junction. Again, take the left fork, winding downhill to a gate at King James Court. Leave the trail and walk one block on the sidewalk to Lindero Canyon Road. The trailhead is to the left. ■

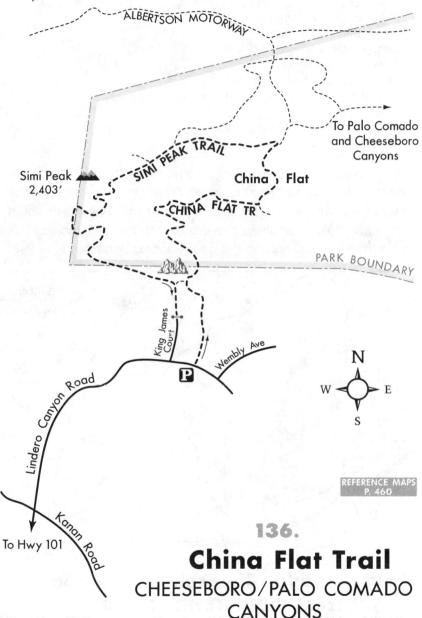

ALBERTSON MOTORWAY

To Palo Comado and Cheeseboro Canyons

SIMI PEAK TRAIL

Simi Peak
2,403'

China Flat

CHINA FLAT TR

PARK BOUNDARY

King James Court

Wembly Ave

N
W   E
S

Lindero Canyon Road

Kanan Road

To Hwy 101

REFERENCE MAPS
P. 460

136.
China Flat Trail
CHEESEBORO/PALO COMADO CANYONS

137. Upper Palo Comado— Cheeseboro Canyons Loop

CHEESEBORO/PALO COMADO CANYONS

Hiking distance: 5-mile loop
Hiking time: 2.5 hours
Configuration: loop
Elevation gain: 800 feet
Difficulty: moderate to slightly strenuous
Exposure: a mix of shaded canyon and open hillsides
Dogs: allowed
Maps: U.S.G.S. Thousand Oaks and Calabasas
    N.P.S. Cheeseboro/Palo Comado Canyons

Palo Comado and Cheeseboro Canyons, in the Simi Hills near Agoura Hills, is a wildlife corridor connecting the Santa Monica Mountains with the Santa Susana Mountains. This north–south corridor allows animals to move between the two ranges. This hike makes a loop around the undeveloped upper ends of Palo

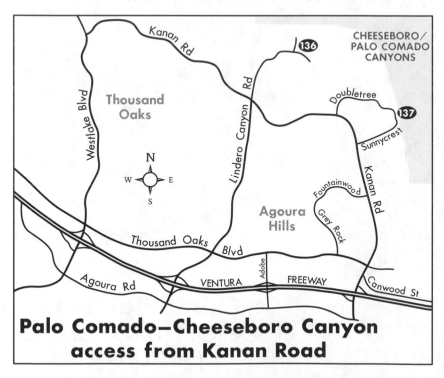

Palo Comado–Cheeseboro Canyon access from Kanan Road

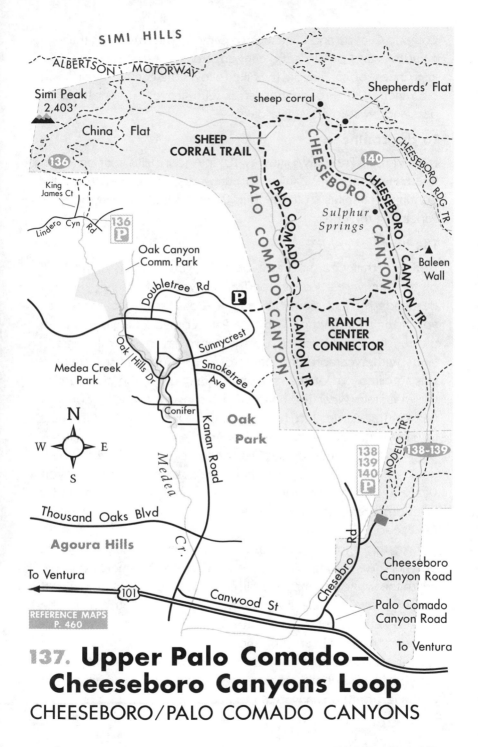

137. Upper Palo Comado– Cheeseboro Canyons Loop
CHEESEBORO/PALO COMADO CANYONS

Comado Canyon and Cheeseboro Canyon. The trail leads through meadows and parallels the canyon streams. After crossing over into Cheeseboro Canyon, the hike follows the canyon floor on an old ranch road through grasslands with groves of stately valley oaks and twisted coast live oaks.

To the trailhead

From Ventura Freeway/Highway 101 in Agoura Hills, exit on Kanan Road. Head north 2.2 miles to Sunnycrest Drive and turn right. Continue 0.8 miles to the "Public Open Space" sign on the right. Park along the curb.

The hike

From the trailhead, hike east past the gate and up a short hill on the Sunnycrest Connector Trail. As you top the hill, the trail descends into Palo Comado Canyon. Cross the stream at the canyon floor to a junction with the Palo Comado Canyon Trail, an old ranch road. Head left up the canyon through rolling grasslands with sycamore and oak groves. At one mile the trail begins to climb out of the canyon, winding along the contours of the mountain. Near the head of the canyon, the Palo Comado Canyon Trail curves left, heading to China Flat (Hike 136). There is an unmarked but distinct path leading sharply to the right at the beginning of this curve—the Old Sheep Corral Trail. Take this path uphill to a couple of ridges that overlook Cheeseboro Canyon. Descend into the canyon a short distance to the corral and a junction at Shepherds' Flat. Straight ahead the trail climbs up to Cheeseboro Ridge.

Take the right fork and follow Cheeseboro Canyon gently downhill. At Sulphur Springs, identified by its smell, walk beneath the white sedimentary cliffs of the Baleen Wall on the east canyon wall. Continue down canyon through oak groves to the posted Ranch Center Connector Trail, 1.3 miles down the canyon on the right. Bear right and wind 1.1 mile up and over the chaparral hillside from Cheeseboro Canyon back to Palo Comado Canyon. Bear right a short distance, completing the loop. Return to the left on the Sunnycrest Connector Trail. ∎

138. Cheeseboro Canyon to Shepherds' Flat

CHEESEBORO/PALO COMADO CANYONS

Hiking distance: 8.6 miles round trip
Hiking time: 4 hours
Configuration: out-and-back with small loop
Elevation gain: 600 feet
Difficulty: moderate to strenuous
Exposure: a mix of shaded canyon and open hillsides
Dogs: allowed
Maps: U.S.G.S. Calabasas
N.P.S. Cheeseboro/Palo Comado Canyons

Cheeseboro Canyon is a lush stream-fed canyon with large valley oaks, gnarled coast live oaks, and sycamores in the Cheeseboro/ Palo Comado Canyons site. The hike follows an old abandoned ranch road on a gentle grade up the forested canyon bottom, from the south end of the park to the north. The trail passes fragrant Sulphur Springs as you pass beneath the Baleen Wall, a vertical rock formation on the east canyon wall. At the upper reaches of the canyon is Shepherds' Flat, a grassland flat and a sheep corral.

To the trailhead

From Ventura Freeway/Highway 101 in Agoura Hills, exit on Chesebro Road. Continue one block straight ahead, past the stop sign, to Palo Comado Canyon Road and turn left. Drive 0.3 miles to Chesebro Road again and turn right. Continue 0.7 miles to Cheeseboro Canyon Road and turn right. The trailhead parking lot is 0.2 miles ahead.

The hike

Take the service road east toward Cheeseboro Canyon to a road split. Bear left on the Cheeseboro Canyon Trail, heading into the canyon past the Modelo Trail and the Canyon View Trail. At 1.3 miles is a junction with the Cheeseboro Ridge Connector Trail (also known as the Baleen Wall Trail). Take the left fork towards Sulphur Springs to another junction with the Modelo Trail on the left. Proceed a short distance on the main trail to a junction. Take the left branch. As you near Sulphur Springs, the white, jagged cliffs of the Baleen Wall can be seen towering on the cliffs to the east. At 3.5 miles, the canyon and trail both narrow as the smell of sulphur becomes stronger. At the head of the canyon is a three-way junction at Shepherds' Flat, the turn-around point.

To return, retrace your steps back on the Cheeseboro Canyon Trail to the Modelo Trail junction. Take the Modelo Trail along the western ridge of the canyon back to the trailhead. ▪

139. Canyon View— Cheeseboro Canyon Loop
CHEESEBORO/PALO COMADO CANYONS

Hiking distance: 4-mile loop
Hiking time: 2 hours
Configuration: loop
Elevation gain: 500 feet
Difficulty: easy to slightly moderate
Exposure: a mix of shaded canyon and open hillsides
Dogs: allowed
Maps: U.S.G.S. Calabasas
      N.P.S. Cheeseboro/Palo Comado Canyons

This loop trail is located in the lower end of the Cheeseboro/ Palo Comado Canyons site. The hike begins on the Canyon View Trail, climbing the east wall of Cheeseboro Canyon to a knoll overlooking Cheeseboro Canyon and the Lost Hills landfill. The Cheeseboro Canyon Trail is an abandoned ranch road that passes through groves of 200-year-old valley oaks, largest of the California oaks. The hike follows the ridge separating Cheeseboro Canyon from Las Virgenes Canyon through native chaparral and coastal sage scrub communities. It then drops back down to the shaded valley oak savannahs, live oak woodlands, and picnic areas on the canyon floor. For a longer loop, the hike can be continued along the ridge to Shepherds' Flat—Hike 140.

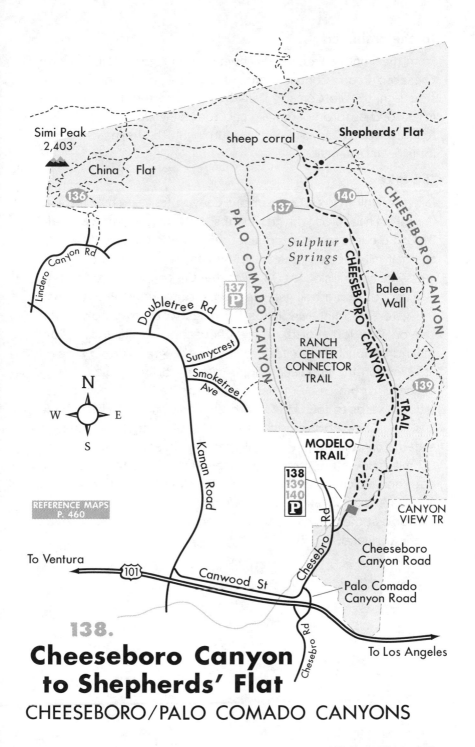

Simi Peak
2,403'

China Flat

Shepherds' Flat

sheep corral

136

140

Lindero Canyon Rd

PALO COMADO CANYON

137

CHEESEBORO CANYON

Sulphur Springs

▲ Baleen Wall

Doubletree Rd

137 P

CHEESEBORO CANYON

Sunnycrest

Smoketree Ave

RANCH CENTER CONNECTOR TRAIL

139

N
W · E
S

Kanan Road

TRAIL

MODELO TRAIL

REFERENCE MAPS
P. 460

138
139
140
P

CANYON VIEW TR

Cheeseboro Canyon Road

To Ventura

101

Canwood St

Chesebro Rd

Palo Comado Canyon Road

To Los Angeles

Chesebro Rd

138.
Cheeseboro Canyon to Shepherds' Flat
CHEESEBORO/PALO COMADO CANYONS

To the trailhead

From the Ventura Freeway/Highway 101 in Agoura Hills, exit on Chesebro Road. Continue one block straight ahead, past the stop sign, to Palo Comado Canyon Road and turn left. Drive 0.3 miles to Chesebro Road again and turn right. Continue 0.7 miles to Cheeseboro Canyon Road and turn right. The trailhead parking lot is 0.2 miles ahead.

The hike

Take the well-marked Cheeseboro Canyon Trail, and hike through the rolling hills filled with groves of stately oaks. Pass the Modelo Trail on the left to a posted junction with the Canyon View Trail at a half mile. Bear right, leaving the canyon floor, and climb the grassy canyon hillside. At 0.9 miles, the Canyon View Trail ends at a T-junction and a trail gate on Cheeseboro Ridge. Pass through the gate. The right fork leads 0.3 miles to an overlook of the canyon. Bear left (north) on the Cheeseboro Ridge Trail. Follow the ridge uphill to a Y-fork, enjoying the great canyon views. Stay left on the undulating ridge, passing power poles. Slowly descend to the Las Virgenes Connector Trail on the right. Stay left 120 yards to the Cheeseboro Canyon Connector Trail on the left. The Cheeseboro Ridge Trail—Hike 140—continues straight ahead along the ridge to Shepherds' Flat. Bear left and descend 0.7 miles down the grassy, sage-covered hillside to the canyon floor and a picnic area. Bear left on the Cheeseboro Canyon Trail, an old ranch road, and stroll through the oak groves, completing the loop at the Canyon View Trail junction. Return down canyon to the trailhead. ■

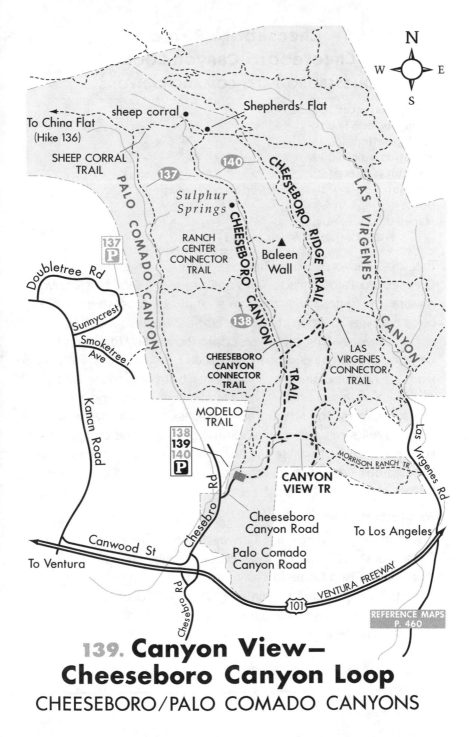

N
W · E
S

Shepherds' Flat

sheep corral •

To China Flat
(Hike 136)

SHEEP CORRAL
TRAIL

137

140

PALO COMADO CANYON

Sulphur Springs •

CHEESEBORO RIDGE TRAIL

LAS VIRGENES CANYON

137
P

Doubletree Rd

Sunnycrest

Smoketree Ave

RANCH CENTER CONNECTOR TRAIL

CHEESEBORO CANYON

▲ Baleen Wall

138

CHEESEBORO CANYON CONNECTOR TRAIL

TRAIL

LAS VIRGENES CONNECTOR TRAIL

Kanan Road

MODELO TRAIL

138
139
140
P

MORRISON RANCH TR

CANYON VIEW TR

Chesebro Rd

Cheseboro Canyon Road

Palo Comado Canyon Road

To Los Angeles

Canwood St

To Ventura

Chesebro Rd

VENTURA FREEWAY

101

Las Virgenes Rd

REFERENCE MAPS
P. 460

139. Canyon View–
Cheeseboro Canyon Loop
CHEESEBORO/PALO COMADO CANYONS

140. Cheeseboro Ridge— Cheeseboro Canyon Loop

CHEESEBORO/PALO COMADO CANYONS

Hiking distance: 10-mile loop
Hiking time: 5 hours
Configuration: loop
Elevation gain: 900 feet
Difficulty: strenuous
Exposure: a mix of shaded canyon and open hillsides
Dogs: allowed
Maps: U.S.G.S. Calabasas
      N.P.S. Cheeseboro/Palo Comado Canyons

This long, canyon-to-ridge loop explores a large tract of the Cheeseboro/Palo Comado Canyons site in the Simi Hills above Agoura. The route travels through a variety of ecosystems, from oak savannahs to open chapparal slopes. The hike leads to the upper canyons along the Cheeseboro Ridge Trail, following the ridge between Cheeseboro Canyon and Las Virgenes Canyon. From the ridge are bird's-eye views into both canyons as well as expansive vistas across the Santa Monica Mountains and the San Fernando Valley. The return trail leads back through Cheeseboro Canyon, following a stream along the drainage. The trail passes by the Baleen Wall, white jagged cliffs that reach upwards to Cheeseboro Ridge. The trail then drops into shaded oak groves before completing the loop.

To the trailhead

From the Ventura Freeway/Highway 101 in Agoura Hills, exit on Chesebro Road. Continue one block straight ahead, past the stop sign, to Palo Comado Canyon Road and turn left. Drive 0.3 miles to Chesebro Road again and turn right. Continue 0.7 miles to Cheeseboro Canyon Road and turn right. The trailhead parking lot is 0.2 miles ahead.

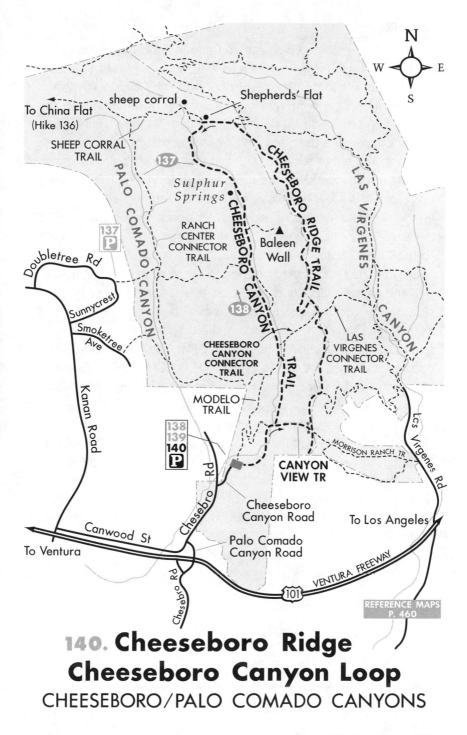

N
W   E
S

To China Flat
(Hike 136)

sheep corral •

Shepherds' Flat

SHEEP CORRAL
TRAIL

PALO COMADO CANYON

137

Sulphur Springs •

RANCH CENTER CONNECTOR TRAIL

CHEESEBORO CANYON

CHEESEBORO RIDGE TRAIL

LAS VIRGENES CANYON

▲ Baleen Wall

138

Doubletree Rd

137 P

Sunnycrest

Smoketree Ave

Kanan Road

CHEESEBORO CANYON CONNECTOR TRAIL

MODELO TRAIL

LAS VIRGENES CONNECTOR TRAIL

TRAIL

138
139
140 P

Chesebro Rd

MORRISON RANCH TR

CANYON VIEW TR

Los Virgenes Rd

Cheeseboro Canyon Road

To Los Angeles

Palo Comado Canyon Road

Canwood St

To Ventura

VENTURA FREEWAY

101

REFERENCE MAPS
P. 460

140. **Cheeseboro Ridge**
Cheeseboro Canyon Loop
CHEESEBORO/PALO COMADO CANYONS

The hike

Take the well-marked Cheeseboro Canyon Trail, and hike through the rolling hills filled with groves of stately oaks. Pass the Modelo Trail on the left to a posted junction with the Canyon View Trail at a half mile. Bear right, leaving the canyon floor, and climb the grassy canyon hillside. At 0.9 miles, the Canyon View Trail ends at a T-junction and a trail gate on Cheeseboro Ridge. Pass through the gate. The right fork leads 0.3 miles to an overlook of the canyon. Bear left (north) on the Cheeseboro Ridge Trail. Follow the ridge uphill to a Y-fork, enjoying the great canyon views. Stay left on the undulating ridge, passing power poles. Slowly descend to the Las Virgenes Connector Trail on the right. Stay left 120 yards to the Cheeseboro Canyon Connector Trail on the left.

Stay to the right (north) on the old ranch road to begin the upper end of the loop. Wind up the ridge and skirt around the right side of a water tank. Gradually descend to the canyon floor and a trail split. Curve left and head west along the base of the mountain to a signed junction at Shepherds' Flat. The Sheep Corral Trail continues straight ahead to China Flat (Hike 136) and Palo Comado Canyon (Hike 137). Bear left on the Cheeseboro Canyon Trail (also called Sulphur Springs Trail), and follow the canyon floor steadily downhill. At Sulphur Springs, easily identified by its smell, walk beneath the white sedimentary cliffs of the Baleen Wall on the east canyon wall. Continue down canyon through oak groves and past shaded picnic areas. Pass the Ranch Center Connector Trail and the Palo Comado Connector Trail on the right, completing the loop at the Canyon View Trail junction. Return down canyon to the trailhead. ■

141. Upper Las Virgenes Canyon Open Space Preserve
from Las Virgenes Trailhead

Hiking distance: 3.3-mile loop
Hiking time: 2 hours
Configuration: loop
Elevation gain: 400 feet
Difficulty: easy
Exposure: mostly exposed with forested pockets
Dogs: allowed
Maps: U.S.G.S. Calabasas · Trails of the Simi Hills map
        Upper Las Virgenes Canyon Open Space Preserve map

The Upper Las Virgenes Canyon Open Space Preserve (formerly the Ahmanson Ranch) is a sprawling, unspoiled landscape in the Simi Hills that straddles the Los Angeles—Ventura county line. Dirt ranch roads lace through the rolling grasslands and oak-studded hills of the 2,983-acre park. The bucolic open space contains nine miles of seasonal streams that form the headwaters of Malibu Creek. The streams flow through the ranch land en route to Malibu Lagoon in the Santa Monica Bay, one of the last remaining coastal wetlands in the county. The diverse land boasts shady streamside riparian habitat, walnut woodlands, valley oak savannah, coastal sage scrub, and native perennial grasslands. The elevations range from 870 feet to 1,840 feet. The open space preserves of Upper Las Virgenes Canyon, Cheeseboro Canyon, and Palo Comado Canyon lie adjacent to each other with a network of inter-connected hiking trails.

    This hike begins at the northern end of Las Virgenes Road in Calabasas. The loop hike begins by following a creekbed through a gorgeous oak woodland, then gently winds through rolling grasslands with great vistas. En route, the trail crosses a saddle and drops into a lush, forested canyon. The trail connects with the adjacent loop to the east—Hike 142.

To the trailhead

From the Ventura Freeway/Highway 101 in Calabasas, exit on Las Virgenes Road. Drive 1.5 miles north to the posted trailhead at the end of the road. Park along the curb.

The hike

Walk through the trailhead gate at the end of the road. Follow the west edge of seasonal Las Virgenes Creek 0.3 miles to a T-junction. Begin the loop to the right on the East Las Virgenes Canyon Trail. Gently wind up the open rolling hills through vast grasslands with distant views up the wide canyon. At a half mile, a short side path drops down to the stream in a pocket of stately oaks. The main trail continues north to a distinct junction by a wooden post. The East Las Virgenes Canyon Trail continues straight ahead to Laskey Mesa and the Victory Trailhead (Hike 142).

Veer left on the two-track trail. Head up the side canyon, and curve around a hill to an 1,100-foot saddle. Drop down into the next drainage to the west to a posted junction at the base of the steep hill. Bear left and cross the canyon bottom to a second saddle with more great vistas of the surrounding hills. Descend to a posted T-junction with the Upper Las Virgenes Canyon Trail. The right fork leads up canyon to Bell Canyon, Runkle Canyon, and to upper Cheeseboro/Palo Comado Canyons.

Bear left and walk gently down canyon among stately stands of oaks. Cross Las Virgenes Creek to a fork with the Las Virgenes Connector Trail, leading one mile to the Cheeseboro Canyon floor (Hikes 138—140). Continue following the canyon floor on the Las Virgenes Canyon Trail, completing the loop at 3 miles. (Along this section, an unsigned one-mile footpath curves up and over the hill, returning to the main trail 40 feet shy of the trailhead.) After completing the loop, return 0.3 miles to the right. ■

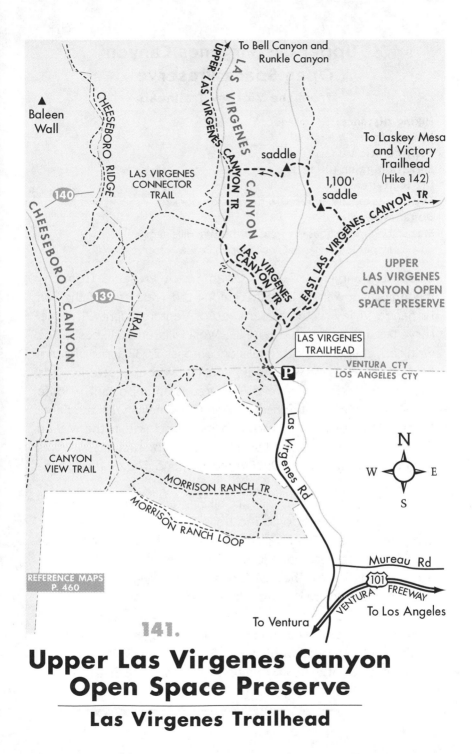

To Bell Canyon and
Runkle Canyon

Baleen
Wall

CHEESEBORO RIDGE

UPPER LAS VIRGENES CANYON TR

LAS VIRGENES CANYON TR

CHEESEBORO CANYON

140

LAS VIRGENES
CONNECTOR
TRAIL

saddle

To Laskey Mesa
and Victory
Trailhead
(Hike 142)

1,100'
saddle

EAST LAS VIRGENES CANYON TR

139

TRAIL

LAS VIRGENES
CANYON TR

UPPER
LAS VIRGENES
CANYON OPEN
SPACE PRESERVE

LAS VIRGENES
TRAILHEAD

P

VENTURA CTY
LOS ANGELES CTY

Las Virgenes Rd

CANYON
VIEW TRAIL

MORRISON RANCH TR

MORRISON RANCH LOOP

N
W E
S

REFERENCE MAPS
P. 460

Mureau Rd

101

VENTURA FREEWAY

To Los Angeles

To Ventura

141.

Upper Las Virgenes Canyon
Open Space Preserve
Las Virgenes Trailhead

142. Upper Las Virgenes Canyon Open Space Preserve
from the Victory Trailhead

Hiking distance: 3.6-mile loop
Hiking time: 2 hours
Configuration: loop
Elevation gain: 400 feet
Difficulty: easy
Exposure: mostly exposed with forested pockets
Dogs: allowed
Maps: U.S.G.S. Calabasas · Trails of the Simi Hills map
  Upper Las Virgenes Canyon Open Space Preserve map

Upper Las Virgenes Canyon Open Space Preserve (formerly the Ahmanson Ranch) is nestled along the west end of the San Fernando Valley on the eastern end of Ventura County. The preserve lies adjacent to Hidden Hills, West Hills, and Calabasas. The wrinkled, chaparral-dotted hills encompass 2,983 acres of open land with groves of valley oak, coastal live oak, cottonwoods, sycamores, and walnut trees. The area is an important wildlife corridor connecting the Santa Susana Mountains with the Santa Monica Mountains. The unspoiled ranchland within the Malibu Creek watershed was used as a backdrop for such classic films as *Gone With the Wind*, *Duel In the Sun*, and *The Charge of the Light Brigade*.

There are more than 15 miles of hiking trails open to hikers, bikers, equestrians, and dogs. The trails are mostly fire roads and some single track. This hike begins from the Victory Trailhead at the western terminus of Victory Boulevard in West Hills in the San Fernando Valley. The hike forms a loop along three trails: Las Virgenes Canyon Trail, Laskey Mesa Trail, and Ahmanson Ranch House Trail. The scenic route crosses gently rolling hills dotted with majestic oaks and circles Laskey Mesa, a broad plateau on the southern portion of the park. From Laskey Mesa are far-reaching vistas of the San Fernando Valley and the Simi Hills.

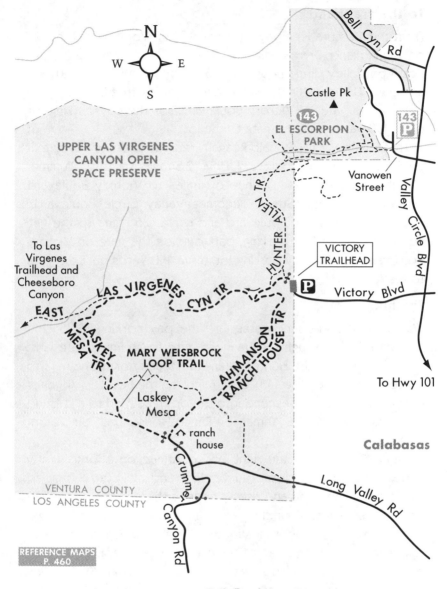

142.
Upper Las Virgenes Canyon
Open Space Preserve
Victory Trailhead

To the trailhead

From the Ventura Freeway/Highway 101 in Woodland Hills, exit on Mullholland Drive/Valley Circle Boulevard. Drive 2.2 miles north on Valley Circle Boulevard to Victory Boulevard. Turn left and drive 0.6 miles to the gated entrance. For free parking, park outside the gate on Victory Boulevard. For the pay parking lot, drive 150 yards past the gate to the lot.

From Highway 118/Ronald Reagan Freeway in Chatsworth, exit on Topanga Canyon Boulevard. Drive 2.5 miles south to Plummer Street. Turn right and continue 6.3 miles to Victory Boulevard. (En route, Plummer Street becomes Valley Circle Boulevard.) Turn right on Victory Boulevard and drive 0.6 miles to the gated entrance. For free parking, park outside the gate on Victory Boulevard. For the pay parking lot, drive 150 yards past the gate to the lot.

The hike

Walk past the entrance gates into the pay parking lot to the trailhead. Pass through the trailhead gate to an immediate junction. To the right, the Hunter Allen Trail heads north one mile to El Escorpion Park (Hike 143). Go straight on the East Las Virgenes Canyon Trail. Gently descend into the open canyon to a U-bend and junction with the Ahmanson Ranch House Trail, our return route.

Begin the loop to the right, and continue on a long, gently winding downward slope. Curve right and make an S-shaped bend with minor dips and rises. Continue through the open, oak-dotted hillsides to a junction at 1.1 mile. The right fork (straight ahead) leads to the Las Virgenes Trailhead (Hike 141) and Cheeseboro Canyon (Hikes 137–140). For this hike, bear left on the Laskey Mesa Trail and steadily loose elevation. At 1.4 miles, ascend the slope and pass under a couple of old growth oaks. Make a sweeping U-shaped bend to a junction with the Mary Weisbrock Loop Trail. Both the Laskey Mesa Trail and the Mary Weisbrock Loop circle Laskey Mesa, a large flat grassland.

For this route, take the right fork (the longer route), and cross the south side of Laskey Mesa. Bear left on the old ranch road and skirt the east side of the mesa to water tanks and a vehicle gate at 2.3 miles. The right fork, straight ahead, passes the ranch buildings and leads out of the park, heading down Crummer Canyon on a paved road. Bear left on the signed Mary Weisbrock Loop Trail, and follow the east side of the mesa 0.3 miles to the east corner of the loop, where the two route options rejoin. Continue straight while overlooking the rolling hilly terrain, and stay left at a Y-fork 60 yards ahead. Curve left to a view of the trailhead and descend to a junction, completing the loop. Return to the trailhead on the right. ■

143. El Escorpion Park

Hiking distance: 2-mile loop
Hiking time: 1 hour
Configuration: loop
Elevation gain: 150 feet
Difficulty: easy
Exposure: mostly exposed with forested pockets
Dogs: allowed
Maps: U.S.G.S. Calabasas
      Trails of the Simi Hills map

El Escorpion Park (also known as Castle Peak Park) is located in the West Hills of the San Fernando Valley. The small park sits in the Simi Hills adjacent to the expansive 2,900-acre Upper Las Virgenes Canyon Open Space Preserve. The three-acre park is open to hikers, bikers, equestrians, and dogs. It has two main trails that run the length of the park along El Escorpion Creek, with a network of connecting trails that leave the park. To the north, a path leads to caves on the hillside canyon wall. Also to the north, a rough, dangerously steep path ascends the south slope of Castle Peak, the prominent rocky mountain towering over the landscape. (The trail gains 1,000 feet in a short distance.) To the south, the El Escorpion Trail connects with the Upper Las Virgenes Canyon Open Space Preserve (Hike 142). A third trail heads west, connecting with the Las Virgenes Trailhead and Cheeseboro Canyon (Hikes 137–141).

To the trailhead

From the Ventura Freeway/Highway 101 in Woodland Hills, exit on Mullholland Drive/Valley Circle Boulevard. Drive 3 miles north on Valley Circle Boulevard to Vanowen Street. Turn left and drive one block to the trailhead on the left, located as the road curves right onto Sunset Ridge Court. Park along the curb.

From Highway 118/Ronald Reagan Freeway in Chatsworth, exit on Topanga Canyon Boulevard. Drive 2.5 miles south to Plummer Street. Turn right and continue 5.5 miles to Vanowen Street. (En route, Plummer Street becomes Valley Circle Boulevard.) Turn right on Vanowen Street, and drive one block to the trailhead on the left, located as the road curves right onto Sunset Ridge Court. Park along the curb.

The hike

Walk through the trailhead gate and curve right. Follow the old dirt road west along the base of the oak-studded hillside to a Y-fork. Begin the loop to the right beneath jagged Castle Peak. Cross the seasonal El Escorpion Creek drainage and veer left, continuing up canyon. A couple of side paths on the right ascend Castle Peak. Connector paths on the left recross the drainage and join the parallel return path to the south. Meander through a mixed forest with palms, oaks, chaparral, and riparian vegetation. At the trail's west end is an open fence that separates the city portion of the park from the Santa Monica Conservancy land. Pass through the fence to a junction. The right fork leads up a side canyon a quarter mile to the base of weather-carved sandstone formations pocketed with caves. This route invites exploration.

Back at the drainage floor, the left (south) fork, leads 100 yards to another junction. The Hunter Allen Trail heads west and curves south, leading one mile to the Upper Las Virgenes Canyon Open Space Preserve at the Victory Trailhead (Hike 142). A short distance past this junction, a path veers right and heads west, winding through the oak-dotted rolling hills and sycamore-lined canyons to Cheeseboro Canyon and the Las Virgenes Trailhead (Hikes 137–141). To return, head back down canyon on the south canyon wall, completing the loop near the trailhead. ■

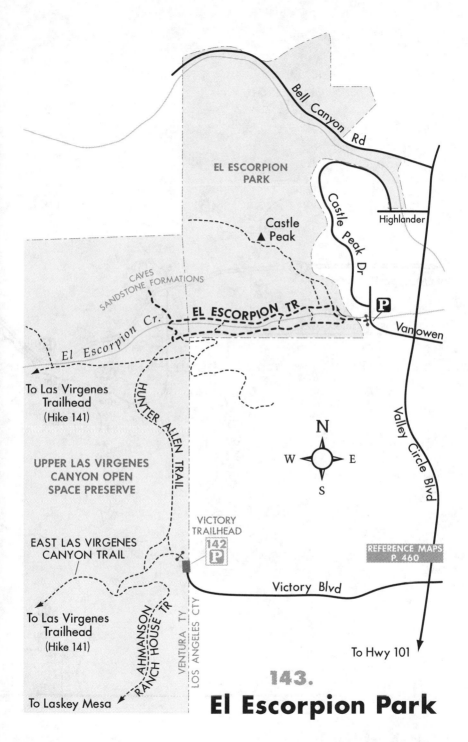

Bell Canyon Rd

EL ESCORPION
PARK

Castle
▲ Peak

Highlander

Castle Peak Dr

CAVES
SANDSTONE FORMATIONS

El Escorpion Cr.

EL ESCORPION TR.

P

Vanowen

To Las Virgenes
Trailhead
(Hike 141)

HUNTER ALLEN TRAIL

UPPER LAS VIRGENES
CANYON OPEN
SPACE PRESERVE

N
W   E
S

Valley Circle Blvd

EAST LAS VIRGENES
CANYON TRAIL

VICTORY
TRAILHEAD
142
P

REFERENCE MAPS
P. 460

To Las Virgenes
Trailhead
(Hike 141)

VENTURA TY
LOS ANGELES CTY

AHMANSON RANCH HOUSE TR.

Victory Blvd

To Hwy 101

To Laskey Mesa

143.
El Escorpion Park

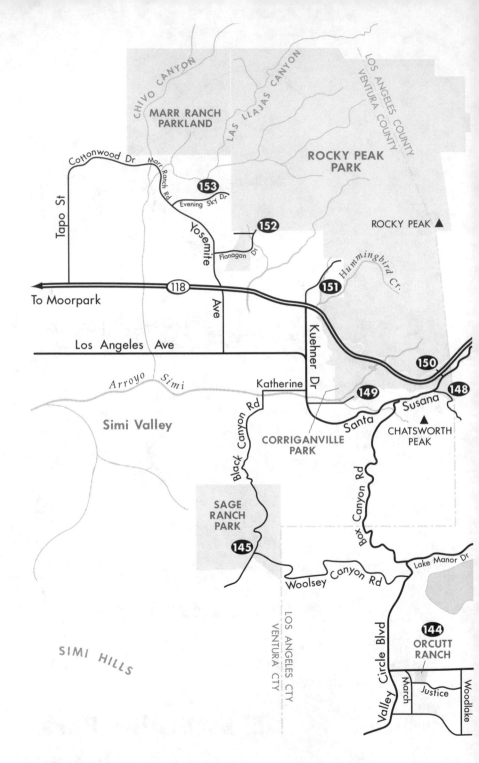

CHIVO CANYON

LAS LLAJAS CANYON

LOS ANGELES COUNTY
VENTURA COUNTY

MARR RANCH
PARKLAND

ROCKY PEAK
PARK

Cottonwood Dr

Morr Ranch Rd

153

Evening Sky Dr

152

ROCKY PEAK ▲

Tapo St

Yosemite

Flanagan Dr

Hummingbird Cr.

151

118

To Moorpark

Ave

Kuehner Dr

150

Los Angeles Ave

Arroyo Simi

Katherine

149

Susana

148

Simi Valley

Black Canyon Rd

Santa

CHATSWORTH
PEAK ▲

CORRIGANVILLE
PARK

SAGE
RANCH
PARK

145

Box Canyon Rd

Woolsey Canyon Rd

Lake Manor Dr

SIMI HILLS

LOS ANGELES CITY
VENTURA CITY

Valley Circle Blvd

144
ORCUTT
RANCH

March

Justice

Woodlake

East Simi Valley
Santa Susana Mountains
Simi Hills

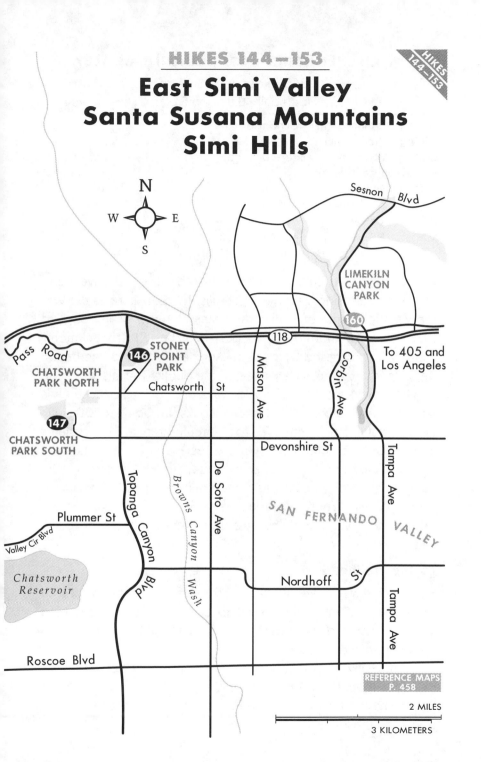

144. Orcutt Ranch Horticulture Center
23600 Roscoe Boulevard
Open daily 8 a.m. to 5 p.m.

Hiking distance: 1 mile round trip
Hiking time: 45 minutes
Configuration: several inter-connecting trails
Elevation gain: level
Difficulty: very easy
Exposure: mostly shaded forest
Dogs: not allowed
Maps: U.S.G.S. Calabasas and Canoga Park
　　　　Orcutt Ranch Horticulture Center map

Orcutt Ranch Horticulture Center is tucked away at the west end of the San Fernando Valley in West Hills. The 200-acre estate was the vacation home of William and Mary Orcutt, dating back to 1917. The tree-studded estate, designated as a historical monument, was purchased by the Los Angeles Parks and Recreation Department in 1966 and opened to the public. The mission-style home with 16-inch thick adobe walls and a large patio area is nestled under the shade of ancient oaks, including a 700-year-old coastal live oak with a 33-foot circumference. Exotic plants and trees are planted on several acres around the former residence. Amid the fountains and statues are rattan palms, cork oaks, dogwoods, sycamores, birch, bunya bunya trees, purple lily magnolias, Chinese wisterias, bamboo, and a rose garden. An orchard of citrus and walnut groves covers the adjacent rolling hills.

To the trailhead

From Highway 118 (Ronald Reagan Freeway) in Chatsworth, take the Topanga Canyon Boulevard exit. Drive 3.2 miles south to Roscoe Boulevard and turn right. Continue 2 miles to the posted park entrance on the left.

From Highway 101 (Ventura Freeway) in Woodland Hills, drive 3.4 miles north on Topanga Canyon Boulevard to Roscoe Boulevard and turn left. Continue 2 miles to the posted park entrance on the left.

The hike

From the parking area, walk to the Parks and Recreation adobe buildings and the Orcutt estate house. After strolling through the patio areas, take the nature trail into the gardens. Dayton Creek flows through the south end of the gardens in a lush woodland. Along the creek are footbridges, statues and benches. Design your own route, meandering through the historic estate and gardens. ▦

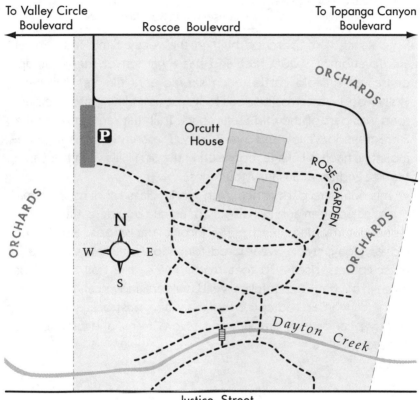

REFERENCE MAPS
P. 484

144.
Orcutt Ranch Horticulture Center

145. Sage Ranch Park

1 Black Canyon Road

Hiking distance: 2.6-mile loop
Hiking time: 1.3 hours
Configuration: loop
Elevation gain: 300 feet
Difficulty: easy
Exposure: mostly exposed
Dogs: allowed
Maps: U.S.G.S. Calabasas
      Santa Monica Mountains Conservancy: Sage Ranch Park

Sage Ranch Park, perched high in the rocky Simi Hills, sits at an elevation of 2,000 feet and has a garden-of-the-gods appearance. The old cattle ranch served as a film set for early Hollywood westerns. Previous to its use as a filming site, the park road was part of the Old Stagecoach Trail that ran between the San Fernando Valley and Simi Valley. The area remains an intermountain habitat linkage, connecting the Simi Hills with the Santa Monica and Santa Susana Mountains.

This 635-acre park is rich with world-class sandstone formations, including an endless display of unique boulders, tilted sandstone outcroppings, and metamorphic backdrops. Sandstone Ridge, a long, steep, weathered formation with caves and natural sculptures, rises 300 feet from the 2.6-mile trail that loops through the park. Beautiful carved boulders and eucalyptus trees fill the canyon. En route, the trail meanders past oak woodlands, prickly pear cactus, bracken and sword ferns, and orange and avocado groves.

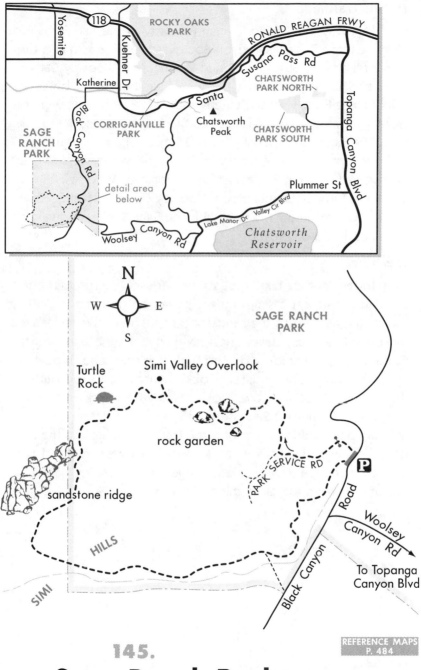

118

ROCKY OAKS
PARK

RONALD REAGAN FRWY

Yosemite

Kuehner Dr

Susana Pass Rd

Katherine

CHATSWORTH
PARK NORTH

Santa

Topanga Canyon Blvd

Black Canyon Rd

CORRIGANVILLE
PARK

Chatsworth
Peak

CHATSWORTH
PARK SOUTH

SAGE
RANCH
PARK

detail area
below

Plummer St

Lake Manor Dr   Valley Cir Blvd

Woolsey   Canyon Rd

Chatsworth
Reservoir

N

W   E

S

SAGE RANCH
PARK

Simi Valley Overlook

Turtle
Rock

rock garden

PARK SERVICE RD

P

sandstone ridge

Road

Woolsey
Canyon Rd

HILLS

Black Canyon

To Topanga
Canyon Blvd

SIMI

REFERENCE MAPS
P. 484

145.

Sage Ranch Park

To the trailhead

From Highway 118/Ronald Reagan Freeway in the San Fernando Valley, exit on Topanga Canyon Boulevard. Drive south and turn right on Plummer Street. Continue 2.4 miles to Woolsey Canyon Road and turn right. (Along the way, Plummer Street becomes Valley Circle Boulevard and Lake Manor Drive.) Continue west on Woolsey Canyon Road 2.4 miles to Black Canyon Road and turn right. The Sage Ranch parking lot is 0.2 miles ahead on the left.

From Ventura Freeway/Highway 101 in the San Fernando Valley, exit on Valley Circle Boulevard. Drive north to Woolsey Canyon Road and turn left. Continue on Woolsey Canyon Road 2.4 miles to Black Canyon Road and turn right. The Sage Ranch parking lot is 0.2 miles ahead on the left.

The hike

From the parking lot, hike west up the park service road. Proceed through the gate, passing orange groves on both sides. At the top of the hill next to the sandstone formations, the trail leaves the paved road and takes the gravel road to the right (north). Continue past a meadow dotted with oak trees and through an enormous garden of sandstone rocks. Watch for a short path on the right to a vista point overlooking Simi Valley. Back on the main trail, the trail parallels Sandstone Ridge before descending into the canyon. Once in the canyon, the trail curves back to the east past another series of large rock formations. Near the east end of the canyon is a trail split. Take the left fork, heading uphill and out of the canyon, back to the parking lot. ▪

146. Stoney Point

11000 Topanga Canyon Boulevard

Hiking distance: 0.7-mile outer loop
Hiking time: 1 hour (allow extra time for exploration)
Configuration: outer loop with several exploratory paths
Elevation gain: 100 feet
Difficulty: easy
Exposure: exposed
Dogs: allowed (a popular place for dogs)
Maps: U.S.G.S. Oat Mountain

Stoney Point (also known as the Stoney Point Outcroppings) is a dramatic sandstone formation that rises more than 300 feet from the valley floor in Chatsworth. The circular landmark is the centerpiece of 76-acre Stoney Point Park. Originally the site of an ancient Indian village, the picturesque formation was designated as a historic-cultural landmark in 1974. It was also used by outlaw Tiburcio Vasquez as a hideout in the 1870s. From the 1930s until today, it has been a popular climbing and bouldering site.

The natural rock outcropping is made up of a maze of weather-carved boulders that merge to form alcoves, caves, and dens. A wide hiking trail circles the perimeter of the mountain, weaving through large boulders dispersed along its base. A small stream trickles southeast of the formation. Numerous side paths lead up the cluster of boulders to an endless display of caves. Several paths also head up to the summit. Many hours can be spent exploring up, over, and around the exposed rocks.

To the trailhead

From Highway 118/Ronald Reagan Freeway in Chatsworth, exit on Topanga Canyon Boulevard. Drive 0.9 miles south to Chatsworth Street, passing the distinct Stoney Point on the left. Turn around and return 0.3 miles on Topanga Canyon Boulevard. Park along the curb.

Stoney Point

The hike

Walk past the vehicle gate and descend to the base of the extraordinary mountain. Many intertwining footpaths weave up and around Stoney Point. Take the wide (main) path, following the southern base of the magnificent formation. Parallel the small stream and the horse stables lined with eucalyptus trees. Meander among the embedded house-size boulders, passing natural caves and alcoves. Continue along the east side of Stoney Point, passing endless routes into the finely etched rocks and caves. At the northeast corner, by the railroad tracks, curve left and climb the slope among additional outcrops and access routes up the mountain. Cross up and over the rise, reaching Topanga Canyon Boulevard by Santa Susana Pass Road. Just before reaching the boulevard, veer left into the massive formation and descend to the sidewalk along the road. For a loop back to the trailhead, follow the paved and gravel path south, paralleling the road for 0.2 miles. ▦

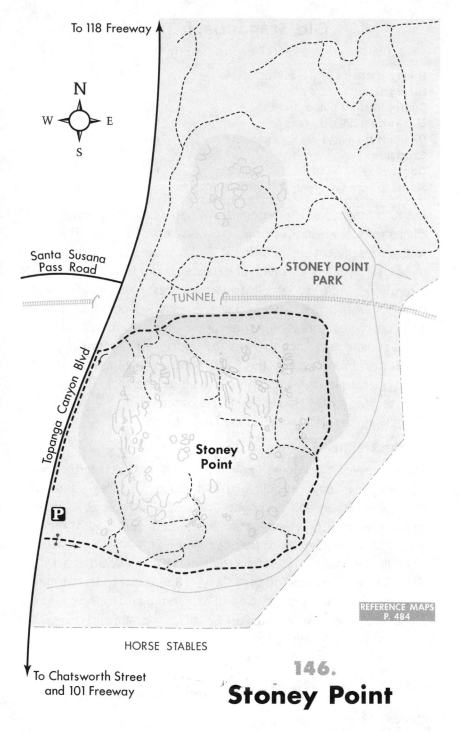

To 118 Freeway

N
W E
S

Santa Susana
Pass Road

STONEY POINT
PARK

TUNNEL

Topanga Canyon Blvd

Stoney
Point

P

REFERENCE MAPS
P. 484

HORSE STABLES

To Chatsworth Street
and 101 Freeway

146.
Stoney Point

147. Old Stagecoach Trail
22360 Devonshire Street

Hiking distance: 2.6 miles round trip
Hiking time: 1.5 hours
Configuration: out-and-back
Elevation gain: 600 feet
Difficulty: easy to slightly moderate
Exposure: exposed hills
Dogs: allowed
Maps: U.S.G.S. Simi Valley East and Oat Mountain

The Old Stagecoach Trail begins in Chatsworth Park South and climbs through an undeveloped portion of the Simi Hills. The trail follows a segment of the historic Santa Susana Stage Road that once linked Los Angeles with San Francisco from 1859—1890. The hike utilizes the old route, lined with interesting formations and bedrock worn down by stagecoach wheels. A web of unmarked, and sometimes confusing, trails weaves through rounded, fractured sedimentary rock to vistas of the city of Chatsworth, the San Fernando Valley, and the Santa Susana Mountains. Near the ridge is a plaque embedded into the sandstone rock. The marker was installed by the Native Daughters of the Golden West in 1937, designating the Old Santa Susana Stage Road.

To the trailhead

From Highway 118/Ronald Reagan Freeway in Chatsworth, take the Topanga Canyon Boulevard exit. Drive 1.5 miles south to Devonshire Street and turn right. Continue a half mile to the end of Devonshire Street and enter Chatsworth Park South. Curve right and drive 0.2 miles to the main parking lot.

From the Ventura Freeway/Highway 101 in Woodland Hills, drive 5 miles north on Topanga Canyon Boulevard to Devonshire Street and turn left. Continue a half mile to the end of Devonshire Street and enter Chatsworth Park South. Curve right and drive 0.2 miles to the main parking lot.

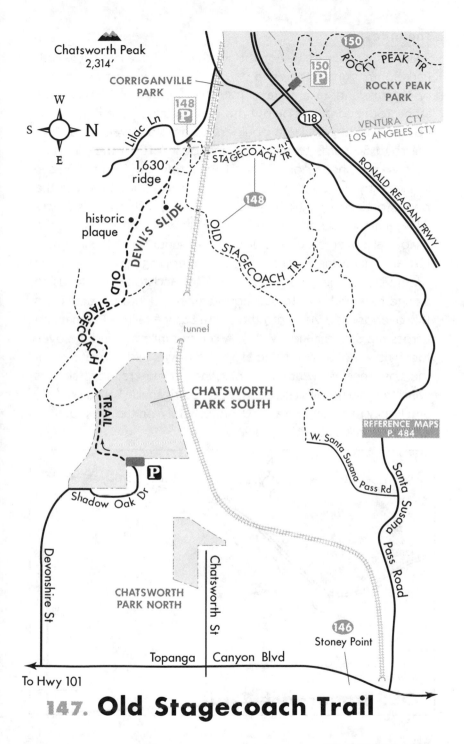

Chatsworth Peak
2,314'

CORRIGANVILLE
PARK

Lilac Ln

W
N
S
E

1,630'
ridge

historic
plaque

DEVIL'S SLIDE

OLD STAGECOACH TRAIL

STAGECOACH TR

OLD STAGECOACH TR

148

150

150 P

118

RONALD REAGAN FRWY

ROCKY PEAK TR

ROCKY PEAK
PARK

VENTURA CTY
LOS ANGELES CTY

148 P

tunnel

CHATSWORTH
PARK SOUTH

REFERENCE MAPS
P. 484

W. Santa Susana Pass Rd

Santa Susana Pass Road

P

Shadow Oak Dr

Devonshire St

CHATSWORTH
PARK NORTH

Chatsworth St

146

Stoney Point

Topanga Canyon Blvd

To Hwy 101

147. Old Stagecoach Trail

The hike

Follow the fire road/trail on the south (left) edge of Chatsworth Park South, skirting the wide park lawn. At the west end of the open grassland, take a gravel path towards the towering sandstone formations, just below the water tank on the right. Wind up the hillside past large boulders to an old paved road. Take the road 50 yards to the right, and bear left on the dirt path by two telephone poles. Climb to the ridge and a junction surrounded by the sculpted rocks. The left fork loops back to the park. Continue straight 50 yards and curve left towards Devil's Slide, a natural sandstone staircase. Follow the east edge of the chaparral-covered slope to an unsigned junction on the left. Bear left and climb the Devil's Slide, stair-stepping up the mountain on the stagecoach-worn bedrock. The sandstone slab leads to a huge rock with a historic plaque cemented into its face. From this overlook is a view into the Santa Susana railroad tunnel and across the San Fernando Valley. A quarter mile beyond the overlook is the 1,630-foot ridge atop the Devil's Slide, located near the Los Angeles—Ventura county line. From here, several trails wind through the hills and connect to Corriganville Park (Hike 149) and Rocky Peak Park (Hikes 150—152). Return on the same path or explore some of the side trails. ▪

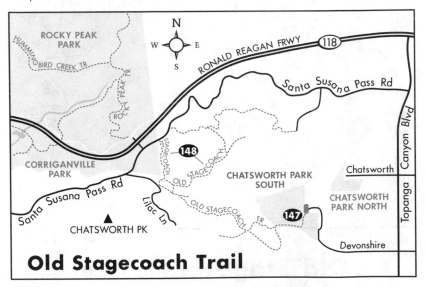

Old Stagecoach Trail

148. Stagecoach Trail Loop

Hiking distance: 2-mile loop
Hiking time: 1 hour
Configuration: loop
Elevation gain: 300 feet
Difficulty: easy
Exposure: exposed
Dogs: allowed
Maps: U.S.G.S. Simi Valley East and Oat Mountain
      Rancho Simi Trail Blazers Stagecoach Trail map

A network of trails runs through the northeast corner of the Simi Hills near Chatsworth. The area, adjacent to the Santa Susana Mountains, straddles the Ventura—Los Angeles county line. This loop begins on the Stagecoach Trail off of Lilac Lane and climbs over a chaparral-covered hill to Santa Susana Pass Road. Along the way, the trail weaves through massive, grey-colored sandstone outcroppings over 70 million years old. This hike continues as a loop with the upper (north) end of the Old Stagecoach Trail, the historic route that once linked Los Angeles with Santa Barbara during the last half of the 1800s. Throughout the hike are a series of magnificent overlooks of the San Fernando Valley, the Santa Susana Mountains, the San Gabriel Mountains, and the Santa Monica Mountains. For a longer hike, the trail can be continued along the lower end of the Old Stagecoach Trail—Hike 147—leading down to Chatsworth Park South.

To the trailhead

From Highway 118/Ronald Reagan Freeway in Simi Valley, exit on Kuehner Drive. Drive 2.8 miles south to Lilac Lane. (Kuehner Drive becomes Santa Susana Pass Road as it curves to the east.) Turn right on Lilac Lane. Continue a quarter mile, and turn left into the dirt parking area.

The hike

The signed trail, located at the back end of the parking area, is the return route. Begin the loop at the front of the parking area on the left (north). Traverse the hillside among gorgeous sandstone boulders. Curve right and drop into a wide gulch as the homes along Lilac Lane disappear from view. Surrounded by a jumble of weather-sculpted outcrops, the path leads to an overlook of Simi Valley, high above the 118 Freeway. The serpentine path curves right to an overlook of Rocky Peak Park (Hike 150). Head east through the low-growing chaparral while marveling at the spectacular landscape. Slowly descend, zigzagging down the hillside to Santa Susana Pass Road at a half mile, located 120 yards east of the 118 Freeway overpass.

Bear right and follow the road 0.1 mile to a fire road, closed off to vehicles by boulders. Bear right, passing the boulders, and gently descend, overlooking the canyon on the left to a Y-fork. The left fork continues down the canyon towards Topanga Canyon Boulevard. (En route, this trail passes through the 500-acre Spahn Ranch. The area was used for western films, including *Bonanza* and *The Lone Ranger.* However, it is best known as the site where serial killer Charles Manson and his infamous cult lived during their 1969 killing spree. All the ranch structures were destroyed in a wildfire one year later. The land is currently owned by the state.)

For this hike, veer right and head up the slope. Curve right and traverse the hillside while expansive views span across the San Fernando Valley. One hundred yards shy of the trailhead parking area is an unsigned fork. Detour left 0.2 miles to an overlook atop a knoll, offering 360-degree vistas across the valley to the San Gabriel Mountains and Santa Monica Mountains. To extend the hike, the trail descends on the Old Stagecoach Road to Chatsworth Park South (Hike 147). ■

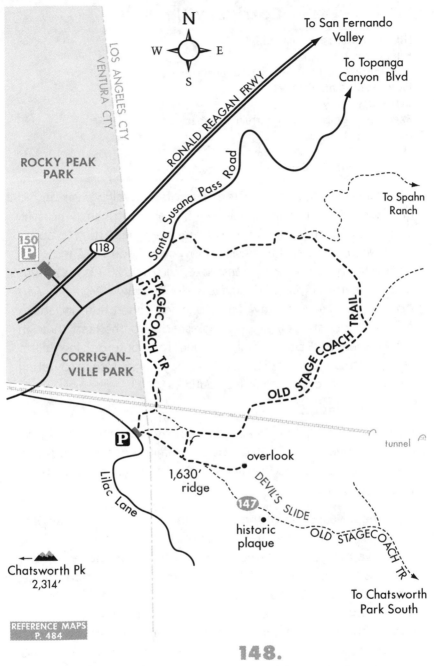

N
W E
S

To San Fernando Valley

To Topanga Canyon Blvd

RONALD REAGAN FRWY

ROCKY PEAK PARK

LOS ANGELES CTY
VENTURA CTY

Santa Susana Pass Road

To Spahn Ranch

150 P

118

STAGECOACH TR

CORRIGAN-VILLE PARK

OLD STAGECOACH TRAIL

P

tunnel

overlook

Lilac Lane

1,630' ridge

DEVIL'S SLIDE

147

historic plaque

OLD STAGECOACH TR

Chatsworth Pk
2,314'

To Chatsworth Park South

REFERENCE MAPS
P. 484

148.
Stagecoach Trail Loop

149. Corriganville Park

Hiking distance: 2-mile loop
Hiking time: 1 hour
Configuration: loop (with optional cut-across trail)
Elevation gain: 100 feet
Difficulty: easy
Exposure: a mix of open terrain and shaded forest
Dogs: not allowed
Maps: U.S.G.S. Simi Valley East
Rancho Simi Open Space: Corriganville Park

Corriganville Park, at the eastern end of Simi Valley, was an old movie ranch. It is named for Ray "Crash" Corrigan, who purchased the ranch in the 1930s. The area was the setting to about a thousand movie and television shows between 1937 and 1965, including *The Lone Ranger, Gunsmoke, The Fugitive, Lassie, Mutiny on the Bounty, African Queen, How the West Was Won*, and *Fort Apache*, to name just a few. Old stone and concrete foundations from the sets still remain. The oak-shaded paths lead through the 225-acre park past prominent sandstone outcroppings, cliffs, caves, a stream, Jungle Jim Lake, and the Hangin' Tree, a towering oak used to "execute" countless outlaws.

To the trailhead

From Highway 118/Ronald Reagan Freeway in Simi Valley, exit on Kuehner Drive. Drive 1.1 mile south to Smith Road and turn left. Continue 0.4 miles into Corriganville Park and park on the left.

The hike

From the far east end of the parking lot, take the wide trail past the kiosk. The forested trail heads northeast up the draw past coast live oaks and sculpted rock formations on the left. Cross a bridge to a junction. The left fork crosses a wooden bridge, passes a pool, and loops back for a shorter hike. Stay to the right to the next junction. The right fork is a connector trail to Rocky Peak Park via a concrete tunnel under the freeway. Curve to the left and cross the stream to another junction. Both trails lead west back to the trailhead. The footpath to the right travels between the sandstone cliffs to a dynamic overlook and a junction. The left fork descends to the old movie sets and the site of Fort Apache. From the sets, cross the bridge back to the parking lot. ▪

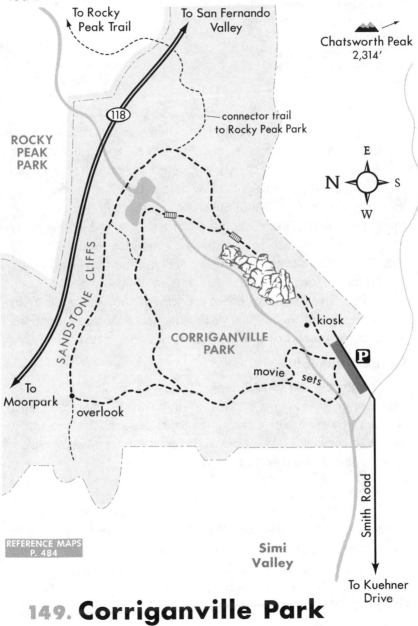

149. Corriganville Park

150. Rocky Peak Trail
ROCKY PEAK PARK

Hiking distance: 5-6 miles round trip
Hiking time: 2.5 hours
Configuration: out-and-back
Elevation gain: 1,100 feet
Difficulty: moderate to strenuous
Exposure: exposed ridge
Dogs: allowed
Maps: U.S.G.S. Simi Valley East

Rocky Peak Park is aptly named for dramatic sandstone forma-tions, fractured boulders, overhangs, caves, and outcroppings. The 4,815-acre wilderness park is located in Simi Valley by Santa Susana Pass. The park is a critical wildlife habitat linkage between the Simi Hills and the Santa Susana Mountains. Rocky Peak Trail follows a winding fire road on the north side of the 118 Freeway to Rocky Peak, which lies on the Los Angeles–Ventura county line. There are a series of vista points along the route and at the jagged 2,714-foot peak, the highest point in the Santa Susan Mountains. The vista points include top-of-the-world views of the San Fernando Valley, Simi Valley, the Santa Monica Mountains, and the many peaks of the Los Padres National Forest.

To the trailhead

From Highway 118/Ronald Reagan Freeway in Simi Valley, exit on Kuehner Drive. Drive 3 miles south to the Highway 118 East on-ramp. (Kuehner Drive becomes Santa Susana Pass Road as it curves to the east.) Turn left, crossing over the freeway, and park 0.1 mile ahead at the end of the road.

The hike

Hike past the trailhead kiosk up the winding fire road to an un-signed trail split at 0.9 miles. Stay to the left on the main trail, hiking steadily uphill to a signed junction with the Hummingbird Creek Trail on the left (Hike 151). Proceed straight ahead on the Rocky Peak Trail, which levels out. The winding trail offers al-ternating views of the San Fernando Valley to the east and Simi

Valley to the west. At the base of the final ascent is a singular, large oak tree. Begin the steep ascent, gaining 450 feet in a half mile, to the Rocky Peak Cutoff Trail. This is a good turn-around spot. However, if you wish to hike to the summit, the trail takes off to the right across the plateau for a half mile to Rocky Peak. The last section of the trail is a rock scramble to the peak. To return, reverse your route. ■

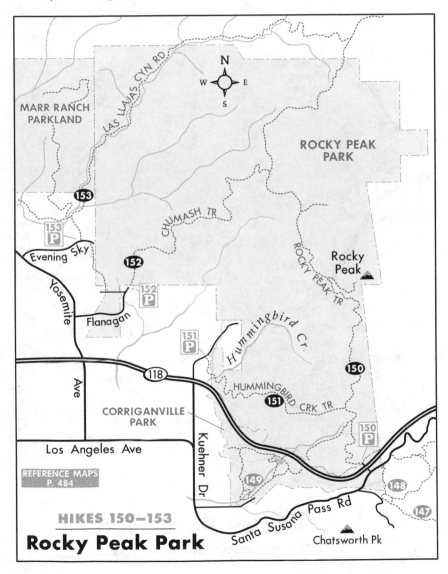

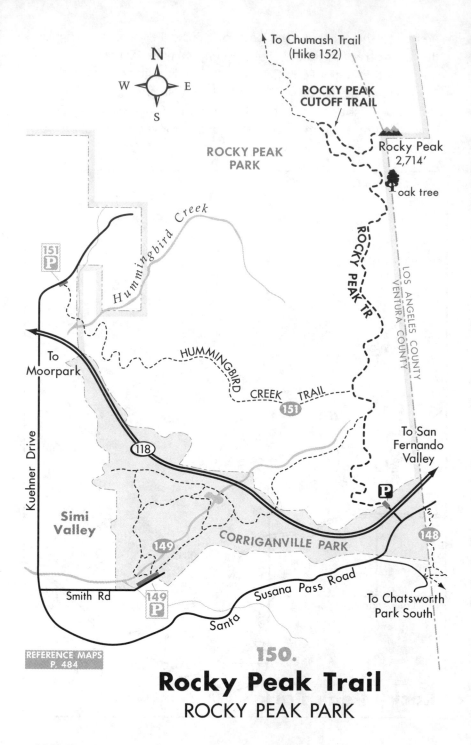

To Chumash Trail
(Hike 152)

**ROCKY PEAK
CUTOFF TRAIL**

Rocky Peak
2,714'

oak tree

ROCKY PEAK
PARK

Hummingbird Creek

151
P

To
Moorpark

HUMMINGBIRD

CREEK   TRAIL
151

ROCKY PEAK TR

LOS ANGELES COUNTY
VENTURA COUNTY

To San
Fernando
Valley

P

Kuehner Drive

Simi
Valley

118

CORRIGANVILLE PARK

148

149

Smith Rd

149
P

Santa   Susana Pass Road

To Chatsworth
Park South

REFERENCE MAPS
P. 484

150.

Rocky Peak Trail
ROCKY PEAK PARK

151. Hummingbird Creek Trail
ROCKY PEAK PARK

Hiking distance: 4.6 miles round trip
Hiking time: 2 hours
Configuration: out-and-back
Elevation gain: 1,000 feet
Difficulty: moderate to strenuous
Exposure: open hillside
Dogs: allowed
Maps: U.S.G.S. Simi Valley East

Rocky Peak Park, in the Santa Susana Mountains, straddles the Los Angeles–Ventura county line at the eastern end of Simi Valley. A network of hiking trails weaves through the 4,815-acre park that is home to deep oak-lined canyons, trickling streams, and massive, sculpted sandstone formations with a moonscape appearance. The Hummingbird Creek Trail, at the base of Rocky Peak, crosses Hummingbird Creek and climbs up a narrow canyon through open chaparral to the Rocky Peak Trail (a fire road), passing stacks of giant sandstone boulders, sculpted caves, and dramatic rock outcroppings.

To the trailhead

From Highway 118/Ronald Reagan Freeway in Simi Valley, exit on Kuehner Drive. Drive 0.3 miles north to the signed trailhead on the right. Park in one of the pullouts alongside the road. If full, additional parking is available just north of the freeway.

The hike

From the trailhead kiosk, head downhill. The trail soon U-turns southeast into the canyon to a defunct rock dam from 1917 and Hummingbird Creek. Proceed past the dam into an oak woodland and meadow. Once past the meadow, the trail crosses Hummingbird Creek and begins the ascent up the mountain through chaparral. Switchbacks lead up to sandstone caves and rock formations. After the rocks and caves, the trail levels out before the second ascent. Switchbacks make the climb easier as it heads up the canyon. At the head of the canyon, the trail levels out and passes more rock formations. The trail ends at a junction with the Rocky Peak Trail. Return to the trailhead by retracing your steps.

To hike farther, the Rocky Peak Trail continues 1.7 miles north to the summit of Rocky Peak—Hike 150. ■

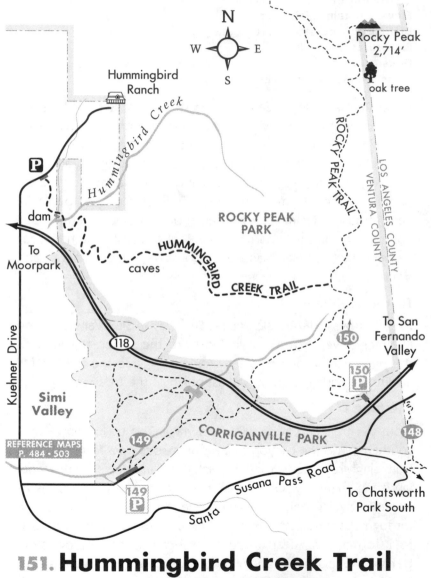

151. **Hummingbird Creek Trail**
ROCKY PEAK PARK

152. Chumash Trail
ROCKY PEAK PARK

Hiking distance: 5 miles round trip
Hiking time: 2.5 hours
Configuration: out-and-back
Elevation gain: 1,100 feet
Difficulty: moderate to strenuous
Exposure: open hillside
Dogs: allowed
Maps: U.S.G.S. Simi Valley East

The Chumash Trail is located in Rocky Peak Park in the Santa Susana Mountains east of Simi Valley. This trail ascends the west flank of Rocky Peak, winding up the chaparral-cloaked mountainside to the ridge north of the peak. En route, the trail passes sculpted sandstone outcroppings, caves, and a series of scenic overlooks and highland meadows. From Hamilton Saddle and the Rocky Peak Trail junction are panoramic views of the Simi Hills, Simi Valley, San Fernando Valley, the Santa Susana Mountains, the Santa Monica Mountains, Blind Canyon, and Las Llajas Canyon.

To the trailhead

From Highway 118/Ronald Reagan Freeway in Simi Valley, exit on Yosemite Avenue. Drive 0.4 miles north to Flanagan Drive and turn right. Continue 0.8 miles to the trailhead at the end of the road.

The hike

Head north past the kiosk along the rolling hills and grassy meadows. The trail climbs steadily as you round the hillside to the first overlook of Simi Hills to the south. Continue uphill through coastal sage scrub, curving left around the next rolling hill and passing sculpted sandstone formations. Arrow signposts are placed along the route. Continue to the east along the edge of the canyon to Hamilton Saddle. From the saddle, the trail sharply curves left (north), gaining elevation before leveling out again at Flat Rock. From Flat Rock, begin the final ascent through chaparral, curving around the last ridge to the top. The trail ends at a junction with the Rocky Peak Trail at an elevation of 2,450 feet. Sixty yards to the left of the junction are views of Blind Canyon and Las Llajas Canyon. Reverse your route to return.

For a longer hike, the Rocky Peak Trail continues 1.3 miles southeast to the summit of Rocky Peak (Hike 150). ■

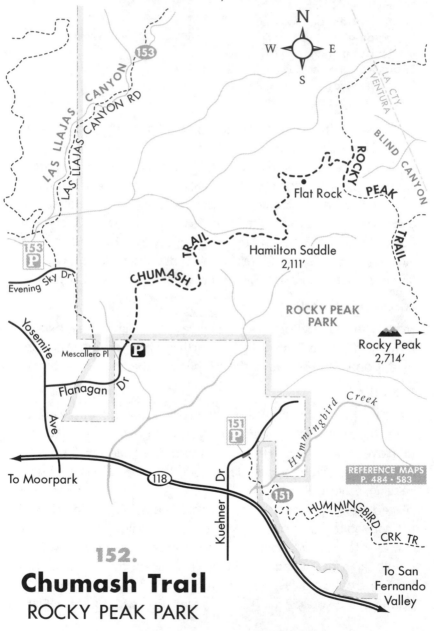

152.
Chumash Trail
ROCKY PEAK PARK

153. Las Llajas Canyon

MARR RANCH PARKLAND · ROCKY PEAK PARK

Hiking distance: 8.8 miles round trip
Hiking time: 4.5 hours
Configuration: out-and-back
Elevation gain: 1,200 feet
Difficulty: strenuous
Exposure: mix of forested canyon and open hillside
Dogs: allowed
Maps: U.S.G.S. Simi Valley East

The Marr Ranch Parkland in Simi Valley is tucked into the foothills of the Santa Susana Mountains adjacent to Rocky Peak Park. The publicly owned parkland and open space encompasses 1,842 acres, which includes Chivo Canyon and Las Llajas Canyon, both stream-fed canyons. The Las Llajas Canyon Road, a vehicle-restricted road, heads up the canyon through scenic, unspoiled landscapes. The hike meanders along the valley floor along the road, parallel to the creek and under groves of old oak trees. The trail climbs out of the canyon on Oil Well Road (part of an active ranch) to Rocky Peak Trail atop the ridge. From the ridge are sweeping vistas, including views of Oat Mountain and its distinctive radio towers.

To the trailhead

From Highway 118/Ronald Reagan Freeway in Simi Valley, exit on Yosemite Avenue. Drive 2.8 miles north to Evening Sky Drive. Turn right and continue a half mile to the signed trailhead on the left. Park along the curb.

The hike

Pass the trailhead kiosk and descend 300 yards on the paved road, dropping into Las Llajas Canyon. At transient Las Llajas Creek, veer to the right and cross over the east fork of the creek. Follow the east side of the main fork, weaving along the canyon bottom as the canyon walls narrow. Pass pockets of oak trees on the easy uphill grade. Cross over the creek at 1.2 miles, then cross over the creek for the third time. Meander past shaded streamside oak groves, continuing up the serpentine canyon. Traverse the north canyon slope above the waterway, then return to the canyon floor. Cross the invisible line from Ventura County into Los Angeles County without noticing an increase in the population. Continue to a Y-fork at 3.4 miles. To the left is a gated access into La Quinta Ranch. Curve right on the Oil Well Road, a partially-paved but mostly dirt road, and ascend the north-facing wall overlooking Las Llajas Canyon. Weave up the hillside, passing oil wells, holding tanks, and grazing cattle. Gain 700 feet over the next mile to the Rocky Peak Trail, a fire road. After savoring the well-earned vistas, return along the same route.

To extend the hike and form a 9.5-mile loop, take Rocky Peak Trail 1.6 miles to the right. Head south to the Chumash Trail. Bear left and descend 2.5 miles (Hike 152) to the Chumash trailhead on Flanagan Drive. Go right on Mescallero Place, and weave to Evening Sky Drive, completing the loop. ■

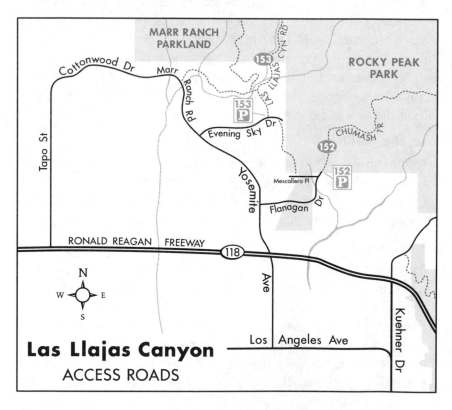

Las Llajas Canyon
ACCESS ROADS

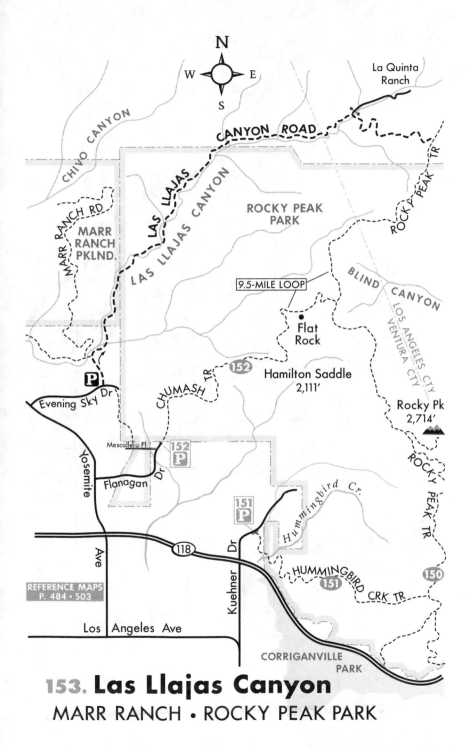

153. **Las Llajas Canyon**
MARR RANCH • ROCKY PEAK PARK

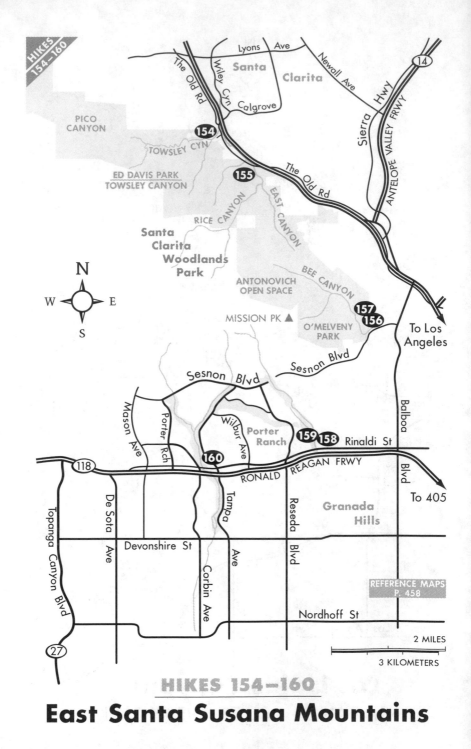

HIKES 154-160

East Santa Susana Mountains

154. Towsley Canyon— Wiley Canyon Loop

ED DAVIS PARK

SANTA CLARITA WOODLANDS PARK

24335 The Old Road · Newhall

Hiking distance: 5.2-mile loop
Hiking time: 2.5 hours
Configuration: loop
Elevation gain: 1,100 feet
Difficulty: moderate to strenuous
Exposure: mostly exposed
Dogs: allowed
Maps: U.S.G.S. Oat Mountain

The Santa Susana Mountains separate the San Fernando and Santa Clarita Valleys. Towsley Canyon sits on the northern slope of the Santa Susana Range, north of the San Fernando Valley and just east of Santa Clarita. This beautiful loop trail explores two canyons in Ed Davis Park, part of the Santa Clarita Woodlands Park system. The undeveloped 6,000-acre park contains hiking, biking, and equestrian trails.

The hike begins in Towsley Canyon on an easy, partially paved road that follows the canyon drainage. The trail then climbs over the mountain ridge that lies between Towsley Canyon and Wiley Canyon on a steep, single-track trail. The scenic trail traverses the mountain slope and drops into Wiley Canyon, following the floor of the beautiful stream-fed canyon.

En route, the hike cuts through a rock-strewn crevice with eroded, water-worn rock formations known as The Narrows. Year-round Towsley Creek ripples through the 20-foot-wide gorge between 200-foot vertical walls of sandstone and conglomerate rock. The trail passes through a variety of ecosystems, including coastal sage scrub, chaparral, riparian vegetation, open grassland, and oak and walnut woodlands. Along the ridge are expansive vistas of the surrounding mountains, canyons, geological formations, and the Santa Clarita Valley.

To the trailhead

From the Golden State Freeway (Interstate 5) in Santa Clarita, exit on Calgrove Boulevard. Head south on Calgrove Boulevard, which quickly becomes The Old Road. Follow the frontage road 0.3 miles to the signed trailhead parking lot on the right.

The hike

Walk past the trailhead kiosk and vehicle gate. Follow the old asphalt road one hundred yards to a signed junction. To the left is Wiley Canyon—the return route. Begin the loop straight ahead, staying in Towsley Canyon. Enter the mouth of the wide canyon on the fire road along an easy uphill grade. At a half mile, pass the Canyon View Loop on the left, a shorter 1.9-mile loop. Continue straight and pass through a vehicle gate, where the dirt path begins.

Pass a crib dam on the left as the canyon narrows. At one mile, the signs of civilization disappear, hidden by the surrounding mountains. Wind up-canyon, passing seasonal pools of water and caves in the eroding cliffs. Cross the drainage and stroll through The Narrows, a water-laced portal. Walk through the boulder-strewn gorge among weather-sculpted rock formations.

Return to the open slopes and traverse the canyon slope. Begin climbing the north canyon wall with the aid of eleven switchbacks. Throughout the climb are stands of walnut trees, then scattered oaks and bay laurel. At 2.3 miles, just before reaching the 2,450-foot summit, a 100-yard side path veers left to a vista point. The views extend across the Santa Clarita Valley to the Los Padres National Forest. Continue up, following the undulating ridge with city vistas to the left and mountain views to the right. Leave the ridge and descend into Wiley Canyon. Weave down the contours of the mountain to the canyon floor. Follow the small waterway downstream, and complete the loop near the trailhead on the right. ▪

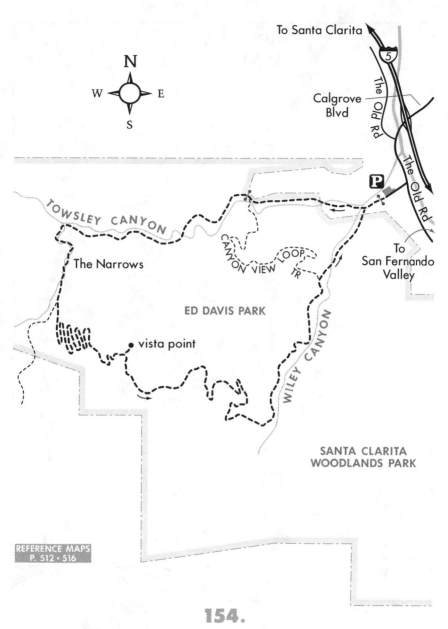

154.
Towsley Canyon–Wiley Canyon
ED DAVIS PARK
SANTA CLARITA WOODLANDS PARK

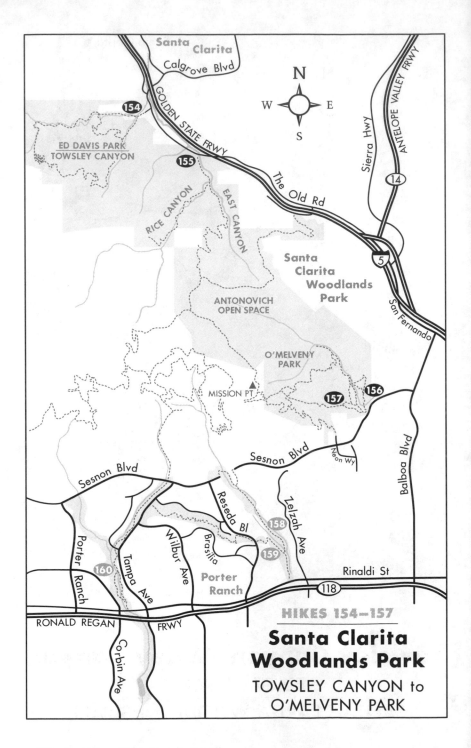

Santa Clarita
Calgrove Blvd
GOLDEN STATE FRWY
154
ED DAVIS PARK
TOWSLEY CANYON
155
RICE CANYON
EAST CANYON
The Old Rd
Sierra Hwy
ANTELOPE VALLEY FRWY
14
5
San Fernando
N
W E
S
Santa
Clarita
Woodlands
Park
ANTONOVICH
OPEN SPACE
O'MELVENY
PARK
MISSION PT
157
156
Sesnon Blvd
Sesnon Blvd
Zeon Wy
Balboa Blvd
Reseda Bl
158
Brasilia
159
Zelzah Ave
Porter Ranch
Porter
Ranch
Tampa Ave
Wilbur Ave
160
Rinaldi St
118
RONALD REGAN FRWY
Corbin Ave

HIKES 154–157

Santa Clarita Woodlands Park

TOWSLEY CANYON to O'MELVENY PARK

155. East Canyon and Rice Canyon

SANTA CLARITA WOODLANDS PARK

24255 The Old Road · Newhall

Hiking distance: 5.6 miles round trip
Hiking time: 3 hours
Configuration: two out-and-back trails
Elevation gain: 1,100 feet
Difficulty: moderate to strenuous
Exposure: mostly exposed
Dogs: allowed
Maps: U.S.G.S. Oat Mountain

East Canyon and Rice Canyon sit on the north-facing slope of the Santa Susana Mountains just south of Santa Clarita. The canyons are included in the 4,000-acre Santa Clarita Woodlands Park, managed by the Santa Monica Mountains Conservancy.

This hike includes two out-and-back trails that lead up both canyons to overlooks. The East Canyon Trail is a dirt fire road that climbs through forested pockets of coast live oak, bay laurel, black walnut, big leaf maple, toyon, and Douglas fir. The hiking, biking, and equestrian trail leads nearly four miles to the Weldon Canyon Motorway, straddling the ridgeline. The trail emerges at an overlook (shy of the ridge), with magnificent views across Santa Clarita Valley.

Rice Canyon, an adjoining drainage to the northwest, diverts from East Canyon and follows seasonal Rice Creek up the canyon bottom to a grassy knoll with an overlook of the canyon and surrounding mountains. The Rice Canyon Trail (for hikers only) winds through the forested canyon at an easy grade, gaining only 300 feet to the plateau dotted with oaks above the canyon floor. En route, the trail leads through open pastoral meadows and groves of oaks, sycamores, cottonwoods, and willows.

To the trailhead

From the Golden State Freeway (Interstate 5) in Santa Clarita, exit on Calgrove Boulevard. Head south on Calgrove Boulevard, which quickly becomes The Old Road. Follow the frontage road one mile south to the signed trailhead on the right (located just before The Old Road goes under I-5.) Park along the right side of the road for free, or pull into the trailhead parking lot on the right for a fee.

The hike

Walk east on the side road, parallel to The Old Road, to the signed trailhead just before of the pay-parking lot. Bear right, head past the botanical garden and vehicle gate, and enter the mouth of East Canyon. Follow the west side of ephemeral East Canyon Creek. At 0.3 miles is a signed trail fork. The right fork heads up Rice Canyon. For now, continue straight, staying in East Canyon while gently climbing past oak groves. The canyon narrows at 0.7 miles and the vegetation thickens. Climb out of the canyon bottom, and wind up the west canyon slope with far-reaching vistas. At 1.8 miles is a short, steep climb. As the path curves left, take the unsigned footpath to the right. Walk 100 yards to a lone majestic oak on a knoll overlooking the fir and pine forest deep in Rice Canyon. Enjoy the great views that span across the Santa Clarita Valley.

To extend the hike along this route, the East Canyon Trail continues less than a mile to the Weldon Canyon Motorway atop the ridge. The left fork traverses the ridge and descends the mountain into Weldon Canyon. The right fork stays on the 3.8-mile East Canyon Trail to its terminus at a trail split. To the right, Bridge Road follows the ridge to Oat Mountain. To the left, Corral Sunshine Motorway leads to Mission Point and O'Melveny Park.

Return down the mountain to the junction at the foot of Rice Canyon. Veer left into Rice Canyon and stroll through the open meadow as the canyon narrows. Enter the shade of the oaks and cross the seasonal drainage. Pass through a small oak-rimmed meadow, then duck back into the forest. Cross the stream four more times, weaving up the canyon. Ascend the west canyon wall to an unsigned Y-fork one mile from the junction. The right fork leads 25 yards to a knoll with a stately oak and a vista of the forested canyon. The left fork heads steeply up the mountain. Return back along the same trail. ■

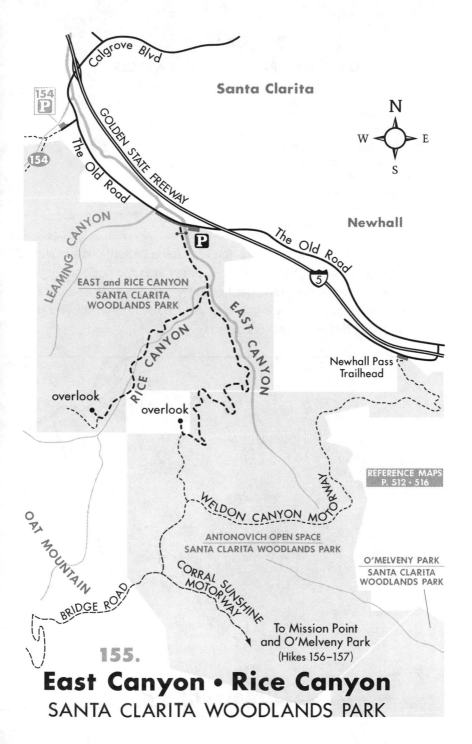

155.

East Canyon • Rice Canyon
SANTA CLARITA WOODLANDS PARK

156. Bee Canyon

O'MELVENY PARK · GRANADA HILLS

17300 Sesnon Boulevard · Granada Hills

Hiking distance: 1.5 miles round trip
Hiking time: 1 hour
Configuration: out and back
Elevation gain: 250 feet
Difficulty: easy
Exposure: mostly exposed
Dogs: allowed
Maps: U.S.G.S. Oat Mountain

O'Melveny Park, located in the Santa Susana Mountains above Granada Hills, encompasses over 672 acres. It is the second largest park in Los Angeles, dwarfed only by Griffith Park. The park contains miles of steep hiking, biking, and equestrian trails along a network of dirt trails and fire roads.

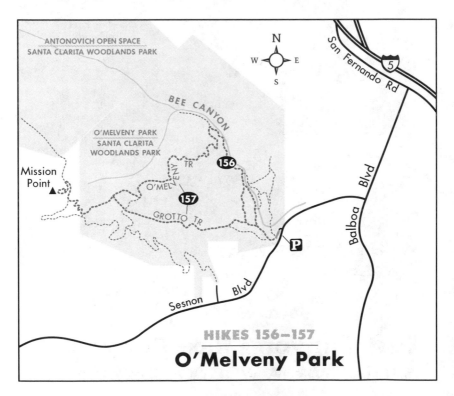

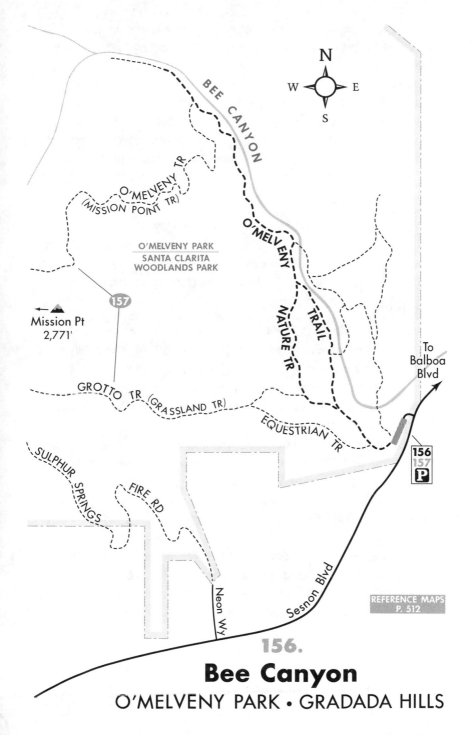

N
W E
S

BEE CANYON

O'MELVENY TR
(MISSION POINT TR)

O'MELVENY

O'MELVENY PARK
SANTA CLARITA
WOODLANDS PARK

157

Mission Pt
2,771'

TRAIL

NATURE TR

GROTTO TR (GRASSLAND TR)

EQUESTRIAN TR

SULPHUR SPRINGS

FIRE RD

To
Balboa
Blvd

156
157
P

Neon Wy

Sesnon Blvd

REFERENCE MAPS
P. 512

156.
Bee Canyon
O'MELVENY PARK • GRADADA HILLS

Bee Canyon, the centerpiece of the expansive park, is a stream-fed box canyon framed with eroding vertical walls that rise over 500 feet. The hike begins in a picturesque picnic ground with sloping lawns, citrus orchards, and eucalyptus groves. Beyond the developed parkland, the Bee Canyon Trail enters the V-shaped gorge in a natural landscape. This is an easy, three-quarter-mile trail up a shaded riparian canyon lined with California walnut trees and live oaks. Continue with Hike 157 if you wish to extend the hike into a strenuous 5.6-mile loop.

To the trailhead

From Highway 118/Ronald Reagan Freeway in Granada Hills, take the Balboa Boulevard exit. Drive 2.3 miles north on Balboa Boulevard to Sesnon Boulevard and turn left (west). Continue a half mile to the signed O'Melveny Park parking lot on the right.

The hike

Walk about 100 yards past the park gate to the signed Nature Trail in a citrus grove. Both the O'Melveny Trail (the main park path) and the nature trail join up again about a quarter mile ahead. Stroll through the tree-shaded picnic grounds among live oaks, eucalyptus, sycamores, walnut trees, and expansive grasslands. Follow Bee Creek on the right to where the two trails merge. Leave the groomed parkland behind and enter undeveloped Bee Canyon as the trail narrows. Follow the creek between the native chaparral slopes on the left and the craggy whiterock cliffs on the right. The barren sedimentary cliffs rise dramatically, towering above the trail. Continue at an easy grade to a left switchback at 0.75 miles.

The Bee Canyon Trail continues straight ahead, but the unmaintained path narrows and the brush soon overtakes the trail. The O'Melveny Trail (referred to as the Mission Point Trail on some maps) sharply bends left and begins the steep ascent to Mission Point (Hike 157). ∎

157. Mission Point

O'MELVENY PARK · GRANADA HILLS

17300 Sesnon Boulevard · Granada Hills

Hiking distance: 5.6-mile loop
Hiking time: 3 hours
Configuration: loop
Elevation gain: 1,500 feet
Difficulty: strenuous
Exposure: mostly exposed
Dogs: allowed
Maps: U.S.G.S. Oat Mountain

Towering Mission Point sits on the east flank of Oat Mountain, high above Granada Hills in the Santa Susana Mountains. The 2,771-foot summit of Mission Point, located in O'Melveny Park, is the highest peak in the mountain range. This strenuous hike gains 1,500 feet in elevation as it climbs up to the point. The reward of the steep hike is a 360-degree vista that spans across the San Fernando Valley, the Santa Monica Mountains, the San Gabriel Mountains, the Santa Clarita Valley, and the Los Padres National Forest. After enjoying the expansive views, the hike makes a return loop down Bee Canyon, a stream-fed box canyon with 500-foot vertical walls.

To the trailhead

From Highway 118/Ronald Reagan Freeway in Granada Hills, take the Balboa Boulevard exit. Drive 2.3 miles north on Balboa Boulevard to Sesnon Boulevard and turn left. Continue a half mile to the signed O'Melveny Park parking lot on the right.

The hike

Walk about 100 yards past the park gate, and bear left on the signed Nature Trail in a grove of citrus trees. Bear left and continue 200 yards, passing the equestrian trail on the left to the posted Grotto Trail (also labeled as the Grassland Trail on some maps). The Grotto Trail is located just after crossing the bridge over the arroyo.

Go left on the Grotto Trail, and leave the landscaped parkland behind. Begin climbing at a steep grade on the exposed grassy slope. The grade temporarily levels out, with great views of the San Fernando Valley to the east. Steadily climb, following a ridge between two parallel coulees lined with California walnut trees, to an unsigned 4-way junction. The right fork is a cut-across to Bee Canyon. Continue straight and head up another steep slope to a T-junction with the wide O'Melveny Trail at 1.3 miles. The right fork (the return route) leads to Bee Canyon.

First, bear left towards Mission Point. Ascend the mountain at a gentler grade while overlooking the valley. From the junction, it is a quarter mile to the fenced park boundary. On the left, the Sulphur Springs Fire Road (also known as the Neon Trail) winds down the mountain to Neon Way. Veer right and zigzag up the partially rock-lined path, parallel to an old iron fence. Pass a distinct grove of four majestic live oak trees. Loop counterclockwise beneath Mission Point to the north side of the mountain. Sharply bear left to the treeless 2,771-foot summit. At the flat top is a bench, a rock memorial, and sweeping panoramic vistas.

Return to the junction at the top of the Grotto Trail. Continue straight ahead on an easy downward slope while overlooking the eroding sedimentary cliffs of Bee Canyon. Gradually wind down the mountain while savoring the views. The trail reaches the floor of Bee Canyon at Bee Creek. Bend right and follow the drainage downstream. Enter the beautiful picnic area and expansive lawns. Complete the loop, returning to the trailhead. ■

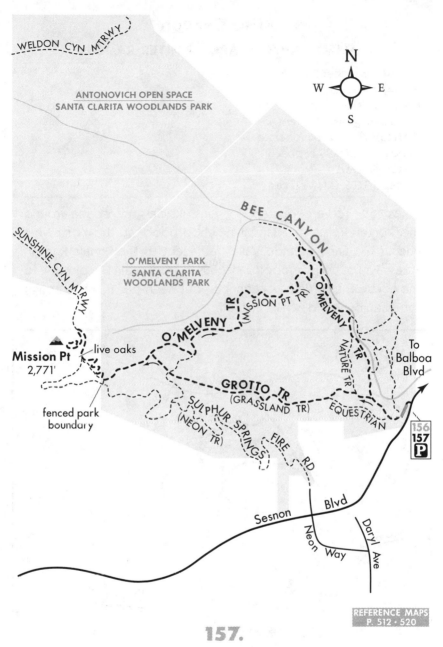

157.

Mission Point

O'MELVENY PARK • GRADADA HILLS

158. Aliso Canyon

ALISO CANYON PARK • PORTER RANCH

Hiking distance: 3.4 miles round trip
Hiking time: 2 hours
Configuration: out and back
Elevation gain: 400 feet
Difficulty: easy to moderate
Exposure: mostly exposed
Dogs: allowed
Maps: U.S.G.S. Oat Mountain

Hikes 158–160 are located along creekside greenspace around the Porter Ranch residential neighborhood at the northwest end of the San Fernando Valley, adjacent to the Ronald Reagan Freeway. The undeveloped Santa Susana Mountains lie directly to the north. The three hikes connect, but each trail is long enough for an enjoyable day hike in itself.

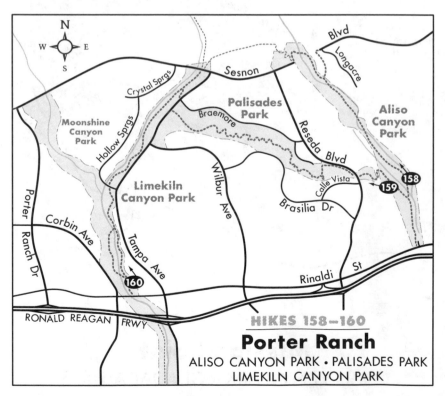

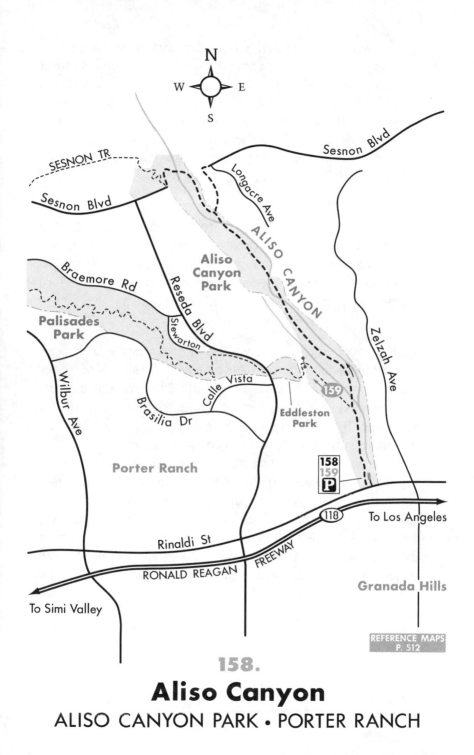

158.
Aliso Canyon
ALISO CANYON PARK • PORTER RANCH

Aliso Canyon is a forested, stream-fed canyon at the eastern end of the trail system. The canyon stretches from Rinaldi Street to Sesnon Boulevard. The scenic oak and sycamore parkland was the film site for the movie *E.T.* This hike begins at Rinaldi Street (a frontage road of the Ronald Reagan Freeway) and heads north up the riparian canyon on the Aliso Canyon Trail. En route are several creek crossings. The trail connects midway with the Palisades Trail (Hike 159) and the Sesnon Trail at the north end.

To the trailhead

From Highway 118/Ronald Reagan Freeway in Northridge, take the Reseda Boulevard exit. Drive one block north on Reseda Boulevard to Rinaldi Street and turn right. Continue a half mile to the signed Aliso Canyon Park on the left at Hesperia Avenue. Turn left and drive 0.1 mile to the trailhead parking lot.

The hike

Cross the footbridge to the west and immediately bear right. Head north into the mouth of Aliso Canyon. Parallel Aliso Creek on the right beneath the cliffs on the left. Stroll through a forest among live oak, sycamore, and bay laurel trees to a Y-fork at a quarter mile. The Palisades Trail (Hike 159) veers to the left. Go to the right, staying in Aliso Canyon. Wind up the canyon, following the waterway through the shade of an oak forest. At 0.8 miles, cross the seasonal drainage two times. The canyon walls widen as the trail crosses the drainage a third time, reaching a Y-fork. The left fork drops back into the canyon, then loops left and climbs to the west canyon rim at the dead-end of Sesnon Boulevard. The right fork climbs out of the canyon to the east rim and exits at Sesnon Boulevard by Longacre Avenue. Return by retracing your steps. ■

159. Palisades Park

ALISO CANYON PARK to LIMEKILN CANYON PARK

PORTER RANCH

Hiking distance: 5.5 miles round trip
Hiking time: 3 hours
Configuration: out and back
Elevation gain: 440 feet
Difficulty: moderate
Exposure: exposed
Dogs: allowed
Maps: U.S.G.S. Oat Mountain

Palisades Park is a 117–acre park in the Porter Ranch neighborhood at the northwest end of the San Fernando Valley, adjacent to the Santa Susana Mountains. (Palisades Park is also known as Wilbur Tampa Park.) The park is highlighted by eroded sedimentary outcroppings that are known as the Palisades.

The curvaceous Palisades Trail connects Aliso Canyon (Hike 158) with Limekiln Canyon (Hike 160). The exposed, undulating bridle trail traverses a cliff-hugging route along the sage-covered hillside, with views across the San Fernando Valley to the Santa Monica Mountains. This hike begins in Aliso Canyon in the shade of oaks and sycamores, then continues westward between Reseda Boulevard and Tampa Avenue.

To the trailhead

From Highway 118/Ronald Reagan Freeway in Northridge, take the Reseda Boulevard exit. Drive one block north on Reseda Boulevard to Rinaldi Street and turn right. Continue a half mile to the signed Aliso Canyon Park on the left at Hesperia Avenue. Turn left and drive 0.1 mile to the trailhead parking lot.

The hike

Cross the footbridge to the west and immediately bear right. Head north into the mouth of Aliso Canyon. Parallel Aliso Creek on the right beneath the cliffs on the left. Stroll through a forest with live oak, sycamore, and bay laurel trees to a Y-fork at a quarter mile. The right fork stays on the Aliso Canyon Trail (Hike 158). Veer left on the Palisades Trail, skirting the west edge of Aliso Canyon. Slowly curve into Palisades Canyon on the right, with a year-round stream and lush riparian foliage. Pass through a vehicle gate and curve left. Steeply climb to the west canyon rim, reaching Reseda Boulevard by Eddlestone Park (just north of Calle Vista).

Carefully cross the road to the signed Palisades Trail. Head up the slope for a couple hundred yards, parallel to Reseda Boulevard. As the road tops a crest, the footpath veers left to a sweeping overlook of the San Fernando Valley. Follow the serpentine, bridle-fenced trail along the sage-covered slope. Perched on the sedimentary bluffs, the path weaves along the contours of the hills above the subdivisions. Drop down the hillside perch to the canyon floor. Skirt the back edge of homes on the left and pine-dotted hills on the right. Follow the rolling terrain to the trail's end at Tampa Avenue by a vehicle gate. Directly across the road is Limekiln Canyon (Hike 160).

To extend the hike into Limekiln Canyon, cross Tampa Avenue and walk 0.1 mile uphill to the right. The signed Limekiln Canyon access is directly across from Braemore Road. ■

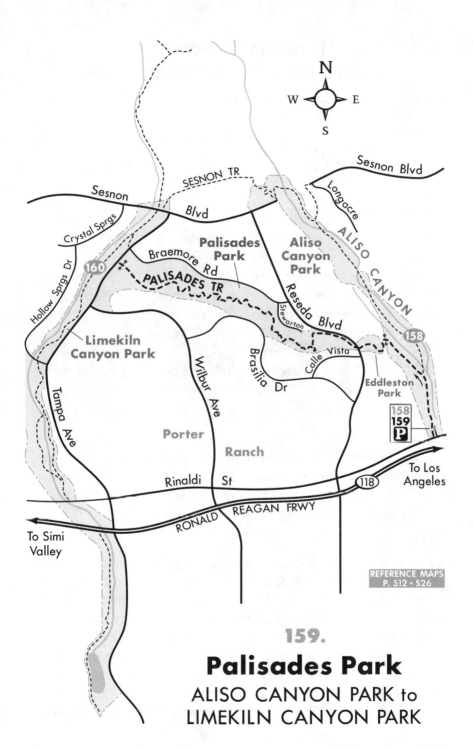

159.
Palisades Park
ALISO CANYON PARK to LIMEKILN CANYON PARK

160. Limekiln Canyon Trail
LIMEKILN CANYON PARK • PORTER RANCH

Hiking distance: 3.6 miles round trip
Hiking time: 2 hours
Configuration: out and back
Elevation gain: 375 feet
Difficulty: moderate
Exposure: mostly shaded
Dogs: allowed
Maps: U.S.G.S. Oat Mountain

Limekiln Canyon—just west of Tampa Avenue in Porter Ranch—is a lush, forested canyon with a year-round stream. The pastoral canyon is tucked in on the lower slopes of the Santa Susana Mountains. Live oak, bay laurel, and sycamore trees fill the shaded canyon, interspersed with pools and lush riparian vegetation along the creek. The Limekiln Canyon Trail is at the west end of the residential trail system, connected to Aliso Canyon (Hike 158) via the Palisades Trail (Hike 159). This path runs the length of Limekiln Canyon, from Rinaldi Street at the south end to Sesnon Boulevard at the north.

To the trailhead

From Highway 118/Ronald Reagan Freeway in Porter Ranch, take the Tampa Avenue exit. Drive one block north on Tampa Avenue to Rinaldi Street and turn left. Continue 0.15 miles to the signed Limekiln Canyon Park on the right. Park along the curb.

The hike

Pass through the vehicle gate by the signed Limekiln Park sign. Descend on the paved path into the stream-fed canyon. Enter the shade in a mixed forest on the wide dirt path. Follow the canyon floor north to a trail split. Both paths follow the creek upstream. The left fork crosses over Limekiln Creek by a gorgeous water-filled grotto on the left. After crossing back over the creek, the two paths merge a short distance ahead. Parallel the stream on the left through groves of oaks, sycamores, and bay laurel. Pass lush pools with scattered palm trees. Traverse the hillside to a Y-fork. The left fork leads only 30 yards to a pool. Stay to the right and gently climb out of the canyon to Tampa Avenue. Continue north, perched on the hillside, and cross under the Hollow Springs Bridge. Climb back up to the shoulder of Tampa Avenue at 0.9 miles. Immediately veer left, staying on the footpath. Descend the slope, then follow the incline back up to Tampa Avenue once again at 1.1 mile. Continue through the pine forest parallel to Tampa Avenue, then descend back into the canyon. At 1.6 miles, pass a trail on the right that leads back up to Tampa Avenue by Braemore Road. The trail ends at Sesnon Boulevard. Return along the same route. ▪

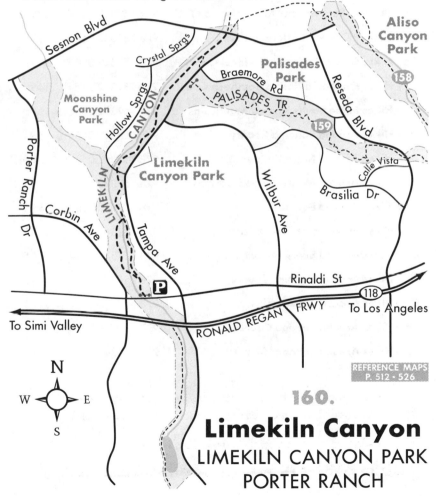

160.

Limekiln Canyon
LIMEKILN CANYON PARK
PORTER RANCH

DAY HIKE BOOKS

Day Hikes In Yellowstone National Park ....978-1-57342-048-8...$12.95

Day Hikes In Grand Teton National Park ....978-1-57342-069-3.... 14.95

Day Hikes In the Beartooth Mountains
Billings to Red Lodge to Yellowstone N.P......978-1-57342-064-8.... 15.95

Day Hikes Around Bozeman, Montana...........978-1-57342-063-1 .... 15.95

Day Hikes Around Missoula, Montana ....978-1-57342-066-2.... 15.95

Day Hikes In Sequoia and Kings Canyon N.P. ...978-1-57342-030-3.... 12.95

Day Hikes In Yosemite National Park ....978-1-57342-059-4 ...13.95

Day Hikes On the California Central Coast ......978-1-57342-058-7.....17.95

Day Hikes On the California Southern Coast ....978-1-57342-045-7 ... 14.95

Day Hikes In the Santa Monica Mountains ....978-1-57342-065-5.... 21.95

Day Hikes Around Sonoma County ....978-1-57342-053-2.... 16.95

Day Hikes Around Napa Valley ....978-1-57342-057-0 ... 16.95

Day Hikes Around Monterey and Carmel ....978-1-57342-067-9 ... 19.95

Day Hikes Around Big Sur ....978-1-57342-068-6.....18.95

Day Hikes Around San Luis Obispo...............978-1-57342-070-9 ... 21.95

Day Hikes Around Santa Barbara ....978-1-57342-060-0 ...17.95

Day Hikes Around Ventura County ....978-1-57342-062-4 ...17.95

Day Hikes Around Los Angeles ....978-1-57342-071-6 .... 21.95

Day Hikes Around Orange County ....978-1-57342-047-1.... 15.95

Day Hikes Around Sedona, Arizona ....978-1-57342-049-5 ... 14.95

These books may be purchased at your local bookstore or
outdoor shop. Or, order them direct from the distributor:

National Book Network

800-243-0495 DIRECT   **800-820-2329** FAX

Day Hikes Around Orange County

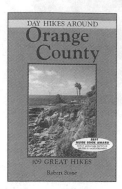

Residents and travelers alike will find this book essential to exploring Orange County. This southern California county is framed by the Pacific Coast on one side while the Santa Ana Mountains run along its backside, offering diverse landscape and scenery.

Despite the presence of the Orange County metropolis, nearly 30% of the county's acreage is parklands, wildlife sanctuaries, national forests, and wilderness preserves. These 106 day hikes provide access to the natural, undeveloped areas, offering hundreds of miles of hiking trails. Highlights include magnificent rock formations, bay-side coves, tidal estuaries, peninsulas, waterfalls, mountain-peak ridge walks, sculpted canyons, and sweeping views from the ocean to the cities.

256 pages • 106 hikes • 1st Edition 2005 • ISBN 978-1-57342-047-1

Day Hikes Around Ventura County

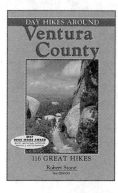

This scenic coastal county lies just north of Los Angeles. The county's unique topography encompasses national forest land, wilderness areas, several mountain ranges, and over 50 miles of coastline. The many communities that lie throughout the area have been thoughtfully integrated within the green space and undeveloped land.

A network of hiking trails weaves throughout the countryside and across the parks, forests, and mountain ranges which form an ecological corridor. Included is an excellent cross-section of hikes, from relaxing beach strolls along the Pacific Ocean to mountain-top hikes with expansive views.

320 pages • 116 hikes • 3rd Edition 2011 • ISBN 978-1-57342-062-4

Day Hikes in the Santa Monica Mountains

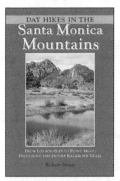

The 50-mile-long Santa Monica Mountains parallel the coastline in southern California, dividing the Pacific coast from the interior valleys. This comprehensive guide includes hikes along the entire range, beginning from its eastern terminus in Los Angeles. A separate section includes the full length of the 68-mile Backbone Trail.

The large variety of hikes accommodates every level of hiking, from short strolls along beach boardwalks to all-day, coast-to-peak hikes. Highlights include fantastic sandstone landscapes, cool canyon retreats, waterfalls, coastal bluffs, lighthouses, and numerous 360-degree overlooks. Several hikes are located in Los Angeles' Griffith Park, including a hike up to the famous "HOLLYWOOD" sign.

480 pages • 138 hikes • 1st Edition 2012 • ISBN 978-1-57342-065-5

Day Hikes On the California Southern Coast

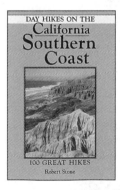

This guide is a collection of the best coastal hikes along 238 miles of southern California coastline, from Ventura County to the U.S.—Mexico border. The area has some of the most varied geography in the state...a blend of verdant canyons, arid bluffs, and sandy coastline.

Discover hundreds of miles of trails in scenic and undeveloped land, despite the expansive urban areas. Highlights include wide sand beaches, marine terraces, rocky headlands, tidal estuaries with coves and caves, sandstone cliffs, lighthouses, great locations for viewing wildlife, expansive dunes, forested canyons, waterfalls, and panoramic overlooks of the coast.

224 pages • 100 hikes • 1st Edition 2004 • ISBN 978-1-57342-045-7

INDEX

ADRIENNE METTER

About the Author

Since 1991, Robert Stone has been writer, photographer, and publisher of Day Hike Books. He is a Los Angeles Times Best Selling Author and an award-winning journalist of Rocky Mountain Outdoor Writers and Photographers, the Outdoor Writers Association of California, the Northwest Outdoor Writers Association, the Outdoor Writers Association of America, and the Bay Area Travel Writers.

Robert has hiked every trail in the Day Hike Book series. With 20 hiking guides in the series, many in their fourth and fifth editions, he has hiked thousands of miles of trails throughout the western United States. When Robert is not hiking, he researches, writes, and maps the hikes before returning to the trails. He spends summers in the Rocky Mountains of Montana and winters on the California Central Coast.